Beyond Gender Binaries

BEYOND GENDER BINARIES

An Intersectional Orientation to Communication and Identities

Cindy L. Griffin

UNIVERSITY OF CALIFORNIA PRESS

University of California Press
Oakland, California

Library of Congress Cataloging-in-Publication Data

Names: Griffin, Cindy L., author.
Title: Beyond gender binaries : an intersectional orientation to communication and identities / Cindy L. Griffin.
Description: Oakland, California : University of California Press, [2020] | Includes bibliographical references and index.
Identifiers: LCCN 2020011873 (print) | LCCN 2020011874 (ebook) | ISBN 9780520297289 (paperback) | ISBN 9780520969698 (ebook)
Subjects: LCSH: Gender identity. | Communication and sex. | Feminist theory. | Women—Communication. | Women's rights. | Rhetoric—Social aspects.
Classification: LCC HQ18.55 .G75 2020 (print) | LCC HQ18.55 (ebook) | DDC 305.3—dc23
LC record available at https://lccn.loc.gov/2020011873
LC ebook record available at https://lccn.loc.gov/2020011874

Manufactured in the United States of America

29 28 27 26 25 24 23 22 21 20
10 9 8 7 6 5 4 3 2 1

Contents

Full Contents

PART III
Intersectionality and Structures of Power

Guides to Communication

Acknowledgments

Beyond Gender Binaries: An Intersectional Orientation to Communication and Identities has been both an individual and a collaborative effort. I am incredibly thankful for the wisdom, insights, encouragement, laughter, and kindness of the many people who assisted me in the journey that resulted in this book. I am especially grateful to Lyn Uhl, executive editor at the University of California Press, who asked me at a key moment in my life, "Have you got a book you'd like to write?" Her guidance, insights, and encouragement were a constant presence throughout this journey, and for these things, as well as her laughter and friendship, I am so thankful. Lisa Colleen Moore, development editor, brought her considerable talents to the project, shaping and clarifying the complex ideas presented here, as well as pushing me to find new ways to bring them to life for the reader. For her amazing skills, support, and encouragement, I am very thankful. UC Press editors Kate Hoffman and Kathleen MacDougall also shared their editing skills and scholarly insights with me during the final stages of this book. To both of these talented individuals, I offer a sincere thank you. I also owe a debt of gratitude to the reviewers who have been a part of this project since it began to take shape and find its way onto the page. The intellects, insights, and suggestions that Suzy D'Enbeau, Suzanne Enck, Rachael Alicia Griffin, Sara McKinnion, Jennifer Sandoval, Derek Sweet, Tahira J. Walker, Issac West, and those who wished to remain anonymous shared with me were invaluable, helping me strengthen the project in ways I could not have done on my own. To these scholars, I offer my heartfelt gratitude. The interlibrary loan staff at Colorado State University, particularly Cristi MacWaters, Maggie Cummings, and Matthew Diven, were always helpful; these rock stars searched, found, downloaded, sent, and reminded me to return a dizzying array of books and articles that inform and support the ideas in this book. For their talents, patience, support, and humor, I am especially thankful.

I am deeply grateful for Teresa Maria Linda Scholz, who shared her insights, warmth, humor, courage, and friendship with me as this project launched. Our paths diverged in ways we did not expect, but her voice remains an important piece of the early conceptualizing of the book. To my Kala Point family, I also express a heartfelt thank you—Valerie and Stanton, Terry and Gerry, Lyn and Ted, Cathi, Nina and Hugh, Roxy and Ray, Nancy and Doug, Laura and Wolfgang, Jani and Mark, Judy, and MJ, your friendship, smiles, and hugs, as well as the frequently asked question, "how's the book going?" encouraged and supported me in quiet and important ways. Several other friends, scattered across the country, were bright spots at various stages of this project—Elisa Varela, Savannah Downing, Min Kyung Kim, and Megan McFarlane, I suspect you didn't realize it, but your laughter and connection to me made the journey brighter. To my immediate family, Mike, Joseph, Kari, Brynn, Tracy, Wendy, John, and Jana (a brilliant intersectional scholar in her own right), thank you for your unending love, support, wordsmithing, and encouragement.

PART I

CONCEPTUAL FOUNDATIONS OF INTERSECTIONALITY

CHAPTER

1

Intersectional Definitions of Identity and Communication

IN THIS CHAPTER YOU WILL FIND . . .

KEY TERMS AND CONCEPTS

- ableist logic
- AFAB/AMAB
- agency
- agender
- aromantic
- ascriptions
- asexual
- avowals
- binary logic
- bisexual
- cisgender logic
- cisgender/cis(gender)/cis
- classist logic
- color-blind logic
- communication
- discourse
- double (multiple) jeopardy
- double (multiple) protection
- essentialism
- gender expression/presentation
- gender fluid
- hearing
- heteronormative logic
- heterosexual/straight
- homosexual
- humanism
- identity
- intersectional approach to communication
- intersectionality
- intersex
- invitational rhetoric
- listening
- marginalized
- pansexual
- power
- privileged
- queer
- skiliosexual
- speaking
- standpoint
- transgender/trans
- truth regime

THE DANGER OF A SINGLE STORY

In her TEDGlobal talk, Nigerian-born novelist Chimamanda Ngozi Adichie shares that she grew up reading British and American children's books.[1] The stories in those books described blue-eyed and blond-haired children playing in the snow and eating apples, with their adult counterparts worrying about the weather and drinking ginger beer. Aspiring to be a writer, Adichie wrote her first stories as a child author about these same characters and situations, despite the fact that "we ate mangos," not apples, never thought about the weather, and she had no idea what ginger beer was. What "this demonstrates," she concludes, "is how impressionable and vulnerable we are in the face of a story, particularly as children." Adichie also relates what her mother told her about their new house boy, Fide. "The only thing my mother told us about him was that his family was very poor." And so, when she discovered the beautiful baskets Fide's mother wove, she was surprised: the only story she had heard was about his poverty and not that his family made beautiful things.

She shares that her college roommate, in the United States, was surprised that Adichie spoke English, knew how to use a stove, and listened to Mariah Carey rather than "tribal music." She explains that her roommate had heard only one story, and hence "she had felt sorry for me even before she saw me. Her default position toward me, as an African, was a kind of patronizing, well-meaning pity. My roommate had a single story of Africa: a single story of catastrophe." But Adichie, too, had fallen prey to a single story: a story of Mexico. She explains, "I remember walking around on my first day in Guadalajara, watching the people going to work, rolling up tortillas in the marketplace, smoking, laughing. I remember first feeling slight surprise. And then, I was overwhelmed with shame. I realized that I had been so immersed in the media coverage of Mexicans that they had become one thing in my mind, the abject immigrant."

Such is the power of representation—the presentation of images and stories that show us people, places, and ideas. Representations are found in stories—in the films, television, YouTube posts, music videos, news reports, and books we listen to, watch, and read. Like a definition, representations put boundaries around people, places, and ideas; they are never neutral. Representations filter "what happened" through a particular lens, often the lens of good and evil, right and wrong, guilty and innocent, and strong or weak. Representations are linked to power, Adichie explains, "the ability not just to tell the story of another person, but to make it the definitive story of that person." When we are only exposed to one story, Adichie explains, representations reinforce a particular story of what is "right" and what is "wrong." It feels like they are telling us what is "true"—but they aren't, they are only telling us a story, a single story told from a particular point of view.

The world, people, and human experiences can seldom be understood as shaped by one factor. Events and conditions of social and political life and the

Figure 1.1 Traditional handmade African baskets. (Source: iStock. Credit: brytta)

self are generally shaped by many factors in diverse and mutually influencing ways. This means that we are never just one identity. This is because a person's **identity** is comprised of the various traits, characteristics, experiences, and histories each of us rely on to answer the question, Who am I? No person can be explained and understood by a single trait. No one is only "tall" or only "smart" because each of us is comprised of a variety of qualities and experiences. Neither can we be explained in terms of binaries placed in opposition to each other: male/female, rich/poor, able/disabled, ethnic/white, native/foreign, educated/ignorant . . . and the list goes on. Our characteristics—the things that make us who we are—are a complex compilation of intersecting features intricately woven together, each with a different and important relationship to our sense of self, our power, or our lack of power in the world. We have to move beyond binary thinking and binary categorizing in order to understand ourselves and other people and to communicate effectively with them.

In their book *Intersectionality,* Patricia Hill Collins and Sirma Bilge propose that "social inequality, people's lives and the organization of power in a given society are better understood as being shaped not by a single axis of social division, be it race or gender or class, but by many axes that work together and influence each other."[2] We all are informed by our past experiences, the groups we identify with, and our cultures and each of these framings privileges a particular slant, take, or way of seeing—that is, until you see or hear a familiar story from a new angle. Adichie's example of her eye-opening travels in Mexico illustrate the invisibility of new angles; we often are unaware of their presence.

This chapter begins by exploring intersectionality, considering what it is, where it came from, and why it matters. The chapter moves on to analyze what intersectional thinking does: what it does to communication, to our understanding of past events, and to future interactions with people, policies, and our ability to act—to have meaningful agency—in the world. The chapter concludes with a call for invitational rhetoric, rhetoric that employs an intersectional lens when entering personal, social, economic, and political conversations. In their book, Hill Collins and Bilge urge us not only to understand just what intersectionality *is,* but to also consider what it *does.* In this book, we take up that charge and explore not only what intersectionality is but also what it does for us as students of gender and of communication.

WHAT IS INTERSECTIONALITY?

Imagine that you are traveling; you are on your way to something interesting or important. As you travel you arrive at a complex intersection. You realize that to get through it, and on to your destination, you must understand how each path meets the others, where each one could take you, and the implications of the crisscrossing paths for your journey. Which avenue do you select first, and why? Do you turn left or right, or move straight ahead? If it's a roundabout, how do you decide which exit will best get you to your destination? Which exits will complicate the journey? Are there several good choices or only one? Are there maps and signposts to help? What if there are none? Is there someone you can ask? On this journey, you've arrived at an intersection of options, crossroads, and pathways that converge and overlap, and you must figure out what each option entails and where it might take you.

Suppose that you navigate successfully through this intersection, only to arrive at another, and then again another—your journey is actually a maze of crisscrossing intersections, one after another. Occasionally, a direct path takes you to your destination, but even so, you find you must negotiate yet another intersection, stopping to consider other travelers, detours, and obstacles to avoid or work your way through, the benefits of choosing one option over others, and the difficulty in doing so. Some trips are easily accomplished; the path seems straightforward and easy, even familiar. Other trips are fraught with complications and frustrations; no matter how you try, you cannot seem to negotiate the maze to get to your destination.

Our identities are like intersections. We are, in fact, made up of multiple identities. Who we are is informed by where we come from, our experiences and habits, our preferences and frustrations, and our daily, weekly, monthly, and yearly journeys. To become the individuals we are now, we have traveled

Figure 1.2 Consider the complex identities of these three women. How might you be similar or different from them? How many different social locations can you identify in this photo and in your own identities? (Source: iStock. Credit: Ridofranz)

through intersection after intersection. Some roads were clear and free of challenges—we moved easily through them—but others entailed conscious choices, careful navigation, confusing and conflicting crossroads, backtracking and reentering, detour after detour, and rarely a signpost or a person around to help. When we consider our identity as an intersection, we acknowledge that the bits and pieces of us as a person might look different, but they operate together, constantly crisscrossing, working in concert to make us who we are. For example, we all have bodies and minds that work in specific ways; we all are expected to identify with particular genders and races; we all are affected by our economic status, our religions, our cultures, our ages, our families. This means that we are never just one identity, because no person can be explained and understood by a single trait. Instead our identities are complex matrices of traits informed by our bodies, minds, genders, races, economic opportunities and resources, religions, sexualities, cultures, and families, and all these influence how we are perceived by others and how we perceive ourselves.

Patricia Hill Collins and Sirma Bilge define **intersectionality** as "a way of understanding and analyzing the complexity in the world, in people, and in human experiences." Communication scholars April Few-Demo, Julia Moore, and Shadee Abdi explain that "intersectionality is a theoretical framework" that helps us "consider how individuals and groups—who are situated in multiple social locations and whose social identities may overlap or conflict in specific contexts—negotiate systems of privilege, oppression, opportunity, conflict and change." Intersectionality has the power to transform our thinking about identities and our understanding of those identities in relation to power. Intersectionality brings our attention to historical forces, how individuals and groups negotiate those forces, and how "interlocking systems of oppression—racism, sexism, classism—configure to form an overarching structure of domination that shapes life for specific individuals, groups, and communities."[3]

The Problems with Essentialist Thinking

Consider a conversation you are having with a colleague. You are female, married, and have just had your first child. You are also Mexican-American, Catholic, from rural Texas, and highly educated with an MBA (Master of Business Administration) from the University of Texas. Your family has large landholdings in the area of Texas where you are from. Your colleague is male, identifies as queer, and white. He is also highly educated with a Bachelor of Science degree in mathematics in computer science from MIT (Massachusetts Institute of Technology), where he received a scholarship. He is urban—from the inner city of Boston—and his family is working class. You are of equal rank at the Center for Digital Inclusion (a nonprofit organization that promotes technological education in marginalized communities) where you both now work, and you have been tasked with presenting a proposal together to the board at the company's headquarters in Philadelphia, Pennsylvania. What are the intersectional issues at play in this conversation?

Nirmala Erevelles, a professor in Social Foundations of Education at the University of Alabama, explains that a person's identity is made up of many identities that are always interacting and being negotiated: they are "concurrently mediated by the politics of race, ethnicity, gender, sexuality, nation," and more.[4] Even as identities are mediated, however, it is easy to slip into essentialism. **Essentialism** claims that there is a fixed and unchanging "essence" to an individual or a group of individuals. Essentialism posits that there is some substance or trait, a core element, that a group of people always possesses. Essentialism suggests that regardless of circumstance or life experience any individual who is said to be a member of that group will possess that trait. The reality, however, is that "individuals can be seen as having multiple 'subjectivities' [sense of self] that they construct from one situation to the next. In other words, people have many choices and considerable agency about who they choose to be."[5] People are far more complex than essentialism would allow.

From an intersectional perspective, the assumption that we can speak of a universal "woman" and a universal "man" is equally flawed. It hinges on **humanism,** which is the "belief that underlying the diversity of human experience it is possible, first, to discern a universal and given human nature," and to speak of that universality in a meaningful way.[6] To argue for a universal "woman" and universal "man" is to advance a logic that says that there is a "female human nature" and a "male human nature." This would mean that there is some characteristic or trait present in every man and a different characteristic or trait present in every woman, regardless of culture, class, religion, circumstance, or geographical location. But we cannot find this universal trait or characteristic: there is nothing we can find in every person we call "man" that is present in every other "man" on this planet and not present in the beings we call "woman." All men are not fundamentally alike, nor are all women. The assumption that they are depends on several problematic logics.

color-blind logic: says race, ethnicity, culture, and the color of one's skin have no effect on how individuals are treated.

cisgender logic: says that every person's gender matches the biological body they were assigned at birth.

heteronormative logic: says that all individuals possess the same sexuality—that is, everyone is, and should be, heterosexual.

classist logic: says that economic conditions, opportunities, and resources are the same, or can be, for every person in a community or country.

ableist logic: says that all bodies and minds function without obstacles or challenges and that they should move about the world as though there are none.

These errors in logic suggest that all women and all men—their bodies, cultures, religions, economies, and political systems—are essentially similar and can be understood through a single lens. But there is no universal "woman" and no universal "man" about whom we can think or speak. There may be commonalities where some intersections align, but the diversity of any person's identity makes it unrealistic to talk about "men" and "women" as if we all share similar histories, experiences, and lives.

Because of their diversity, women encounter the forces of sexism differently: the more mainstream a woman's identities are (that is, she is white, cisgender, able-body, heterosexual, affluent, and Christian), the easier she moves through intersections; the less mainstream, the more challenging the journey. Similarly, all men do not move through the world with equal ease: the more mainstream a man's identities are, the easier he moves through intersections; the less mainstream, the more challenging the journey.

When we engage an intersectional perspective, we are trying to understand the combination of identities of people—as individuals and as members of groups—as their identities shift and change in relation to power, access, equity, and respect. We are interested in understanding how each of us interact with other people and how we are linked to our history. By "history" we mean more than a static or linear record of facts. By history we mean that *what* has happened and *how* those events influence us today are intimately linked to structures of power and privilege. As cultural studies scholar Stuart Hall explains, identity is not simply a "matter of being," it is very much a matter of becoming. Our ideas about race, ethnicity, gender, sexuality, ability, age, and nationality, for example, did not come from nowhere. Our ideas about these aspects of identity came from events in the past and the stories told or not told about those events. Identity "becomes" because these stories frame our understandings—we don't exist outside of them; in fact, we are the products of the stories. This is to say, identities have histories, they have a past as well as a future. They come from somewhere and, as such, are "subject to the continuous 'play' of history, culture and power."[7]

The Benefits of Intersectional Thinking

It is helpful to think of intersectionality as both an orientation to a communication interaction as well as a tool with which to communicate. When we orient ourselves intersectionally, we begin to name the complexity of our identities as well as the complexity of the identities of other people. When we think of intersectionality as a tool, we see that it is foundational in naming that complexity. Let's examine the conversation between the two colleagues introduced earlier in this section. Orienting ourselves intersectionally, and using intersectionality as a tool for analysis, we see that the man has the privilege of gender and race; he is male and he is white. Some might consider that being a white male would give him social advantage and opportunity, and certainly these identities offer some. But he is also from a working class background, and he may have a working class Boston accent. This exposes his socioeconomic roots in a way that may not be to his advantage. In addition, he identifies with a marginalized group in terms of his sexuality. Thus, he is carrying a "double jeopardy" as well as a "double protection." None of these characteristics individually tell you who this person is because he is an amalgam of these features and others. To assume at the outset that his gender and race give him all the power would be inaccurate. On the other hand, if you are the Mexican-American woman, these factors might make you assume you are in a disadvantaged position, especially considering your recently acquired status as a working mother. But you also come from a well-to-do family, are heteronormative, and have a superior education, with an advanced degree. There are real advantages and disadvantages to particular statuses, but we are not just one thing. Intersectionality brings richness and increased accuracy to our conversations, helping us embrace and engage complexity rather than denying and ignoring it.

Intersectional thinking benefits students of communication and gender in three very concrete ways: first, intersectionality helps us avoid essentialist thinking about identity. Second, we can recognize that individuals possess multiple identities. Third, we can acknowledge that those multiple identities mean something—they are important for how an individual can move through the world.

1. Intersectionality helps us avoid essentialist thinking.
2. Intersectionality calls attention to complexity and multiplicity.
3. Intersectionality acknowledges the importance of multiple identities.

By calling attention to the complexities and multiplicity of any one person's identity, intersectional thinking highlights the ways these complexities and multiplicities are intertwined and interlocking. To view an individual intersectionally means that we acknowledge that an individual may have more than one **privileged** identity and may enjoy special advantages based on those identities. To view an individual through an intersectional lens is also to acknowledge that having more than one oppressed and **marginalized** identity may mean being relegated to a disadvantaged or powerless identity.

double (multiple) protection: Intersectional thinking involves understanding that privilege is not one essentialist identity but rather provides "double" and "multiple" social protections. Intersectional thinking addresses the racial, masculine, heteronormative, financial, able-body, sexual, sexed, cisgender, and religious advantages and benefits that also are very real material aspects of people's lives.

double (multiple) jeopardy: Intersectional thinking involves understanding that marginalization is not one essentialist identity but rather includes "double" or "multiple" social jeopardy.[8] Intersectional thinking addresses the racism, sexism, heterosexism, economic inequities, ableism, homophobia, transphobia, religious persecution, and more, that are very real and material aspects of very real and human people.

Cherríe Moraga gives this example of multiple jeopardy: "In this country, lesbianism is a poverty—as is being brown, as is being a woman, as is being just plain poor." Moraga continues, "The danger lies in ranking the oppressions. *The danger lies in failing to acknowledge the specificity of the oppressions.*"[9] Intersectionality acknowledges the specificity of oppressions. Acknowledging the specificity of oppressions requires that we recognize the reality of all of our identities as intersectional. To acknowledge a specific oppression (for example, race, gender, poverty, sexuality) is to show awareness of something, to recognize and accept its existence; its opposite is to deny and dispute. Responding to Moraga's challenge to acknowledge, rather than ignore or rank, the specificity of the oppressions takes courage and honesty. Not all individuals move through the world with equal ease. Furthermore, most of the stories and histories told to and consumed by mainstream U.S. citizens do not acknowledge oppressions, nor link them to structural and systemic problems. Rather, they deny, dispute, and even erase them.

1.1. GUIDE TO COMMUNICATION

Developing an Intersectional Vocabulary

1. Consider the "single story" you may have heard about a group of people. This single story may be about people from a country other than your own or about people who live in your own country. What information does this story give you about those people? Have you taken the time or had the opportunity to discover whether or not this story reflects the complexity of the people it is about? If so, what can you add to the single story to increase its intersectionality? If not, log into TED and see if you can find those intersectional stories.
2. Sketch or draw an image of your view of intersectionality. Use the definition offered in this section as well as the material you have read and/or discussed as a class. Compare your view with several of your classmates. Discuss the similarities and differences in your views and images.
3. Consider your own identities through an intersectional lens and make a list of your various identities that you feel are significant—for yourself and to others. Make a list of the times in the last week that those identities have made life easier or harder for you.
4. Make a list of the new vocabulary and ways of communicating you are developing. Consider whether there are terms and phrases you will no longer use, and whether there are new terms and phrases you will need to help you communicate about identity complexities.
5. Identify several current issues or events that have caught our national attention recently, or that have been a topic of controversy for some time. Using intersectionality as a tool, name the complexities inherent in that issue or event.

The benefit of intersectionality, in sum, is that it helps us expresses the multilayered nature of our experiences, histories, cultures, politics, and daily lives. Intersectionality moves us beyond overly simplistic language to help us engage the richness and challenges that we face in today's complex and multidimensional world.

WHAT IS COMMUNICATION?

Communication often is defined as the use of symbols (words, sounds, images, gestures, facial expressions, and the like) with a goal of exchanging messages with other people. Although this definition feels adequate—it seems clean and clear—its simplicity hides the complex nature of communication and the processes of communicating with other people. This is because communicating with others involves several acts, which aren't always clear and clean. Communication involves

> **hearing** others, which is recognizing that sounds and images are coming your way, and that often we do not want to acknowledge the presence of other people, especially if they upset or disturb our view of how things are or should be;
>
> **listening** to others, which is the process of giving thoughtful attention to another person's words and messages, even when we may not like what we are being asked to be thoughtful about; and
>
> **speaking** with others, which is the process of asking questions and sharing information, and sometimes we may be uncomfortable or afraid to ask questions as well as uneasy about sharing certain information.

Intersectionality shows us that communication and the act of communicating with other people is much more nuanced than a simple definition allows.

Defining Communication Intersectionally

When we use an intersectional lens, we can see that the simple definition of communication offered above fails to capture the complexity of the majority of our interactions with others. It fails to recognize that, while we may exchange messages with others, we always stand in a matrix of identities that affect our communication. When viewed intersectionally, we see communication as a more nuanced, complex, and often challenging exchange. In each interaction, identities will be combined and arranged differently—some will be more respected than others, some will be more influential than others, some will have more resources at their disposal, some will be perceived more positively than others.

At times, the process of avowal is in place in our communication with others. **Avowals** are the identities we have freely or consciously chosen. When avowals are at work, we engage in attempts to portray and present ourselves in ways that are consistent with our chosen identities. If we identify as a cisgender woman or man, or as gender queer, for example, we attempt to behave in ways that are consistent with those identities. Our verbal communication—the things we say to and share with others—and our nonverbal communication—the clothes we wear and the gestures and postures we adopt—confirm our chosen identities. Because we want others to see us as having the identity we avow—as being cisgender or gender queer—we communicate in ways that we see as consistent with those identities.

At other times, however, the process of ascription is at work. **Ascriptions** are the assigning of identities to others, whether or not the person actually

Figure 1.3 Compare your own agency in communication and in public spaces with that of this woman. What similarities and differences can you identify? (Source: iStock. Credit: adamkaz)

presents and portrays those characteristics. When we ascribe identities to others, we often fall prey to stereotypes. Our assumptions are clichés: a person looks poor, so they must be lazy; a person looks Asian, so they must not speak English; a person looks Hispanic, so they must be an illegal immigrant; a person looks Muslim, so they must be dangerous; a person looks white, so they won't understand racism. When we engage in the process of ascription, we aren't communicating with someone; we are making judgments about them, without exploration, investigation, or conversation.

When we define communication through an intersectional lens, we also come to understand power and agency in new ways. In the context of communicating with others, **power** can be defined as the amount of authority, control, influence, and credibility a person has in any interaction. When we consider power and communication intersectionally, we recognize that in any interaction, some combinations of identities will wield more power than other combinations of identities. Agency is a second term worth exploring intersectionally. **Agency** can be defined as the ability a person has to act freely and without constraint in our exchanges. Like power, agency is present in all of our interactions with other people as well as in how we move about in the world. Sometimes individuals with a lot of power also have a lot of agency in a communication exchange; those with more authority often have more agency. However, power and agency can shift such that those who once had little power and agency now have more: strikes and protests, occupations and reclamations, all can shift the balance of power and agency—temporarily or long term—as can exposing wrongdoings or unethical or unsustainable practices, laws, and customs.

When defined through an intersectional lens, communication is the creation and exchange of messages that recognize (or refuse to recognize) that our complex and multifaceted identities affect power and agency in different and important ways. How we hear, listen, and speak; the identities which we avow or are ascribed to us; the measure of power and agency we have, can gain, or are given or allowed to express in any interaction—all are always involved in our communication with other people, whether we acknowledge that involvement or not.

Communication and Hierarchies of Value

Intersectionality helps us see that the symbols we use to communicate are always infused with hierarchies of value and individuals are always positioned differently along those hierarchies. Sociologist Michael Kimmel describes these hierarchies metaphorically as a strong headwind. When we communicate, or even move in and around the world, some of us face that headwind directly and are constantly pushing against it, yet we often make little headway. Others have the strong wind at their backs and thus move easily through an exchange with little awareness that there even is a wind, rarely acknowledging the ways "we are sustained, supported, and even propelled by that wind."[10] To adequately understand communication—and its successes and failures—our definition must include a recognition of this strong wind. We must acknowledge the ways this wind, an elegant metaphor for our power and agency, inhibits and/or sustains us: we must come clean about power and privilege and the ways they blow with or against our attempts at message exchange.

When we communicate with other people, we engage in practices and systems of power and privilege. The messages we craft and negotiate are infused with symbols that reflect our own power and privilege as well as our view of the power and privilege held by our fellow communicators. Consciously or unconsciously, each of us taps into, employs, and deploys hierarchical structures and social codes. These hierarchies and social codes define what we see as normal and salient—what is right and important—and they often go unexamined and unexplored. An **intersectional approach to communication** involves noticing, examining, and exploring the presence of hierarchies and power differences—in effect, the privilege present or absent in our interactions with others.

Discourse and Truth Regimes

We all organize our worlds through our relationships with numerous, and complex, discourse systems and practices. **Discourse** refers to the ways we use language to establish belief systems, ways of knowing, and even what we can or cannot say. We use these discourse systems in ways that help us organize our worlds. How we collect and group together various facts and ideas, how we organize them into coherent statements, and how we make claims based on that organized collection of facts and ideas reflects how our communication captures complexity.[11] When we engage with others, we consciously and unconsciously engage particular discourses: we value certain groupings of ideas and practices and we see others as problematic or unacceptable. If we have the courage to define communication through an intersectional lens, however, we may open up doors for new kinds of logics, new ways of understanding people and places, and new ways of living in and moving through the intersections.

Discourse encompasses what are called truth regimes. **Truth regime** refers to a collection of statements and claims society accepts and makes function as true. We engage, for example, in discourses of science, religion, medicine, education, health, and economics, as well as discourses of identity, citizenship, and rights. These are the "sites in which knowledge is produced."[12] Each of these discourses reflects what a society accepts as right and true. Consider the following discourses, which establish truth regimes, or collections of statements and facts that have come to be considered as "true" and "real":

Discourse of Science: Knowledge can be organized into testable explanations and predictions about the universe.

Discourse of Religion: The universe can be understood and explained via supernatural or transcendental principles and practices.

Discourse of Medicine: The science and practice of diagnosis, treatment, and prevention of disease is the most productive means of treating illness.

Discourse of Education: The acquisition of knowledge occurs through study, storytelling, discussion, teaching, training, and research.

Discourse of Health: The well-being of an individual can be determined by their metabolic efficiency and ability to adapt to changing physical, mental, psychological, and social conditions.

Discourse of Economics: Societies can be explained and understood through an analysis of the production, distribution, and consumption of goods and services.

Discourse of Identity: Individuals possess and express an understanding of themselves via their physiological, psychological, and social relationships to others.

Discourse of Citizenship: A person's status can be determined by their being a legal member of a sovereign state or nation.

Discourse of Rights: Standards exist, and can be established, that determine an individual's legal, political, social, and personal freedoms and entitlements.

1.2. GUIDE TO COMMUNICATION

Discourse, Power, and Agency

1. Make a list of the identities you avow and another list of those that have been ascribed to you. Do not put your name on that list, yet. As a class, compile two lists: a list of the avowed identities of all the people in your class and another list of the ascribed identities.
2. What kind of "strong winds" are present for some of these identities, yet absent for others? Discuss the differences, hierarchies, and amount of agency and power in each of these lists.
3. Review the list of discourses of "truth regimes" (on science, religion, medicine, education, health, economics, identity, citizenship, rights) presented in this chapter. Now select a contemporary, and contentious, issue we face today. Map out the arguments around this issue and identify which discourse regimes they fall into. What kinds of claims emerge from these different truth regimes? What are the communication obstacles we face and in what ways might defining communication intersectionally help us communicate more effectively and less contentiously?

These discourses frame and organize the ways individuals are encouraged to think, act, and believe. Although they can be enormously helpful, assisting us as we organize our thoughts and methods of understanding, they also can be highly problematic. Truth regimes can be so tightly organized that they prevent us from seeing what is new, what has been present but ignored, and even innovative ways of organizing knowledge. In addition, truth regimes often are at odds with one another: discourses of science are often in conflict with discourses of religion; and discourses of rights, citizenship, and identity are often organized and supported in vastly different ways. For example, when some individuals challenged the accepted way of understanding our own earth—as flat or round, as being the center of the universe or just one of many planets in that universe orbiting around a sun—centuries ago, those individuals were shunned, mocked, and ridiculed. Today, we see conflicting truth regimes at work when we consider the contentious discourses around climate change or immigration. The truth regimes of science, economics, and religion are foundational in arguments around climate change, while the discourses of citizenship, identity, rights, and economics frame the arguments around immigration.

Truth regimes are representations that communicate to us—send us information—from a particular bias. One way to understand this bias is through the concept of a standpoint. A **standpoint** is the view or perspective through which something is being observed or explained. Standpoints frame things in particular ways: from an economic standpoint, it might make excellent sense to dump wastewater into a river or lake; from an environmental standpoint, however, it makes no sense at all. For those interested in communication and intersectionality, identifying and exploring the standpoint from which a thing is represented is paramount. We want to look for new angles that might initially be invisible but, when recognized, will reveal the complexities and nuances inherent in an intersectional approach to communication.

GENDER IDENTITY: COMMUNICATION BEYOND BINARIES

Intersectional thinking helps us see the binary nature of most of our assumptions, and thus communication, about identities. Binary thinking establishes an either/or framework that assumes something consists of two parts and can be best explained by those two parts. For example, to think in binaries is to assume a person should identify with only one of their identity categories and no more than one: female or male, for example, but not female and queer, or female and biracial, or female and Jewish, or female and poor, and so on. Although it is tempting to think that binaries simplify our complex world, making it easier for us to organize our lives, they actually are very problematic. Binary logics encourage hierarchies—one part of the equation usually comes first, is seen as better, and holds more cultural capital. Whiteness—whether referring to a racial identity or a skin color—has been privileged over all other racial identities and skin colors. Cisgender maleness has been privileged over cisgender femaleness, heterosexuality over homosexuality, able bodies over disabled bodies, cisgender over transgender or gender queer, and so on.

Thinking—and communicating—intersectionally moves us beyond these binary categories, helping us address the influences of a myriad of factors that affect who we are: our genders, races and ethnicities, sexualities, physical and mental abilities, economic opportunities, religions, and even our countries of origin and the ways they impact our lives. Elizabeth Rahilly, in her longitudinal study of transgender children, illustrates how communicating through the lens of gender binaries reinforces certain truth regimes. In a gender binary truth regime there is a category called "men" and a category called "women." When a person is born, she is either female and, therefore, a "woman," or he is male and, therefore, a "man." Male bodies will identify as male; female bodies will identify as female. Yet transgender, queer-identified, and intersex individuals tell us that this **binary logic** is a social construct and not an immutable fact—individuals are born with male bodies and do not identify as men—they identify as women and female, or both male and female, or neither—and individuals are born with female bodies and identify as masculine and male, or both male and female, or neither.

Individuals with intersex conditions also tell us that a gender binary identity is a social construct, not a biological reality, and reveals a truth regime at work. The

American Psychological Association states that as many as 1 in every 1,500 children are born with an intersex condition, and the Organization Intersex International (OII-USA) shares that an intersex "condition is about as common as having red hair (1–2 percent)."[13] An intersex condition means that an individual is born with ambiguous genitalia and as such, is not easily placed into the male/female paradigm, or is born with a condition that manifests at puberty, such as an extra X chromosome or an insensitivity to testosterone. Binary logics and the gender binary truth regime tell us that we should "fix" individuals who do not fit our either/or thinking—it's the individual who is the problem and not the binary logic. Rather than reflecting the complex, sometimes messy, often unpredictable nature of being human, gender binaries and their accompanying logics constrain our thinking and limit what we can know about ourselves as human beings.

If you are interested in beginning to develop a nonbinary vocabulary for gender identities, consider the following terms, which may be new to you. Keep in mind that in this first list, these terms refer to a person's gender identity—that is, a person's own sense of being male, female, neither of these, both, or other gender(s). These terms help us understand not only gender binaries, but also how powerful, and invisible, those binaries might be for some as well as how obvious they are for others—in short, they are truth regimes.

cisgender/cis(gender)/cis: an adjective that indicates that a person "identifies as their sex assigned at birth." A cisgender woman, for example, is someone who, at birth, is said to be "a girl" and identifies as a girl or woman throughout her life.

transgender/trans: a term that indicates that a person does not identify with the sex assigned to them at birth. A transgender man, for example, is someone who, at birth, is said to be "a girl" but does not identify, or exclusively identify, as a girl or woman throughout their life.

AFAB/AMAB: acronyms that mean "assigned female at birth" and "assigned male at birth." "No one, whether cis or trans, gets to choose what sex they're assigned at birth" and the acronyms call attention to that fact, providing more respectful labels than "biologically male," "female bodied," or "'born male/female,' which are defamatory and inaccurate."

intersex: a term that describes people born with "a combination of chromosomes, gonads, hormones, internal sex organs, and genitals that differs from the two expected patterns of male or female."

queer: a term that refers to groups of people who have "marginalized gender identities and sexual orientations who are not cisgender and/or heterosexual." The term has a "complicated history as a reclaimed slur."

gender expression/presentation: a term that refers to a person's "physical manifestation" of their gender. This is done through clothing, hair, voice, body, and more. A person may present as female, male, neither, both, and more.

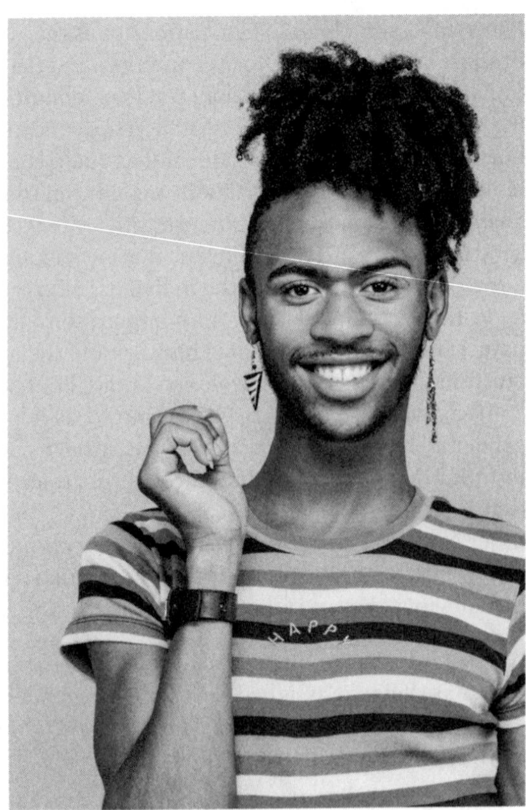

Figure 1.4 Consider the nonbinary identities this young person is presenting. What terms might you select to describe those identities? (Source: iStock. Credit: CarlosDavid.org)

agender: a term that describes people who do not "have a gender," who describe their gender as "neutral," or have little affiliation with our "traditional system of gender."

gender fluid: a term that describes a person with fluid or changing gender identity.[14]

All of these terms refer to people's gender identity—their experiences of themselves as gendered beings in bodies that have been labeled for them at birth. These labels help us move away from binary thinking—and instead make a space for people to describe their own experiences and identities.

These terms help us think about identity in important ways and reflect on philosopher and gender theorist Judith Butler's theory of the performance of our gender identities. Butler suggests that gender is a social and historical construct—it is not a biological given. We "perform" gender, and our ideas of correct performances come, in part, from the repetition of certain performances over time. They also come from being disciplined—punished or not rewarded—for what are considered incorrect performances. Social codes and norms "regulate" gender performances, and discourses play a key role in this regulation.[15] Our language reinforces ideas of gender identity and is often at odds with a person's avowed gender identity.

Other terms help us understand the binaries constructed around our sexuality—that is, who we are attracted to physically, emotionally, spiritually, and romantically. In this second list, the terms help us speak more clearly about our sexual orientation, which is a term that describes the type of romantic, sexual, and emotional or spiritual attraction a person has. Thinking only in binary terms, we would describe someone as either heterosexual or homosexual. When we want to move outside this binary truth regime, however, we find a number of helpful terms:

aromantic: a person who has little or no romantic attraction to others and/or has little interest in romantic behaviors.

asexual: a person who has "little or no sexual attraction to others and/or a lack of interest in sexual relationships/behavior."

bisexual: a person who is emotionally, physically, and sexually attracted to both men/males and women/females.

heterosexual/straight: a person who is primarily attracted to people of the "opposite sex."

homosexual: a person who is primarily attracted to people of the "same sex."

pansexual: a person who experiences sexual, physical, romantic, and spiritual attractions to people across all gender identities.

skoliosexual: a person who is primarily attracted to "genderqueer, transgender, transsexual, and/or non-binary people."[16]

Nonbinary vocabularies for gender identities and sexualities add richness to our communication. They help us remember that overly simplistic labels, like male/female or gay/straight, for example, do not address the complexity of who we are. This expanded terminology helps us understand that our identities are social and historical constructs and not biological givens. When we add nonbinary vocabulary into our communication with other people, we move away from the disciplining effect of binary language. People's identities are not incorrect performances of humanity, they are honest expressions of who they are.

INVITATIONAL RHETORIC

In this chapter, you have explored the way intersectionality opens up the idea of gender and communication and engages relations of power. By defining terms, we are not simply naming or narrowing what that term means; we are entering a social, economic, and political conversation. Definitions set boundaries around concepts that are always informed by power and politics. If you doubt this, consider the definition of "man." When advanced by Thomas Jefferson in the United States Declaration of Independence in 1776, the definition of "man" in the phrase "all men are created equal" did not include all men but, instead, only a very select group of them. At that time, Jefferson "owned about 200 slaves" and "never set any of them free, even upon his death."[17] At that time, "men" referred to white, property owning, cisgender, heterosexual, and Christian men—or those who could pass for all of these things. This definition of "men" did not include indigenous or African American men, because they were defined as inferior "savages" and "brutes" or "devils" and not fully human. It also did not include any women at all; all white women were considered the property of men in 1776; women of color fell into the same category as did men of color, not fully human.

Nearly a century later, the abolitionist and former slave Sojourner Truth countered this categorization of women in a speech she gave at the Women's Rights Convention of 1851. That speech became famous for this simple question, "Aren't I a woman?" With this question, she challenged several truth regimes:

> Nobody ever helps me into carriages, or over mud-puddles, or gives me any best place! And arn't I a woman? Look at me! Look at my arm! I have ploughed, and planted, and gathered into barns, and no man could head me! And arn't I woman? I could work as much and eat as much as a man—when I could get it—and bear the lash as well! And arn't I a woman?

In this speech, Truth identified with and engaged the intersecting oppressions of race, gender, and class. She saw that her oppression as a black woman and former slave excluded her, and women like her, from not simply the definition of "woman" but also "human." This exclusion meant that she, and other black women freed from slavery, were seen as not deserving basic rights: access to the justice system, the right to locate and reunite with their children, and even the right to be considered fully human. Before the term intersectionality became a part of our vocabulary, Truth expertly engaged the perspective. She successfully entered our justice system, becoming the first African American woman and former slave to sue the United States government for the return of her children, who had been sold into slavery (securing the release of many of them), and she challenged white women and men's assumptions about their own definitions of "woman" and "human." At one point, "men" and "women" meant a specific class of men and women. Truth challenged these definitions and the privileges they held in her declaration of her womanhood.

But Truth is not the only person to engage in the challenge of truth regimes before the term intersectionality came into our vocabulary. In "Six Reasons Every Indian Feminist Must Remember Savitribai Phule," Deepika Sarma

1.3. GUIDE TO COMMUNICATION

Nonbinary and Invitational Communication

1. Consider the nonbinary vocabulary you have been exposed to in this section. Identify the terms you would use to describe your own gender and sexual orientation. How often do you use these terms? Why do you or don't you use them in conversation with other people?
2. How important do you feel these nonbinary terms are? If you wanted to have an invitational conversation about their importance with someone who felt different than you did about their importance, how might you begin that conversation? How would you stay invitational rather than argumentative throughout the conversation?

relates the history of Savitribai Phule, who, in the 1850s, and with her husband, spearheaded a social justice campaign in India. The Phules engaged the perspective of intersectionality in robust ways. They "confronted several axes of social division, namely cast, gender, religion, and economic disadvantage or class." The Phules fought against laws that prevented widows from remarrying or from being pregnant as a widow (older husbands often died during a younger wife's child-bearing years). They fought against laws and cultural and religious practices that left widows in poverty, with incredible food insecurity and poor health. They also fought against the forced shaving of a widow's head, to mark her as a widow and thus undesirable.[18] At similar times, women in India, the United States, and other parts of the world were engaging an intersectional perspective to call out practices of power and exclusion that were harmful, painful, and unnecessary—and they had men helping them.

Some discourses are at odds with others, just as the Phules' and Truth's discourses on human value were at odds with the dominant discourses of their time. There are several ways we can engage these differences. We can argue with one another, pitting individuals and ideas against each other as we attempt to secure the correctness of our views over the views of other people. This kind of absolutist rhetoric—"I'm right/you're wrong"—rarely persuades anyone. We are rightly suspicious of arguments crafted and presented to achieve "the best" or "the right" view or position. Although this style of interaction can be productive and informative, if we constantly argue with others, if we are forced to pick one view as the "best" view, we can become discouraged because we are not allowed to embrace the nuances and complexity of issues. An alternative approach is to engage in a rhetoric that assists us in communicating intersectionally, which helps us identify binary and hierarchical logics. This kind of rhetoric is called invitational rhetoric and can be used as an invitation to learn. With **invitational rhetoric,** the goal is not to change a person or their view but instead to understand the experiences, histories, and ways of making sense of the world from their perspective. Using invitational rhetoric, we engage in conversations that allow an intersectional orientation in our communication with other people; conversations that have a goal of sharing perspectives, conveying ideas, and exploring beliefs and meanings. We exchange messages with others in order to explore, respectfully, the intersecting identities of that person and how those identities inform their worldviews.

When we use invitational rhetoric, we explore the threads, strands, paths, inroads, and exits that make up a person's identity. We engage other people in an exchange of meaning, an exchange that is rooted in an honest desire to understand, explore, clarify, explain, and share. When we use invitational rhetoric, our interactions do not have to lead to agreement or seeing "eye-to-eye." When people use invitational rhetoric, they gather information, respectfully, by engaging with others, exchanging ideas with them, listening to new facts and perspectives, and sharing differing opinions and views. Although they may be moved to a new view or position, or they may become more secure in their original stance, the goal is a responsible, respectful, and real engagement of ideas and views so that understanding the diversity and complexity of experiences is enhanced and enriched.[19] Intersectionality and invitational rhetoric can help us avoid the pitfalls and dangers inherent in Adiche's "single story." As an orientation to understanding and a tool for analysis and naming, invitational rhetoric and intersectionality invite us to explore issues, people, and experiences openly and honestly while we embrace the complexity present in all of our lives.

Resources

Chimamanda Ngozi Adichie, "The Danger of a Single Story," filmed July 2009 in Oxford, TEDGlobal video, 18:34, https://www.ted.com/talks/chimamanda_adichie_the_danger_of_a_single_story/transcript.

Sue Austin, "Deep Sea Diving . . . In a Wheel Chair," filmed November 2012 in Washington, DC, TEDxWomen video, 9:23, https://www.ted.com/talks/sue_austin_deep_sea_diving_in_a_wheelchair.

Kimberly Crenshaw and Abby Dobson, "The Urgency of Intersectionality," filmed October 2016 in San Francisco, CA, TEDWomen video, 18:42, https://www.ted.com/talks/kimberle_crenshaw_the_urgency_of_intersectionality.

Mellody Hobson, "Color Blind or Color Brave," filmed March 2014 in Vancouver, British Columbia, TED2014 video, 14:03, https://www.ted.com/talks/mellody_hobson_color_blind_or_color_brave.

Lee Mokobe, "A Powerful Poem About What It Feels Like to Be Transgender," filmed in May 2015 in Monterey, CA, TEDWomen 2015 video, 4:12, https://www.ted.com/talks/lee_mokobe_a_powerful_poem_about_what_it_feels_like_to_be_transgender.

Clint Smith, "The Danger of Silence," filmed July 2014 in New York, NY, TED@NYC video, July 2014, 4:11, https://www.ted.com/talks/clint_smith_the_danger_of_silence#t-238376.

Notes

1. Chimamanda Ngozi Adichie, "The Danger of a Single Story," filmed July 2009 in Oxford, TEDGlobal video, 18:34, https://www.ted.com/talks/chimamanda_adichie_the_danger_of_a_single_story/transcript.
2. Patricia Hill Collins and Sirma Bilge, *Intersectionality* (Cambridge, MA: Polity Books, 2017), 2.
3. April L. Few-Demo, Julia Moore, and Shadee Abdi, "Intersectionality: (Re)Considering Family Communication from Within the Margins," in *Engaging Theories of Family Communication: Multiple Perspectives*, ed. Dawn O. Braithwaite, Elizabeth A. Suter, Kory Floyd, 2nd ed. (New York: Routledge, 2017), 175, 177.

4. Nirmala Erevelles, *Disability and Difference in Global Contexts: Enabling a Transformative Body Politics* (New York: Palgrave Macmillan, 2011), 26.
5. Hill Collins and Bilge, *Intersectionality,* 125.
6. Leela Gandhi, *Postcolonial Theory: A Critical Introduction (*New York: Columbia University Press, 1998), 27.
7. Stuart Hall, "Cultural Identity and Diaspora," in *Identity: Community, Culture, Difference,* ed. Jonathan Rutherford (London: Lawrence and Wishart, 1990), 225.
8. Francis Beale, "Double Jeopardy: To Be Black and Female," in *The Black Woman: An Anthology,* ed. Toni Cade Bambara (1970; New York: Washington Square Press, 2005), 109–122.
9. Cherríe Moraga, "La Güera," in *This Bridge Called My Back: Writings by Radical Women of Color,* ed. Cherríe Moraga and Gloria Anzaldúa (New York: Kitchen Table: Women of Color Press, 1983), 29; emphasis in original.
10. Michael S. Kimmel, "Toward a Pedagogy of the Oppressor," in *Privilege: A Reader,* ed. Michael S. Kimmel and Abby L. Ferber, 2nd ed. (Boulder: Westview Press, 2010), 1.
11. Michel Foucault, *The Archaeology of Knowledge,* trans. A. M. Sheridan Smith (New York: Pantheon, 1972); Michel Foucault, *The Order of Things: An Archaeology of the Human Sciences* (New York: Pantheon, 1970); Paul Chilton, *Analysing Political Discourse: Theory and Practice* (New York: Routledge, 2004).
12. Jill Mattuck Tarule, "Voices in Dialogue: Collaborative Ways of Knowing," in *Knowledge, Difference, and Power: Essays Inspired by Women's Ways of Knowing,* ed. Nancy Goldberger, Jill Tarule, Blythe Clinchy, and Mary Belenky (New York: Basic Books, 1996), 286.
13. "Answers to Your Questions about Individuals with Intersex Conditions," American Psychological Association, last modified 2006, accessed February 2, 2017, https://www.apa.org/topics/lgbt/intersex.pdf, and "How Common Is Intersex? An Explanation of the Stats," OII-USA, The United States Affiliate of the Organization Intersex International (OII), last modified April 1, 2015, accessed February 2, 2017, http://oii-usa.org/2563/how-common-is-intersex-in-humans/.
14. LGBTQ+ Definitions, Trans Student Educational Resources, accessed April 2018, http://www.transstudent.org/definitions/ and Sasafrass Lowrey, "A Guide to NonBinary Pronouns and Why They Matter," HuffPost, November 8, 2017, accessed April 2018, https://www.huffingtonpost.com/entry/non-binary-pronouns-why-they-matter_us_5a03107be4b0230facb8419a.
15. Judith Butler, *Gender Trouble: Feminism and the Subversion of Identity* (New York: Routledge, 1990); Judith Butler, *Bodies That Matter: On the Discursive Limits of Sex* (1993; London: Routledge, 2011); and Judith Butler, *Undoing Gender* (New York: Routledge, 2004).
16. "Comprehensive List of LGBTQ+ Vocabulary Definitions," accessed April 2018, http://itspronouncedmetrosexual.com/2013/01/a-comprehensive-list-of-lgbtq-term-definitions/.
17. Matt Brundage, "The Meaning of Thomas Jefferson's Phrase 'All Men are Created Equal,'" accessed February 19, 2018, https://www.mattbrundage.com/publications/jefferson-equality/.
18. Hill Collins and Bilge, *Intersectionality,* 4.
19. George Kennedy, "A Hoot in the Dark: The Evolution of General Rhetoric," *Philosophy and Rhetoric* 25, no. 1 (1992): 1–21; Gregory J. Shepherd, "Communication as Influence: Definitional Exclusion," *Communication Studies* 43, no. 4 (1992): 203–219; Sonja K. Foss and Cindy L. Griffin, "Beyond Persuasion: A Proposal for an Invitational Rhetoric," *Communication Monographs* 62, no. 1 (1995): 3–18; Kathleen J. Ryan and Elizabeth J. Natalle, "Fusing Horizons: Standpoint Hermeneutics and Invitational Rhetoric," *Rhetoric Society Quarterly* 31, no. 2 (2001): 69–90; Krista Ratcliff, *Rhetorical Listening: Identification, Gender, Whiteness* (Carbondale: Southern Illinois University Press, 2005); Jennifer Emerling Bone, Cindy L. Griffin, and T. M. Linda Scholz, "Beyond Traditional Conceptualizations of Rhetoric: Invitational Rhetoric and a Move Toward Civility," *Western Journal of Communication* 72, no. 4 (2008): 434–462.

CHAPTER

2

Intersectional Explorations of Discourses of Rights

IN THIS CHAPTER YOU WILL FIND . . .

KEY TERMS AND CONCEPTS

- ad hominem attack
- aggrieved
- capitalism
- entitlement
- feminism
- first wave feminism
- imperialist
- misogyny
- monolithic view of human experience
- outrage
- patriarchy
- second wave feminism
- third wave feminism
- white supremacy

GENDER EQUALITY IS YOUR ISSUE, TOO

"I am reaching out to you because I need your help," explained UN Women Goodwill Ambassador Emma Watson in her "HeforShe" speech at the United Nations headquarters in 2014.[1] "We want to end gender inequality," and to do that, she explained, "we need everyone to be involved," not just women. Watson shared that as she travels, speaking about feminism and advocating against gender inequality, she continually hears that feminism is about hating men. She says, "If there is one thing I know for certain, it is that this has to stop. For the record, **feminism** by definition is: 'The belief that men and women should have equal opportunities. It is the theory of the political, economic and social equality of the sexes.'" The inequalities women face are clear, Watson notes, but men also are disadvantaged by this lack of gender equality. In fact, they are "imprisoned by gender stereotypes" that keep them unwilling to reach out for help when facing mental illness, underappreciated for their roles as parents, and unable to express sensitivity. "Men," she states, "I'd like to take this opportunity to extend your formal invitation" to enter the feminist conversation around gender equality, because "gender equality is your issue, too."

Watson, and countless other feminists like her, want people to understand the ways feminist thinking can change lives—for the better. She wants people to recognize that "we have to stop defining each other by what we are not and start defining ourselves by what we are." Gender exists on a "spectrum, and not as two opposing sets of ideals," and it is time we all recognize this. But with so much negative press surrounding feminism, what it is and what it can do, this has become difficult. In this chapter, we explore the evolution of feminism and feminist thinking—its contributions and its dilemmas—and the ways that evolution has moved our thinking beyond a binary logic of human rights. We then turn to an exploration of patriarchy and patriarchal discourses of rights. We consider in particular the American Dream, the concept of entitlement, and discourses of outrage. The chapter concludes with ways intersectionality can assist us in moving beyond outrage and toward respectful, open, and honest communication.

FEMINISM AND DISCOURSES OF RIGHTS

A quick survey of feminism in the United States and its history of achievements can help us see the ways it has changed lives—positively. Many of these changes we never stop to think about. We assume that education, jobs, and even having one's own bank account have always been open to everyone—when indeed, they have not. We know that some people could not cast a vote, wear pants, or even ride bicycles, but we often assume that common sense rather than feminism was key in correcting those social codes that seem silly to us

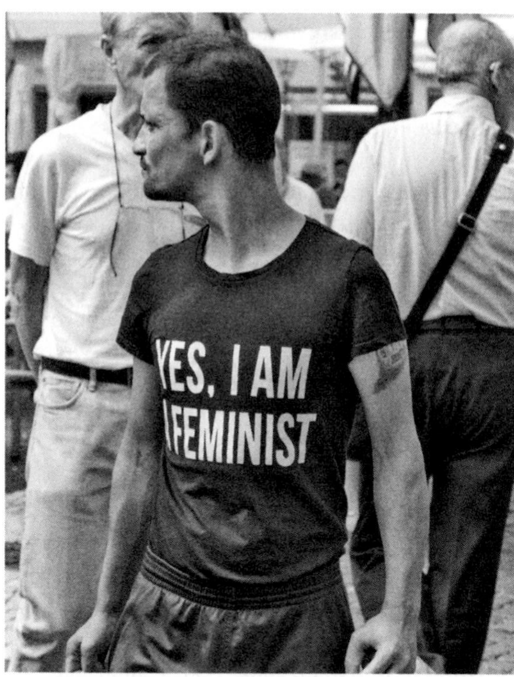

Figure 2.1 This man, from Augsburg, Germany, is proud to avow himself a feminist. Do you know many men who openly claim this identity? (Source: iStock. Credit: graemenicholson)

today. Most people know very little about the feminist movement, which, as Australian feminist Dale Spender points out, has been with us for centuries.[2] Because feminist efforts span such a long period of time, it is difficult to present its rich history with brevity. Even so, we can get a sense of some of the accomplishments of the feminist movement in the United States and understand that these accomplishments have benefited more people than we realize. The metaphor of waves (i.e., surges of water that push things forward, then retreat, then push forward again) has been the most prominent way we talk about feminism and the causes advanced and measured around "the rights of women," so we explore those waves here. In what follows, we trace the evolution of feminist thinking in the United States.

First Wave Feminism

Scholars mark the beginning of the first wave of the U.S. women's movement as 1840, when Elizabeth Cady Stanton and Lucretia Coffin Mott were barred entry to the World Anti-Slavery Convention in London—because they were women. Although women were an influential force in the abolition movement, their leadership was largely accepted as an extension of their moral and religious domestic roles. Outrage at women's involvement in the public sphere of politics from certain male quarters of the movement sparked voluminous (male) debate at the convention, and Mott and Stanton, among other women, were ultimately seated in a separate area, not in the main auditorium, behind a curtain. They could listen, but they were not allowed to speak. After having traveled 3,000 miles, Stanton and Mott's second-class status at this convention inspired them to hold their own convention, on their American home ground—this time, specifically to promote women's rights.

This first wave is said to have ended around 1925—a few years after women secured the right to vote with the passage of the Nineteenth Amendment to the Constitution in 1920. In **first wave feminism,** concern for public welfare extended beyond suffrage to include a variety of issues, and feminists fought for many of the rights we take for granted today: the right of access to public meetings and spaces, the right to an education, the right to own property, the right to divorce and keep custody of their children, and the right to birth control, which involved decriminalizing contraceptives. Feminists in the first wave took up temperance, the unionization of women (and the elimination of sweatshops), child labor reform, improved conditions for new immigrants living in overcrowded slums, and antilynching campaigns in the South, among other social issues. It was during this first wave that Sojourner Truth delivered her famous "Arn't I a Woman" speech and Jane Addams and Ellen Gates Starr established the Hull House, where "recently arrived immigrants from Europe" could not only "hear readings from books," but have their children attend kindergarten and their teenagers join clubs and attend classes.[3] Margaret Sanger, Ethel Bryne, and Fania Mendel spearheaded efforts to make birth control legal and available, and Mary McLeod Bethune became the president of the National Association of Colored Women's Clubs. The activism and advocacy by feminists during this first wave led to many "firsts": the first women physicians, lawyers, scientists, professional athletes, pilots, elected political representatives, and a Nobel Prize recipient, Marie Curie, first for physics in 1903 and then for chemistry in 1911.

To accomplish these gains, first wave feminists relied on certain discourses and actions. They organized, spoke publicly, wrote letters to government officials, peacefully marched in cities and protested in front of public buildings, engaged in hunger strikes, petitioned congress and the president, and wrote pamphlets, handbooks, books, and even a Declaration of Rights and Sentiments, invoking in its title both the Declaration of Independence and the Bill of Rights. Its principal author was Elizabeth Cady Stanton. The declaration, commonly referred to simply as the Declaration of Sentiments, inaugurated the first convention for women's rights, held in 1848 at Seneca Falls, New York. It stated, "We hold these truths to be self-evident: that all men and women are created equal. . . ." Seventy-three years after the convention, feminists introduced the Equal Rights Amendment to Congress in 1921, an amendment to the constitution that would have added the sentence "Equality of the rights under the law shall not be denied or abridged by the United States on account of sex" (the amendment was never ratified).

Rather than hostile or anti-male, as they often are characterized, these efforts were overwhelmingly peaceful, carefully organized, and pro-rights, in the face of resistance and antagonism from public officials, heads of organizations and industries, heads of churches and social organizations, and even the women's own families. The discourse of this first wave is often described as that of access: the right to be allowed in, to have a voice, and to be seen as fully human.

Second Wave Feminism

The second wave of feminism is sometimes marked as beginning with the 1949 publication of *The Second Sex* by French philosopher Simone de Beauvoir. *The Second Sex* catalogs the second-class status of women throughout history and deconstructs how the idea of what is "feminine" (*myth de la femme*) is used against women to keep them subservient. The most famous line of the book—"One is not born, but rather becomes, a woman"—inspired a generation of feminists to reject traditional subservient roles for women and instead to embrace independence, including reproductive freedom, sexual freedom, and economic freedom. Translated into English in 1953, the work heavily influenced Betty Friedan's *Feminine Mystique,* which helped launch second wave feminism in the United States. While the second wave of feminism built on the successes of first wave feminism, the civil rights movements of the 1950s and 60s also informed this movement. The *Feminine Mystique* was published in 1963, the same year as the March on Washington for Jobs and Freedom where Martin Luther King, Jr. gave his famous "I Have a Dream" speech. Scholars mark the second wave of the feminist movement in the United States as occurring from the 1960s to the 1990s.

The women's movement of the sixties and seventies glorified a unified "sisterhood" advancing through collective action, such as that sponsored by the National Organization of Women (NOW), founded in 1965. Movement leaders such as Betty Friedan, a founding member of NOW, promoted a redefinition of traditional sex roles and the liberation of women from domestic labor to pursue meaningful careers. In 1970, the prominent feminist leader Susan Brownmiller wrote in her *New York Times* article, "Sisterhood Is Powerful," that the issue of gender inequality is women's "fundamental oppression in a male-controlled society."[4] Issues not explored included race and how it affected experiences of oppression, or class and how the idea of career as an opportunity was radically different for poor and working class women, who had always worked outside the home.

In this second wave, feminists focused on a range of issues. They expanded their professional options by breaking into jobs once thought to be "male only" occupations. White feminists began to acknowledge that a person's race, class, sexuality, and physical abilities—and not just sex or gender—strongly influenced hiring and retention practices. Advocacy for the right to work outside the home also led to efforts for federally subsidized childcare options and exposed what we now call "the wage gap" (paying white men more than men of color and women of any color for the same job). Because of the efforts of second wave feminists, President John F. Kennedy signed the Equal Pay Act in 1963, making it illegal to pay women and men different salaries for the same work. The Civil Rights Act of 1964 banned employment discrimination on the basis of race, color, religion, sex, or national origin. These efforts also resulted in a familiar metaphor, the glass ceiling, which identifies the "unseen, yet unbreachable barrier that keeps minorities and women from rising to the upper rungs of the corporate ladder, regardless of their qualifications or achievements."[5]

The second wave also brought sexual harassment, interpersonal violence, and date-rape into our national conversation. Second wave feminists are responsible for Title IX of the Education Amendments of 1972, which makes "discrimination under any education program or activity receiving Federal financial assistance" illegal and thereby securing a place for women's athletics, among other things, in our high schools, colleges, and universities. In 1973, the Supreme Court upheld a woman's right to privacy in *Roe v. Wade,* which legalized abortion as a private decision between a woman and her doctor. Across college and universities, feminist advocated for, and succeeded in establishing, women's studies classes, centers, and programs. Because of second wave feminists, "take back the night" marches (against sexual and domestic violence) became common events nationwide, and two phrases, "the personal is political" and "consciousness raising," became a part of our discourse around personal experiences of sexism.

Second wave feminists also protested against such cultural spectacles as the Miss America Pageant and, in addition to establishing NOW, founded such organizations as the National Black Feminist Organization. The novelist and social activist Alice Walker coined the term "womanism" to better explain black women's orientation to feminism. Audre Lorde published poetry that called attention to racism, sexism, classism, and homophobia. Bell hooks published her first full-length book, *Ain't I a Woman: Black Women and Feminism,* in 1981. In the 1980s, the Combahee River Collective—an Afrocentric lesbian and feminist organization headquartered in Boston and critical of white feminism—rejected what now is known as a **monolithic view of human experience** that implied all human experience could be best explained through a single lens. Phrases like "all humans are . . ." represent monolithic thinking, they explained. More specifically, the monolithic thinking of early feminism involved the idea that all women had the same experience and that this single lens on experience was that of a cisgender, able-body, heterosexual, economically secure, Christian, white person's identity. Other experiences were seen as variations on this "norm." In "A Black Feminist Statement," the Combahee River Collective articulated the need for a more multifaceted understanding of identity: "We believe

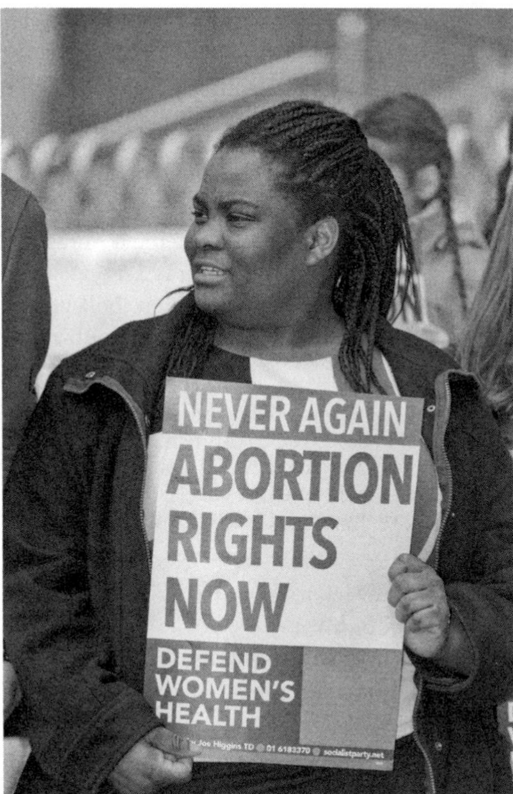

Figure 2.2 Second wave feminists brought the conversation about reproductive rights to the public's attention. Even though the Supreme Court upheld a woman's right to reproductive choice in 1973, feminists, like this young woman, are still fighting to protect those rights today. (Source: iStock. Credit: Sebastian Kaczorowski)

that sexual politics under patriarchy is as pervasive in Black women's lives as are the politics of class and race. We also often find it difficult to separate race from class from sex oppression because in our lives they are most often experienced simultaneously."[6] Writing in 1984, bell hooks echoed these views and explained that the assertion "all women are oppressed" is inherently flawed because it

> implies that women share a common lot, that factors like class, race, religion, sexual preference, etc., do not create a diversity of experience that determines the extent to which sexism will be an oppressive force in the lives of individual women. Sexism as a system of domination is institutionalized but it has never determined in an absolute way the fate of all women in this society.[7]

In the 1980s, second wave feminists founded film and production companies such as Women Make Movies, while the Guerilla Girls donned gorilla masks to protest the lack of representation of women in the arts. Second wave feminists engaged in numerous—peaceful—public demonstrations, marches, and rallies. Their music and art began to receive public support, and they caught the attention of many with their street performances, humor, manifestos, and willingness to speak out—in print or in public.

These efforts were overwhelmingly reasoned, organized, respectful, and much needed, and the discourses coming from second wave feminists do have a particular tone. Second wave feminism can be characterized as producing discourses focused on increasing access to mainstream society as well as naming the **misogyny** (contempt for and even hatred of women) that made it so difficult for women to be seen as credible and capable. Popular media coverage of second wave feminism tended to mock, trivialize, and portray second wave feminists as angry and anti-male. But the problem is not men, bell hooks explains, it is sexism; hooks adds that, like most feminists, she is not anti-male but, rather, anti-sexism.

> All of us, female and male, have been socialized from birth to accept sexist thought and action. As a consequence, females can be just as sexist as men. And while that does not excuse or justify male domination, it does mean that it would be naïve and wrong minded for feminist thinkers to see the movement as simplistically being for women against men . . . we need to be clear that we are all participants in perpetuating sexism.

When we come "closer and know firsthand what feminist movement is all about . . . you will see: feminism is for everybody."[8]

Second wave feminism, in sum, identified sexist assumptions, practices, laws, and norms, highlighting ways of living and thinking that were antithetical to our country's explicit commitment to equality. However, women of color feminists in the 1980s strengthened this contribution significantly by challenging the popular slogan of "sisterhood is powerful" advanced by Friedan, Brownmiller, and others in the 1960s and 70s. Black feminist legal scholar Kimberlé Crenshaw introduced the term intersectionality and began to develop a theory of intersectionality as a rejection of a system in which political, legal, and media practices relied on seeing only a single aspect of a person's identity—only gender, for example, but not race or class; only race, for example, but not gender or class. She notes that this "single axis" definition of a person resulted in policies and practices that severely disadvantaged certain individuals.[9]

Crenshaw's work, which grew out of her experiences with minority women seeking respite from violent and abusive relationships and the shelters that were supposed to provide them that respite, transformed feminist thinking. Feminists began to articulate a far more nuanced view of identity and its many relationships to rights, and this intersectional thinking influenced what has come to be called third wave feminism.

Third Wave Feminism

Variously described as a reaction against first and second wave feminism, pushing back against media claims that feminism had outlived its usefulness, and galvanized by Anita Hill's charges in 1991 of sexual harassment against Clarence Thomas (and his appointment to the U.S. Supreme Court, regardless), the third wave of feminism is said to have its beginnings in the late 1980s and early 1990s. Several things set **third wave feminism** apart from the previous waves. First, the intersectional theories, voices, and writings of Cherríe Moraga, Gloria Anzaldúa, bell hooks, Chela Sandoval, Audre Lorde, Maxine Hong Kingston, and many other feminists of color had a profound influence on young feminists who came of age in the 1980s; many third wave feminists were keen to challenge binary and exclusionary thinking and embrace intersectional theories and practices. Second, the 1990s were said to be the era of "post-feminism," a media creation that posited that feminism had achieved gender equity and sexism was a thing of the past. Far from correct, in this supposedly "post-feminist" era, young feminists had to become "a strong enough force" to be able not only to create their own identities but to resist post-feminist attempts to dismantle the significance of them. Third, because of the internet and social media outlets, feminist activism and feminist conversations could take place in an entirely new ways—and third wave feminists were eager to use these tools.[10]

Scholar and activist Emi Koyama suggests that understanding the third wave is not so much about what "third wave feminism is" but rather "how calling ourselves 'third wave' enables us to do what we cannot do otherwise."[11] In the decades since the 1990s, third wave activism has included marches to Washington, DC in support of reproductive freedom as well as the worldwide Women's March in protest of the election of Donald J. Trump; gender neutral public bathrooms; the Third Wave Fund, led by young activist women of color as well as queer and trans people under the age of thirty-five; #MeToo; #BlackLivesMatter; consumer boycotts of sexist, racist, and homophobic food industries; the publication of books and anthologies including *Manifesta: Young Women, Feminism, and the Future, Colonize This! Young Women of Color on Today's Feminism, To Be Real—Telling the Truth and Changing the Face of Feminism,* and *Listen Up—Voices from the Next Feminist Generation;* support for feminist rock, punk, and hip hop by musicians such as the Indigo Girls, Ani DiFranco, the Riot Grrls, Nicki Manaj, Rihanna, Princess Nokia, Cardi B, and Rapsody; the Lilith music festival; feminist blogs; safety apps for cell phones that discussed physical and mental health, reproductive cycles, parenting, and more; zines including *Bust* and *Bitch;* and "Girlies," who reclaim such "feminine" things as "knitting, the color pink, nail polish, and fun" as well as "their right to a cultural space once deemed the province of men; for example . . . porn and judgment-free pleasure and sex."[12]

As with the first and second waves, the third wave contains contradictions, but these young feminists are more open about them. Third wave feminism is grounded in both Third World activist Chela Sandoval's call for a "new subjectivity that honors race" and also Rebecca Walker's proclamation that feminists must face and embrace the "contradictions and complexities of our feminist

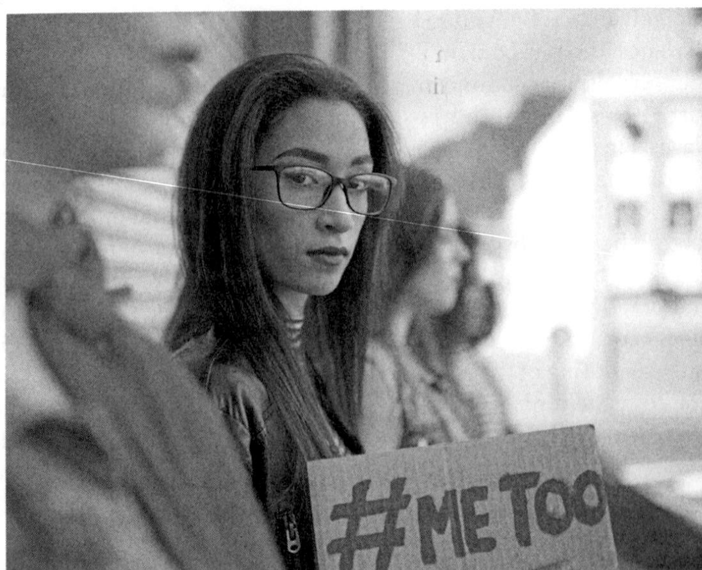

Figure 2.3 #MeToo is one example of the many issues we can credit third wave feminism for bringing to the public's attention. How many other important issues has third wave feminism brought to the public's attention? (Source: iStock. Credit: Tassil)

lives."[13] Walker coined the phrase third wave in a 1992 *Ms.* magazine article written in response to the Anita Hill hearings: "I am not a post-feminist feminist, I am the Third Wave."[14]

Although third wave feminism shares a commitment to move beyond binary thinking, like all of the waves, it is not perfect. Feminist author Amber Kinser suggests that "while the third wave as a group may be stronger at pluralistic thinking in some ways than second wave as a group, in other ways third wave is weaker."[15] In the name of inclusiveness, third wave feminism runs the risk of inviting "practically any claims to feminist membership." Kinser suggest that this can lead to depoliticization and co-optation rather than feminist activism.[16] Moreover, in "U.S.–Third World Feminism," Chela Sandoval suggests that "hegemonic feminism," which is largely the monolithic thinking of the non-intersectional feminism of the second wave, plagues us still. If we are to be successful in the third wave, we must "shatter the construction" of any one approach to or framing of feminism "as the single most correct site where truth can be represented." Moraga and others in the second wave paved the way for naming the "specificity of the oppressions" (e.g., gender, race, class, sexuality),[17] in order to, as Sandoval urges, "re-center" various framings and approaches to understanding oppression "depending on the kinds of oppression to be confronted."[18]

Sharing the words of Chicana feminist Aida Hurtado, Sandoval takes women of color and especially queer women of color off the margins in an effort to re-center the discourse around them. Hurtado explains the "political skills required by women of color are neither the political skills of the White power structure that White liberal feminist have adopted nor the free spirited experimentation followed by the radical feminists." More like "urban guerillas trained through everyday battle," women of color's "fighting capabilities" are rarely understood nor are they "codified anywhere for them to learn." How to cope is the strategy that needs to be codified and learned. On an everyday basis, minority women "measure and weigh what is to be said and when, what is to be done and how, and to whom . . . daily deciding/risking who it is we can call an ally, call a friend (whatever that person's skin, sex, or sexuality)," and they must also track how these situations constantly differ and change.[19] Feminists must "read the current situation of power" and self-consciously choose to adopt "the ideological form best suited to push against its configurations, a survival skill well known to oppressed peoples."[20]

We often talk about "the rights of women" in relatively uncomplicated ways when examining the metaphor of the first and second waves of feminism; we conceptualize "women" as a large and homogenous group of individuals and see "rights" as something each woman is denied in the same way. The intersectional third wave, however, recognizes that these previous "waves of feminism" were often dominated by cisgender, middle and upper class, able body, heterosexual white women.[21] Some scholars consider that we may be entering a fourth wave, perhaps exemplified by popular figures like Beyoncé, whose song "Flawless" embraces feminism, femininity, sexuality, self-respect, ethnicity, independence, and female aspiration all at the same time because, as Beyoncé has said, "We're not all just one thing. Everyone who believes in equal rights for men and women doesn't speak the same, or dress the same, or think the same."[22] In her "Flawless" performance, Beyoncé quotes novelist Chimamanda Adiche's TEDx speech, "Why We Should All Be Feminists." The quotation, flashed across a big screen with Chimamanda's voiceover, is about how we teach girls to "have ambition . . . but not be too successful," to "aspire to marriage" when we "don't teach boys the same," and that ideas of sexuality do not need to be examined and challenged.[23] If feminists are to move into a fourth wave of advocacy they will have to engage intersectional ideas and orientations fully. Adiche's ending words must be more than this familiar definition of feminism: "Feminist: the person who believes in the social, political and economic equality of the sexes." That definition also needs to be explicitly centered in a commitment to intersectionality and nonbinary ideas of identity.

While first, second, and third wave feminisms were and are not perfect by any means, feminists have helped many people see that their assumptions, and our laws, did and do not uphold the commitment to equality for all. The achievements of feminism and the feminist movements are significant and because of this, their contributions are worth respectful consideration and engagement.

2.1. GUIDE TO COMMUNICATION

Exploring Intersectional Feminist Discourses of Rights

1. There likely are other things you have learned or heard about feminism and feminist movement not presented in this section. As a class, make a list of these other ways of thinking about feminism. Where does this knowledge come from? Whose perspective is being presented? Is this information oriented toward intersectional thinking?
2. Search for descriptions and images of fourth wave feminism. Who are the spokepersons? What are they suggesting? How does this emerging fourth wave add to the conversation about intersectional approaches to gender equality?
3. Watch L. B. Hannahs, "What It's Like to be a Trans Gender Dad," filmed April 2017 in Gainesville, FL, TEDxUF video, 13:36, https://www.ted.com/talks/lb_hannahs_what_it_s_like_to_be_a_transgender_dad#t-645267s. What insights about avowals and ascriptions do you gain from Hannahs's story?

PATRIARCHY AND DISCOURSES OF RIGHTS

To fully understand patriarchy, bell hooks declares, we must acknowledge that patriarchy is "the single most life-threatening social disease" of the contemporary moment.[24] In contrast to feminism, patriarchy has never been described as occurring in waves or as a movement. Instead, patriarchy is a daily presence in our lives, and this presence often goes unnoticed.

Wikipedia defines patriarchy as "a social system in which males hold primary power and predominate in roles of political leadership, moral authority, social privilege and control of property."[25] Hooks takes this definition to feminist and intersectional levels by defining **patriarchy** as "a political-social system that insists that males are inherently dominating, superior to everything and everyone deemed weak, especially females, and endowed with the right to dominate and rule over the weak and to maintain that dominance through various forms of psychological terrorism and violence."[26] With this definition, hooks is saying that patriarchy shapes "the values of our culture. We are socialized into this system, females as well as males."[27]

Hooks uses the phrase "imperialist white-supremacist capitalist patriarchy" to describe the complexity of patriarchy and highlight its far-reaching aspects. This phrase asks us to consider "the interlocking political systems that are the foundation of our nation's politics," a politics rampant with sexist oppression.[28]

Although the phrase seems intimidating and complicated, and on many levels it is, much of its power and truth comes from its intersectional foundations. Here is how we can begin to understand this complex association of terms.

imperialism: to encourage and practice absolutist, hawkish, dictatorial, colonizing, and authoritarian practices and solutions to local as well as global issues. Imperialism encourages domination and empire-building. It sees the takeover of countries, colonies, peoples, and nations as a good thing. Imperialism supports and encourages the ideas, belief systems, and cultural norms of a more powerful entity, erasing the ideas, belief systems, and cultural norms of the less powerful entity.

white supremacy: entails the privileging of white people and white ways of thinking, including the belief that white individuals are superior to all other racial groupings. White supremacy includes systemic racism, racist language, violence directed at non-whites or white allies, as well as the more recent "white nationalist" groups who are "offended by what they see as excessive political correctness" and who consider themselves a part of "the new, embattled White minority."[29]

capitalism: an economic system that celebrates private ownership, profits, competition, and the accumulation of wealth. Capitalism depends on an abundance of low-wage-earning workers, whose wages are not reciprocal to the profits made by those employing the workers. Those who support capitalism are often challenged to address the tensions between profit seeking and earning with ethical and sustainable approaches to that seeking and earning.

To describe patriarchy, as hooks does, through the feminist and intersectional lenses of imperialism, racism, and capitalism, is to have the courage and honesty to acknowledge the specificity of oppressions called for in the Combahee River Collective's statement. Hooks's inclusion of white supremacy, capitalism, and imperialism point out that patriarchy is an ideology that has spread far and wide. Its reach extends to the way we interact with those we see as "American," and those we consider "other." It infects our understanding of commerce and the economy within the United States as well as how we do business globally.

But what does all this mean for students of communication? An intersectional exploration of the very familiar story of the American Dream is an excellent way to begin to unpack patriarchy. Exploring the American Dream intersectionally helps us understand the patriarchal narrative emerging from a select group of Americans and its impact on us all.

The American Dream and Promises Made

In *Angry White Men: American Masculinity at the End of an Era,* Michael Kimmel describes the American Dream and its link to an idealized version of

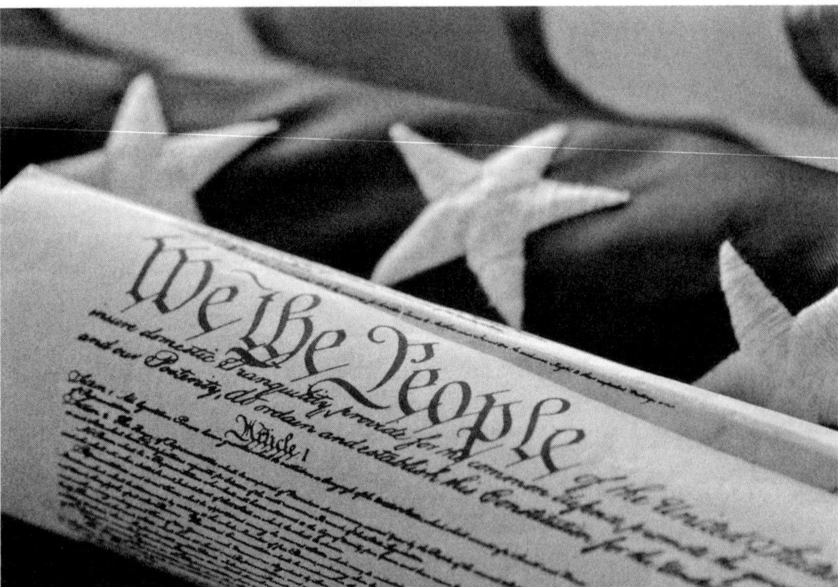

Figure 2.4 Take a moment to reflect on the promises made in the United States constitution. Which of these promises do you take for granted, which do you feel are threatened, and which promises are denied to you or other people? (Source: iStock. Credit: alancrosthwaite)

masculinity for men in the United States. The American Dream tells us that if people work hard enough, they can achieve success. In this dream, everyone has an equal chance to succeed because our founding fathers proclaimed "all men" as created equal. Both our Declaration of Independence and the Constitution ensure this equality, our government makes laws that protect this equality, and ours is the Promised Land, the land of hard work, upward mobility, and dreams that "really do come true."[30] Kimmel explains that this American Dream promised us abundance, prosperity, economic freedom, boundless opportunity, and unlimited upward mobility.[31]

Kimmel's research pointed out that a particular group of individuals, specifically cisgender, able body, heterosexual white men, "believed that this was the terra firma of American masculinity." More than any other group of men, this dream was "the ground on which [white, cisgender, able body, heterosexual] American men have stood for generations." Because all men were said to be equal, if they worked hard enough and overcame obstacles, they could prosper. The dream is grounded in the belief that, because the United States is the land of freedom and opportunity, anyone can succeed. Opportunities to do so are available to all: failing to work hard and lack of determination are the only things standing in a person's way.

This dream of success defined masculinity—real men showed up, put in an honest day's work, and returned home at the end of the day to read the paper, perhaps discipline a wayward child, and then enjoy a nice dinner prepared for and served to them. Today, however, many of these men feel "like a carpet [is] being snatched from under their feet."[32] In a very short span of time, Kimmel explains, many white, cisgender, able body, heterosexual men went from feeling like the father who knew best, the breadwinner and head of the family, and the apple of the nation's eye, to feeling "stiffed," as Susan Faludi describes the emotion. Many of these men now are feeling as though they have "lost 'a useful role in public life, a way of earning a decent and reliable living, appreciation in the home, respectful treatment in the culture.' They're feeling emasculated—humiliated."[33] The dream promised success but, instead, they've received what feels like the last place in line. Today these men

> feel like their voices are silent, drowned in the din of other voices shouting to be heard by a federal government that seems increasingly hard of hearing. Maybe, they imagine, their voices are not even silent, but silenced—deliberately suppressed to give others a chance. We, who were raised to believe our voices would be heard, are actually being told to be quiet. Surely, that's not fair.[34]

Kimmel believes that American men actually do "have a lot to be angry about." We live in a system that "promised a lot of rewards if [men] played by the rules." If men were

> good, decent, hardworking men, if they saddled up, or, even more accurately, wore the harness themselves, they could feel the respect of their wives and children; if they fought in America's wars and served their country fighting fires and stopping crime, they'd have the respect of their communities. And, most important, if they were loyal to their colleagues and workmates, did an honest day's work for an honest day's pay, then they'd also have the respect of other men.[35]

Contrary to this promise, however, are decades of the downsizing of corporations, the outsourcing of jobs once central to achieving this promise, and the rampant foreclosing of homes because of unethical lending practices that put corporate profits above human security and dignity. The events of recent decades have not just threatened this group's belief in their right to economic security but perhaps most keenly for this group of people, exposed the American Dream as only a dream and not a certainty.

But aren't women angry too? Kimmel's research suggests that a certain group of white, cisgender, able body, heterosexual women are also angry. We see them on television and at rallies, we hear them on talk shows and radio. Their anger is slightly different, and there are fewer of them compared to men. Kimmel explains that these "angry American women" are angry because they want "their men to be the traditional heads of households, able to support their families. They want to be *moms,* not 'women.'"[36] They worry about their children in a world in which the once promised American Dream no longer delivers. In the words of one of these women, who is a mother of three children, "I think I'm angry because I'm so afraid. I'm afraid that we are bankrupting our children. We're spending so much, in debt up to our eyeballs, and who's going to have to pay for that? My kids. Their kids. We're going to leave them a complete mess—a debt ridden country where immigrants feed off our taxes like we're goddamned breast-feeding them. It's just wrong. It's all upside down."[37]

The result of these dramatic changes is that there is a group of native-born white, cisgender, able body, heterosexual men, and white, cisgender, able body, heterosexual women who are feeling like the very thing their fathers "entrusted" to them, or were "supposed to entrust" to them, has been stolen. A "birthright" has been lost. What was promised is no longer available and this has left some feeling enraged. Carol Gilligan, feminist, ethicist and psychologist, explains that the "hallmarks of loss are idealization and rage" and under that rage, she shares, is "immense sadness."[38] When we feel loss, we often romanticize what we thought we once had—we see the best, erase the worst, and in short, view what was lost as more wonderful than it actually was. We see the past as perfect, the present as uncertain and wrong, and the future as frightening. When something we thought we once had, and should have had, is taken away we may feel violated and cheated: "the smoldering rage which comes from being cheated" will be extended "to the society which allowed us to be so cheated."[39]

Entitlement and the Loss of a Birthright

Kimmel explains that the feeling of being cheated can move from sadness to intense rage when there is a powerful sense of having been wronged and of what he calls being "aggrieved." To be **aggrieved** is to feel ignored and treated unfairly. We are aggrieved when we feel that something that we thought was rightfully ours is taken away. We feel aggrieved when we feel deceived—as though we've been cheated. Citing psychologist Carol Tavris, Kimmel says that that in order to feel wronged, a person must have wanted what was promised. A person must want what they "don't have and feel that they deserve" what they did not get.[40]

The strength of a person's feeling wronged—feeling aggrieved—depends on their sense of entitlement. **Entitlement** is the belief that you were supposed to have something: someone promised you something you very much wanted to have. Indeed, you came to feel that it was your right to have this thing, so powerful was the promise and compelling your desire to have it. The promises that lead to entitlement can come from any number of places, certainly from our friends and family, but also from our media, educational and religious systems, popular culture, politicians, even the grand story of the American Dream. Aggrievement can occur when a person's sense of entitlement—their sense of "I should have had that" or "that's mine" and not yours or theirs—is strong.

With regard to many cisgender, heterosexual, able body, white men in America today, their sense of "that was mine" is strong: for some, the threat to "my job" and "my right" looms large. And the threat, indeed the promise not delivered, challenges the very foundation of their manhood and masculine identities. Kimmel shares that it is a fact that the American Dream is not coming true for many in this group of angry men. Hard work today does not necessarily ensure a good job or the ability to provide for one's family or upward mobility. For some white, cisgender, able body, heterosexual men, Kimmel explains, changing cultural, social, and economic dynamics have, indeed, hit hard.

Although it is reasonable to be angry when a promise made to you goes unfulfilled, why isn't everyone angry in the ways this group is? What is driving this aggrieved entitlement? Kimmel explains that "those who already have something believe they are entitled to it."[41] Those who never had that thing never really felt entitled to it. The sense of violation is far different when something has been yours, without challenge or question, from the start. Kimmel shares that as he listened to this group of men, he understood their anger and felt empathy for them: "they were right, they had lost something." Their "feelings *are* real. They cannot be dismissed with a casual wave of a hand. But at the same time, their feelings may not be *true*—they may not provide an accurate assessment of their situation."[42] The discourses explaining the reasons for feeling aggrieved and the solutions to that feeling of being wronged may not be sound.[43]

From Entitlement to Outrage

In "From Incivility to Outrage: Political Discourse in Blogs, Talk Radio, and Cable News," Sarah Sobieraj and Jeffrey Berry expose one genre of a discourse of entitlement. Sobieraj and Berry analyzed the discourse of **outrage,** which they define as

> a particular form of political discourse involving efforts to provoke visceral responses (e.g., anger, righteousness, fear, moral indignation) from the audience through the use of overgeneralizations, sensationalism, misleading or patently inaccurate information, ad hominem attacks, and partial truths about opponents, who may be individuals, organizations, or entire communities of interest (e.g. progressives or conservatives) or circumstance (e.g. immigrants).[44]

Sobieraj and Berry examined cable television, talk radio, political blogs, and newspaper columns to uncover not just the presence of outrage, but what it looks and sounds like, as well as who produces the discourse. What they discovered is fascinating:

- 100 percent of the television episodes contained the discourse of outrage.
- 98 percent of the talk radio programs contained the discourse of outrage.
- 82 percent of the political blogs and newspaper columns contained the discourse of outrage.

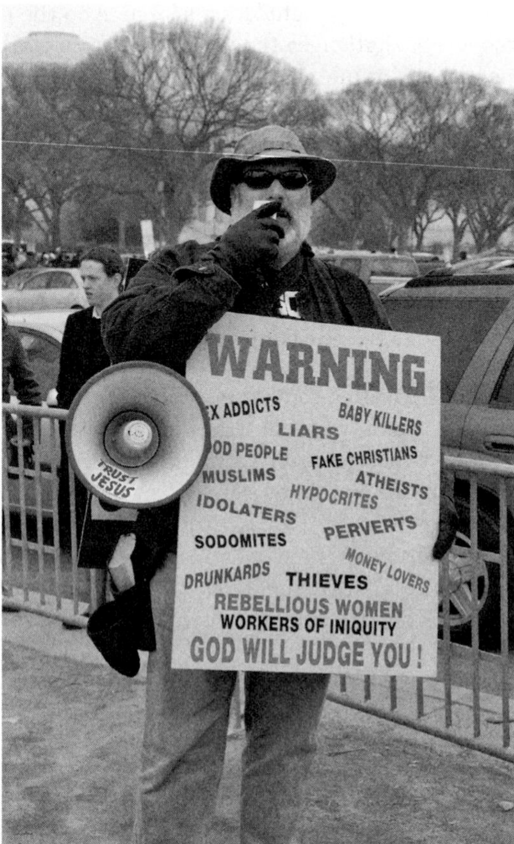

Figure 2.5 How many different forms or styles of outrage rhetoric is this protestor using? Can you identify what this person feels entitled to and what promises are going unfulfilled for him? (Source: iStock. Credit: Joel Carillet)

Outrage comes from people on both "the right" and "the left," but spokespeople from what we know as "the right" engage in significantly more outrage discourse, as well as a wider range of styles, than those we identify as from "the left."

Outrage discourse takes various forms or styles: insulting language, name calling, emotional display and emotional language, verbal fighting/sparring, character assassination, misrepresentative exaggeration, mockery/sarcasm, conflagration, ideologically extremizing language, slippery slope arguments, belittling, and use of obscene language. The most common forms of outrage, however, are mockery, followed closely by misrepresentative exaggeration and insulting language. For example, commentators on "the left" used outrage rhetoric to mock members of the conservative Tea Party coalition during the Obama years by describing them as staging a "decade long toga party, safeguarding our money with the diligence and sobriety of the fraternity brothers in 'Animal House.'" Those on "the right" misrepresented and exaggerated the efforts of former Senator Alan Specter, the moderate Republican from Pennsylvania (who later became a Democrat), for bringing economically advantageous projects to Pennsylvania, stating that he was stabbing future generations in the back with his "porkzilla package which appears purposely designed to break capitalism by crushing our economy." From both parties, such labels as "asinine," "idiotic," "moron," "partisan hack," "hack-in-the-box," and "Obamabots" are used to describe politicians and citizens.[45]

Who are the audiences for this outrage rhetoric? Researchers have identified two traits, overwhelmingly male and conservative, as consistent across the millions of weekly listeners. Beyond this, however, the best and most consistent description of who listens is a person who is interested in sidestepping "the messy nuances of complex political issues in favor of melodrama, misrepresentation, exaggeration, mockery and improbable forecasts of impending doom. Outrage talk is not so much a discussion as it is verbal competition, political theatre with a score card."[46] Consumers of outrage talk are not defenders of free speech or advocates of a robust criticism of important issues. They are, instead, interested in "misinformation" and appeals to emotion that "fan the flames of intolerance, promote and entrench polarization, or create a generalized mistrust of government."[47]

Sobieraj and Berry conclude that to understand the impact of this outrage discourse, we "must consider the many ways that hostility and disrespect permeate the political landscape."[48] As students of communication, identities, and intersectionality, moreover, we also must consider the ways this hostility infects our understanding of aggrieved entitlement, human rights, and human dignity. Outrage discourse makes what are already difficult conversations for many people even more difficult.

Much of the outrage talk we hear focuses not just on political candidates and their parties, but also on race, class, and gender. According to one outrage television and radio personality, the election of Barack Obama as president meant that to get ahead you must "hate white people." Obama's presidency meant that rather than safety on the school bus for white kids, they now get beat up, with the "black kids cheering." And "of course, everybody says the white kid deserved it: he was born racist."[49]

Those who advocate for the rights of working class and poor women such as Sandra Fluke, a Georgetown University law student, also are targets of outrage discourse. Fluke testified before a Democratic congressional panel on the question of whether or not health insurance should cover the cost of contraception. She explained the costs of contraception ($3,000) per year, described the medical necessity of contraceptives beyond birth control (for example, preventing dangerous cysts from growing on women's ovaries), and the interrogation received by women students at her university as they requested prescriptions for contraception (they were told they were lying about their symptoms). Those

2.2. GUIDE TO COMMUNICATION

Moving beyond Outrage

1. Discuss the American Dream with other students in your class. Develop a list of the promises made in this dream. Bring the Declaration of Independence and the Constitution into your discussion if you think they will help you understand this dream.
2. Once you have a strong idea of what the American Dream promises, identify the sources of that dream—that is, how has it been communicated to us? Identify as many sources as you can: news, politics, public and private institutions, people, stories, movies, music, and the like. How often are we exposed to this dream?
3. bell hooks provides a complex definition of patriarchy. Take time in class to explore this definition carefully, honestly, and respectfully. If you are uncomfortable with her definition, consider why. Write one of your own, or amend her definition, so that you think it describes patriarchy more accurately.
4. Collect examples of outrage discourse from a variety of sources and perspectives (that is, the "left" and the "right" as well as other "positions"). Bring these to class and share them or post them so that you can discuss them with your fellow students. The citation for the article in this chapter is Sarah Sobieraj and Jeffrey M. Berry, "From Incivility to Outrage: Political Discourse in Blogs, Talk Radio, and Cable News," *Political Communication* 28, no. 1 (2011) and you can find it online from your library. What types of outrage are you seeing in the examples you are exploring? Pretend that you are the sender of the outrage and that you want to communicate with the person you are outraged at. How might you do so? Now pretend you are the receiver of the outrage and want to communicate with the sender. How might you do so?

on "the right" labeled Fluke a "slut and a whore for having so much sex." Rush Limbaugh, "as a tax payer," demanded "that she provide high-quality videos of her sexual escapades," explaining that "if we are going to pay for your contraceptives and thus pay for you to have sex, we want something. We want you to post the videos online so we can all watch."[50]

When we mock, scorn, and insult other people, we are engaging in a discourse of ridicule and humiliation. Discourses of ridicule and humiliation do more than shut down conversations—they set the parameters of how someone is able to enter that conversation, and if they are able to enter it at all. When we are slandered—by what are usually called **ad hominem attacks** (against the person rather than focused on the issue or idea)—we are faced with several problems: do we attempt to salvage our reputation, redirect the content of the argument back to the original issue, or ignore the attack? Can we accomplish any of these? Do we have access to the same platforms as our attacker? Is there a willingness to engage the ideas at all? Or, is the goal of an ad hominem attack to silence someone so that the attacker does not have to communicate with them in any meaningful and humane way?

But beyond these perplexing and confusing questions and styles of communication is the loss of a dream, the feelings of being wronged, and the fear that the world is slipping out of control. How do we engage this loss and fear in productive ways? How do we address the failed promise—the undelivered dream some hold tightly to? How can our communication begin to bridge what seem to be huge chasms of difference and division? Could intersectionality help?

INTERSECTIONALITY AND DISCOURSES OF RIGHTS

How might we engage in discussions and conversations about some of our most precious tenets: the truths we hold to be "self-evident" that tell us "all [people] are created equal; that they are endowed by their Creator with certain unalienable rights; that among these are life, liberty, and the pursuit of happiness"?[51] In later chapters we explore the ways many of these unalienable rights have been defined and the ways they have been conceptualized to include some individuals and not others. Here, however, we consider two contrasting approaches to rights, feminism and patriarchy, and the discourses coming from them.

From intersectional feminism, we hear claims to two rights, one promised by our Constitution and Declaration of Independence, the other not necessarily: the right to access and inclusion and the right to freedom from misogyny and other forms of hatred. We are exposed to the ways that binary either/or thinking can block our understanding of complexity, and we are offered new vocabularies with which to speak about people and identities. We hear that sexism as an ideology is the problem, not men as a group of individuals, and that feminism is a movement that, although not perfect, has benefits for more than a select group of women.

From patriarchy, we hear the discourse of the American Dream: the assurance of opportunity and upward mobility. We speak of a promise made and not delivered and the anger that can be present as a result of that broken promise. We learn that not everyone felt entitled to that promise, but for those who did, the feeling of being wronged is powerful. Our feeling wronged, or aggrievement, is expressed through outrage, a vocabulary that relies on mockery, misrepresentation, exaggeration, and insult. In this outrage discourse, the goal is silencing other people and putting them down rather than engaging with them in open and reasoned conversation.

What can intersectionality bring to these two different approaches? When we engage in discussions of rights intersectionally, we can do the following with our communication: identify and refuse to engage in outrage discourses, because they belittle people and ideas. We can, instead, take ownership and responsibility for our communication and engage in informed conversations about issues and dilemmas. As communicators who engage an intersectional lens, we can work to understand the complexity of identities and the ways that complexity has been erased or ignored. We can bring an understanding of that complexity to our conversations as we discuss questions of rights, access, inclusion, and the meaning of our founding documents. What can intersectionality bring to our communication? It can, in the words of Luvvie Ajayi, author, speaker, and digital strategist, help us get "comfortable being uncomfortable" and "commit ourselves to telling truths to build bridges" because "bridges that aren't based on truth will collapse."[52]

Resources

Laura Bates, *Everyday Sexism* (New York: Thomas Dunne Books/Saint Martin's Press, 2016).

bell hooks, *Feminism Is for Everybody: Passionate Politics* (New York: Routledge, 2017).

Cherríe Moraga and Gloria Anzaldúa, eds., *This Bridge Called My Back: Writings by Radical Women of Color* (London: Pluto Press, 2000).

Elizabetta Povoledo, Raphael Minder, and Yonette Joseph, "International Women's Day 2018: Beyond #MeToo, Pride, Protests, and Pressure," *New York Times*, March 8, 2018, https://www.nytimes.com/2018/03/08/world/international-womens-day-2018.html.

Emma Watson, "Gender Equality Is Your Issue, Too," United Nations Speech on Gender Equality, New York, September 20, 2014, https://www.unwomen.org/en/news/stories/2014/9/emma-watson-gender-equality-is-your-issue-too.

Notes

1. Emma Watson, "Gender Equality Is Your Issue, Too," United Nations Speech on Gender Equality, New York, NY, September 20, 2014, UN Women, https://www.unwomen.org/en/news/stories/2014/9/emma-watson-gender-equality-is-your-issue-too.
2. Dale Spender, *Women of Ideas and What Men Have Done to Them* (London: Pandora Press, 1982).
3. "Hull House," VCU Social Welfare History Project, Virginia Commonwealth University, February 26, 2018, https://socialwelfare.library.vcu.edu/settlement-houses/hull-house/.
4. Susan Brownmiller, "Sisterhood Is Powerful," *New York Times*, March 15, 1970, https://www.nytimes.com/1970/03/15/archives/sisterhood-is-powerful-a-member-of-the-womens-liberation-movement.html.
5. Federal Glass Ceiling Commission, "A Solid Investment: Making Full Use of the Nation's Human Capital," Washington, DC: Department of Labor, 1995, 13–15, https://www.dol.gov/oasam/programs/history/reich/reports/ceiling2.pdf.
6. Combahee River Collective, "A Black Feminist Statement," in *This Bridge Called My Back: Writings by Radical Women of Color*, ed. Cherríe Moraga and Gloria Anzaldúa (New York: Kitchen Table: Women of Color Press, 1983), 213.
7. bell hooks, *Feminist Theory: From Margin to Center*, 2nd ed. (Boston: South End Press, 2000), 5.
8. hooks, *Feminism Is for Everybody: Passionate Politics* (London: Pluto Press, 2000), x.
9. Kimberlé Crenshaw, "Mapping the Margins: Intersectionality, Identity Politics, and Violence against Women of Color," *Stanford Law Review* 43 no. 6 (1991): 1241–1299, and "Demarginalizing the Intersection of Race and Sex: A Black Feminist Critique of Antidiscrimination Doctrine, Feminist Theory and Antiracist Politics," *University of Chicago Legal Forum* (1989): 139–167.
10. Amber Kinser, "Negotiating Spaces for/through Third-Wave Feminism," *NWSA Journal* 16, no. 3 (2004): 131, 134.
11. Emi Koyama quoted in Kinser, "Negotiating Spaces," 136.
12. Jennifer Baumgardner and Amy Richards, *Manifesta: Young Women, Feminism, and the Future* (New York: Farrar, Strauss, and Giroux, 2000), 78–80.
13. Kinser, "Negotiating Spaces," 131.
14. Kinser, "Negotiating Spaces," 131.
15. Kinser, "Negotiating Spaces," 141.
16. Kinser, "Negotiating Spaces," 143.

17. Cherríe Moraga, "La Güera," in *This Bridge Called My Back: Writings by Radical Women of Color,* ed. Cherríe Moraga and Gloria Anzaldúa (New York: Kitchen Table: Women of Color Press, 1983), 29.
18. Chela Sandoval, "U.S.–Third World Feminism: The Theory and Method of Oppositional Consciousness in the Postmodern World," *Genders* 10 (1991): 14.
19. Sandoval, "U.S.–Third World Feminism," 14–15.
20. Sandoval, "U.S.–Third World Feminism," 15.
21. Some scholars have critiqued the wave metaphor as limiting. See for example, Kimberly Springer, "Third Wave Black Feminism?" *Signs* 27, no. 4 (2002): 1059–1098, and Michelle Sidler, "Living in McJobdom: Third Wave Feminism and Class Inequity," in *Third Wave Agenda: Being Feminist, Doing Feminism,* ed. Leslie Heywood and Jennifer Drake (Minneapolis: University of Minnesota Press, 1997), 25–39.
22. Beyoncé, quoted in Caitlyn Callegari, "Beyonce Explains What Being A Feminist Means to Her and It Goes Way Beyond the Label," *Bustle,* April 6, 2016, https://www.bustle.com/articles/152215-beyonce-explains-what-being-a-feminist-means-to-her-it-goes-way-beyond-the-label.
23. Chimamanda Adichie, "Why We Should All Be Feminists," filmed December 2012 in London, TEDxEuston video, 29:19, https://www.ted.com/talks/chimamanda_ngozi_adichie_we_should_all_be_feminists?language=en.
24. bell hooks, *The Will to Change: Men, Masculinity, and Love* (New York: Washington Square Press, 2004), 17.
25. See https://en.wikipedia.org/wiki/Patriarchy.
26. hooks, *Will to Change,* 18.
27. hooks, *Will to Change,* 23.
28. hooks, *Will to Change,* 17.
29. Carl Skutsch, "The History of White Supremacy in America," *Rolling Stone,* August 19, 2017, https://www.rollingstone.com/politics/politics-features/the-history-of-white-supremacy-in-america-205171/.
30. Harold Arlen, composer, and Yip Harburg, lyricist, "Somewhere Over the Rainbow," 1939.
31. Michael S. Kimmel, *Angry White Men: American Masculinity at the End of an Era* (New York: The Nation Institute, 2017).
32. Kimmel, *Angry White Men,* 13.
33. Kimmel, *Angry White Men,* 13.
34. Kimmel, *Angry White Men,* 23.
35. Kimmel, *Angry White Men,* 26.
36. Kimmel, *Angry White Men,* 63.
37. Kimmel, *Angry White Men,* 65.
38. Kimmel, *Angry White Men,* 23.
39. Kimmel, *Angry White Men,* 25.
40. Kimmel, *Angry White Men,* 23.
41. Kimmel, *Angry White Men,* 24.
42. Kimmel, *Angry White Men,* x.
43. Kimmel, *Angry White Men,* xi.
44. Sarah Sobieraj and Jeffrey M. Berry, "From Incivility to Outrage: Political Discourse in Blogs, Talk Radio, and Cable News," *Political Communication* 28, no. 1 (2011): 20.
45. Sobieraj and Berry, "From Incivility to Outrage," 29–30.
46. Sobieraj and Berry, "From Incivility to Outrage," 20.
47. Sobieraj and Berry, "From Incivility to Outrage," 23.
48. Sobieraj and Berry, "From Incivility to Outrage," 35.
49. Rush Limbaugh, quoted in Kimmel, *Angry White Men,* 40.
50. Kimmel, *Angry White Men,* 40.
51. The Declaration of Independence, July 4, 1776.
52. Luvvie Ajayi, "Get Comfortable with Being Uncomfortable," filmed November 2017 in New Orleans, LA, TEDWomen video, 10:14, https://www.ted.com/talks/luvvie_ajayi_get_comfortable_with_being_uncomfortable/transcript.

CHAPTER

3

Intersectional Approaches to Privilege and Its Impact on Communication

IN THIS CHAPTER, YOU WILL FIND . . .

KEY TERMS AND CONCEPTS

- ableism
- aesthetics of human disqualification
- alliances
- anti-Semitism
- coalitions
- classism
- collective guilt
- colorphobia
- ethnocentrism
- guilt
- heterosexism
- homophobia
- individual guilt
- Islamophobia
- knapsack of privileges
- nativism
- Negrophobia
- phobia
- racism
- religious imperialism
- sexism
- transphobia
- unearned privileges
- xenophobia

ASKING INTERSECTIONAL QUESTIONS

If we are to understand our own intersectional identities, as well as the intersectional identities of others, we must ask ourselves questions—questions that are informed by the intersections in which we stand. Because we move through these intersections differently, the ways we are asked to negotiate them differs. If we can begin to name and examine the specificity of the oppressions some groups of individuals experience, as well as the specificity of protections other groups take for granted, we may take a step toward improving our communication. Understanding privilege, and learning to communicate about it, prevents us from ignoring or denying our differences. As more informed communicators, we can learn skills necessary to talk about our own intersectional identities, and the intersectional identities of others—with respect, interest, and agency.

In this chapter we explore our intersectional identities, how they are or are not linked to privilege, and the hierarchies this can create. By examining our own complex intersectional identities, and our feelings about them, we are better able to see the myriad ways we are taught to be ignorant of our privileges, as well as the ways privilege intersects with the value we assign to other people. The chapter concludes with a discussion of the ways we might use communication to build alliances and coalitions with others as we embrace our intersectional identities.

PRIVILEGE AS A KALEIDOSCOPE OF UNMARKED ADVANTAGES

Although the word *privilege* makes many people uncomfortable, to be privileged is to enjoy special advantages, and almost all of us enjoy some privileges throughout our lives. In her attempts to understand male privilege in the 1980s, Women's Studies professor Peggy McIntosh invigorated a conversation about white privilege. McIntosh realized that she could not, in good conscience, focus exclusively on "male" privilege, she also had to grapple with her own white, cisgender, heterosexual privilege. Referencing the Combahee River Collective's recognition "that the major systems of oppression are interlocking,"[1] McIntosh shares a piece of her struggle: "I was taught to see racism only in individual acts of meanness by members of my group, never in invisible systems conferring racial dominance on my group from birth."[2] McIntosh explains that if we are to "redesign systems" of unearned privilege and even "unsought dominance," we must "first acknowledge their colossal unseen dimensions."[3]

Using a definition similar to that for male privilege, McIntosh defines white privilege as "an invisible package of unearned assets which I can count on cashing in each day, but about which I was 'meant' to remain oblivious. These **unearned privileges** are like an invisible weightless knapsack of special provisions, assurances, tools, maps, guides, codebooks, passports, visas, clothes, compass, emergency gear, and blank checks."[4] McIntosh's work prompted

Figure 3.1 Our privileges are like this kaleidoscopic image: Privileges might be static for a moment or two, but then they rapidly shift to a new alignment as we interact with different people in different situations. (Source: iStock. Credit: Evgenia22)

scholars to explore privilege as it relates to a range of identities: masculinity, masculinity and sport, black masculinity, heterosexuality, economic class, culture, religion, and even college admission standards.[5] Thanks to their work, we can extend the metaphor of the invisible, weightless knapsack of special provisions to other identities as well: the privileges that come with being cisgender; with one's religion, race or ethnicity; with sexual orientation and sexuality; with age and size; with language, country of origin, and more.

It is no secret that privileges that are granted to you on the basis of your identities can be hard to spot—in fact, the more privileges a person has, the more they have been taught not to name them or to even identify them as privileges. We are meant to remain ignorant of them. We are meant to deny the reality of them as privileges and to assume that if we simply work hard enough we too will enjoy them. But as Paul M. Terry, professor of Education, Leadership and Policy Development notes, "We cannot begin to develop a sensitivity and understanding of others until we begin to look internally and understand how we have become the individual we are."[6]

Unearned Privileges

To help you unpack the invisible knapsack you may possess, take the following ten quizzes.[7] Rank your answers on a scale of 1 to 4, from "no/almost never" to "yes/almost always"; this scale is described above each quiz. Total your score at the end of each quiz, and then add all of your scores together after you have competed all ten quizzes.

1. Privileges Earned through Social Norms

1 = no/almost never 2 = occasionally 3 = often 4 = yes/almost always

____You can and do speak first, and often longer than others, in conversations or meetings without being judged negatively.

____You are less likely to be interrupted when you are speaking.

____You are automatically assumed to know what you are talking about, regardless of the topic.

____You can be sure people won't criticize you for being a single parent or for having "too many children."

____You can be sure people won't be surprised when you tell them you are a parent.

____You can easily find neighborhoods and workplaces in which people approve of you, your family, and your household.

____You can be quite relaxed when walking around, driving, or eating out, and you will feel welcome and safe pretty much everywhere you go.

____You can be sure that people won't ask you "What are you?" or "Where are you from? No, really where are you from?" very often.

____You can speak English without people complimenting you on your skill at speaking English.

Total Score____ (36 points possible)

2. Privileges Earned through Sex and Relationships

1 = no/almost never 2 = occasionally 3 = often 4 = yes/almost always

____You are more likely to be congratulated or praised for having lots of sex, rather than shamed for it.

____You can be open about enjoying having sex without people feeling automatically entitled to having sex with you.

____You can be sure you won't be asked "How do you do it?" when talking about sex, and that people won't be surprised that you actually do have sex.

____You can say "no" to sex and be fairly sure it will not be taken as a "yes."

____You can hold hands, hug, or even kiss your romantic partner in public without people staring at you or indicating that they feel uncomfortable.

____You are not expected to change your last name when you get married.

____You can be fairly certain that people won't worry about what your child will look like, or the color of her or his skin before that child is born.

____You have a long history of being able to marry the person you love, legally, and without scrutiny or fear.

Total Score____ (32 points possible)

3. Privileges Earned through Public Safety and Security

1 = no/almost never 2 = occasionally 3 = often 4 = yes/almost always

____You can be fairly sure you won't be the target of street harassment.

____You can be fairly certain you won't be the victim of interpersonal violence.

____You can be fairly certain you won't be held accountable for preventing rape or keeping it from happening.

____You can be fairly certain you won't be asked "Why were you there?" or "What were you wearing?" or "How much did you have to drink?" if you are the victim or target of harassment or violence.

____You can stand in a crowed area or use public transportation without worrying about being groped, verbally or physically assaulted, or making others feel afraid or uncomfortable.

____You can be fairly sure that if you are pulled over or stopped by the police, it is not because of one or more of your identities.

____You can be fairly sure you won't be detained, or even removed from your workplace, by authorities and been made to show legal documentation of your right to be in a country or for proof of citizenship.

Total Score____ (28 points possible)

4. Privileges Earned through Environmental Conditions

1 = no/almost never 2 = occasionally 3 = often 4 = yes/almost always

____Your neighborhood has regular trash services and people rarely leave broken furniture outside or on the sidewalks.

____Your neighborhood is free of toxic waste and is far away from a toxic waste site.

____Your neighborhood has well-maintained parks and affordable recreational facilities nearby.

____Your neighborhood has a lot of open space for you to walk, explore, or relax in safely.

____You live in a neighborhood that has regulations about where you can park, how long you can leave a car unattended, and those who live there abide by those rules.

____You can read all the street signs, stop signs, and other helpful notices because they are in your native language or are free of graffiti and undamaged.

____Your neighborhood is free of graffiti, and when there is graffiti, it is removed quickly.

____You can easily get into buildings, over curbs, across thresholds, around corners, into bathrooms, and up sets of stairs.

Total Score____ (32 points possible)

5. Privileges Earned through Health and Body

1 = no/almost never 2 = occasionally 3 = often 4 = yes/almost always

____You can age naturally without being accused of "letting yourself go."

____You are usually taken seriously by doctors and other health care providers when you tell them your symptoms.

____You rarely have your physical symptoms attributed to psychological factors.

____You have health insurance.

____You can be fairly sure you won't make people uncomfortable, or end up in special education classes, because of the way your body moves or your mind works.

____You are unaware that medical and pharmaceutical research has spent far more time exploring and treating the symptoms and diseases your body presents than investigating the symptoms and diseases of those who do not share your same identities.

____You are only labeled "retarded" or "a freak" as a joke.

____You can easily find attractive and comfortable clothing in mainstream stores.

Total Score____ (32 points possible)

6. Privileges Earned through Media Practices

1 = no/almost never 2 = occasionally 3 = often 4 = yes/almost always

____Your identities are present in media and are portrayed as "strong," "capable," and "good."

____Your identities are present in influential media outlets at every level—from actors to camera crews, to writers and directors, as well as producers and owners of studios.

____You, and people with similar identities as you, are more likely to be published and read.

____Your identities are often portrayed in film and television and they are rarely objectified or presented as sex objects.

____Your identities, when they are portrayed in film and television, are less likely to be cast as hardened criminals or prisoners.

____Your identities, when they are portrayed in film and television, are less likely to be the comic relief or the tragic figure.

____Your identities, when they are portrayed in film and television shows, almost never have the lines "What should we do now?" or "Help me!"

Total Score____ (28 points possible)

7. Privileges Earned through Politics and Law

1 = no/almost never 2 = occasionally 3 = often 4 = yes/almost always

____Most of your identities are reflected in and shared by the majority of people holding elected office.

____Most of your identities are reflected in and shared by the majority of individuals who make and uphold the law.

____You can express strong political views and opinions without people labeling you negatively, accusing you of taking things too far, or "having an agenda."

____Your identities have been clearly included and named in the U.S. Constitution as well as its Amendments.

____People with your identities have pretty much always had the right to vote, own property, and live as free human beings.

____You, and people with identities similar to yours, regularly get shorter or more lenient jail or prison sentences as compared to people with identities different from yours.

Total Score____ (24 points possible)

8. Privileges Earned through the Workplace and Economy

1 = no/almost never 2 = occasionally 3 = often 4 = yes/almost always

____You, and individuals with identities similar to yours, are securely at the top of the hierarchy of wage earnings.

____You, and individuals with identities similar to yours, have a much lower risk of living in, or ending up in, poverty.

____You can choose to have a profession and a family with less risk of people accusing you of neglecting your family or neglecting your job.

____You and your family thought and talked about professions and careers, rather than jobs and wages.

____You can spend little time and less money on your professional appearance without having people think you are unprofessional or "not put together."

____You shop at secondhand clothing stores because it's fun, not because that is what you can afford.

____You are praised when you speak out against harassment or inequities at work, especially when they relate to gender, sex, race, ability, religion, or the like.

____You are more likely to have your work cited, to be praised for your accomplishments, and to receive awards of recognition.

____You are fairly sure that you will be competitive on the job market because of your appearance, the way you speak, and the way you move.

Total Score____ (36 points possible)

9. Privileges Earned through Childhood and the Educational System

1 = no/almost never 2 = occasionally 3 = often 4 = yes/almost always

____You receive more attention from your teachers and professors, often are called on first, and may even raise your hand to answer a question, even if you don't know the answer and haven't studied.

____Your teachers and professors assume you are intelligent, motivated, and articulate.

____Your energetic behavior is praised rather than considered disruptive and a problem to be remedied.

____Your identities, and the contributions of people who share your same identities, are reflected in the curriculum throughout your education.

____Your native language, as well as the native language of your parents, is the language used to teach the curriculum in schools.

____At school, you could afford to eat pretty much what you wanted for lunch, and the food you ate was very similar to what everyone else was eating.

____You have always known you would go to, and could afford to go to college—others in your family have done so for generations.

Total Score____ (28 points possible)

10. Privileges Earned through Norms for Religions

1 = no/almost never 2 = occasionally 3 = often 4 = yes/almost always

____If you are religious, your holy texts are considered safe and accepted by mainstream culture as legitimate.

____You are likely to find stories and images of important figures and events in holy texts that reflect or share your identities, if you are religious.

____You are able to be open about the majority of your identities with authorities like rabbis, clergy, and Imams, if you are religious.

____Your church, or the buildings that house your church, are safe places to worship because people rarely attack the buildings or the people in them.

____You are less likely to be harassed, threatened, hurt, or even killed when you are dressed in clothing that reflects your religious beliefs.

Total Score____ (20 points possible)

Total Overall Score ____ (296 total points possible)

Unpacking Your Own Invisible Knapsack and Improving Communication

All of the questions in the quizzes relate to a privilege—an unearned advantage. Because these privileges are unearned, they do not and did not involve work; instead, they accrue based on a person's identities—they were and are given to us because of our ascribed and avowed identities. The more mainstream our identities, the more unearned privileges we have. This means that the higher your own score is, the more unearned advantages you have in your invisible knapsack; conversely, if your scores are low, you have fewer unearned advantages in your invisible knapsack. There is an additional piece to consider, however. The more surprised you are by your scores, the more unaware you have been about these unearned assets. If a high score surprises you, you likely did not realize that the privileges were yours. If a low score surprises you, you may not have realized that there are privileges not available to you.

White, cisgender, heterosexual, able body, economically secure, Christian people often have difficulty acknowledging their unearned assets. It can be confusing to realize that privilege has fueled many of the successes this group has accomplished. It also can be hard to imagine that other people's experiences—the difficulties they encounter as they seek to advance—are the result of a lack of privilege. Although political commentators such as Ben Shapiro suggest that capitalism and meritocracy, and not privilege, create the differences in a total

Figure 3.2 Take time to consider the privileges you do or do not have in your invisible knapsack. How aware of their presence or absence were you? What will you do with this new information about your ascribed and avowed identities? (Source: iStock. Credit: Harbucks)

score, there are too many advantages unrelated to capitalism or meritocracy in the lists above to support this claim.[8] Regardless of how hard someone may have worked, the reality of life is that many of our identities make our movements seamless—while the intersections of other identities, regardless of our hard work, make that movement difficult if not sometimes impossible.

Individual and Collective Guilt

When confronted with a high score, people often feel guilty. To feel **guilt** is to feel agitated: we may have caused harm to someone and we accept responsibility for that harm.[9] Guilt can be an uncomfortable emotion because it holds us accountable for our actions—we become responsible for them. Harming another person, intentionally or unintentionally, rarely feels good. Our **individual guilt** tells us that we've done something wrong and we can respond by fixing it—and often we do. But sometimes guilt is a collective matter—a lot of people with similar identities did something wrong—a lot of people are responsible for that wrongdoing. Although we may be able to hide or ignore our individual guilt, **collective guilt** and its accompanying responsibility, once identified, is harder to mask or ignore. Even though we may not like feeling guilty,

3.1. GUIDE TO COMMUNICATION

The Language of Privilege

Take a moment to review your scores on the privilege quizzes. Select one or two of the quizzes and consider how this information may change how you interact with the people around you. You can use the following questions to help you develop an intersectional approach to communication.

1. What privileges do I have that might be influencing my interactions with others?
2. What privileges don't I have that might be influencing my interactions with others?
3. Given the privileges that are present and/or absent in my knapsack, what are my communication challenges?
4. What new information do I need to assist me in working respectfully and openly through these challenges?

collective guilt actually may have positive outcomes that go beyond individual guilt. This is because when we feel guilty collectively, that feeling "may create a motivation to establish a more egalitarian relationship."[10]

Collective guilt can help us frame inequality in life-changing ways. This is because our newly understood perspective "highlights an aspect of the [privilege] that typically goes unnoticed." The "pride" we may have felt at our higher status and our accomplishments is undercut. That feeling of pride over our successes now contains a "taint of illegitimacy" as we begin to name and understand the "unearned benefits derived from structural inequality."[11] We explore structural inequality in detail in chapter 4, but for our purposes in this chapter, we can think about structural inequality as the ways unearned privileges are made to seem "normal." Linda Martín Alcoff, a professor of philosophy at Hunter College, City University of New York, explains that what is "normal" or "common sense"—which may be invisible to many people—is in reality "culturally constituted." Unearned privileges belong to some people not because of their talents or work ethic but because of "past historical beliefs and practices of a given society or culture."[12] What is normal is actually a product of the processes of history and not, in fact, simple human nature.

Unpacking our knapsack of privileges can move our conversations about identities and inequality beyond individual statements like, "I'm not racist /sexist/homophobic/classist" and the like. Naming the various ways some people are privileged far more than others—the structural advantages and disadvantages we experience—is yet another step in improving our communication. Our **knapsack of privileges,** as McIntosh shares, are meant to remain invisible. When we make them visible we continue to develop new discourses and to improve our chances of productive communication with other people.

PRIVILEGE AND THE AESTHETICS OF HUMAN DISQUALIFICATION

In *Disability Aesthetics,* Tobin Siebers, professor of English and Comparative Literatures, discusses an **aesthetics of human disqualification.** Disqualification, Siebers explains, is a "symbolic process" that "removes individuals from the ranks of quality human beings, putting them at risk of unequal treatment, bodily harm, and death." Although we are hesitant to admit this, Siebers suggests "we do believe that nonquality human beings" exist.[13] Individuals with disabilities fall into this category because they display "markers of inferiority" that, although culturally constructed, are said to be "biological" in nature. We prefer, Siebers explains, "to fix, cure, or eradicate the disabled body rather than the discriminatory attitudes" and structural barriers present in our society.[14] We disqualify more than just people we consider to have a disability, however. Consider the idea, for example, of the "deserving poor" (those who are poor through "no fault of their own," perhaps through a disability that makes it impossible for someone to work) versus the "undeserving poor" (those who are considered "too lazy to work" or to have squandered their livelihood on drugs). These notions of deserving and undeserving often invisibly infuse social attitudes. Consider the following isms.

sexism: argues that certain sexes and genders are inferior mentally and physically to others.

racism: holds that some individuals are inferior to others because of skin color, bloodlines, and physical features.

classism: allows us to rank groups by family lineage and economic status.

ableism: supports the idea that some individuals are inferior based on mental and physical attributes.

anti-Semitism: encourages prejudice and discrimination toward Jewish people.

ethnocentrism: urges us to evaluate and denigrate other cultures based on the standards and customs of one's own.

heterosexism: teaches us to hold prejudiced attitudes and engage in discriminatory practices against homosexuals and queer-identified people.

nativism: supports policies and attitudes that protect the interests of native-born or established inhabitants over those of immigrants or those who do not fit the stereotype of native-born or documented citizen.

religious imperialism: perpetuates the systemic and systematic prejudice or discrimination against people who practice religions other than Christianity.[15]

Figure 3.3 Just like this bartender, people resist and overcome the aesthetics of human disqualification every day. (Source: iStock. Credit: SolStock)

At this moment in time, Siebers says, our aesthetics of human disqualification "justifies discrimination, servitude, imprisonment, involuntary institutionalization, euthanasia, human and civil rights violations, military intervention, compulsory sterilization, police actions, assisted suicide, capital punishment, and murder."[16] The aesthetic of disqualification, in short, describes "how individuals are disqualified . . . found lacking, inept, incompetent, inferior, in need, incapable, degenerate, uneducated, weak, ugly, underdeveloped, diseased, immature, unskilled, frail, uncivilized, defective, and so on."[17]

Disqualification and Phobias

Disqualification fuels our phobias. A **phobia** is a fear of someone or something that in fact poses no real threat of danger or harm to us. When we are phobic, we attach a nonrational dread, panic, hatred, or dislike to someone, some group, or something knowing that, in reality, that person, group, place, or object can do no actual harm to us. Phobias are learned responses, which means there is no biological or physiological origin to them (as would be the case with a peanut allergy, for example). Phobias are politically and ideologically informed and motivated, and they are rooted in the aesthetics of disqualification. The first phobias to be named as phobias were "colorphobia" and "Negrophobia." Nineteenth-century anti-slavery abolitionists coined these terms to "not only contest the slave system, but unearth an emotional basis for slavery's persistence." For abolitionists, **colorphobia** and **Negrophobia** were dangerous diseases, similar to being bitten by a rabid dog. These rabies-like phobias, they argued, could make a person "mad" and surround them with a "furious insanity," causing them to support and advocate slavery rather than see its inhumanity. This disease could be passed on to others, abolitionists reasoned; for example, as Canadians were "becoming unfriendly to black fugitives from the South," they were said to have "caught from us the contagion of negro-phobia."[18]

The terms "colorphobia" and "Negrophobia" held considerable power for a short time and were used to "shame racist acts, persons, and policies in the North and South alike." However, they soon were co-opted, and arguments emerged suggesting that individuals with these phobias "could not help themselves." Abolitionists began to see that the terms were making it difficult to talk about white supremacy, and that if "Southern slaveholding had anything to do with fear, it wasn't so much a fear of people of color as it was a fear that white supremacy might be exposed, challenged, and demolished."[19]

The term "phobia" emerged again as a powerful tool when gay rights activist George Weinberg coined the term "homophobia" in his 1972 publication, *Society and the Healthy Homosexual.* The term became "the go-to 'descriptor for the intolerant' and a rallying point for gay liberation worldwide."[20] "Homophobia" captured a "whole point of view and of feeling" and reminded us, Weinberg explains, that phobias were not "only about fear," but also about hierarchies of power that certain individuals did not want exposed.[21]

Unmasking Phobias

If the abolitionists and Weinberg are correct, that phobias based on identities are about hierarchies of power we wish to keep hidden, then what might the four terms listed below—and other similar identity-based phobias—suggest about what we are hiding? What hierarchies of power are being masked within these four terms that we might unmask? Consider the following definitions, designed to *unmask* those power hierarchies.

homophobia: refers to the power heterosexual individuals hold to define and impose on others a view of heterosexuality as the "correct" or "right" sexuality. Homophobia legitimizes hate speech and hate crimes, legislation that discriminates against the LGBTQ community, the exclusion and/or discrimination of individuals based on sexuality, and minimizes the damages done by this political ideology.

transphobia: refers to the power people whose biological sex matches the sex they were assigned at birth, known as cisgender individuals, hold to impose a binary definition of identity on others. Transphobia holds that we can define individuals as "real men" or "real women," refuse to acknowledge a transgender person's avowed identity, and engage in hate speech, hate crimes, and discriminatory practices and legislation against transgender people.

Islamophobia: refers to the power people of Christian and other non-Muslim faiths hold to define and impose a particular view of religion and religious practices on others. Islamophobia legitimizes hate speech and hate crimes against Muslim people, the defacement of holy texts and buildings, and the harassment of Muslim individuals.

xenophobia: refers to the privileging of a person's place of birth over all other factors, granting individuals born in a particular country the power to create hostile conditions for individuals considered to be "non-native"—that is, individuals born in one country but residing in another. Xenophobia invokes the idea that some groups of particular national origins are undesirable and legitimizes the strict control and monitoring of national borders to keep these undesirable people from entering. Xenophobia supports the dehumanizing of individuals from different countries through expressions of hostility and hatred toward them; the establishment of structures and legislation designed to prevent immigration, relocation, or asylum; and the removal of all non-native-born individuals from a country—regardless of their legal status or citizenship.

When we think and speak in terms of "isms" and "phobias," we engage in the aesthetics of human disqualification, categorizing some individuals as better and more human than others. We identify some people as "nonquality human beings," as inferior, flawed, incorrect, inappropriate, and unwelcome. But, as Patricia Hill Collins notes, "we now know that few people can achieve that mythical norm of being wealthy, white, male, [cisgender], heterosexual, American, able-bodied, and Christian that Western social institutions tout as being natural, normal, and ideal." Hill Collins shares that most of us fall somewhere outside those categories because our identities are far more complex and intersecting than this mythical norm allows.[22]

THE POSSIBILITY OF ALLIANCES AND COALITIONS

Because so many of us do fall outside this mythical norm, we might do well to consider and even embrace the understanding of power promoted by Aimee Carrillo Rowe, the author of *Power Lines: On the Subject of Feminist Alliances.* In her book, she describes power as political and relational. Carrillo Rowe explains this understanding through the metaphor of power lines:

> Power lines are those heavy cables carrying vital bits of data that gain relevance as they connect people across time and space. . . . Sometimes they are weighty wires scooping up and down. . . . Sometimes power lines run underground, invisibly

> transmitting power from place to place. . . . Power lines criss-cross the globe. . . . They are intentionally constructed. Without our recognition they do the invisible work of enabling the messy connectivity of lives.[23]

Carrillo Rowe uses this power-line metaphor to explain the **alliances** and **coalitions** that are possible across, among, and between our racial groupings. She suggests, "Like so many webs criss-crossing the globe, feminist alliances are also power lines that connect us to one another and to circuits of power."[24] But we have not acknowledged this fact, particularly under the monolithic presentation of women as a unified and homogenous group, based on color-blind logics and binary truth regimes, and our ignorance and denials of individual, collective, and structural privileges.

Carrillo Rowe notes that "the insistence that race does not matter" is contradicted "by relational choices. Whites make virtually every major life decision around issues of race: whom they or their children may love, where they might work or go to school, what neighborhood they live in, who their friends and colleagues are. The lines that connect us to others are not neutral: they are neither natural nor innocent."[25] They are, in fact, political. Alliances and coalitions that are able to "span the lines of power" are intentional rather than automatic. They "must be consciously made" as well as "fought for."[26]

Extending Carrillo Rowe's metaphor to the range of identities we each possess, we might now attend to how we do, or do not, communicate about the webs of power present in every interaction. Carrillo Rowe urges us to acknowledge that if we are "guilt ridden," then we are owning an important and long-overdue "loss of innocence."[27] If our scores on the privileges quiz are high in certain areas—or even across several areas—we may begin to feel guilty. Guilt is our signal that something is off but that it can be righted or attended to. Guilt signals a wrong that could have been prevented or even now can be fixed. In his exploration of war crimes and crimes against humanity, political and cultural sociologist Eric Gordy shares that

> One of the frequently stated goals of confronting the recent past is to assure that the events that marked it will not be repeated. This effort requires asking questions that go deeper than the investigations required for criminal prosecution. The principal questions deal with causes: how was an environment maintained that made the commission of crimes possible? Generating answers to these questions requires research into social and political history, but also demands uncomfortable self-interrogation. Was the ideological justification that legitimated criminal activity widely shared? To what extend did people acquiesce to the regime that was responsible for these crimes? How widespread was knowledge about crimes and their perpetrators? Did citizens have the capacity to change the regime or its policy?[28]

Gordy explains that these questions help us distinguish between guilt and responsibility.

In taking responsibility for our communication, we intentionally lose our innocence about privilege and take steps toward becoming allies. Using an

3.2. GUIDE TO COMMUNICATION

An Intentional Loss of Innocence

As you conclude this section on human disqualification, phobias, and power lines, consider all that you have been exposed to and asked to digest. To improve your communication with other people, ask yourself the following questions:

1. In what ways do I engage the discourses that disqualify other people?
2. What phobias do I possess and what hierarchies do they depend on?
3. How might my beliefs in "nonquality human beings" be affecting my ability to listen and communicate with other people?
4. Are there alliances and coalitions I might be willing to create and establish that could help me understand the complexity of identity and the illusion of "normal"?

intersectional orientation, we analyze the ways we may be privileged and the ways we may be oppressed. We acknowledge the visible and invisible inequalities with empathy and respect. We unmask the power and privilege that lurks behind perceptions of some individuals as inferior, flawed, or unwelcome. We build coalitions and invite others to do the same. Carrillo Rowe explains that, as intersectionally oriented feminists, we must "build alliances to link our lives together, to transmit power, and potentiality for the purpose of transforming power. Through their mindful construction, these alliances function as sites where 'power over' may be remade as 'power with' and 'power to.'"[29]

Resources

Luvvie Ayayi, "Get Comfortable with Being Uncomfortable," filmed November 2017 in New Orleans, LA, TEDWomen video, 10:47, https://www.ted.com/talks/luvvie_ajayi_get_comfortable_with_being_uncomfortable#t-609272.

Isaac Lidsky, "What Reality Are You Creating for Yourself?" filmed June 2016 in Banff, Alberta, TEDSummit video, 11:41, https://www.ted.com/talks/isaac_lidsky_what_reality_are_you_creating_for_yourself.

Susan Robinson, "How I Fail at Being Disabled," filmed December 2016 in New York, NY, TED Residency video, 7:44, https://www.ted.com/talks/susan_robinson_how_i_fail_at_being_disabled.

Priya Vulchi and Winona Guo, "What It Takes to Be Racially Literate," filmed November 2017 in New Orleans, LA, TEDWomen video, 12:13, https://www.ted.com/talks/priya_vulchi_and_winona_guo_what_it_takes_to_be_racially_literate.

Notes

1. Combahee River Collective, "A Black Feminist Statement," in *This Bridge Called My Back: Writings by Radical Women of Color*, ed. Cherríe Moraga and Gloria Anzaldúa (New York: Kitchen Table: Women of Color Press, 1983), 210.
2. Peggy McIntosh, "White Privilege and Male Privilege: A Personal Account of Coming to See Correspondences through Work in Women's Studies," in *Privilege: A Reader*, ed. Michael S. Kimmel and Abby L. Ferber, 2nd ed. (Boulder: Westview Press, 2010), 25.
3. McIntosh, "White Privilege," 25.
4. McIntosh, "White Privilege," 14.

5. See, for example, Michael S. Kimmel and Abby L. Ferber, eds. *Privilege: A Reader,* 2nd ed. (Boulder: Westview Press, 2010); and Paula Rothenberg, *Invisible Privilege: A Memoir about Race, Class, and Gender* (Lawrence: University Press of Kansas, 2000).
6. Paul M. Terry, "Preparing Educational Leaders to Eradicate the 'isms,'" Paper presented at the Annual International Congress on Challenges to Education: Balancing Unity and Diversity in a Changing World," July 10–12, 1996, 1, http://files.eric.ed.gov/fulltext/ED400612.pdf.
7. Portions of this list are compiled and adapted from McIntosh, "White Privilege and Male Privilege, 13–26; Jewel Woods, "The Black Male Privileges Checklist," in Kimmel and Ferber, ed., *Privilege: A Reader,* 27–38; and Maisha Z. Johnson, "160+ Examples of Male Privilege in All Areas of Everyday Life," Everyday Feminism, February 25, 2016, http://everydayfeminism.com/2016/02/160-examples-of-male-privilege/.
8. Ben Shapiro, "Ben Shapiro Destroys the Concept of White Privilege," YouTube video, 21:04, November 28 2015, YAFTV, https://www.youtube.com/watch?v=rrxZRuL65wQ.
9. Adapted from Adam A. Powell, Nyla R. Branscombe, and Michael T. Schmitt, "Inequality as Ingroup Privilege or Outgroup Disadvantage: The Impact of Group Focus on Collective Guilt and Interracial Attitudes," *Personality and Social Psychology Bulletin,* 31 no. 4 (2005): 509.
10. Powell et al., "Inequality," 510.
11. Powell et al., "Inequality," 510.
12. Linda Martín Alcoff, *Visible Identities: Race, Gender, and the Self* (New York: Oxford University Press, 2006), 180, 185.
13. Tobin Siebers, *Disability Aesthetics* (Ann Arbor: University of Michigan Press, 2010), 23.
14. Siebers, *Disability Aesthetics,* 24–25.
15. "List of Isms," Interrupting Oppression, posted November 11, 2014, http://interrupting-oppression.tumblr.com/post/102351553722/list-of-isms.
16. Siebers, *Disability Aesthetics,* 23–24.
17. Siebers, *Disability Aesthetics,* 23.
18. Don James McLaughlin, "The Anti-Slavery Roots of Today's '-Phobia' Obsession," *New Republic,* January 29, 2016, https://newrepublic.com/article/128719/anti-slavery-roots-todays-phobia-obsession.
19. McLaughlin, "Anti-Slavery Roots."
20. Amanda Hess in McLaughlin, "Anti-Slavery Roots."
21. George Weinberg in McLaughlin, "Anti-Slavery Roots."
22. Patricia Hill Collins, *On Intellectual Activism* (Philadelphia: Temple University Press, 2013), 66.
23. Aimee Carrillo Rowe, *Power Lines: On the Subject of Feminist Alliances* (Durham, NC: Duke University Press, 2008), 1.
24. Carrillo Rowe, *Power Lines,* 1, 176.
25. Carrillo Rowe, *Power Lines,* 1–2.
26. Carrillo Rowe, *Power Lines,* 2.
27. Carrillo Rowe, *Power Lines,* 176.
28. Eric Gordy, *Guilt, Responsibility and Denial: The Past at Stake in Post Milosevic Serbia* (Philadelphia: University of Pennsylvania Press, 2013), 14–15.
29. Carrillo Rowe, *Power Lines,* 1.

PART

II

FEMINIST INTERSECTIONAL ORIENTATIONS TO RIGHTS

CHAPTER

4

Intersectional Approaches to Personhood and Citizenship

IN THIS CHAPTER, YOU WILL FIND . . .

KEY TERMS AND CONCEPTS

- civility
- coverture
- eugenics
- hierarchy of humanness
- human rights
- social polarization
- universal moral respect

THE RIGHT TO BE CONSIDERED FULLY HUMAN

What makes someone human? Who decides? Law professor Patricia J. Williams tells a story of her great-great grandmother, a young woman sold as a slave to a white man, that reveals the powerful, and negative, effects of the hierarchies of humanness used to grant and deny personhood:

> A few years ago, I came into the possession of what may have been the contract of sale for my great-great-grandmother. It is a very simple but lawyerly document, describing her as "one female" and revealing her age as eleven; no price is specified, merely "value exchanged." My sister also found a county census record taken two years later; on a list of one Austin Miller's personal assets she appears again, as "slave, female"—thirteen years old now with an eight-month infant.
>
> Since then I have tried to piece together what it must have been like to be my great-great-grandmother. She was purchased, according to matrilineal recounting, by a man who was extremely temperamental and quite wealthy. I try to imagine what it would have been like to have a discontented white man buy me, after a fight with his mother about prolonged bachelorhood. I wonder what it would have been like to have a thirty-five-year-old man own the secrets of my puberty, which he bought to prove himself sexually as well as to increase his livestock of slaves. I imagine trying to please, with the yearning of adolescence, a man who truly did not know I was human, whose entire belief system resolutely defined me as animal, chattel, talking cow. . . . I try to envision being casually threatened with sale from time to time, teeth and buttocks bared to interested visitors.[1]

William's great-great grandmother existed as property, as an animal to be owned, a non-person. She had no control over her life or her dignity as a human being. We know that the discourses circulating at that time convinced many people that this was normal. The logic of such discourses of humanness used to defend and promote slavery did powerful work: people were held in unacceptable conditions for centuries because of that discourse. But what does it take to deny someone the identity of fully human? An intersectional orientation to discourses of humanness helps us recognize that slavery is but one among many horrific examples of the discourse of human undesirability.

For centuries in the United States, and elsewhere, people used particular criteria to establish someone as human, or to disqualify them, and treat them in inhumane ways. To understand this part of our history, and to consider whether we still struggle to grant individuals the status of human, in this chapter we explore conceptualizations of *human, person,* and *citizen* in the United States through an intersectional lens. Our intersectional orientation to identity and communication helps us recognize, and begin to understand, how conceptualizations of who was considered fully human have changed over time—and how we can cultivate a discourse of civility and respect that promotes the full recognition of humanness.

Figure 4.1 Can you name the hierarchies of humanness that are reflected in these shackles, which were used to restrain people the United States deemed not fully human and thus as property to be owned? (Source: iStock. Credit: BMBPhotoArt)

THE RIGHT TO PERSONHOOD: HIERARCHIES OF HUMANNESS

If you were asked to name the specific traits and characteristics that define a human being as a person, what would those traits be? Depending on the discursive regime used, individuals have offered different answers. Biologists might have one view, legal experts another, social psychologists yet another, and religious leaders yet another view. To answer this question, we could consider the following criteria:

- Is our humanness or personhood dependent on holding membership in a biological species? Are we genetically human?
- Is our humanness dependent on other people with whom we share a history as well as "a cultural background, roles, [and] relationships"? Are we human because we are members of a community of other people?

- Does our personhood and humanness rely on having a body, a soul, a "perceived future and a transcendent or spiritual dimension"? Is there a divine or mystical element to humanness and personhood?
- Is personhood and humanness something we acquire over time, through a legal status that allows us the right to vote or serve in the military, for example?
- Is personhood determined by the participation in certain activities—owning land or property; looking, dressing, or moving about the world in a particular way; possessing certain documents, such as birth certificates, visas, green cards, and passports; or even having committed a crime?[2]

Can we lose our humanness or personhood because of some activity, way of looking, acting, or documentation or the lack of it? Is personhood some combination of all of these factors? None of them? We have looked at hierarchies of value and power in previous chapters. How do such factors as gender, sexuality, race, ethnicity, national origin, religion, education, profession, class, ability (physical and mental) influence the idea of what it means to be fully human? Are these factors related to a **hierarchy of humanness**—that is, do some traits make some individuals more fully human, more of a person, than others? What factors contribute to an individual's humanity being recognized and what factors are at work when it is not?

When we use the word *human* in this context we are looking at the features—physical, social, and legal—that establish an individual as a "person." Although the word *person* has been with us for a long time, in her exploration of treatment for individuals with dementia, Jan Dewing suggests that "the concept of what a person is in Western culture has undergone dramatic changes over time." These dramatic changes include our understanding of "personhood" as linked to the following factors.

Morality: If individuals did not conform to the standards of morality in place in a given era, they could be deemed less than human.

Spirituality: If individuals did not adhere to particular forms of spirituality and religion, they could be considered less than human.

Ability: If individuals did not possess a particular kind of body, they could be treated as not fully human.

Reason: If individuals did not possess a particular functioning of the brain, they were considered less than human.[3]

When we take an intersectional orientation to the definitions of *human* or *person,* we acknowledge that some people have had to fight for the right to be recognized as fully human and thus a person, while others have not—as is illustrated by the opening story in this chapter.

The negative impact of slavery on those who were made slaves and their descendants is clear; but the impact of owning other humans—the impact of slavery on slaveholders and their descendants—is rarely a topic of conversation and debate. What traits might an owner of slaves—a white male and his family—possess that would make their ownership of another human possible and desirable? Is it subscribing to hierarchies of humanness, binary logics of human/non-human, entitlement, and more? What language could be used to explain these traits and logics? What intersectional words would describe the person who treated another human being as a slave and what would those words tell us? In all probability, they would tell us a good deal about a long legacy of dehumanization that affects us even today.

CRITERIA FOR PERSONHOOD: THE DISCOURSE OF UNDESIRABLE TRAITS

When groups of people are able to establish the criteria for personhood and humanness, powerful discourses circulate that normalize those criteria. People talk as though the criteria are true, societies function as though they are natural, and laws make claims for the existence of a "normal" and an "ideal" person. But what does this talk of desirable/undesirable traits look like? How does what we say in our homes, towns and cities, churches, and social clubs become dominant aspects of our everyday lives? U.S. history provides many examples; one that helps us understand the privilege and power that come with the identity of "person" and "human" can be found in what were called the laws of **coverture.**

Beginning in the 1600s, the laws of coverture gave no married women any legal status of their own: she could not own property, sign contracts, write a will, or even keep her own wages. Upon divorce, she had no rights to her children. These laws continued through the late 1800s, and for almost three hundred years, all married women—no matter their race, class, physical ability, religion, or cisgender identities—were considered to be inferior to men—religiously, intellectually, and legally.[4] The laws of coverture, in short, made married women the property of men.[5] Their inferior status was codified into legal decisions, which secured the control of married women by men both privately and publicly.

There are other examples of the power to deny someone the status of personhood, and they are, perhaps, less well known. In earlier periods individuals who were poor, had a physical or mental disability, or were not white also had no legal status of their own—they were not considered fully human, or people. This status of "disqualified human" gave individuals with power the right to control these individuals. If this sounds preposterous or impossible, consider the practices that justified the sterilization of the "feebleminded," the poor and illiterate, those called "promiscuous," as well as immigrants, "troublemakers," African American and Hispanic women, Native American women, transgender individuals, and the incarcerated.

"Feebleminded," Poor, and "Promiscuous" Women

In 1906, doctors sterilized fourteen-year old Carrie Buck, a cisgender white woman who grew up poor in Virginia. Buck's father, a tinner, died when Buck was quite young and authorities removed her from her mother's care at the age of three. Buck attended local schools where "her records indicate normal progress each year" and at the age of fourteen, her foster family took her out of school to help with housework. Raped by the nephew of her foster parents, Buck's family believed that the pregnancy "was evidence of promiscuity and thus of feeblemindedness." In 1923, Virginia laws allowed the foster family to commit Buck to the Colony for Epileptics and Feeble-Minded. Doctors then sterilized Buck's daughter, arguing that the trait of feeblemindedness is hereditary and that "sexual sterilization could thus prevent the transmission."

Buck was not alone, however. The discourse around sterilization in the early twentieth century conflated the categories of "disability" and "sexual deviance" (including being labeled "promiscuous," which Buck was), sending the "feebleminded" to sanatoriums, where they could be sterilized.[6] Doctors working for the state of Virginia forcibly sterilized approximately 8,300 Virginian women, including Buck's younger half-sister. Released from the Virginia institution in 1927, Buck, who had been misdiagnosed, lived an independent and productive life. Her daughter, adopted by the same foster family, "was an honor student when she died of enterocolitis" at the age of eight.[7]

Immigrants

Driven in part "by anti-Asian and anti-Mexican prejudice," the state of California performed the most forced sterilizations during a nation-wide eugenics craze that began in the early 1900s. Under what were called Asexualization Acts, the state of California forcibly sterilized more than 20,000 Asian and Mexican men and women. A team of epidemiologists, historians, and digital humanists, led by University of Michigan professor Alexandra Minna Stern, located archival records that revealed that "patients with Spanish surnames were much more likely to be sterilized than other patients," and that "often the focus was on minors, people as young as 7."[8] Initially, Stern explains, more men were sterilized than women. But, "by the 1930s, that patterned started to change," and by the 1940s and 1950s, women were more likely to be sterilized than men. Individuals were sterilized under the diagnosis of "mental disease," which could be anything from "not conforming to social norms," to being poor, lacking education, and not speaking "sufficient English."[9]

Troublemakers

White, cisgender, and male, Willis Lynch, sterilized by the state of North Carolina at the age of fourteen, "is one of 7,600 victims of North Carolina's eugenics program" that took place between the 1929 and 1974. One of seven children raised by a single mother, authorities sent Willis, who described himself as "mean" and often in trouble for fighting, to the Caswell Training School for the Mentally Handicapped at the age of eleven. Willis's mother "consented to the procedure when the Welfare Department threatened to take away the benefits that provided for the rest of her children."[10] Given a diagnosis of "feeblemindedness" as justification for the sterilization, Wills, now "retired from a career that included military service, farming, plumbing, handyman work, and auto repair," plays country music at a nearby VFW hall, performing "a few of the 60 or 70 songs he knows by heart," and shares, "I never figured out why they did that to me."[11]

Black and Hispanic Women

Between 1933 and 1983, southern states adopted the practice of what civil rights activist Fanny Lou Hamer called "Mississippi appendectomies,"[12] her label for "unnecessary hysterectomies performed at teaching hospitals in the south on women of color as practice for medical students."[13] The National Council of Negro Women states that "bitter experience has taught the Black woman that the administration of justice in this country is not colorblind. Black women on welfare have been forced to accept sterilization in exchange for a continuation of relief benefits and others have been sterilized without their knowledge or consent."[14] The abuses of the teaching hospitals in the south are not unique; however, as a director of obstetrics and gynecology at a New York municipal hospital reports, in "most major teaching hospitals in New York City, it is the unwritten policy to do elective hysterectomies on poor black and Puerto Rican women, with minimal indications, to train residents."[15]

In 1973, the Montgomery Family Planning Clinic sterilized Minnie Lee Relf, involuntarily, at the age of fourteen, and her mentally disabled sister, Mary Alice, age twelve. The two African American girls had received birth control shots from the clinic two years earlier, and their mother, who could not read or write, believed she was consenting to continued shots. The "clinic decided that the girls should be sterilized, as they were poor, black, and living in public housing." With the assistance of the Southern Poverty Law Center, the Relf family filed a lawsuit. The district court found that an "estimated 100,000–150,000 poor people had been involuntarily sterilized annually."[16]

Native American Women

Between the 1960 and 1980, doctors working for the Indian Health Services sterilized 25–50 percent of native women between the ages of fifteen and forty-four.[17] Doctors told these women that the procedures were reversible, and the women were given improper consent forms, coerced into signing, or sterilized without knowledge or permission. The rationale for these sterilizations included higher birth rates among Native American women as compared to white women: 1.79 births for white women as compared to 3.79 for Native women.[18] "What may be the most disturbing," Gregory Rutecki, MD, states, is that "*it was physicians and healthcare professionals in the IHS who coerced these women.* It was they who abandoned their professional responsibility to protect the vulnerable through appropriate, non-eugenic indications for surgery and informed consent prior to the procedures."[19]

Transgender Individuals

Forced sterilization is not a travesty of the past, however. Fourteen countries in Europe require transgender individuals to be sterilized before they can receive legal documents that reflect the gender identity with which they identify.[20] Japan's government recently upheld laws that require the sterilization of transgender people if they wish to have the legal documentation that reflects the gender identity they avow. A transgender man in Japan explains, "I don't want to [have surgery], to be honest. However, I have to just because it's a requirement . . . I feel pressured to be operated on—so terrible." And a transgender woman shares, "Of course I want to change the gender on my official family register, and have relationships with my significant other. . . . But the walls that I have to overcome are just too big."[21] The Human Rights Commission has defined this forced sterilization as a violation of basic human rights and as "coercive, humiliating, and unnecessary." Activists and those working with the Human Rights Commission explain that it is time to get "trans people and trans issues outside the medical framework because no gender identity is pathological or can be determined by someone else."[22]

Inmates

The United States also continues to practice unethical sterilization procedures. Between 2006 and 2010, California's prisons "oversaw the forced sterilization of 148 women inmates."[23] In 2015, Tennessee attorneys offered sterilization as an alternative to fifteen years in prison to a mentally ill woman facing charges in the neglect and undetermined cause of death of her infant.[24] And in 2017, a Tennessee judge offered shorter sentences for inmates if they underwent sterilization procedures. Craig Klugman, a bioethicist at DePaul University, explains that prisoners are "a vulnerable population lacking many freedoms of others. A reduced sentence in return for a surgical procedure violates autonomy, social justice, the right to determine what happens to one's body, and procreative liberty."[25]

What do these sterilization practices tell us about those "in power" in (and outside) the United States? One discursive regime is particularly helpful in understanding the mind-set of those who forced sterilization on so many. **Eugenics** is the practice of selective breeding in an attempt to eliminate "undesirable" genes from a gene pool. To accomplish this selective breeding, certain kinds of people must be prevented from having children, that is, sterilized. To justify this selective breading, certain people must be understood as "undesirable" and disqualified as being human. In fact, Adolph Hitler, in Nazi Germany, found the eugenics program in the United States so compelling that he used these practices as a model for his own attempts to exterminate Jewish people, people who were gay and lesbian, or others who he felt were expendable or could be made examples of. Historian William Deverell explains the ideology behind eugenics discourse: "If you are sterilizing someone, you are saying, if not to them directly, 'Your progeny are inassimilable,'"—that they are unacceptable and should not be allowed to exist.[26]

What were and are the criteria used to develop the arguments that validate these so-called undesirable traits? How is it that physicians and health care professionals abandoned their commitment to ethical procedures informed by the principle of "first, do no harm?" To meet the criteria for "undesirable," you could

- grow up in conditions of poverty
- be Asian, Mexican, or Puerto Rican
- be Black and female
- be Native American and female
- be undereducated or poorly educated
- not speak English "properly"
- not conform to social norms
- have a mental disability
- be assigned the labels of feeblemindedness and/or promiscuity—however inaccurately
- be transgender
- be incarcerated

Any of these traits or conditions were and are grounds for sterilization, and authorities create and circulate a discourse that sanctions the procedure—without the individuals' informed consent or with undue pressure to agree to the procedures. Certainly, people possessing these traits did and do not feel unacceptable or that they had or have undesirable traits. Yet they were and are told—through the language of misinformation, deception, manipulation, and force—and shown—through sterilization procedures—that, indeed, they were and are undesirable.

An intersectional orientation to discourses of humanness helps us recognize that slavery (see the story that opened this chapter), is only one among the many horrific examples of the discourse of human undesirability. Race, sex and gender, class, sexuality, physical and mental ability, and incarceration all are given central roles in this discourse. Those identity categories, however complex they actually are, are reduced to simple conceptualizations of identity. Race is problematic if it is not "white"; class is problematic if it is not economically secure; sex is problematic depending on your race or class; gender is problematic if it is not cisgender; physical and mental ability are problematic if they do not match what is considered "normal"; and incarceration strips people of their right to freely choose what happens to their bodies. Historically, the standards for what is desirable, and thus human, were profoundly non-intersectional. In fact, these standards reflect the identities of those who are white, economically secure, cisgender men who are of "normal" intelligence and physical ability. Those standards are with us today even though, as women-of-color feminists have pointed out for decades, very few people fit this restrictive ideal.

THE RIGHT TO CITIZENSHIP: THE DISCOURSE OF BELONGING

The discourse of "unacceptable humans" does not stop with the stripping away of someone's dignity, their right to bring children into the world, or the horrific practices that constitute and legitimize eugenics. This discourse also informs notions of citizenship and belonging. In the United States, citizenship allows individuals to participate in the making of laws and policies, the running of governments and communities, the acquisition of land and other material wealth—participation in most everything that makes this society function. It also informs the protections an individual can expect, that is, the right to proper medical care, to be free from assault and violence, and even the kinds and lengths of prison sentences.[27] The discourse of what is unacceptable has influenced ideas of citizenship for people living in the United States in important ways.

The Constitution does not, as Barbara Young Welke, professor of law and history, explains "define who was a citizen. Rather, citizenship, like personhood, was given shape and meaning largely by state law."[28] And these laws were rooted in hierarchies of privilege and power as well as regimes of dependency and control. The story of who belonged (and who belongs now) in and to America, of who could be a citizen, is a story of a power and privilege that is entrenched in "abled, racialized, and gendered terms."[29] Those who belonged were able-body, cisgender, white men, and they "alone were fully embodied legal persons, they were America's 'first citizens,' they were the nation."[30] Even though more than five million Native American people lived on this continent long before white settlers arrived, our self-described "first citizens" saw the presence of those here long before them as an enormous problem. Ascribing these individuals the identity of "undesirable," the newcomers used both active and passive methods of extermination: military violence and widespread

Figure 4.2 This canceled stamp reflects the realities that citizenship and belonging in the United States were defined by those in power, rather than by the Native American people who lived on the continent long before settlers arrived. (Source: iStock. Credit: traveler1116)

disease. In just a little more than 500 years, less than one million Native people remained. Our founding fathers communicated clearly in both word and deed that Native Americans did not "belong."

The founding fathers of this nation also created laws, social norms, and material conditions that protected "able white male privilege not simply up to the Civil War, but after it as well."[31] Consider these examples.

> The law of coverture stated. "By marriage, the husband and wife are one person in law; that is, the very being or legal existence of the woman is suspended during the marriage."[32]
>
> The law of slavery "constructed blacks as property to be claimed by whites" and miscegenation laws disallowed inter-racial marriage between whites and non-whites, ensuring that "white claims to land" and inheritance were secure.[33]
>
> After the emancipation of slaves, Black Code laws "bound blacks to white-owned land" by requiring "all freedmen, at the beginning of each year, to have written evidence of their employment contract" for that year and made "leaving that employment subject to arrest."[34]
>
> The laws of dispossession made it legal for white men to take land from Native Americans and to establish white settlements across the nation, regardless of who already lived there.
>
> Laws made it acceptable to take custody of an Indian child and place him or her under apprenticeship and to "arrest and hire out to the highest bidder Indians found loitering, drunk, or 'guilty' of any number of other offenses."[35]

> Laws controlled the labor of "paupers and beggars" by defining their labor as "not labor at all." So, if a boy or man sold newspapers on street corners, he could be driven from his corner, or any corner, and his means of earning an income could be confiscated or destroyed.
>
> Laws sanctioned the refusal of entry into the country to "various unstable individuals," which included "persons with abnormal sex instincts" as well as individuals with "defects" described as "poor physique," "undersized," "deficient in muscular development," or "physically degenerate."[36]

Those with privilege determined who belonged, where they belonged, and who could and who could not share in the responsibilities and enjoy the privileges of citizenship.

In fact, our founding fathers also legislated "human nature" and codified that assumed nature into law. In 1876, Supreme Court justice Oliver Wendell Holmes embraced the English self-defense law of "to the wall." This law referred to a man's obligation to have a wall at his back before defending himself. Having one's back up against a wall meant that a man had no recourse but to defend himself; fighting was his only means of protection or survival. Justice Holmes approved of this notion and determined that a man did, indeed, have an obligation to have his back against the wall before retaliating. However, Justice Holmes took the "to the wall" principle a step further, arguing that "the law 'must consider human nature and make some allowances for the fighting instinct at critical moments.'" This meant that a man could experience "momentary madness," for example, and justifiably kill his wife's lover, should he find them in bed together or chance to meet him on the street—or he could justifiably whip his slave for misbehaving.

The "human nature" and "man" to which Justice Holmes referred, in reality, were a cisgender white man and his so-called nature: the "black slave and the married woman had no right to resist with deadly force a master's or a husband's physical assault."[37] As Welke explains, for centuries Indians, blacks—slave or free—and women of any color or race were "so far inferior that they had no rights which the white man was bound to respect."[38]

Our laws are not simply rules for directing behaviors, however. They are the frameworks for the discourses that legitimize our practices and shape our conversations, discussions, and disagreements. Laws speak to and about priorities, beliefs, and truth regimes. The founding laws of our nation, were, in effect, grounded in discourses that legitimized hierarchies of humanness, with cisgender white males occupying the privileged spot at the top. Justice Holmes's legalization of "momentary madness" in the guise of "human nature" is but one example of the cementing into the law the dynamics of privilege and subordination and the citizen/not citizen dichotomy that are with us to this day. Laws respond to ideas of unacceptability and, with regard to citizenship, are filtered through two questions: Who belongs? and Does belonging depend on there being others who do not belong?[39]

CRITERIA FOR INCIVILITY: DISCOURSES OF SOCIAL POLARIZATION

Humans have a need for social belonging, states Lilliana Mason, associate professor of Government and Politics at the University of Maryland. We are "hard-wired to cling to social groups," she states, and for good reasons. Humans categorize in order to understand the world—plants are different from animals, which are different from minerals, and so on. But we also categorize for social cohesion. Without that cohesion, Mason explains, "we would have a hard time creating societies and civilizations." At their best, categories help us "understand ourselves and our place in the world." At their worst, they help us exclude and rank, avoiding meaningful communication and interaction with our fellow human beings. The desire to form groups is not the problem, says Mason; instead, our tendency to form exclusive groups is what creates problems. This is because the sense of exclusivity can hide our inclination to "evaluate our various groups with an unrealistic view of their relative merits."[40] Because others in our exclusive group are similar to us, we tend to see those who are not in our group as inferior.

Mason's work revolves around our two-party political system and, although we might want to think our groupings of personhood and citizenship are relics of the past, they aren't: Republicans and Democrats have begun grouping and ranking personhood and citizenship in different yet troublingly familiar ways. Both parties have experienced an increase in the loyalty of its party members to the party itself: Democrats are more strongly identified as Democrats and Republicans are more strongly identified as Republican than ever before. To rephrase: both parties have a stronger sense of exclusivity than in previous decades. This has led to two phenomena. The first is that party allegiance is strongly linked to personal identity. The Republican party is "now solidly conservative, middle class or wealthy, rural, churchgoing, and white." The Democratic party is now "firmly aligned with identities such as liberal, secular, urban, low-income, Hispanic, and black."[41] The second phenomenon is that "members of both parties negatively stereotype members of the opposing party, and the extent of this partisan stereotyping has increased by 50 percent between 1960 and 2010."[42]

"Across the electorate," Mason notes, "Americans have been dividing with increasing distinction into two partisan teams. . . . They view the other party as more extreme than their own, while they view their own party as not at all extreme." The majority of people in both parties "hold *very* unfavorable views of their partisan opponents," preferring to "live in neighborhoods with members of their own party, expressing less satisfaction with their neighborhood when told that opposing partisans live there."[43] Mason defines this phenomenon as **social polarization,** which she explains is "defined by prejudice, anger, and activism on behalf of that prejudice and anger. These phenomena are increasing quickly—more quickly, in fact, than the level of our policy disagreements. We act like we

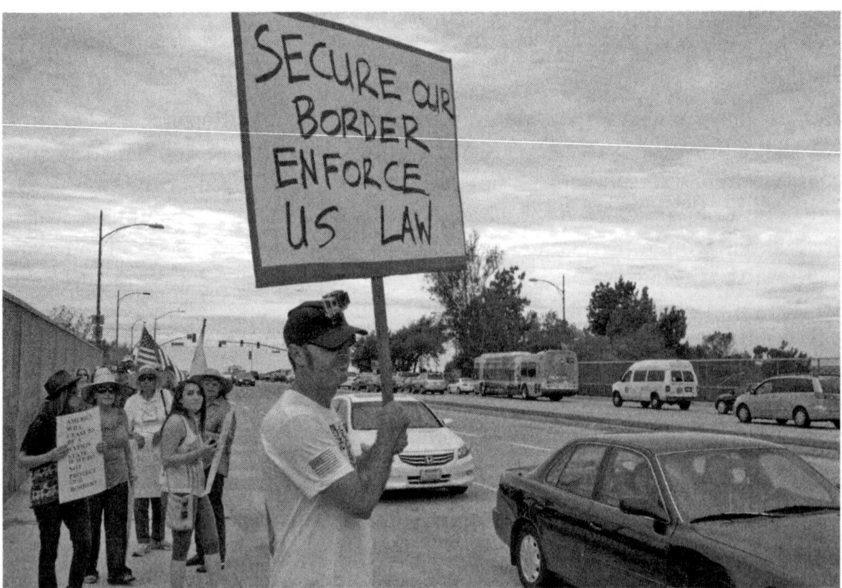

Figure 4.3 Who is said to belong in the sign held by this protester? What kind of categorization and social cohesion is the language on the sign advocating for? (Source: iStock. Credit: DnHolm)

disagree more than we really do." Mason adds that "our conflicts are largely over who we think we are rather than over reasoned differences of opinion."[44] Our disagreements are based on our group identifications, rather than reasonable conversation, discussion, and exploration of dilemmas and problems.

As each party has grown more homogenous, the cross-cutting of social identities, and thus the need to communicate with individuals who are different from us, has diminished. Consider the following divisions.

Gender: A little more than half of women voters (56 percent) identify with the Democratic Party, while a little more than half of male voters (56 percent) identify with the Republican Party.

Race: The parties are now so divided by race that simple racial identity can often predict party identity. Black, Hispanic, and Asian voters are overwhelmingly Democratic; white voters are more likely to lean toward the Republican Party.

Religion: Between 1989 and 2000, the Republican Party became "firmly affiliated with conservative Christianity" while the Democratic Party remained secular.

Education: Those voters with college experience tend to affiliate with the Democratic Party while those without college are split evenly between the parties.

> *Age:* Millennials (born between 1981 and 1996) are more likely to identify as Democratic or Independent than any other age group. Generation X (born between 1965 and 1980) and Baby Boomers (born between 1946 and 1964) are equally divided between the parties, and the Silent Generation (born between 1928 and 1945) leans just slightly toward the Republican party.[45]

We are lining up according to several primary identities—gender, race, religion, education, and age—which influence the cultural norms we avow. Equally as interesting, however, is that our news and entertainment preferences mirror these divisions: TiVo Research and Analytics discovered in 2012 that, of the top twenty shows watched by Republicans and Democrats, not a "single network show appeared on both lists."[46] In an interesting series of binaries, Republican/Democrat preferences are, respectively, *Washington Times*/*Washington Post,* Macaroni Grill/Chuck E. Cheese's, Land Rovers/hybrids, and Amstel Light/cognac.[47]

Democrats and Republicans "have grown so different from each other that cooperation is receding as a perceived value." This affects not just our dislike or even loathing of one another, it affects the way we see the world and the way we "think about other citizens."[48] To be clear, it is not the party affiliation that is the problem, nor our various identities, per se, that are tripping us up: it is the homogeneity of identities within each of the political groups. Never before have we been so non-diverse as political parties. "This has generated an electorate that is more biased against and angry at opponents, and more willing to act on that bias and anger." When any group grows more "socially homogeneous, their members are quicker to anger and tend toward intolerance." But beyond this anger and intolerance of those not in one's own group is an intense commitment to winning as well as a refusal "to give an inch to the other side."[49]

Our discourses related to controversial issues reflect not just our views of one another, but the various people who are affected by the complex issues we struggle with today: food security, safe and affordable shelter and housing, meaningful and economically sustainable employment, access to health care, questions of family planning and security into old age, expressions of sexuality, adequate education, the care of our environment, and more. Incredibly controversial today are the issues of migration and immigration. Using this particularly complex topic as a case study, set aside your opinions on the issue and instead consider the following nouns, adjectives, and adverbs used by Republicans and Democrats to define the dispute.

> *Republican terminology:* alien, illegal, criminal, invasion, flood, pollution, infection, infestation, balkanization, disease, burden, raids, arrest, detain, criminally prosecute, zero tolerance, mass detention, border security, deportation, assault on the American worker, our jobs, Latin onslaught, decline of folks who look like you and me, purity, homeland security, identity theft, fraud and abuse, mass legal immigration, chain migration,

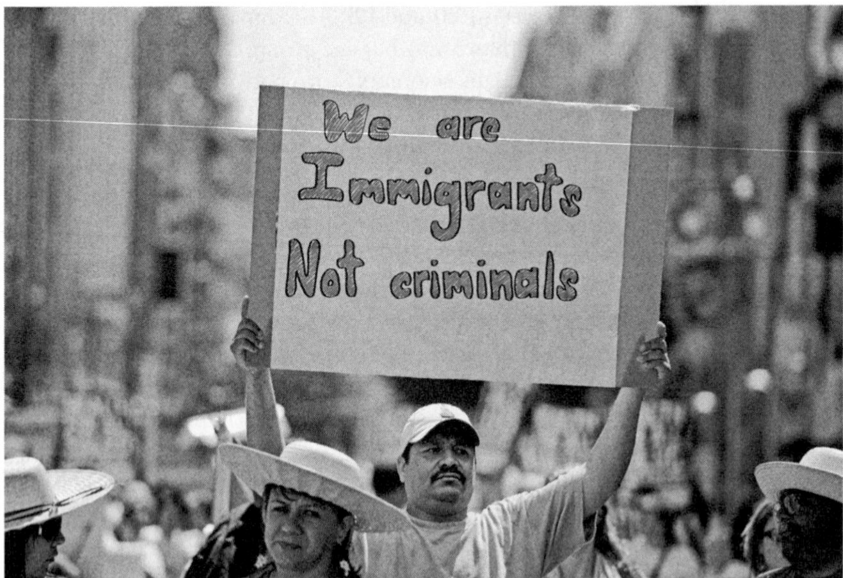

Figure 4.4 How are we being asked to understand the identities described in the sign of this protester? What ideas of belonging and citizenship are being advocated in this sign? (Source: iStock. Credit: anouchka)

> low-skilled immigrants, growing problem of alien minors, Unaccompanied Alien Children (UACs), and loopholes.
>
> *Democratic terminology:* nation of immigrants, foreign born and U.S. born, unauthorized immigrant population, Mexican legal residents, length of residence, green cards, work permits, visas, mixed status families, Deferred Action for Childhood Arrivals (DACA), unauthorized LGBT adult immigrants, asylum, integral to nation's economy, innovation, entrepreneurship, technological change, graduates, facts matter, fake news, undocumented Americans, less likely to commit crimes, healthy immigrant thesis, motivated, ambitious, and people.[50]

If you look carefully at these lists, only five words actually refer to migrating and immigrating human beings as people: folks, children, families, adults, and people. The other 125 terms ascribe identities to their humanness, or perceived lack of it. Not only are we using terms that cast humans as insider/outsider, but we are using terms that deny those humans any meaningful humanity.

Does this language have much to do with our ideas of personhood and citizenship? The answer of course is yes. "In the communication discipline, studies have long focused on power-defining discourses to show that naming is power. The discursive power to name someone . . . is in the ability of words to control how people are represented."[51] Our words matter. Words describe our identities, affect how we think about ourselves and other people, and as we talk, we expose our fundamental assumptions about ideas of personhood and citizenship. Our words raise, for students of communication and intersectionality, questions about humanness and personhood—and ultimately citizenship. Can an "alien" be a person and a citizen? What does it mean to be an illegal person?[52] Does place of birth determine personhood? Or, does place of birth combined with place and length of residence matter more? If you arrived to that place as a child, are you less human? If you have a well-paying job, are an entrepreneur, or technologically talented, are you more of a person? Who decides?

If, as Michael Wolf and his colleagues suggest, both parties are fiercely committed to party identity, and "enormous numbers of strong partisans" are "ready to go to war," what is the battle we are fighting?[53] When we talk about food security, education, medical care, or migration and immigration, are we talking about actual people and human rights, or are we relying on and engaging in polarizing narratives? The language we use to understand people and their complex identities informs our view of their humanness.

HUMAN RIGHTS, CIVILITY, AND UNIVERSAL MORAL RESPECT

Viewed through the lens of intersectionality, our decisions about who is human, a person, and a citizen have been profoundly influenced by discourses of exclusivity and hierarchy. Our history of slavery, coverture, sterilization, dispossession, and ownership inform our conversations about humanness, personhood, and citizenship today. They inform our discussions of human rights. But what are **human rights?** The United Nations defines them as "rights inherent to all human beings, regardless of race, sex, nationality, ethnicity, language, religion, or any other status. Human rights include the right to life and liberty, freedom from slavery and torture, freedom of opinion and expression, the right to work and education and many more. Everyone is entitled to these rights, without discrimination."[54] Does our conversation about any of the complex issues we face today mirror the UN declaration? Or, do these conversations reflect our desire to win, to be a member of a winning party, more than a desire for the guarantee of human rights?

If we are committed to human rights, which most of us in this country are, can our conversations begin to change? Can we communicate about complex issues respectfully, as an invitation to understand more fully? Can we address issues of residency, citizenship, employment, food, taxes, and health care by attending to our intersecting identities and without re-inscribing hierarchies of humanness? Can we communicate more civilly, even as we disagree about who belongs? The term *civility* has been defined in a number of ways, ranging from a false veneer of politeness with which we hope to silence and stifle disagreement to an anything-goes approach in which people say whatever they want, without fear of consequences. From feminist and intersectional lenses, however, we can define **civility** as "the care and concern for others, the thoughtful use of words and language, and the flexibility to see many sides of an issue."[55] When we are civil, we do not need to agree. Instead, we make a commitment to listen to people with identities much different from our own. We pay attention to their experiences and ideas, take responsibility for our own words and their impact on other people, and consider, respectfully, the concerns and needs of people with vastly different identities. When we are civil, our communication reflects a commitment to human rights rather than human hierarchies.

What does civil communication, despite differences, look like? Consider two polarizing statements regarding the costs of immigration:

> *The New York Times* reports that "57 percent of all voters said 'immigrants strengthen the economy,' while 35 percent say 'they are a burden.'"[56] Journalist Thomas Edsall states that "first generation immigrants cost the United States about $57 billion; second generation immigrants add about $30 billion a year; third generation immigrant families contribute about $223 billion a year to government finances." And, "expelling the estimated 11 million undocumented immigrants [currently in the U.S] would cost almost $900 billion in lost revenue over a decade."[57]
>
> *The Washington Times* explains that "the Department of Health and Human Services paid over $1.4 billion last year to care for nearly 41,000 Unaccompanied Alien Children (UACS) in its Facilities."[58] Additionally, journalist John Binder explains that "job growth for foreign born workers is growing more than twice what it is for native born American Citizens." That growth translates to 2.7 percent for foreign-born men as compared to 1.7 percent for native born male workers. This means that "immigrants continue to have advantages over native born Americans when it comes to their rapidly growing employment opportunities."[59]

How might we respond civilly to these contrasting statements?

Social polarization paves an easy path to animosity, facilitating hostility, hatred, bitterness, and ill will. Civility paves a different path, one that is invitational, complex, and often difficult to navigate. In *Situating the Self,* philosopher Seyla Benhabib advances the notion that we "ought to treat each other as concrete human beings" worthy of respect and of being listened to. In essence, "we ought to *respect* each other as beings whose standpoint is worthy of equal consideration (the principal of universal moral respect)."[60] Although Benhabib's notion of **universal moral respect** seems like common sense, that kind of respect has not always been offered. If we are to understand our profound disagreements today, we must engage our histories intersectionally, civilly, and

Communication Checklist for Civility

When we engage one another with civility, we do not begin by defending our own position. As we struggle to engage with other people civilly, we take time to communicate with other people rather than argue with them. Our goal is not to prove we are correct and they are wrong—that can happen at another time, if necessary.

- ✓ *Explore the claims.* Take time to explore the claims, statistics, sources of information, biases, and omissions from both sides. What is being said? What support is offered? What is left out? How is each argument progressing logically and emotionally?
- ✓ *Consider the source.* We must also consider the identities, privileges, values, histories, needs, commonalities, and differences of those making the statements. Who is asking for change? What kind of change is this person asking for? What are the experiences and background of this person—what identities do they bring to the conversation?
- ✓ *Share perspectives.* We share perspectives, information, and our identities in the spirit of exploring options and ideas.
- ✓ *Find common ground.* We find some common ground and express care and concern for our fellow human beings—even as we disagree.
- ✓ *Unpack differences respectfully.* We unpack and explore our differences as respectfully and honestly as is possible.
- ✓ *State understanding as goal.* We accept that the goal of civil communicators is not to defend our position but rather to understand issues as fully as possible—as intersectionally as possible.

4.1. GUIDE TO COMMUNICATION

Civility and Universal Moral Respect

Before you enter conversations and discussions about personhood, citizenship, rights, and respect, take time to consider the following questions:

1. What hierarchies of identity and humanness are present?
2. What undesirable traits are being said to exist?
3. Are laws or practices being advocated that frame or define identities, rights, belonging, and even human nature in hierarchal ways?
4. In what ways could invitational rhetoric, civility, and intersectional orientations be added productively to this conversation?
5. Are there times when incivility, argument, and flat-out disagreement during conversations about personhood and citizenship are warranted? If so, describe and explain those moments.

invitationally. We must have the courage to do so, recognizing that we have positioned one another differently on hierarchies of value. Intersectional, invitational, and civil exchanges hold the promise of de-polarization and of finding points of agreement and respect, even as we disagree.

Resources

Oskar Eustis, "Why Theatre Is Essential to Democracy," filmed April 2018 in Vancouver, British Columbia, TED2018 video, https://www.ted.com/talks/oskar_eustis_why_theater_is_essential_to_democracy.

"On a 'Eugenics Registry,' a Record of California's Thousands of Sterilizations," National Public Radio Weekend Edition Sunday, December 18, 2016, http://www.npr.org/2016/12/18/505000554/on-a-eugenics-registry-a-record-of-californias-thousands-of-sterilizations.

Michael Rain, "What It's Like to Be the Child of Immigrants," filmed November 2017 in New York, NY, TED Residency video, 7:55, https://www.ted.com/talks/michael_rain_what_it's_like_to_be_the_child_of_immigrants.

Theo E. J. Wilson, "A Black Man Goes Undercover in the Alt-Right," filmed December 2017 in Denver, CO, TEDxMileHigh video, 18:21, https://www.ted.com/talks/theo_e_j_wilson_a_black_man_goes_undercover_in_the_alt_right?referrer=playlist-dissecting_cultures_of_hate.

Notes

1. Patricia J. Williams, *The Alchemy of Race and Rights: Diary of a Law Professor* (Cambridge, MA: Harvard University Press, 1991), 17–18.
2. Jan Dewing, "Personhood and Dementia: Revisiting Tom Kitwood's Ideas," *International Journal of Older People Nursing* 3 (2008): 5.
3. Dewing, "Personhood and Dementia," 5.
4. Sara M. Evans, *Born for Liberty: A History of Women in America* (New York: Free Press, 1989), 22.
5. Barbara Young Welke, *Law and the Borders of Belonging in the Long Nineteenth Century United States* (New York: Cambridge University Press, 2010), 27.
6. Jess Whatcott, "Sexual Deviance and Mental Defectiveness in Eugenics Era California," Notches (blog), March 14, 2017, http://notchesblog.com/2017/03/14/sexual-deviance-and-mental-defectiveness-in-eugenics-era-california/.
7. J. David Smith, "Carrie Buck (1906–1983)," *Encyclopedia Virginia: A Publication of the Virginia Foundation for the Humanities*, accessed February 23, 2017, http://www.encyclopediavirginia.org/Buck_Carrie_Elizabeth_1906–1983#start_entry.
8. NPR Staff, "On a 'Eugenics Registry,' A Record of California's Thousands of Sterilizations," *National Public Radio Weekend Edition Sunday*, December 18, 2016, accessed March 1, 2017, http://www.npr.org/2016/12/18/505000554/on-a-eugenics-registry-a-record-of-californias-thousands-of-sterilizations.
9. NPR Staff, "On a Eugenics Registry."
10. Belle Boggs, "For the Public Good: The Shameful History of Forced Sterilization in the U.S.," *The New South: Long Reads*, August 2013, accessed March 1, 2017, https://longreads.com/2014/11/19/for-the-public-good/.
11. Boggs, "For the Public Good."
12. Serena Sebring, "Sterilization–Black Women," Mississippi Appendectomy, last modified November 25, 2007, accessed March 1, 2017, https://www.uvm.edu/~lkaelber/eugenics/MS/MS.html.
13. Lisa Ko, "Unwanted Sterilization and Eugenics Programs in the United States," PBS Independent Lens, January 29, 2016, accessed March 8, 2017, http://www.pbs.org/independentlens/blog/unwanted-sterilization-and-eugenics-programs-in-the-united-states/.
14. Editorial, The National Council of Negro Women, *Black Woman's Voice* 2, no. 2 (January/February 1973), quoted in "Mississippi Appendectomy," https://mississippiappendectomy.wordpress.com/2007/11/19/black-women-in-the-1960s-and-1970s/.
15. Dorothy E. Roberts, quoted in "Sterilization–Black Women," Mississippi Appendectomy, https://mississippiappendectomy.wordpress.com/2007/11/19/black-women-in-the-1960s-and-1970s/.
16. D'Army Bailey, "June 27, 1973—Relf Sisters Sue Clinic for Involuntary Sterilization," *Voices of the Civil Rights Movement, Moments in Civil Rights History*, YouTube video, 2:43, accessed March 8, 2017, https://www.youtube.com/watch?v=Sy8jRV0vmn4.
17. Jane Lawrence, "The Indian Health Services and the Sterilization of Native American Women," *The American Indian Quarterly* 24, no. 3 (Summer, 2000): 400; and Gregory W. Rutecki, "Forced Sterilization of Native Americans: Late Twentieth-Century Physician Cooperation with National Eugenic Policies," *The Center for Bioethics and Human Dignity, Trinity International University*, October 8, 2010, accessed March 9, 2017, https://cbhd.org/content/forced-sterilization-native-americans-late-twentieth-century-physician-cooperation-national-eugenic-policies.

18. Lawrence, "Indian Health Services," 404.
19. Rutecki, "Forced Sterilization," emphasis in original.
20. Transgender Europe (TGEU), Trans Rights Europe Map 2018, https://tgeu.org/wp-content/uploads/2018/05/MapB_TGEU2018_Online.pdf.
21. Human Rights Watch, "Japan: Compelled Sterilization of Transgender People," March 19, 2019, https://www.hrw.org/news/2019/03/19/japan-compelled-sterilization-transgender-people.
22. Liam Stack, "European Court Strikes Down Required Sterilization for Transgender People," *New York Times*, April 12, 2017, https://www.nytimes.com/2017/04/12/world/europe/european-court-strikes-down-required-sterilization-for-transgender-people.html.
23. Lea Hunter, "The U.S. Is Still Forcibly Sterilizing Prisoners," Talk Poverty, August 23, 2017, https://talkpoverty.org/2017/08/23/u-s-still-forcibly-sterilizing-prisoners/.
24. Stacey Barchenger, "A Dead Baby, an Ill Mother and a DA's Intervention," *Tennessean*, March 17, 2015, updated April 1, 2015, https://www.tennessean.com/story/news/crime/2015/03/17/jasmine-randers-committed/24870929/.
25. Craig Klugman, "Sterilization for Prisoners Is Not New and Shows that Studying History Is Essential," BioEthics, August 2, 2017, https://www.bioethics.net/2017/08/sterilization-for-prisoners-is-not-new-and-shows-that-studying-history-is-essential/.
26. William Deverell, quoted in Lisa Ko, "Unwanted Sterilization and Eugenics Programs in the United States," January 29, 2016, accessed March 8, 2017, http://www.pbs.org/independentlens/blog/unwanted-sterilization-and-eugenics-programs-in-the-united-states/.
27. E. Johanna Hartelius, ed., *The Rhetorics of U.S. Immigration: Identity, Community, Otherness* (University Park: Pennsylvania State University Press, 2015).
28. Barbara Young Welke, "Law, Personhood, and Citizenship in the Long Nineteenth Century: The Borders of Belonging," in *The Cambridge History of Law in America*, vol. 2, ed. Michael Grossberg and Christopher Tomlins (New York: Cambridge University Press, 2010), 348.
29. Welke, *Law and the Borders of Belonging*, 34.
30. Welke, *Law and the Borders of Belonging*, 5.
31. Welke, *Law and the Borders of Belonging*, 2.
32. Welke, "Law, Personhood, and Citizenship," 348.
33. Welke, "Law, Personhood, and Citizenship," 354.
34. Welke, "Law, Personhood, and Citizenship," 354.
35. Welke, *Law and the Borders of Belonging*, 32.
36. Welke, *Law and the Borders of Belonging*, 151.
37. Welke, *Law and the Borders of Belonging*, 25.
38. Welke, *Law and the Borders of Belonging*, 35.
39. Welke, *Law and the Borders of Belonging*, 1.
40. Lilliana Mason, *Uncivil Agreement: How Politics Became Our Identity* (Chicago: University of Chicago Press, 2018), 9.
41. Mason, *Uncivil Agreement*, 26.
42. Mason, *Uncivil Agreement*, 3.
43. Mason, *Uncivil Agreement*, 3.
44. Mason, *Uncivil Agreement*, 4.
45. Compiled from Mason, *Uncivil Agreement*, 40, and Pew Research Center, "Wide Gender Gap, Growing Educational Divide in Voters' Party Identification," March 20, 2018, https://www.people-press.org/2018/03/20/1-trends-in-party-affiliation-among-demographic-groups/.
46. Mason, *Uncivil Agreement*, 43.
47. Mason, *Uncivil Agreement*, 44.
48. Mason, *Uncivil Agreement*, 44, 47.
49. Michael R. Wolf, J. Cherie Strachan, and Daniel M. Shea, "Forget the Good of the Game: Political Incivility and Lack of Compromise as a Second Layer of Party Polarization," *American Behavioral Scientist* 56, no. 12 (2012): 1689.
50. Compiled from D. Carolina Nuñez, "War of the Words: Aliens, Immigrants, Citizens, and the Language of Exclusion," *Brigham Young University Law Review*, vol. 2013, no. 6 (2014): 1519; Hartelius, *Rhetorics of U.S. Immigration*; "The Facts on Immigration Today: 2017 Edition," Center for American Progress, April 20, 2017, https://www.americanprogress.org/issues/immigration/reports/2017/04/20/430736/facts-immigration-today-2017-edition/; Kent A. Ono and John M. Sloop, *Shifting Borders: Rhetoric, Immigration, and California's Proposition 187* (Philadelphia: Temple University Press, 2002); Mark Ellis and Richard Wright, "The Balkanization Metaphor in the Analysis of U.S. Immigration," *Annals of the Association of American Geographers*, 88 no. 4 (1998): 686–698; Leo R. Chavez, *Covering Immigration: Popular Images and the Politics of the Nation* (Berkeley: University of California Press, 2001); Otto Santa Ana, *Brown Tide Rising: Metaphors of Latinos in Contemporary American Public Discourse* (Austin: University of Texas Press, 2002); "Anti-Immigrant Arguments Against Immigration Reform," Anti-Defamation League, 2017, https://www.adl.org/resources/backgrounders/anti-immigrant-arguments-against-immigration-reform; Jason DeParle, "The Anti-Immigration Crusader," *New York Times*, April 17, 2011, https://www.nytimes.com/2011/04/17

/us/17immig.html; and Daniel Costa, David Cooper, and Heidi Shierholz, "Facts about Immigration and the U.S. Economy: Answers to Frequently Asked Questions," *Economic Policy Institute,* August 12, 2014, https://www.epi.org/publication/immigration-facts/; https://www.numbersusa.com.

51. Claudia A. Anguiano, "Dropping the 'I-Word': A Critical Examination of Contemporary Immigration Labels," in Hartelius, *Rhetorics of U.S. Immigration,* 95.
52. Anguiano, "Dropping the I-Word," 95.
53. Wolf, Strachan, and Shea, "Forget the Good of the Game," 1689.
54. The United Nations, "Human Rights," http://www.un.org/en/sections/issues-depth/human-rights/.
55. Cindy L. Griffin, *Invitation to Public Speaking,* 6th ed. (Boston: Cengage, 2018), 2.
56. Thomas B. Edsall, "What Does Immigration Actually Cost Us?" *New York Times,* September 29, 2016, https://www.nytimes.com/2016/09/29/opinion/campaign-stops/what-does-immigration-actually-cost-us.html.
57. Edsall, "What Does Immigration Actually Cost Us?"
58. "Report: Growing Alien Minor Problem Costly to Taxpayers," *Washington Times,* May 31, 2018, https://www.numbersusa.com/news/report-growing-alien-minor-problem-costly-taxpayers.
59. John Binder, "Job Growth for Foreign Workers Rising Twice as Fast as for Native Born Americans," Breitbart, June 2018, http://www.breitbart.com/big-government/2018/06/01/job-growth-for-foreign-workers-growing-twice-as-fast-as-for-native-born-americans/.
60. Seyla Benhabib, *Situating the Self: Gender, Community and Postmodernism in Contemporary Ethics* (New York: Routledge, 1992), 31.

CHAPTER

5

Intersectional Approaches to Safety in Public Spaces

IN THIS CHAPTER, YOU WILL FIND . . .

KEY TERMS AND CONCEPTS

- crime myths
- criminalization
- cyber cesspools
- cyber harassment
- cyberstalking
- demonize
- gang injunctions
- gentrification
- hate crimes
- hate speech
- hypercriminalization
- punitive social control
- street harassment
- scapegoating
- youth control complex

THE RIGHT TO SAFETY

Sophie Sandberg founded Catcalls of NYC when she was a freshman at New York University. Growing up in New York, Sandberg shares that catcalls, a daily occurrence in her and her friends' lives, always made them very uncomfortable, feeling confused and powerless. On her popular Instagram account, @CatcallsofNYC, Sandberg receives messages from people around the world recounting the street harassment they experience and Sandberg posts those messages in chalk on the sidewalks of New York City. The catcalls she chalks on sidewalks include: "Smile, lady, you'll look prettier," "Sexy girl. Excuse me. Yo," "Call me when you're legal, doll," "Oh, so you gonna just ignore me? You ugly anyway," "Turn around and let me see your face, b*tch," "I want to cum on your face," "Hey, Mexico, F*** you, Mexico," "Lift up your dress and show us your pussy," "Nice chinky eyes," and "F*** her without a condom, bro." For Sandberg, street harassment is more than a mere annoyance. She explains that it has "shaped my experience in public space. It has affected my confidence and comfort walking down the street. It has silenced me—I've never felt comfortable responding to cat calls, as much as I'd like to tell these men off."[1]

To be safe in the world is to be able to move about without fear and threat of danger. To be safe is to feel secure and confident that you can get from one place to another free from menace and harm. Although all individuals feel more or less safe in certain circumstances, the complex identities we bring to public spaces are powerful forces in securing our safety. These identities are of particular interest for students of intersectional communication because they suggest that some individuals are seen as having less right to safety and security than others. When we view the right to safety through a non-intersectional lens, we are told that women, as compared to men, are not safe in public spaces.

When we view the right to safety through intersectional and feminist lenses, we can tell a much more complex—and accurate—story: our identities line up in certain ways to make us all more or less safe or unsafe in a range of spaces. In this chapter we explore that lack of safety both on our streets and online as well as the discourses that perpetuate the normalization of unsafe spaces. We also examine the myriad ways masculinity is policed on our streets, particularly with regard to men of color. In addition, we discuss some of the ways harassment, hate speech, and the policing of masculinity contradict values many people see as important to democracy and to basic human rights. The words we use to communicate are important because, when used with thoughtfulness and care, they can counterbalance harassment, hate speech, and the policing of masculinity.

Figure 5.1 If you could chalk one of Sophie Sandberg's messages on this sidewalk in Harlem, New York, which one would you choose? Why would you make that choice? (Source: iStock. Credit: Torresigner)

DISCOURSES OF HARASSMENT AND HATE

In *Stop Street Harassment,* Holly Kearl suggests that "public harassment motivated by racism, homophobia, transphobia, or classism—types of deplorable harassment that men can be the target of and sometimes women perpetrate—is recognized as socially unacceptable behavior." In contrast, Kearl states, "men's harassment of women," usually "motivated by gender and sexism," often is not viewed in this same way. But is there a difference? Do we see some types of street harassment as deplorable and others as acceptable? Kearl suggests that the harassment of women when they are in public spaces—walking on the street, riding on the bus or subway, standing on street corners or enjoying pubic parks or performances, is normalized and tolerated. This type of public harassment often is described as a bit of fun, just joking, and even something positive.[2] Yet, our intersectional orientation tells us that public harassment of individuals based on racism, homophobia, transphobia, and classism also is normalized and tolerated.

Street harassment rarely is funny for the targets of this harassment, and the identities of "women" and "men" must be complicated to fully understand the damage done to people's sense of, and right to, safety on the streets. **Street**

harassment "ranges from physically harmless leers, whistles, honks, kissing noises, and nonsexually explicit evaluative comments, to more insulting and threatening behavior like vulgar gestures, sexually charged comments, flashing and stalking, to illegal actions like public masturbation, sexual touching, assault and rape."[3] Although we regularly dismiss street harassment as "only a trivial annoyance," Kearl's research on street harassment reveals that across countries, ages, and identities, it may be serious enough to force people to choose among the following options.

- avoid routes: Street harassment can cause someone to avoid particular routes to and from work, school, and social activities.
- stay at home: Street harassment can cause someone to stay at home rather than go out for even the most basic of necessities, such as food or personal care.
- move out: Street harassment can cause someone to move out of neighborhoods or change jobs because their routes are riddled with harassment.

Street harassment, in sum, is no joke: it causes people to be afraid and constrained, and these are not trivial matters.[4]

Heath Fogg-Davis, a professor of political science at Temple University, explains, "Just as rape is not about sex, street harassment is not about flirtation or courtship. Both acts are meant to assert male dominance over women in situations where women appear vulnerable, and both leave psychological wounds on women's lives that are rarely tended to, let alone acknowledged."[5] The existence of both rape and street harassment suggests that we live in cultures that expect safety for some identities, while normalizing the lack of safety for others.

The Many Faces of Street Harassment

Before we consider the types of street harassment individuals endure, consider how prevalent street harassment is. Across all studies, findings show that between 80 to 100 percent of women between the ages of eleven and eighty, regardless of the country they are living in or visiting, report experiencing street harassment. One third to one half of those women report experiencing street harassment daily.[6] Street harassment communicates a perpetrator's and a culture's acceptance of inequality, sending a message that the individual being harassed can be interrupted, touched, followed, insulted, harmed, or even killed, simply for the identities they avow or are ascribed. Consider the statistics in table 5.1 regarding types of street harassment and the percentage of women—broadly defined—experiencing it.

Although the broad sweep of statistics gives us information about the prevalence of street harassment, an intersectional orientation complicates these numbers and types of harassment much further. When viewed intersectionally, we see that harassment goes beyond gender to include the following aspects.

Table 5.1 Street Harassment Statistics

Type of Street Harassment	Percentage of Women Experiencing It
Leering	95%
Honking and whistling	94%
Sexist comments	87%
Vulgar gestures	82%
Sexually explicit comments	81%
Kissing noises	77%
Following	75%
Blocking paths	62%
Sexual touching or grabbing	57%
Masturbating	37%
Assaulting	27%

SOURCE: Holly Kearl, *Stop Street Harassment: Making Public Places Safe for Women* (Santa Barbara: Praeger, 2010), 11–15; "Street Harassment Statistics," 2015, https://www.ilr.cornell.edu/news/street-harassment-statistics; and "Statistics—Street Harassment Studies," 2018, http://www.stopstreetharassment.org/resources/statistics/sshstudies/.

Race: Women of color often experience street harassment based on sex and race or ethnicity.

Sexuality: Lesbian and bisexual women often experience street harassment based on sex and sexual identity, if they are open about, or are perceived to have, those identities.

Gender nonconformity: Gender nonconforming individuals often experience street harassment that includes not only slurs but also physical assault.

Poverty: Individuals with fewer economic resources often experience more street harassment because they cannot afford cars, taxis, or other forms of private transportation, or live in unsafe neighborhoods with higher crime rates.

Working/living on the street: Homeless women and sex workers are vulnerable to street harassment by other people on the streets as well as police and clients, and are assumed to be sexually available because they are on the streets.

Ability/disability: People with disabilities are often targeted because they are seen as more vulnerable, yet asexual, and unable to fight back, speak out, escape, or unlikely to be believed.[7]

Public transportation: In terms of verbal harassment on public transportation, between 70 to 90 percent of women from approximately thirty different countries say they have been the targets of, or witnessed, verbal harassment.[8]

Figure 5.2 Although women on commuter trains, such as this one in Beijing, report extremely high rates of harassment, police often fail to take the issue seriously. In Tokyo, however, police created a mobile phone app that screams "Stop it!" and provides a message that commuters can send to police which says, "There is a molester. Please help." In the private sector, businesses also are responding. One company developed a stamp that allows commuters to mark the perpetrator with invisible ink that officials can later detect under ultraviolet light. (Source: iStock. Credit: John Crux)

Whether it happens daily, weekly, or monthly, street harassment causes an overwhelming number of women to feel unsafe. Legal scholar Cynthia Grant Bowman shares that cisgender and heterosexual men often don't see street harassment and may be inclined to dismiss its prevalence and severity. They don't see the harassment because when they are with women as they walk or travel to and from locations, other men do not harass women. However, when women are alone or with other women, "there is a tremendous amount of hostility that just comes off the sidewalks of the city."[9]

The Many Faces of Cyber Harassment

Cyber harassment is defined as "the intentional infliction of substantial emotional distress accomplished by online speech that is persistent enough to amount to a course of conduct rather than an isolated incident." Cyber harassment includes "threats of violence, privacy invasions, reputation-harming lies, calls for strangers to physically harm victims, and technological attacks."[10] It can include **cyberstalking,** which involves installing spyware on a victim's computer so that the stalker can track all of the victim's interactions on the internet. This means that a stalker can track someone's purchases, personal and professional e-mails, and reading and entertainment habits. What's more, by installing GPS in a victim's car, the stalker can follow her to the store, place of worship, or coffee shop. Wherever you are, Danielle Keats Citron, a professor of law at Boston University, explains, "there is the stalker and you can't imagine how the stalker knew that you were going to be there."[11]

The internet's many features make cyber harassment profoundly disruptive to the lives of its victims. Posts can go viral in days or even minutes, attracting "hundreds of thousands of readers," and the post itself can never be removed. "Posters often compete to be the most offensive, the most abusive," and for the victim, "fear can be profound." When your address, phone numbers, email, and social media addresses are made public, many victims say, "I don't want to go out alone . . . because I don't know what might happen." Others move to high security buildings attempting to avoid what victims most dread: "rape and real-world stalking."[12] Some go into hiding, route mail to post office boxes, use fake names when they travel and, if they are public personalities, no longer maintain public calendars of appearances and speaking events.[13]

Victims also change schools and move to new towns, lose jobs and their professional clientele, are denied internships, close blogs and lose advertising revenue, and shut down social media platforms. In today's world of online business and marketing, these are death sentences to a person's professional success. But there is even more damage. Victims of cyber harassment "incur legal fees, child care costs, and moving expenses. The average financial impact of cyberstalking is more than $1,200." A former computer science professor reports that "online harassment at the hands of her former student and his highly skilled hacker supporters" cost her "thousands of dollars in legal fees, hundreds of hours of lost work time, the dismantling of [her] chosen career," and made it so that she could no longer use the degrees she "worked so hard to obtain."[14]

When someone is harassed online, Keats Citron explains that "it feels like the perpetrator is everywhere." Consider the following forms of cyber attack:

- Email inboxes are flooded with demeaning and threatening messages.
- Employers receive anonymous emails falsely accusing the victim of misdeeds.
- False online advertisements provide victims' contact information and offers for sex.
- Derogatory websites are put up to damage the victim's personal and professional identity and relationships.
- Videos of interactions and actions by the victim are posted online, without the victim's knowledge or consent.
- Nude photos of the victim appear on sites devoted to exacting revenge and often go viral.

- False message boards and blogs accuse victims of having sexually transmitted infections, mental illnesses, or criminal records.
- Social security numbers and medical conditions are published.
- Victims are stalked online and in real time.
- Threats of rape and physical assault are rampant, and harassers describe in detail the violence they plan to inflict on victims.
- Harassers encourage other people to inflict this same violence on the victim.[15]

Keats Citron, who has studied cyber harassment and stalking for almost a decade, explains that "cyber harassment and cyber stalking incidents are devastating *and* endemic. Thousands upon thousands of . . . incidents occur annually in the United States." Twenty percent of adults experience cyber harassment and stalking, including "persistent harassing e-mails, and other unwanted online contact," and close to 75 percent of them are women.[16] Keats Citron also shares that in her 2014 study, women of color were the most likely to be harassed; the group least likely to have been harassed was white males (see table 5.2).

As these statistics reveal, women are more likely to be harassed, particularly if they are women of color. Additionally, the harassment of women online usually involves violent sexual threat:

- When women are harassed, they are "equated with their sexual organs," threatened with rape and other forms of violence, and often described as diseased.
- When women are harassed visually, doctored images of violent sex acts are posted on sites, and the images usually are accompanied by verbal descriptions of the violence to be done to the victim.

Sexual orientation and nonconforming gender identity also contribute to the likelihood of cyber harassment. College students identifying as lesbian, gay, bisexual, queer, and transgender are more than twice as likely to be cyber-harassed than heterosexual students. When men are victims, they are disproportionately accused of being gay, accused of posing as women and threatened with rape, accused of being sex offenders, or have their religious affiliations demeaned.

Age and time spent on the internet may be factors in cyber harassment as well. For young people, the more time spent online, the more likely the victimization. In addition, college students report more cyber harassment than real-time face-to-face harassment. Almost 60 percent of victims have no previous relationship with the harasser. And, even though there is a harasser, "cyber harassers leave scant clues about their identities."[17]

Cyber cesspools, defined as "sites that encourage users to post abusive material about specific individuals usually to make profit through ad sales," are becoming common. Cyber cesspools promote shaming and degradation, urging users to "post gossip, which tends to involve deeply personal, homophobic,

Table 5.2 Cyber Harassment by Gender and Race

Respondents	Percentage Who Have Experienced Harassment
Females of color harassed online	53%
White females	45%
Males of color	40%
White males	31%

SOURCE: Danielle Keats Citron, *Hate Crimes in Cyberspace* (Cambridge, MA: Harvard University Press, 2014), 14.

misogynistic, and racist" attacks on individuals. They encourage "sexually explicit posts and images," known as "revenge porn," and include the names, addresses, and contact information of the victim. The operator of one cyber cesspool reports that he earns $3,000 a month from advertising revenue on his site.[18] The "more embarrassing and destructive" the posts, explains yet another cesspool site operator, the more money to be made. Acknowledging that even though he didn't want anybody to commit suicide as a result of his site, "if it happened, he would be grateful for the publicity and advertising revenue it would generate."[19]

Similar to street harassment, cyber harassment is often described as "no big deal," and just a part of online life. Victims are said to be overreacting and even deserving of the abuse—after all, they were online. Death threats are dismissed and trivialized: "It's not as if those cowards will actually act on their threats," explains one site operator. Victim blaming is common as well: if you share a photo of yourself, nude or otherwise, it's your fault as to what happens with it. Blogging about controversial topics is "an invitation to abuse." Sharing one's race is an invitation for trouble: "If you want to get into somebody's face with your race, then perhaps you deserve a bit of flak." Responding to doctored pictures of women, naked with nooses beside them, being suffocated by lingerie, one operator shared, "Evidently, there are some people who don't much like her. . . . Get a life, this is the Internet."[20]

Deborah Hellman, a law professor at the University of Virginia, explains that demeaning someone is to "insult," put down, or "diminish and denigrate" them. "It is to treat another as lesser." Demeaning is wrong, Hellman explains, because "the fact that people are of equal moral worth requires that we treat them as such. We must not treat [others] as lesser beings" when it causes them harm, Hellman states. But equally importantly, she notes, we must not treat them as lesser beings "even when doing so causes them no harm."[21] Those who engage in street and cyber harassment or who dismiss these attacks as normal or inconsequential, are communicating a clear message. That message states that not everyone has the right to feel safe. When viewed through an intersectional lens, street and cyber harassment become not just what happens when someone is out in public or has their privacy violated or destroyed via the internet but rather, they are acts of domination and humiliation directed at people with particular identities. Street and cyber harassment have very gendered, raced, and classed components. They are directed at people based on perceived sexuality, ability, and transgender and gender queer identities. Because of this, we must return to the claim that opened this section, that "public harassment motivated by racism, homophobia, transphobia, or classism . . . is recognized as socially unacceptable behavior." When filtered through an intersectional lens, we can understand that cyber harassment has not been viewed as unacceptable and deplorable—in fact, it is a regular occurrence, usually with little consequence for the harassers.

HATE SPEECH

Hate speech is defined as speech that "puts people down based on their race or ethnic origin, religion, gender, age, physical condition, disability or sexual orientation" and is comprised of words, images, and sounds "that are used to terrorize, humiliate, degrade, ambush, lacerate, pummel, assault, and injure."[22] In short, hate speech causes a person, because of their identities, to feel threatened, ambushed, insulted, hurt, and silenced.[23] Hate speech can take any number of forms: spray paint on walls, fences, or billboards; late night and/or anonymous phone calls and texts; crude messages or professionally printed flyers stuffed under doors, left in mail boxes, or placed where the intended recipient will see them; words and sounds shouted by people from automobiles, buses, and taxis; threats and/or putdowns shouted in public spaces or via tweets, hashtags, and other social media; and, of course, messages sent through private social media accounts as well as public media outlets.

Rather than an exercise of a person's right to free speech, as hate speech is so often categorized, Anthony Cortese, professor of sociology, explains that hate speech is a performance of "prejudice, bigotry, racism, misogyny, homophobia, ageism, bias, and xenophobia."[24] Cortese describes the hate messages that take the form of flyers and graffiti as not simply "hateful but also spineless" because "the receiver of the hate message is not able to respond directly to the sender of the message. With anonymous hate speech, the victim cannot verbally defend himself or herself." But, when hate speech is delivered face to face, it seldom is an "invitation to politely chat," Cortese cautions. Verbally "countering hate aggressors is not always the best option. In fact, many hate crimes began just like this: The victim replies—and is then physically assaulted or murdered."[25]

Richard Delgado and Jean Stefancic, both professors of law, suggest that hate speech, whether direct or indirect, harms more than just the individuals at which it is aimed. Hate speech also harms the perpetrators sending the message. Delgado and Stefancic explain that "bigots suffer when their narrow, categorical thinking etches in a little deeper. They fail to develop a universal moral sense that extends to all persons. They can easily develop a mildly paranoid mentality with respect to the group they disparage." This mentality leads the perpetrators to believe that, "if they [their victims] are so bad, perhaps they will do bad things to me and my friends."[26]

Discourses of Demonization

Individuals who use hate speech engage a rhetoric of demonization. To **demonize** is to try to make an individual or a group of people seem evil. Bernadette Calafell, a scholar of critical cultural communication, explains that in making a person seem evil, we turn them into monstrosities. Our anxieties about "race, class, gender and sexuality," Calafell shares, are evident in the ways we see and describe people who seem different from, and thus frightening to, ourselves.[27] Perpetrators of hate speech make public the traits they see as unacceptable in someone or some group, regardless of the inaccuracies of their assessments of those traits. They define those traits as warranting disrespect and denigration, in effect saying, "I believe that not 'everybody is entitle to the same measure of respect.'"[28] Those who use and support hate speech are saying that, indeed, there is a hierarchy of humanness at work, and that they are higher on that hierarchy than the targets of their hate and bigotry. The perpetrators of hate speech "fail to learn one of life's most useful lessons—that people of other races and types are just like my own; some good, some bad."[29]

Who are the targets of hate speech?

- African American men are the most frequent targets, followed closely by all other racial and ethnic minorities
- Lesbian, gay, bisexual, transgender, and queer-identified individuals who are out or who are ascribed one of those identities
- Anyone who is physically or mentally "different"
- Individuals with obvious non-Christian religious affiliations

The harms of hate speech are physical as well as psychological. Contrary to the childhood adage "words can never hurt me," the physical harms of hate speech include "rapid breathing, headaches, raised blood pressure, dizziness, rapid pulse rate, drug-taking, risk-taking behavior and even suicide." The psychological harms include "damaged self-image, lower aspiration level, and depression."[30] When children are the targets of hate speech, the impact is especially troublesome. Children who are the targets of hate speech may respond forcefully as a way to defend themselves. This behavior often is labeled as aggressive, rather than as legitimate forms of self-defense, and the label may follow them throughout their years in school. Additionally, without proper support systems, children may internalize the messages delivered by the hate speech and, without guidance and support, come to see themselves through a lens of shame or despair.[31]

What happens when hate speech escalates and turns into a hate crime? **Hate crimes** are defined as a "traditional offense like murder, arson, or vandalism with an added element of bias," that is, when the perpetrator targets a victim because of their identities.[32] The data on hate crimes reveal that race (58 percent of hate crimes), religion (21 percent of hate crimes), and sexual orientation (18 percent of hate crimes) comprise the majority of the motivations for this hateful bias. Statistics from the Bureau of Justice show that most hate crimes toward LGBTQ individuals are not reported because individuals fear being outed to family or employers or, if they are reported, are not classified as hate crimes by local enforcement jurisdictions. Additionally, the National Coalition of Anti-Violence Programs reports that black or Hispanic transgender women are the most likely group to be murdered in a hate crime, suggesting that the violence occurs at the "intersections of racism, sexism, and transphobia."[33] Hate crimes also are on the rise:

- Religiously motivated hate crimes rose by almost 23 percent in 2015.
- Anti-Semitic hate crimes rose more than 9 percent in 2015.
- Attacks on Muslim-Americans "rose an eye-popping 67 percent" in 2015, the second largest surge "following the 9/11 terrorist attacks in 2001."[34]

Delgado and Stefancic believe that society at large suffers from hate speech and hate crime. They explain that "when hate . . . goes unpunished" it is "a visible, dramatic breach of one of our most deeply felt ideals, that 'all men are created equal.' A society in which some, but not all, must run a gauntlet of racial abuse and stigmatization scarcely exemplifies this ideal." An insult grounded in hate "conveys to all who hear or learn about it" that society is willing to tolerate the claim "that equality and equal respect are of little value."[35] This is because "racial insults and name-calling evoke and call up" specific and violent histories, among them "lynching, Indian wars, and signs barring Latinos and blacks," but also sexual violence and assault, the denial of basic human rights as well as institutional, structural, and systemic oppressions. The recipient of hate speech and crime is more than "likely to know of this history and recognize the cultural weight—and maybe veiled threat—behind it."[36]

When hate speech and hate crime go unchecked, that is, when they are tolerated, a society is saying that it is willing to accept the legitimacy of these violent histories, and the possibility that they may come around again. Judith Butler, philosopher and gender theorist, offers the idea of "ungrievable" to explain this acceptance. Butler suggests that for some people, "a life that was not supposed to have existed at all," or was not supposed to have existed in the public sphere, is often seen as a life not worth grieving over.[37] Heath Fogg-Davis wonders whether those who harass others believe that certain individuals should have more freedom and comfort in our public spaces than others, and that people should not feel bad about this disparity. Do those who harass believe that

- Some lives are less valuable than others?
- Identities that "fit no dominant frame for the human" are less than human?
- A less than human and even "ungrievable" identity justifies the level of verbal and physical violence experienced on our streets?

Is there, Fogg-Davis wonders, a message of "dehumanization" actively "at work in the culture"?[38]

POLICING MASCULINITY: VIOLENCE AGAINST BLACK AND LATINO BOYS AND MEN

Victor Rios, a professor of sociology at the University of California, Santa Barbara, grew up in the ghetto of Oakland, California. After receiving his PhD from the University of California, Berkeley, Rios returned to his hometown to explore the violence and punitive policies the young men living in Oakland face, a city known for its gang violence. Rios undertook an ethnographic study—that is, he spent time with the young men he was studying, listening to their conversations and stories, observing their interactions with police, teachers and principals, parents and friends—seeking to "understand the social forces that impacted the community where I was raised." Rios's interests were not the violence committed by the young men but rather, the "culture of punishment," a material and discursive regime that "shaped the ways in which young people organized themselves and created meanings of their social world."[39] This led Rios to identify institutions and structures that labeled the everyday and mundane behaviors of these young men as "criminal" rather than commonplace and ordinary.

Criminalizing Normal Behaviors

In attempting to understand the social forces that governed the lives of young men in Oakland, Rios saw a discursive regime that he came to call the **youth control complex.** This complex is a "coherent system in which schools, police, probations officers, families, community centers, the media, businesses, and other institutions systematically treat young people's everyday behaviors as criminal activity." Activities that would be normal for young men in other spaces and places were labeled as deviant, problematic, and criminal in the areas of Oakland in which these young men lived. Rios labels this the **criminalization** of normal behaviors, a process by which essentially harmless and benign styles and behaviors of moving through a day are "rendered deviant and are treated with shame, exclusion, punishment, and incarceration."[40]

Figure 5.3 Consider the youth control complex and the criminalization of normal behaviors that both Victor Rios and Ana Muñiz mention. How do enjoyable behaviors, such as riding bicycles with a group of friends, come to be considered criminal activities? (Source: iStock. Credit: Marco_Plunti)

Ana Muñiz, director of the Dream Resource Center at the University of California, Los Angeles, identifies these harmless behaviors as including, but not limited to, "congregating in groups of two or more, standing in public for more than five minutes, wearing certain clothing and making certain gestures." Other everyday behaviors are also labeled criminal: carrying flashlights, cell phones, pagers, or marbles; standing on balconies, sitting on roof tops, climbing trees or fences, and riding bicycles.[41] Police and school authorities have unlimited discretion in determining which behaviors are criminalized, such that young men can be stopped for "looking like a gang member" or "drug dealer"; appearing too nervous or, the converse, too relaxed; speaking up to defend one's self, or again conversely, not speaking up to defend one's self; and even being too tall or physically mature and thus intimidating to the person in charge. Muñiz attests that these are normal adolescent behaviors as well as items of play and adventure. Yet, these young men, unlike white youth in urban or rural areas, can be and are "arrested if they engage in any of these activities."[42]

Sociologists and criminologists do not dispute that violence happens in impoverished communities. What we want to attend to, as students of intersectionality and communication, however, is the discursive regime that prompts the hypercriminalization of young minority men. Rios says that "it is obvious that the majority of young people living in poverty are not delinquent."[43] But discourses of hypercriminalization have a profound impact on our perceptions of these youth as well as on their own "perceptions, worldviews, and life outcomes." Through **hypercriminalization,** everyday styles of interaction, behavior, and communication are marked as "deviant and are treated with shame, exclusion, punishment, and incarceration" such that all minority youth in a particular demographic area are seen as disrespectful of authority and transgressive in their actions.[44] Before a young man of color even commits a crime, Rios notes, he is "harassed, profiled, watched, and disciplined."[45] The youth control complex relies on **punitive social control**—that is, constant surveillance and punishment, regardless of the transgressive nature of the action such that "individuals come to feel stigmatized, outcast, shamed, defeated, or hopeless as a result of negative interactions and sanctions imposed by individuals who represent institutions of social control."[46]

But how do some groups of young men come to be labeled as in need of social control when they are on our streets, while others are not? Certainly, young men of any racial or ethnic grouping congregate in groups of more than two, stand in public for more than five minutes, sit on rooftops and climb fences or trees, carry cell phones or flashlights, and ride bicycles. So why are young men of color seen as suspect and criminal when they engage in these benign activities while young white men are not? Statistics show that it is actually young white men who are more likely to be engaged in illegal behaviors than are young men of color. Moreover, far fewer young men of color are actually members of a gang then we are led to believe. Michelle Alexander, in *The New Jim Crow,* shares the following facts about crime rates, drug use, and incarceration:

- Rates of drug crime are relatively similar across races.[47]
- If there is any disparity in these rates, it is reflected in our white youth, who are more likely to engage in drug crime than are people of color.[48]
- Studies repeatedly find that white youth use cocaine at seven times the rate of black youth, crack cocaine at eight times the rate of black youth, and heroin at seven times the rate of black youth.[49]
- The majority of drug dealers and illegal drug users in the United States are white (there simply are more white people living in the United States); however, 75 percent of those imprisoned for illegal drug use are black and Latino.[50]
- Black youth and men are incarcerated for drug use at rates twenty to thirty times that of white youth and men.[51]

Statistics regarding gangs reveal the following:

- Only 2 to 3 percent of the youth population (ages five to seventeen) are members of a gang.[52]
- 73 percent of those youth are members of a gang for less than three years. Most who join, leave.[53]

- Only 24 percent of gang members stay in a gang approximately four to seven years.
- Only 1 to 3 percent of individuals stay in gangs longer than seven years. Typically, those individuals either joined a gang before the age of thirteen or after the age of eighteen.[54]

Why, then, the intense focus on so many young men of color, when so few are involved in gangs or crime? And why are their behaviors and styles of interacting criminalized, but not those of their white peers?

Crime Myths and Scapegoating

Crime myths explain a piece of this disparity and mistreatment. Criminologists Victor Kappeler and Gary Potter explain that **crime myths** are myths that "organize our views of crime, criminals, and the proper operation of the criminal justice system."[55] They are fictions, yet they are myths that are told and retold countless times as truth. These fabrications teach us what to believe, rather than what is in fact true. Kappeler and Potter note that when we subscribe to a crime myth, we usually are unaware that we are doing so. A crime myth—which is a lie and a distortion about who commits a crime—is used so frequently to organize people's responses to crime that it feels real to them, regardless of its lack of truth.

Crime myths rely on the most sensationalized, worse-case scenarios of a crime, presenting the exceptions as the rule. They force our attention on the horrific, and the rare, and away from what is most common in any genre of crime. Kappeler and Potter explain, "Using the worst case to characterize a social problem [gang membership, for example] encourages us to view that case as typical and to think about the problem in extreme terms."[56] Thus the horrific and brutal actions of one gang or a few gang members, for example, become the only story we hear and come to believe as true of all gangs and their members, and even all young minority men.

When filtered through an intersectional lens, we can see that the discourses of crime myths are doing dangerous work. The political, economic, legal, and social injustices, policies, and practices that make gang membership, however slight and short it might be, seem attractive—the actual roots and sources of the problems—are erased. The black or Hispanic youth become the problem and the danger, not the youth control complex, hypercriminalization, excessive surveillance, and lack of respect and opportunity.

Rios describes a second piece of this puzzle, the puzzle of the excessive policing of youth of color and the inattention to white youth engaged in exactly the same behaviors. Rios observes that when economies get tough and unemployment rises, when cultures clash, or when gentrification is desired, our "media and politicians create scapegoats." **Scapegoating** is the act of blaming someone for a problem that is not of their making. When we scapegoat, we can blame individuals for the problem, rather than institutional, structural, and systemic racism or classism. Instead of focusing on the problematic larger structures and systems (discussed in chapter 10), Rios explains that we are encouraged to worry and even panic about "black muggers, AIDS, pregnant teens, gang members." We scapegoat those who can be "deemed a threat to mainstream society" and are encouraged to view the "threat" as the source of the problem.[57]

The crime myth narrative tells us that it is not the fault of our economy, our unemployment rates, our absence of affordable housing, or underfunded schools, it's the young black or Hispanic criminal or drug addict who are the problems. Rios shares that politicians and media are "central players in determining who or what becomes the moral panic of the time. They generate support for an increase in spending on crime or a decrease in spending on welfare for the 'undeserving' poor."[58] They sell us stories, regardless of their truth, expanding on "coverage of isolated events," resorting to "unreliable statistics," and creating epidemics where none exist.[59] There are two final components to this hypersurveillance of youth of color to explore as we consider the right to safety on our streets: the cultural and economic upheaval of gentrification and the pressure of gang injunctions.

Gentrification and Gang Injunctions

An intersectional orientation to gentrification and gang injunctions helps us understand how different groups of people are affected differently by economic and cultural upheavals that circulate narratives about what should be done. In Rios's neighborhood in Oakland, for example, and the Cadillac-Corning neighborhood in Los Angeles, these narratives circulated widely. During the 1990s, wealthy neighborhoods were being developed next to poor neighborhoods. As supposedly "nicer," and whiter, neighborhoods came to border supposedly "bad," and minority, neighborhoods, those in the white neighborhoods pushed to have the minority neighborhoods "cleaned up."[60] The result was **gentrification,** the process of renovating impoverished neighborhoods.

Gentrification is discursive, that is, it tells a particular kind of story about neighborhoods, but it also is profoundly material. Gentrification leads to the displacement of individuals who, having lived in a neighborhood they once could afford, are forced to move. As rents increase, families on limited incomes are driven out of an area and must find different housing, at an affordable rate. But gentrification does not just force low-income individuals and families to move. The discourse of gentrification created something known as a "gang injunction" for police and prosecutors. Muñiz explains that **gang injunctions** "are civil lawsuits against neighborhoods based on the claim that gang behavior is a nuisance to nongang-involved residents. Injunctions then restrict the movements of those labeled gang members."[61] Recall that only 2 to 3 percent of

Figure 5.4 Gentrification often leads to the displacement of those who lived in the neighborhood before its transformation. Compare gentrification to the forced removal of Native people mentioned in chapter 4. Are there similarities or differences between these two approaches to "improvement"? (Source: iStock. Credit: andipantz)

the youth population are involved in gangs, yet an injunction labels an entire neighborhood as a gang-infested nuisance. Indeed, police officers have not just "the discretion to decide who is served with an injunction," but the ability to add as many names of those they "suspect" to be a member of a gang as they want. The result is hundreds of young boys—and even "John Does," who may be "identified at a later point"—are labeled as members of gangs, regardless of the accuracy of that label or membership.[62]

It is significant that the first gang injunctions in Los Angeles were not issued in the areas of the highest rates of murder, assault, or crime. In fact, they were issued in the Cadillac-Corning area, not known for its crime but rather for the gentrification of the neighborhoods bordering the district. The low-income and predominately black residents of Cadillac-Corning were not criminals. Instead, they were a "threat to the boundaries of white, middle- and upper-class areas" near them. Muñiz explains:

> Despite the sanitization of race in gang injunctions policy, fear of black men and stereotypes about black families were central to the rationale for the injunction. The injunction was meticulously designed to control the movement of black youth by criminalizing activities and behavior that is unremarkable and legal in other jurisdictions. Thus, the injunction shored up racial boundaries.[63]

Injunctions allow police to remove youth from public spaces or to seriously curtail their movement through that space. Youth who fit the mythic profile of a gang member—in short, any young man of color—are subject to "stops, detainment, and enhanced sentencing" regardless of their innocence. Those who associate with a supposed gang member (this could be your brother or cousin, neighbor, best friend, or acquaintance, for example) are "subject to the same treatment." Thus, entire neighborhoods, complete with families and friends, "become entangled in gang injunction restrictions or torn apart by prohibitions on socializing."[64]

Although many groups fit the description of "gang," Muñiz notes, they rarely are treated in the same way black and Latino youth are. Fraternities fit this definition, as do "conspiring Enron executives, and corrupt police." Moreover,

> The Los Angeles Sheriff's Department admits they have groups of deputies that have a collective name, group tattoos, and an internal hierarchy through which deputies advance by brutalizing jail inmates and civilians on the street. The most notorious of these sheriff gangs is the Jump Out Boys. Instead of using the term "gang," however, the Sheriff's Department refers to them as "cliques". . . . No white supremacist groups have gang injunctions . . . [and] while the predominantly Latino motorcycle group the Mongols is enjoined from wearing their logo, the Hells Angels remain unrestrained.[65]

Muñiz reports that gang injunctions quickly "became a mass factory. Let's [hand] out gang injunctions to give cops the chance to stop anybody for any reason." But not just "anybody," an intersectional orientation reveals. Gang injunctions are rare in the neighborhoods with the highest rates of crime; they are, however, frequently "instituted where borders separating black and white, wealthy and working class [are] becoming porous."[66]

A Discursive Regime of Danger

The research by both Muñiz and Rios illustrates the discursive regime that allows us to label almost any action taken, movement made, or item of clothing worn by black and/or Latino youth as suspect and criminal. This regime has sanctioned a surveillance that goes "beyond the bounds of duty" and appropriateness. Young men of color are marked by schools, neighbors, and the police as dangerous at a very young age, and this mark follows them into adulthood. These young men, Rios suggests, are living in an untenable world, one where they can only make mistakes (who among us has not jay-walked or stood on a street corner talking with a friend for more than five minutes?) because any movement is seen as suspicious and labeled as criminal. The youth control complex "becomes a unique formation . . . taking a toll on the mind and future outcomes" of young black and Latino men. "This complex is the combined effect of the web of institutions, schools, families, businesses, residents, media, community centers, and the criminal justice system, that collectively punish, stigmatize, monitor, and criminalize young people in an attempt to control them."[67]

There are serious material consequences for these young men: "police harassment, exclusion from businesses and public recreation spaces, zero-tolerance policies that lead to detention rooms, school suspensions, and incarceration." Black and Latino boys are followed in stores, "stopped by police for matching the description of a criminal gang member," ignored at school by counselors and teachers, and "not expected to make it to college."[68] When teachers, counselors, security, and law enforcement are challenged as racist and engaged in racial profiling, they "can justify their behaviors by saying something like, 'That was not racist, I was following the law.'" These consistently negative encounters can "lead young people to become adversarial toward the system, to lose faith in it, to resist against it, to build resilience skills to cope." The reality, Rios says, is that the majority of these young men actually are "striving for dignity, demanding to be treated as fellow citizens who are innocent until proven guilty." They want, like most of us, to be treated fairly, and to be granted the right to move safely about the streets.[69]

THE ABSENCE OF DEMOCRACY

Harassment, hate speech, and the policing of the movements of select groups of people fly in the face of certain intrinsic values important to democracy and to the protection of basic human rights. Even "those who do not take part in the system of [hateful and harassing] speech may find themselves demoralized when they realize how often social norms of equality" and goodwill are "breached and how far we are as a group, from living in an egalitarian, humane society."[70] Jeremy Waldron, professor of law and philosophy at the New York University School of Law, unpacks this demoralizing breach of social norms protecting equality. To the targeted individual, hateful communication says,

> Don't be fooled into thinking you are welcome here. The society around you may seem hospitable and nondiscriminatory, but the truth is that you are not wanted, and you and your families will be shunned, excluded, beaten, and driven out, whenever we can get away with it. We may have to keep a low profile right now. But don't get too comfortable. Remember what has happened to you and your kind in the past. Be afraid.[71]

And to society at large, hateful and harassing communication says,

> We know some of you agree that these people are not wanted here. We know that some of you feel that they are dirty (or dangerous or criminal or terrorist). Know that you are not alone. Whatever the government says, there are enough of us around to make sure these people are not welcome. There are enough of us around to draw attention to what these people are really like. Talk to your neighbors, talk to your customers. And above all, don't let them join in.[72]

Waldron explains that the point of hate and harassing speech, as well as hypersurveillance, is not to exercise the right to free speech but rather "to make these messages a part of the permanent visible fabric of society" such that the individuals "who are targeted are never quite sure when they will encounter them." The point of hateful, harassing speech and hypersurveillance is "to communicate hostility, discrimination, exclusion, and even violence, to call up those histories, and undermine and threaten a person's dignity."[73]

Evoking the travesty of the Holocaust, Delgado and Stefancic remind us what this kind of communication can do: "Whom we will oppress, we first demonize," because such demonization rationalizes the violence that comes later.[74] The cumulative effect of "months and years of denigration" and demonization makes the violence or death "natural and palatable."[75] They share the reflections of American philosopher Sidney Hook that a Holocaust could happen under extreme circumstances anywhere:

> I believe any people in the world, when roused to a fury of nationalistic sentiment and convinced that some individual or group is responsible for their continued and extreme misfortune can be led to do or countenance the same things the Germans did. I believe that if conditions in the U.S. were ever to become as bad psychologically and economically as they were in Germany in the 1920s and 1930s, systematic racial persecution might break out. It could happen to the blacks, but it could happen to the Jews, too, or any targeted group.[76]

When we subscribe to a discursive regime of demonization, and of denying people basic human rights and protections, we denigrate and violate other people. When we ignore or fail to challenge the discursive regime of demonization, we run the risk of being coopted by that discursive regime. Either way, basic principles of democracy are compromised when the right to move freely in public spaces is denied. Although the Holocaust may be viewed as a travesty of the past, it models for us the dangerous discursive regimes that remain a part of our present.

THE WORK OUR WORDS DO

In 1998, linguist and communication scholar Deborah Tannen posed a powerful question: are we using words, or are words using us? Tannen states that "words matter. When we think we are using language, language is using us." She shares the thoughts of one of her colleagues, Dwight Bolinger, who explained that "language is like a loaded gun: It can be fired intentionally, but it can wound or kill just as surely when fired accidentally."[77] Legal scholar Stephen Carter adds: "Racial insults hurt. Sexual harassment hurts. Religious bigotry hurts. The pains are genuine and deep." Taking one example, Carter explains that racial epithets communicated through hate speech are "devoid of any utility other than to do harm."[78]

Tannen (and numerous scholars across disciplines) notes that the "terms in which we talk about something shape the way we think about it—even what we see."[79] When we demonize someone, we see the demon and not the person. When we trivialize hate and hurt, we see hate and hurt as trivial. When we post something anonymously, we perform a cowardly act of avoiding responsibility for our communication. When we use subtle yet demeaning words and phrases, we are putting a person or their culture down. Are we engaging in our right to free speech, or are we engaging in the practice of free harassment, hate, and profiling?

But aren't we free to say anything we like? Isn't that one of the guarantees of our founding documents and more than two hundred years of subsequent legal decisions? Viewed from a non-intersectional lens, the answer is a qualified "yes." We can, for example, yell "fire" in a crowded theatre when there is no fire—but we may be arrested for spreading false panic. We are free to yell, but there are consequences. If the false claim of "fire" has repercussions for the perpetrator, then why do hate speech and harassment have none? Is the false claim of "fire" in a crowded public space (where people might be harmed if they panic and try to escape) so different from false claims posted about someone online or the harmful words leveled at someone in public? Aren't they all frightening, damaging, and hurtful?

Words do work. The words we utter craft a world and a view of our place in that world. They surround us with images and reveal our beliefs and values about identities and where people belong. They avow but they also ascribe. From the orientations of intersectionality and feminism we might reply to the question of our freedom to say anything we like with an even more nuanced "yes." We may be free to say what we want, but the discourses of harassment, hate, and policing are inconsistent with our founding principles. They ascribe demonized identities to other people and run counter to our democratic values. An intersectional approach to safety in public spaces reveals that we extend the right to safety on the streets to some people, but not to other people.

We can notice and challenge discourses of harassment, hate, and policing by communicating that our commitment to our right to free speech does not supersede considerations of human safety, dignity, and respect. We can identify the difference between what we are "free" to say and the harms done by that saying. When we normalize harassment and hate speech, we communicate that we do not care what kind of work our words are doing—or that we do care, and we want our words to do the work of harm. When we challenge discourses of harassment and hate, we make a statement that we do not accept the harm that occurs.

5.1. GUIDE TO COMMUNICATION

Communicating Safety Intersectionally

As you explore intersectional communication related to safety in public spaces and places, consider the following questions:

1. Discuss free speech in the context of street and cyber harassment. Are these forms of communication protected under the First Amendment to our Constitution?
2. Make a list of the words you use to describe groups of people who avow identities different from your own. Write them down so that you can spend time unpacking their meanings and considering their impact if you use them in your everyday communication.
3. As a class, discuss the phrases "it's just a joke" and "it's no big deal." Consider when those phrases diminish and trivialize the harms being done to someone and the differences between saying those phrases to someone else and having them said to you.
4. Reflect on Anthony Cortese's statement that hate speech is seldom an invitation to politely chat. Could there be ways of communicating our dislike of someone that are invitations to conversation? What might those ways of communicating look like? What can feminism and intersectionality add to conversations about our dislike of other people?
5. Consider Meera Vijaynn's call for women to speak out against gender violence in her TED talk, "Find Your Voice Against Gender Violence," TEDxHousesOfParliament, 2014, https://www.ted.com/talks/meera_vijayann_find_your_voice_against_gender_violence. What might be the implications of responding to her call for you, your friends and family, and society at large?

The realities of street harassment, cyber harassment, hate speech, and the policing of certain youth contradict several of our nation's most foundational principles and frameworks: Our inalienable right to life, liberty, and the pursuit of happiness has not been granted to all. Identities play a key role in the granting or denying of those rights. Harassment, hate, and biased policing are not normal styles of communication—they are not funny or trivial, neither are they the inevitable outcome of a dislike or mistrust of someone. Harassment, hate, and the hypercriminalization of young men of color are learned and, as such, they can be unlearned. To be clear, the goal of ensuring safety on the streets for human beings, no matter their identities, is not to "love everyone." It is, instead, to be committed to communicating respectfully with our fellow human beings. Cynthia Grant Bowman shares that for centuries, public leaders have recognized that "the power of locomotion," that is, the "security to move about in public," is "one of the most basic civil rights."[80] Yet it is denied to many of us as a result of our identities.

Resources

Violet Blue, *The Smart Girl's Guide to Privacy* (San Francisco: Digita Publications, 2014).

Declaration of Independence, https://www.archives.gov/founding-docs/declaration-transcript, and the Constitution of the United States, https://www.archives.gov/founding-docs/constitution-transcript.

Hollaback!, https://www.ihollaback.org, and Black Lives Matter, https://blacklivesmatter.com.

Sally Kohn, *The Opposite of Hate: A Field Guide to Repairing Humanity* (Chapel Hill: Algonquin Books, 2018).

Sally Kohn, "What We Can Do about the Culture of Hate," filmed November 2017 in New Orleans, LA, TEDWomen 2017 video, 17:38, https://www.ted.com/talks/sally_kohn_what_we_can_do_about_the_culture_of_hate?referrer=playlist-dissecting_cultures_of_hate.

Meera Vijaynn, "Find Your Voice Against Gender Violence," filmed June 2014 in London, TEDxHousesOf-Parliament video, 13:51, https://www.ted.com/talks/meera_vijayann_find_your_voice_against_gender_violence.

Notes

1. Alanna Vagianos, "These Are the Explicit Things Men Say to Women on the Street," HuffPost, December 1, 2017, https://www.huffpost.com/entry/street-harassment-project_n.
2. Holly Kearl, *Stop Street Harassment: Making Public Places Safe for Women* (Santa Barbara: Praeger, 2010), 5–6.
3. Kearl, *Stop Street Harassment,* 3.
4. Kearl, *Stop Street Harassment,* 5.
5. Hawley [Heath] G. Fogg-Davis, "Theorizing Black Lesbians within Black Feminism: A Critique of Same-Race Street Harassment," *Politics and Gender,* 2 (2006): 65.
6. Kearl, *Stop Street Harassment,* 9. See also Stop Street Harassment, "Statistics—The Prevalence of Street Harassment," accessed March 13, 2017, http://www.stopstreetharassment.org/resources/statistics/statistics-academic-studies/.
7. Kearl, *Stop Street Harassment,* 45–61.
8. Stop Street Harassment, "Statistics—the Prevalence of Street Harassment."
9. Cynthia Grant Bowman, "Street Harassment and the Informal Ghettoization of Women," *Harvard Law Review* 106, no. 3 (January 1993): 519, note 8.
10. Danielle Keats Citron, *Hate Crimes in Cyberspace* (Cambridge, MA: Harvard University Press, 2014), 3.
11. Keats Citron, *Hate Crimes,* 4.
12. Keats Citron, *Hate Crimes,* 5.
13. Keats Citron, *Hate Crimes,* 6–7.
14. Keats Citron, *Hate Crimes,* 10.
15. Compiled from Danielle Keats Citron, *Hate Crimes,* 3–4; and Keats Citron, "Addressing Cyber Harassment: An Overview of Hate Crimes," *Journal of Law, Technology and the Internet* 6 (2015): 1–12.
16. Keats Citron, *Hate Crimes,* 12.
17. Keats Citron, *Hate Crimes,* 51.
18. Keats Citron, *Hate Crimes,* 50.
19. Keats Citron, *Hate Crimes,* 52.
20. Keats Citron, *Hate Crimes,* 73–79.
21. Deborah Hellman, *When Is Discrimination Wrong?* (Cambridge, MA: Harvard University Press, 2008), 29–30.
22. Anthony Cortese, *Opposing Hate Speech* (Santa Barbara: Praeger, 2006), 1.
23. Cortese, *Opposing Hate Speech,* 2.
24. Cortese, *Opposing Hate Speech,* 2.
25. Cortese, *Opposing Hate Speech,* 1.
26. Richard Delgado and Jean Stefancic, *Understanding Words that Wound* (Boulder: Westview Press, 2004), 16.
27. Bernadette Marie Calafell, "Monstrous Femininity: Constructions of Women of Color in the Academy," *Journal of Communication Inquiry* 36, no. 2 (2012): 113.
28. Stephen L. Carter, *Civility: Manners, Morals and the Etiquette of Democracy* (New York: HarperPerennial, 1998), 120.
29. Delgado and Stefancic, *Understanding Words that Wound,* 16.
30. Delgado and Stefancic, *Understanding Words that Wound,* 13.
31. Richard Delgado and Jean Stefancic, "Four Observations about Hate Speech," *Wake Forrest Law Review* 44 (2009): 363, http://wakeforestlawreview.com/wp-content/uploads/2014/10/Delgado_LawReview_01.09.pdf.
32. Hate Crimes, https://www.fbi.gov/investigate/civil-rights/hate-crimes.

33. Haeyoun Park and Iaryna Mykhyalyshyn, "L.G.B.T. People Are More Likely to Be Targets of Hate Crimes Than Any Other Minority Group," *New York Times*, June 16, 2016, https://www.nytimes.com/interactive/2016/06/16/us/hate-crimes-against-lgbt.html?_r=0.
34. Camila Domonoske, "Hate Crimes Rose in 2015, with Religious Bias a Growing Motivation, FBI Data Shows," National Public Radio, November 14, 2016, http://www.npr.org/seForctions/thetwo-way/2016/11/14/502036699/hate-crimes-rose-in-2015-with-religious-bias-a-growing-motivation-fbi-data-shows.
35. Delgado and Stefancic, *Understanding Words that Wound*, 16–17.
36. Delgado and Stefancic, *Understanding Words that Wound*, 16.
37. Judith Butler and Nelly Kambouri, "Judith Butler—Ungrievable Lives," Monthly Review Online, May 21, 2009, https://mronline.org/2009/05/21/judith-butler-ungrievable-lives/.
38. Fogg-Davis, "Theorizing Black Lesbians," 58–59.
39. Victor M. Rios, *Punished: Policing the Lives of Black and Latino Boys* (New York: New York University Press, 2011), xii-xvi.
40. Rios, *Punished*, xiv.
41. Ana Muñiz, *Police, Power, and the Production of Racial Boundaries* (New Brunswick, NJ: Rutgers, 2015), 35, 48.
42. Muñiz, *Police, Power*, 34.
43. Rios, *Punished*, 11.
44. Rios, *Punished*, xiv.
45. Rios, *Punished*, xv.
46. Rios, *Punished*, xiv.
47. Michelle Alexander, *The New Jim Crow; Incarceration in the Age of Colorblindness* (New York: Free Press, 2010), 6.
48. Alexander, *New Jim Crow*, 7.
49. Alexander, *New Jim Crow*, 99.
50. Alexander, *New Jim Crow*, 98.
51. Alexander, *New Jim Crow*, 7.
52. David C. Pyrooz and Gary Sweeten, "Gang Membership Between Ages 5 and 17 in the United States," *Journal of Adolescent Health* 30 (2015): 4, http://jjie.org/wp-content/uploads/2015/02/Pyrooz_Sweeten_Gang-Membership-Between-Ages-5-and-17-Years-in-the-United-States.pdf.
53. David C. Pyrooz, "'From your First Cigarette to Your Last Dyin' Day': The Patterning of Gang Membership in the Life-Curse," *Journal of Quantitative Criminology* 30 (2014): 361, 364, doi: 10.1007/s10940-013-9206-1.
54. Amanda B. Gillman, Karl G. Hill, and J. David Hawkins, "Long-Term Consequences of Adolescent Gang Membership for Adult Functioning," *American Journal of Public Health* 104, no. 5 (2014): 938–945.
55. Victor Kappeler and Gary Potter, *The Mythology of Crime and Criminal Justice*, 4th ed. (Long Grove, IL: Waveland Press, 2010), 2.
56. Kappeler and Potter, *Mythology of Crime*, 9.
57. Rios, *Punished*, 7.
58. Rios, *Punished*, 7.
59. Kappeler and Potter, *Mythology of Crime*, 10.
60. Muñiz, *Police, Power*, 15–32.
61. Muñiz, *Police, Power*, 33.
62. Muñiz, *Police, Power*, 33–34.
63. Muñiz, *Police, Power*, 35.
64. Muñiz, *Police, Power*, 38.
65. Muñiz, *Police, Power*, 46.
66. Muñiz, *Police, Power*, 53.
67. Rios, *Punished*, 39, 40.
68. Rios, *Punished*, 41.
69. Rios, *Punished*, 39–41.
70. Delgado and Stefancic, *Understanding Words that Wound*, 17.
71. Jeremy Waldron, *The Harm in Hate Speech* (Cambridge, MA: Harvard University Press, 2012), 2.
72. Waldron, *Harm in Hate Speech*, 2–3.
73. Waldron, *Harm in Hate Speech*, 5.
74. Delgado and Stefancic, *Understanding Words that Wound*, 23.
75. Delgado and Stefancic, *Understanding Words that Wound*, 24.
76. Sydney Hook, in Delgado and Stefancic, *Understanding Words that Wound*, vi.
77. Deborah Tannen, *The Argument Culture: Stopping America's War of Words* (New York: Ballantine, 1998), 14.
78. Carter, *Civility*, 163.
79. Tannen, *Argument Culture*, 14.
80. Grant Bowman, "Street Harassment," 520–521.

CHAPTER

6

Intersectional Approaches to Safety in Private Spaces

IN THIS CHAPTER, YOU WILL FIND . . .

KEY TERMS AND CONCEPTS

- bystanders who intervene
- historical trauma
- hypermasculine ideologies
- interpersonal violence
- lack of useful vocabulary
- male emotional funnel system
- rape culture
- rape myths
- sexual violence
- scripts
- societal trauma
- unrapeable myth

IN PRAISE OF INSUBORDINATION

In her book chapter, "In Praise of Insubordination, or What Makes a Good Woman Go Bad," Inés Hernández-Avila (Nez Pierce/Tejana), professor of Native American Studies at the University of California, Davis, asks why both the heterosexual and gay men of her communities "argue that women really mean yes when they say no? Why do you try to justify your violence by insisting that the woman asked for it? Don't you see that this argument leaves you no defense when the victim of a rape or beating is your mother, your sister, your lover, your wife, your daughter, your granddaughter or your friend? Suddenly you will find yourself hearing someone say, 'She really asked for it,' or, 'She meant yes'—and worse, you will find yourself believing it."[1]

"Through whose eyes have we seen the dynamics of dating and courtship," Hernández-Avila asks. With regard to those who identify as female or as women, Hernández-Avila wonders

> Why can't more of us remember that we deserve to know pleasure and love? Why do so many of our women of all ages allow themselves to be coopted and succumb to mistreatment and degradation for the sake of having a partner, for the sake of having a spouse—of either sex? How did so many of us become convinced that violence is eroticism? When did we come to feel worthless, undesirable, and crazy, as if something were dreadfully wrong with us, as if the fault were ours because we do not enjoy violent sex that is called by the name of *passion,* that is called by the name of love? What makes it so hard for us to say, "I was raped"? We must claim our power and give value to every aspect of ourselves, including our sexuality.[2]

THE RIGHT TO SAFETY IN PRIVATE SPACES

If we were to assess a person's safety in the places in which they live and socialize, what conditions would we measure? Would we be concerned with the level of verbal, physical, and sexual aggression or violence that occurs? The narratives that circulate regarding that aggression and violence? The ways we might improve our communication about the overwhelming lack of safety that millions of people—worldwide—experience in their private spaces? Perhaps all of these and more? In the discussion that follows, we explore the profound lack of safety individuals may experience in the private spaces they occupy. We begin with a discussion of interpersonal violence, sexual violence, and the perpetrators of that violence. We then turn to a discussion of the intersections of power and oppression as they constrain our communication and understanding of this absence of safety in private spaces. The chapter concludes with an exploration of the ways we might change the conversation about interpersonal and sexual violence so that our understanding of this violence is more intersectional and accurate.

INTERPERSONAL AND SEXUAL VIOLENCE

In order to begin to fully understand interpersonal and sexual violence, we have to expose ourselves to painful aspects of their presence. The material you are about to read on interpersonal and sexual violence exposes us to some of that pain and is especially sensitive. In the next two sections, you are exposed to definitions and descriptions of various types of interpersonal and sexual violence. As you read, please take care to proceed cautiously and carefully. The information may cause you to feel uncomfortable, upset, and even to recall unpleasant and painful experiences. Please acknowledge your feelings. If the material stimulates anxiety and/or feelings you are struggling to manage, please reach out to your instructor, a mental health professional, or trusted friends and family.

Defining Interpersonal Violence

Interpersonal violence is defined as the intentional use of physical force or power, threatened or actual, against a family member, spouse, dating partner, cohabitating partner, roommate, friend, or acquaintance. Interpersonal violence "either results in or has a high likelihood of resulting in injury, death, psychological harm, mal-development, or depravation."[3] The National Coalition Against Violence reports that over ten million Americans are victims of interpersonal violence annually; the World Health Organization reports that interpersonal violence "occurs in all countries, irrespective of social, economic, religious or cultural group."[4] Using a binary framework for reporting their data, the World Health Organization explains that violence "against women—particularly intimate partner violence and sexual violence—is a major public health problem and a violation of women's human rights."[5] Decades of research indicate that interpersonal violence can take many forms (see table 6.1).

Defining Sexual Violence

Sexual violence is defined as a "sexual act committed against someone without that person's freely given consent." Sometimes called sexual assault, sexual abuse, or molestation, sexual violence is a complex phenomenon that affects hundreds of thousands of people each year.[6] Sexual violence includes rape, the most studied form of sexual violence, as well as numerous other forms of violation. Because of this complexity, the Centers for Disease Control and Prevention (CDC) divides sexual violence into explicit categories:

- Forced penetration of a person, either attempted or completed
- Alcohol/drug-facilitated penetration of a person, either attempted or completed

Table 6.1 Forms of Interpersonal Violence

Type of Violence	Actions
Physical violence	Use of force causing injury, including hair pulling, punching, kicking, slapping, stabbing, choking, forcing drugs or alcohol; making someone hurt physically; causing injury or even death
Sexual violence	Sexual assault, molestation, rape, unwelcome touching; coercing someone into not using contraception; coercing someone into having sex with others
Financial violence	Controlling the finances, preventing someone from going to school or taking a job
Emotional/psychological violence	Undermining someone's worth by insulting, humiliating, criticizing, and destroying their self-esteem; threatening, intimidating, or fear-causing behaviors; controlling behaviors such as needing "permission" to go out or talk to someone; monitoring cell phone or social media accounts; extreme jealousy and insecurity; isolating them from community, family and friends; blackmail
Verbal violence	Screaming, shouting, swearing, name calling, insulting, often accompanied by emotional and psychological abuse;posting insulting and humiliating information on social media accounts
Stalking violence	Loitering, watching, following; persistent phone calls, texts, emails; unwanted love letters or gifts
Spiritual violence	Mocking, ridiculing, putting down religious and spiritual beliefs and practices; not allowing someone to participate in spiritual or religious events, practices, and worship
Legal violence	Refusing to sign, file, or give access to papers that confer legal status; hiding mail or documents necessary to obtain legal status; threatening to deport; threatening to take away or harm children; violating restraining orders that protect the person and their children

SOURCE: "Types of Domestic Violence," FindLaw, accessed March 20, 2017, http://family.findlaw.cobam/domestic-violence/types-of-domestic-violence.html; "Forms of Abuse," Domestic Violence Prevention Centre, accessed March 20, 2017, http://www.domesticviolence.com.au/pages/forms-of-abuse.php; and "Teen Dating Violence," Weave, accessed March 20, 2017, http://www.weaveinc.org/post/teen-dating-violence.

- Forced acts in which a person is made to penetrate another person, either attempted or completed
- Alcohol/drug-facilitated acts in which a person is made to penetrate another person, either forced or completed
- Forced acts of penetration, either attempted or completed, because of a misuse and abuse of authority, or resulting from verbal pressure or intimidation by another person
- Unwanted sexual contact
- Unwanted sexual experiences that occur verbally (i.e., sexual harassment) or visually (i.e., exposure to pornography)[7]

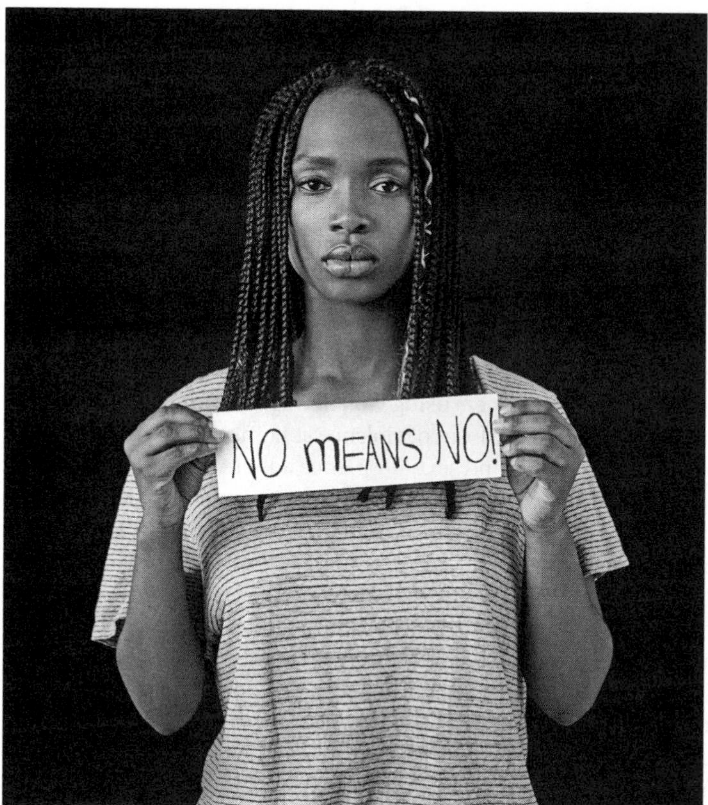

Figure 6.1 Take a moment to reflect on Inés Hernández-Avila's question: Why do some men insist that when a woman says "no" she really means "yes"? (Source: iStock. Credit: Chardy Penn)

Targets and Perpetrators of Interpersonal and Sexual Violence

Intersectional and feminist orientations tell us that the male/female binary used for decades to understand interpersonal violence is grossly inaccurate. We know that low-income women of color, girls and young women of color, indigenous women, disabled women, and LGBQ and transgender individuals are overwhelmingly the targets and victims of interpersonal and sexual violence—worldwide.[8] As any of these identities intersect with others, the rate of targeting and victimization increases. This is true not just in the United States, but globally.[9] On college campuses, we know that lesbian, bisexual, and queer-identified women report "significantly higher" incidences of physical dating violence, "sexual assault, and unwanted pursuit victimization [e.g., stalking]" than cisgender and heterosexual women and even gay, bisexual, or queer-identified men.[10] This does not mean that economically secure, cisgender, heterosexual, able body, white women or men, or men of color are not targets of sexual or interpersonal violence: they are. What it does mean is they are far less likely to be the targets of this violence.

Even though we might wish to be able to identify offenders and construct a profile of them, the U.S. Department of Justice shares that there is no such thing as an offender profile. Nonetheless, studies of the perpetrators of interpersonal violence seem to agree that several traits are common, many of them embedded in cultural and societal expectations for masculinity.[11] Among those who are interpersonally violent, we see high levels of callousness, a lack of empathy and remorse, impulsivity, irresponsibility, anti-social behaviors, and emotional deficiencies.[12] Additionally, they are more likely to be men who subscribe to male privilege and believe that women are, and should be, subordinate to men.[13] Studies of offenders outside the United States suggest that perpetrators are more likely to have "witnessed their fathers using violence against their mothers," and to be men "who experienced some form of violence at home as children."[14]

Perpetrators of interpersonal and sexual violence adhere to **hypermasculine ideologies.** Hypermasculine ideologies tell us that men must be dominant over women in a relationship, heterosexual relationships are inherently adversarial, and gender nonconforming individuals are deviant and, as such, a threat to masculine ideals. These hypermasculine individuals are likely to "discount refusals for sexual activity" and to believe that they can persuade their target to have sex with them.[15] They also believe that their friends and peers "are using coercive behavior to obtain sex," whether they actually are or not.[16] Perpetrators of interpersonal and sexual violence also "have a strong sense of entitlement"—to people's bodies and to sex—and are willing to use power and control to get what they want from another person, to make them behave in the ways they want, and to commit acts of sexual violence, even though they know those acts are illegal and harmful.[17] They often subscribe to homophobic and transphobic beliefs, and regardless of the identity of the person violated, perpetrators of interpersonal and sexual violence are overwhelmingly the acquaintances, neighbors, dating partners, friends, and/or family members of that person.

Ryan McKelley, professor of clinical/counseling psychology and a licensed psychologist, offers a possible explanation for this hypermasculine willingness to hurt others. In his work on masculinity and social connectedness, McKelley describes a **male emotional funnel system,** which reduces the wide range of emotions that a person may experience to a single emotion: anger. McKelley explains that all humans experience a range of emotions. Tests of our autonomic nervous systems support this fact: when we are exposed to stimulus that should engage our emotions, our bodies automatically react emotionally and we cannot control or shut down these responses. The expression of those emotions, however, is socially controlled and highly limited for boys and men. In a binary world, a world that valorizes hypermasculine ideologies—boys are encouraged to be tough, strong, and stoic and to never cry or show fear: they must accept pain and hurt without expression or acknowledgement. The most

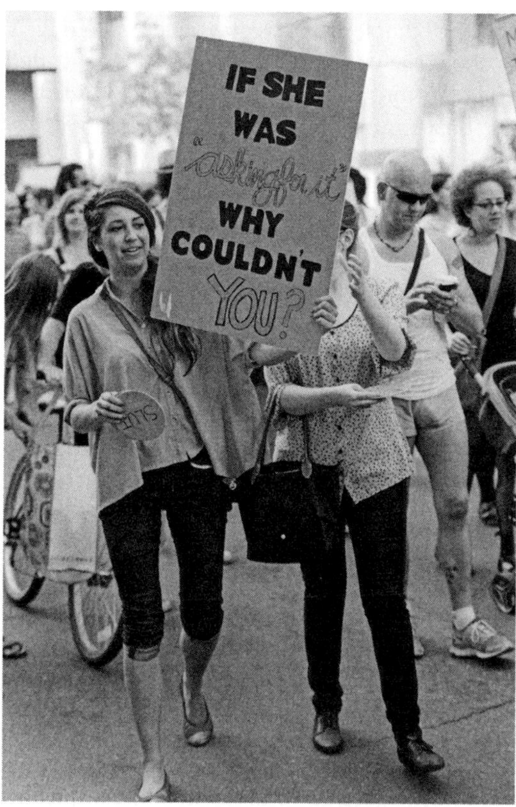

Figure 6.2 Hypermasculine ideologies often result in flawed assumptions about who is entitled to someone else's body. At a Slut Walk, in Toronto, this protestor's sign challenges the hypermasculine ideology of dominance and entitlement. (Source: iStock. Credit: jentakespictures)

insulting words for boys in this binary and hypermasculine environment are *fag, sissy, wimp, crybaby,* and *girl.* This means that even though all people experience a range of emotions, in a binary world, boys, who grow up and become men, often are socialized to deny them.

For boys, common human emotions—such as humiliation, embarrassment, powerlessness, shame, fear, loneliness, regret, hurt, and anger—are filtered and then distilled down to anger and aggression, the two emotions a binary society is willing to tolerate in boys, or even deem acceptable. Over time, not only can boys become disconnected from the full range of human emotions, they also lose their ability to detect, care about, and respond to them in others. The result, McKelley surmises, may be that hypermasculine men are able to hurt the people they know because they have lost the ability to recognize or to care about hurt, shame, humiliation, and fear in others, and even in themselves.[18]

When we filter hypermasculinity and the male emotional funnel system through feminist and intersectional lenses, we come to understand that masculinity and emotions are far more complex than we have been encouraged to believe. If we can begin to talk about the ways humans, regardless of gender identity, experience a full range of emotions, we may be able to help turn the tide on these hypermasculine and constraining influences on men and boys.

INTERSECTING SYSTEMS OF POWER AND OPPRESSION

A person's safety in private settings is more complicated than being in a relationship or having contact with a perpetrator. Safety, and its presence or absence, is in constant interaction with complex "systems of power and oppression."[19] These systems circulate, informing our choices and the discourse with which we can speak about the experiences of sexual and interpersonal violence. They reside in what are known as rape myths and scripts, societal and historical traumas, and social and cultural norms that often constrain people's ability to speak out, get help, or make sense of interpersonal and sexual violence. We take up those systems of power and oppression next, investigating the ways they silence or confuse our communication about safety in private spaces.

Rape Myths and Rape Scripts

Myths are false beliefs about something and, although they can take the form of wonderful stories that catch our imagination, they are in fact untrue. Rape myths are the stories told in a society about sexual violence and sexual assault. They circulate in our families, communities, workplaces, entertainment outlets, and our legal and political ideologies and practices. They are especially prevalent among fraternities and athletics on college campuses.[20] Rape myths originate from binary ways of thinking about identity and communicate very misleading views of rape and sexual violence. Even people who are not the perpetrators of this violence often subscribe to these myths. To explore whether you and your peers are prone to accepting rape myths, answer the following questions:[21]

Women routinely lie about rape. (true/false)

Only "certain kinds" of women are raped. (true/false)

Although most women wouldn't admit it, they generally find being physically forced into sex a real turn-on. (true/false)

If a woman doesn't fight back, you can't really say that it was rape. (true/false)

Men from nice middle-class homes almost never rape. (true/false)

Women who wear low cut tops or sexy clothing are just asking for trouble. (true/false)

If a woman has no bruises, scratches or marks, rape probably didn't really happen. (true/false)

Women tend to exaggerate how much rape affects them. (true/false)

Boyfriends almost never rape their girlfriends. (true/false)

Stranger rape is the most common kind of rape. (true/false)

Women who claim they were raped just have emotional problems or want to get back at men. (true/false)

Rape is rare in middle and high schools. (true/false)

Rape happens when a man's sex drive gets out of control. (true/false)

Although many people respond to each statement with *true,* the accurate response to each statement is *false.* These statements reflect **rape myths,** which permeate our culture with "attitudes and beliefs that are generally false but are widely and persistently held" to be true about rape. Those attitudes and beliefs "serve to deny and justify male sexual aggression" and make the naming of rape as "rape" confusing for some.[22]

Rape myths, which are included in many people's everyday conversations about sexual assault, as well as in our media representations of rape, evolve into scripts, specifically scripts for sexual interactions and scripts for rape. **Scripts** are "cognitive structures that guide behaviors in social situations" and are not inherently harmful, in fact they are very common for a range of situations in which we find ourselves. For example, individuals have scripts for shopping, going to church, riding a bus, and the like. Scripts "define individuals' roles in social situations" and "shape expectations for how others should behave in that situation." They tell us who pays and who accepts our money when we shop, who stands in front of the congregation when we attend religious services, who drives and determines where and when to stop when we take public transportation, and so on.

Similar to rape myths, common sexual scripts follow a non-intersectional and binary logic. They tell us who initiates the sexual activity (he does) and who is the gatekeeper (she is). With respect to sexual assault, we find that within "these [binary] scripts, men are presumed to have strong, difficult-to-control sexual urges" and "multiple partners," while women are "presumed to desire relationships and intimacy" and "to have much weaker sexual urges." If they have multiple partners or enjoy sex, they "are viewed as deviant in some way."[23] These scripts, their binary logics, and the myths they emerge from, focus attention on the female victim. If an experience does not match the script for rape, then the experience "gets disqualified" as "real rape" even though it matches the legal definition of rape.[24]

Rape myths and scripts have made it difficult to discuss sexual violence accurately: we lack a comprehensive vocabulary for this violence. That is, we often are faced with an inability to name an experience of sexual violence in ways that make sense to the person violated. In her work on sexual violence, communication scholar Kate Lockwood Harris focused on the word *rape.* Through interviews with young women whose experiences fit the legal definition of rape,

Lockwood Harris came to realize that "the word *rape* carries with it a framework" that created an overly simplistic binary—"rape" (horrific acts of sexual violence) versus "not rape" (consensual sex)—and that binary often erased the complexity of the experience. For some of the women she interviewed, the ability to name the violation so definitively was helpful and they could stop blaming themselves for the violence. For others, however, the label of rape left "little room to identify the nuance and the complexity of the experience."[25]

This meant that these women were constrained in two ways. First, the label of rape "reduced their ability to view themselves as agents in the moment of violence."[26] It forced the women to see themselves as victims rather than agents, as statistics rather than individuals who have the potential to make choices. For these women, labeling a sexual act as "rape" lumped together so many kinds of nonconsensual sex that they were unable "to speak about ambiguous, contradictory parts of their experiences."[27] Second, the label of rape forced the women into a litigious mode—they felt they had to attempt to prosecute the perpetrator if they named the experience as such, and many did not want to pursue that route. As one of the participants explained, "women are not going to say anything because it is a long-term relationship and you have an attachment to that person. And sure, they did something you didn't like, but that's no reason to send them to jail."[28]

For these women, the label of rape demanded "that a whole person be condemned. Although the women in the study readily affixed judgment to the man's behavior, they did not want to conflate that behavior with an identity."[29] The **lack of useful vocabulary** with which to describe and understand rape as sexual violence, Lockwood Harris concludes, erases the "real and important differences between" the actual experiences of rape and "the clearest cultural images of rape." The common cultural images, one participant explains, are "like Lifetime movies" that perpetuate myths of dangerous "sickos" abducting and assaulting women. They fail to speak to the reality that the perpetrators often are people the victim felt an attachment to and even wants or needs to maintain a relationship with.[30] The women in Lockwood Harris's study are calling for "a more nuanced vocabulary for their experiences," one that acknowledges the "varied types of harm" and that departs from "the most overtly and brutally violent cases of forced sex."[31]

The Unrapeable Myth

Our attitudes also are shaped by a myth that defines some women as **unrapeable.** Not unrapeable in the sense of being too pure, but as being so sexually promiscuous and sexually motivated that any sex, whether consensual and self-selected or not, is welcome sex. As troubling as this may sound, consider the following backstory. Historically, "ethnic minority women's bodies have been systematically and routinely objectified, exoticized, and devalued."[32] For African American women, as just one example, these practices have led to severe outcomes. For women held in slavery, "institutionalized rape" was a real and frequent part of their lives. "African American women" were raped by slaveholders, the sons of slaveholders, and anyone else who might be a free male and inclined to rape, and they "had no legal or social protections"—in fact, they were not regarded as "legitimate victims of rape." Indeed, they were regarded as not fully human, more animal-like in desires and, as such, unrapeable. The myth of their "hypersexual nature," too, which circulated widely during slavery (and beyond), was said to have "led them to desire men's sexual advances and enjoy forced sex."[33]

This abuse and violation continued after the emancipation of slaves, as "the job most frequently available to African American women" was as domestic workers. "It is well documented that as maids and washer women, African American women were routinely the victims of sexual assault committed by the Caucasian men in the families for which they worked."[34] Not only are rape myths and sexual scripts muddling our understanding of sexual assault and rape, but we continue to subscribe to traumatic historical legacies that name some women as more legitimately victims of rape than others. Before you reject this claim, consider that although "legalized slave labor and the resulting sexual violation [slavery] has ceased . . . judges and juries tend to impose harsher penalties (i.e., longer sentences) for men who rape White women as compared to Black women."[35] The myth being subscribed to is that black women are not seen as legitimate victims of rape or sexual assault.[36]

This unrapeable myth is also with us in other realms. Consider several of the common unrapeable myths about sex workers: Sex workers can't be raped, no harm occurs to them if they are assaulted or harassed, and they actually deserved to be raped;[37] sex workers are engaged in criminal behaviors, so what does it matter if they are raped; and they aren't credible or trustworthy enough to be believed.[38] The result of these myths includes not just the trauma involved in sexual assault and violence experienced by sex workers but also the underreporting of sexual assault and violence on the part of sex workers as well as the under-prosecution of the perpetrators of that violence.

In other cases, the unrapeable myth appears in slurs describing women as not desirable enough for someone to want to have sex with them. When Brazilian politician Jair Bolsonaro (who became Brazil's president in 2019), said that human rights critic Maria do Rosario "isn't worth it, because she's ugly, she's not my type; I would never rape her," he was using the unrapeable myth to back his claim. In another context, comedian Damon Wayans defended actor Bill Cosby against his accusers by saying they were "unrapeable" because they were in a relationship with Cosby, suggesting the relationship implied consent (even though Cosby allegedly used drugs to help him subdue the women).[39] Although Wayans questioned the financial motivations of Cosby's accusers, he also walked back his comments, saying that "for anybody who was raped by Bill Cosby, I'm sorry. And I hope you get justice," and indeed Cosby was later found guilty.

To change the narrative and lessen the power of these rape myths and scripts, we can follow the lead of high school journalist Sabrina Nelson, who explains **rape culture** as "blaming the victim rather than rapist for the assault, and saying that the victim did something to provoke the attack. Rape culture teaches women to not get raped, rather than teaching men not to rape. Rape culture involves sympathizing with the rapist [rather than the victim]."[40] Concerns about how accusations (or a conviction) can ruin the rapist's future and his career (if he is white) reveal a hierarchy of who is more fully valued; women are blamed for the attack because she should have known better than to be at that party, to drink so much, to wear that outfit. In such instances, some consider that by such behavior women give up their right to be treated as fully human.

Societal and Historical Traumas

The dysfunctional legacies that drive our misunderstandings of rape and sexual violence are present in still other ways. Societal and historical traumas help us understand why. Thema Bryant-Davis, Heewoon Chin, and Shaquita Tillman, scholars at Pepperdine University, suggest that societal trauma helps explain this low reporting rate for cisgender, transgender, lesbian, bisexual, and queer-identified women of color. They share that "the sexual assault of ethnic minority women in the United States often occurs within a context of societal trauma." Societal trauma is often called "intergenerational trauma, race-based trauma, sexism, racism, classism, heterosexism" as well as "cultural violence, political and racial terror and oppression." **Societal traumas** are viewed as "interpersonal and systemic emotional, verbal, and physical assaults by those with power and privilege against members of marginalized" groups.[41]

Societal traumas, of which slavery, forced sterilization, and rape culture are three examples, are ignored, denied, minimized, and misrepresented by those in positions of power. Those with privilege and control, in essence, keep these traumas from being a part of the larger conversation. Societal traumas are minimized or misrepresented in textbooks, left out of the historical record, explained away as "not really that bad," and mocked or misrepresented in popular culture. Victim blaming, placing responsibility for the violence on the victim rather than the perpetrator, also is a frequent response to societal trauma by those in power.

A second example helps explain the severe impacts of trauma on a particular group of people and the ways that trauma can affect experiences and reports of rape. Native American women experience some of the highest rates of sexual assault of any ethnic group.[42] Because of the diversity of Native American populations, and the absence of published research, "it is difficult to get an accurate picture of the violence against women in Indian country."[43] However, scholars interested in understanding sexual assault in Native communities have used the concept of historical trauma to begin to understand this

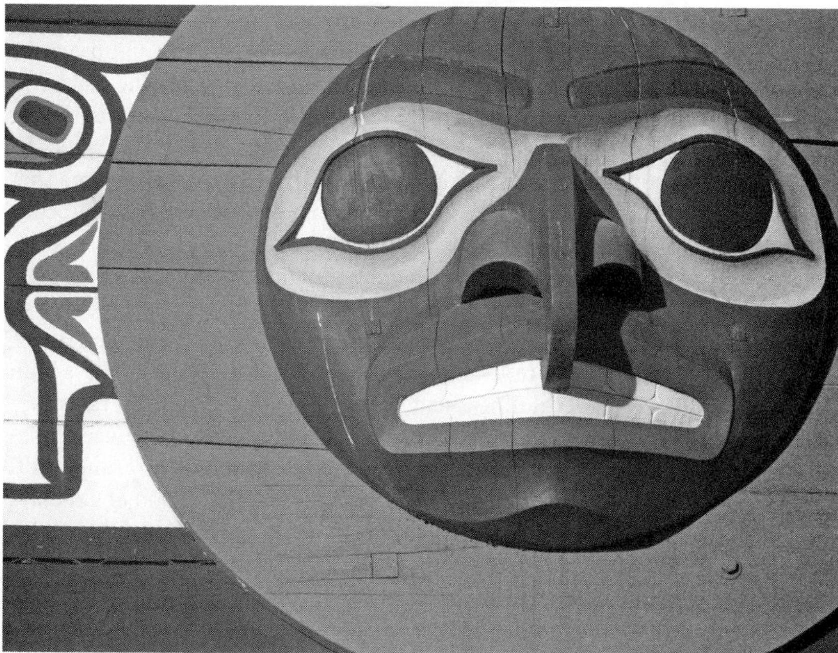

Figure 6.3 Totems pay respect to cultural beliefs and practices, tell a story of ancestors or important events, and recount family lineage. Totems are placed in strategic places and reveal complex and symbolic messages. Their meanings often are only known to those who created them, or to those who share a history and knowledge of certain events. When those in a culture are subjected to historical trauma, totems may preserve and tell their stories. (Source: iStock. Credit: Miranda1066)

violence. **Historical trauma** unpacks societal trauma by calling attention to the material, emotional, spiritual, and psychological impacts of that trauma. Historical trauma is defined as the loss of both old and young people, who are "depositories of cultural, spiritual, and medicinal knowledge and hope for the future," the loss of subsistence economies, territories and game, homelands, kinship systems, language and family systems as well as genocide and forced relocation to reservations and urban areas.[44]

Historical trauma explains the ways in which American Indian and Alaskan Native peoples have experienced "community massacres, genocidal policies, pandemics from the introduction of new diseases, forced relocation, forced removal of children through Indian boarding school policies, and prohibition of spiritual and cultural practices." More recently the forced sterilization of Native women (between 1970 and 1980), dumping of toxic waste on tribal lands, exploitation and destruction of sacred sites, and the prohibition of whaling and fishing traditions generate extremely high levels of stress, mourning, and trauma in contemporary communities. Taken together, "these events amount to a history of ethnic and cultural genocide."[45] Scholars of American Indian and Native Alaskan trauma label this "historical trauma" because it captures the collective and compounding nature of the trauma, illustrating that "events occurring at different time periods (often across generations) come to be seen as parts of a single traumatic trajectory." Historical trauma helps explain how events that may have occurred in the distant past continue to have "clear impacts on contemporary individual and familial mental health and identity."[46]

Responses to this historical trauma include individual symptoms of "PTSD and guilt, anxiety, grief" and depression. At the familial level, a breakdown of family communication is common. At the community level, "traditional culture and values" are lost, as are "traditional rites of passage." The result is high rates of alcoholism, "physical illness (e.g., obesity), and internalized racism."[47] Although there is considerable resiliency and positive coping in the face of historical trauma, survivors display higher levels of anxiety, mistrust, and guilt, more difficultly managing anger, and somatization (the conversion of a mental state into a physical illness). Children of survivors of historical trauma "may have more difficulty expressing emotions and regulating aggression, feel guilty, be more self-critical, and experience psychosomatization" (illness caused by extreme mental stress and anxiety).[48]

Cultural and Social Norms

Cultural and societal norms also can help explain the under-reporting of sexual violence for Native women, in particular, and ethnic minority women, in general. With regard to Native women, Ethnic Studies scholars Roe Bubar and Pamela Jumper Thurman explain, "the tribal community has a significant impact on how Native women are empowered, protected, or oppressed in their respective homelands. In urban reservation communities, isolation (physical, political, spiritual, and communal) can seal the fate of many Native women in violent relationships." Moreover, cultural norms privilege "self-sufficiency and taking care of problems within the family"; hence, seeking help from outsiders, who have a history of exploiting Native communities, is unacceptable. This is compounded by "culturally incompetent law enforcement" from outside the tribal community, but even within tribal enforcement, an abused woman may avoid reporting abuse because the abuser may actually be a relative of the tribal authority. In addition, because identifying the offender may fuel stereotypes, many Native women stay put and silent.[49]

For many ethnic minority women, the cultural mandate to protect male offenders within one's own racial groupings is powerful.[50] Bryant-Davis and her colleagues explain, "when the perpetrator of sexual assault is an African American male, African American women may feel ambivalent about what to disclose to others about the sexual assault and the identity of their assailant. Historically, false accusations of sexual assault against African American males have perpetuated their unfair treatment in many domains, including work, schools, and the criminal justice system."[51] Latina women, too, portrayed in popular culture as hypersexual and passionate, as well as flirtatious and teasing, may be unwilling to report a rape or sexual assault because of "fear that they will not be believed," fear of police, and fear of reinforcing the "machismo and marianismo standards" and stereotypes. For Asian American and Pacific Islander women, the combination of tradition, culture, and philosophical ideologies may prevent women from reporting an assault. The emphasis on "group harmony, suppression of conflict, indirect communication, and avoidance of loss of face," combined with high levels of acceptance of rape myths, may help explain the reasons that the reporting of rape within this population is so low.[52]

The reality of losing one's children also can never be underestimated. In situations in which cisgender women must leave their homes to save their lives, the risk of losing custody of the children is very real. The courts have a long history of defining cisgender and heterosexual women's escape to safety as abandonment, and of granting custody of the children to the man who remained in the home. When the target of the violence is gender nonconforming, transgender, lesbian, bisexual, or gay, the risk of losing one's children is equally high. If a target is undocumented, the fear is compounded by the real prospects of deportation, which may include the loss of children or even contact with other members of the family.[53] The risks of escalating violence, should someone report or leave the situation, are also troubling. Although existing research focuses on the broad category "women," studies show that when abused women do leave, they run a very high risk of being stalked and even murdered by the abuser. Approximately "4,000 women die each year due to domestic violence" and "75 percent of the victims are killed as they attempted to leave the relationship or after the relationship had ended."[54] This statistic is even more formidable for Native American women. According to the Indian Law Resource Center, "On some reservations, indigenous women are murdered at more than ten times the national average."[55]

Social norms and sanctions around sexuality also are confounding factors in the reporting of interpersonal violence. Lesbians, bisexual individuals, gay men, and queer-identified people who are keeping their identities secret from the outside world may fear the repercussions of being outed more than the abuse, so fear of homophobic and queerphobic backlash may outweigh the abuse experienced. People can lose their jobs, their families, and even their social standing if they report the violence and abuse. The fear that stereotypes proclaiming the inherent equality in lesbian relationship will be damaged is also present for some individuals. The pressure to uphold the stereotype may be so great that the violence is not reported to authorities.[56]

Communication scholar Stephanie Huston Grey explains that "trauma often entangles individuals in a massive knot involving psychology, culture, experience, relationships, history and communication. Not only does this knot bind individuals, but it also can fragment them from some allegiances while meshing them with others as their recollections of the traumatic events collide with their local cultures, diverse encounters, and disparate beliefs."[57] Huston Grey suggests that "people come to understand trauma only after they articulate it."[58] Through communication, experiences are named and externalized. Emotions also are released via language and the result is that individuals can begin to develop strategies to cope with the trauma. We live in a society, however, that constrains conversations in two ways: the trauma is either silenced and erased or the violence is eroticized. Huston Grey shares that when experiences and emotions are exploited "for ratings or economic gain," and when the vocabulary available with which to describe trauma is embedded in myth and inaccurate terminology, the trauma remains unexplained and misunderstood.

As students of intersectionality, we cannot accept the violence done to individuals using the vocabularies that are familiar and currently available. Instead, we must begin to expose their inaccuracies and develop more complex and nuanced ways of talking about interpersonal and sexual violence. In the next section, we explore how we might begin to do so.

THE LIE OF ENTITLEMENT

Terrance Crowley, instructor and trainer with Men Stopping Violence, challenges the normalcy of a rape culture with what he calls the lie of entitlement. Crowley explains, "my [white male] privilege always gives me permission to frame my perceptions as the truth. This lie of entitlement—my privilege to describe the reality of women—gives a rape culture its life. Patriarchy is predicated on this lie and on our protective silence."[59] The lie of entitlement is a labyrinth, Crowley explains, a labyrinth that exists in offices and homes, in boardrooms and classrooms, in athletics and military, in entertainment industries and politics, in churches and courtrooms, on the streets and in cars, everywhere men gather, work, and play. So powerful is this labyrinth, says W.J. Musa Moore-Foster, that "it is not uncommon in a patriarchal society supportive of rape that men can boast about their misdeeds (sometimes in the company of women) with little fear of retaliation or ostracism."[60]

To speak against this lie of entitlement is to "break with patriarchy," to tell the truth, and to challenge rape culture at its very foundation. Crowley offers this hope:

> If I go on to name the lie, if I break ranks with the patriarchy by acknowledging that I cannot know the reality of those subordinated by the system of values that entitles me, that system is no longer seamless; its existence is endangered. . . . If I let my mind run wild, I can see men naming the lie of privilege in such numbers that this system of values begins to unravel. As it unravels, the rape culture begins to transform into one of respect and dignity for women.[61]

Figure 6.4 What lies of entitlement are being told in this image? How might you begin to construct a different version of masculinity from the one presented here? (Source: iStock. Credit: Peopleimages)

Crowley acknowledges that imagining the destruction of rape culture is difficult. This difficulty lies in the reality that

> to stop lying means nothing less than changing what it means to be a man . . . my proclivity is to consolidate my power as a man—not to write this essay, not to blow the whistle on myself. Silence feels easy. I don't feel like a man when I'm not in control. I feel confused and vulnerable. It frightens me to say it out loud: As long as men control women's bodies, a rape culture will continue. As long as men get to define the sexuality and eroticism of women, a rape culture will continue. As long as men link sexual excitement with control, domination, and violence, a rape culture will continue.[62]

Privilege continues when people remain silent, Crowley reminds us. This legacy of silence, of saying nothing about what rape culture costs us, or the ways it harms us, maintains superiority: "Men can stop the lie of our inherent superiority in its tracks by simply not acting as if it were true. I do not mean to imply that what is simple will be easy. It is extremely difficult for me. But the process begins with the acknowledgment of privilege; the terms of my privilege are that I do not have to acknowledge it."[63]

We must say, out loud, that "the standards of gender identity are contrived to accommodate [male] privilege. The male/female dichotomy is based on relatively minor biological differences that are eroticized, fetishized, mythologized, and exploited to declare men and women opposites." Crowley states that the male/female dichotomy, as false as it is, makes it difficult for us to see that people who identify as men are not more rational, more intelligent, and more moral than those who identify as women or as gender queer. But rape culture requires this dichotomy, it requires that we believe the binary structure and see men as superior to women, that we "deify the masculine" and "necessarily vilify women." The degradation of women, Crowley concludes, but also of transgender, lesbian and gay, and queer-identified people, "not only makes attack permissible, it makes it a moral imperative."[64] We must say, out loud, that no one is entitled to anyone else's body; no one is any higher on any hierarchy of humanness that may be said to exist.

Unraveling rape culture and making spaces safe requires admitting that our current construct of masculinity is "antifemale, antiwomanist, antifeminist, and antireason. This flawed socialization of men is not confined to the West but permeates most, if not all, cultures in the modern world," explains Haki Madhubuti. Madhubuti, a poet, publisher, editor and educator, continues:

> If we men of all races, cultures, and continents would just examine the inequalities of power in our own families, business, and political and spiritual institutions and decide today to reassess and reconfigure them in consultation with the women in our lives, we would all be doing the most fundamental corrective act of a counterrapist.[65]

REWRITING THE SCRIPTS

To change our rape culture we must change our language—about rape, sex, gender, race, sexuality, class, religion, the body, and more. But to do that, we must begin to talk about safety in private and public spaces in informed and intersectional ways. We must challenge the continual media representations of men of color as sexual predators and of white men as entitled to women's bodies. These presentations have "sadly produced" among men of color such pain and "a defensive, knee-jerk reaction to discussing rape as if the mere mention of it were self-incriminating."[66] Among white men, these representations have shielded them from being the focus in discussions of sexual predation and violence. We must also challenge the images of sexual and interpersonal violence against queer-identified, transgender, gay, lesbian, or bisexual individuals as "legitimate forms of humiliation" because of their identities and sexualities.[67]

This challenge is only a part of the struggle to change our language and write more complex and intersectional scripts. Because, as Inés Hernández-Avila, whose words opened this chapter, explains, if "I criticize the men or women of the Native American and Chicana/Chicano community who are perpetuating oppressive regimes of being, I am said to be 'airing dirty laundry,' perpetuating negative stereotypes, or being co-opted by the man-hating feminist agenda." Our loyalties to our communities are challenged as a way to silence our challenges to patriarchy. When the "unconscionable maltreatment" of women by men is raised, rather than silencing the spokesperson, *we should listen.* Speaking out does not mean "I do not love my communities, or that I do not want to honor them or respect them. It is because I love them and care for them that I challenge all of us to unlearn the doctrine of subordination to which we have been subjected intentionally as colonized peoples."[68] Speaking out means we are willing to assume an active role in challenging the normalization of the absence of safety in private spaces for far too many people. We become more than bystanders, individuals who simply stand by passively doing nothing. Instead, we become **bystanders who intervene:** we educate and train ourselves to frame issues intersectionally, to speak out against violence and injustices, and to do so in ways that do not unnecessarily jeopardize our, or other people's, safety.

W.J. Musa Moore-Foster notes that if we "are to survive as a people with a moral foundation, men's attitudes about women must be fundamentally overhauled." This is true not just for black men, or just men of color, however, but for all people. Speaking to men as a group, Moore-Foster suggests that language can change and the rewriting of the scripts must happen. Men must "resist the temptation to use [their] strength to coerce women and children or express anger in threatening ways." They must reexamine their "lexicon of intimacy. . . . The expressions I've heard are more related to acquisition than to sharing. Many of them are baleful synonyms for aggression, disrespect, and devaluating that objectify the partners as well as the deed. This is the language of demeaning work, violence, narcissism and alienation."[69] Moore-Foster shares that the shaming of women must stop and youth must be reeducated about sexual violence. Men, regardless of race or ethnicity, must identify the core of the hurt that produces their rage. Men of color as well as white men "must set about cleansing [their] souls of the toxic levels of rage and alienation. Healing ourselves is an important preparation in the struggle for justice."[70] Finally, every male, as a bystander who intervenes, must speak out and take action against the depiction of violence against women.[71]

Hernández-Avila shares Paulo Freire's work from *Pedagogy of the Oppressed* to explain "how a person who is oppressed internalizes the oppressor." Both Freire and Hernández-Avila explain that when someone internalizes the oppressor, they come to believe that the oppressor, or in this case, the scripts embedded in our rape culture, are true. Hernández-Avila states that "the oppressor becomes a part of the person, so much so that the oppressed person adheres to the oppressor and sees the world only through the oppressor's eyes," however misguided and cruel those eyes may be. Even as we come to know that the scripts we have learned so well are damaging and hateful, learning what steps to take instead, what scripts to create and engage, can be challenging.[72] Hernández-Avila says that to be free of these damaging scripts, we must embrace a holistic perspective and engage those scripts. She suggests that for a holistic healing to occur, we reject the myths of entitlement: "Male entitlement. White skin entitlement. Class entitlement. Heterosexual entitlement. Youth entitlement. Ability entitlement. Adult entitlement. Employer entitlement.

6.1. GUIDE TO COMMUNICATION

Exposing the Lie of Entitlement

Explorations of the right to be safe in private and social settings, that is, free from interpersonal and sexual violence, expose some painful truths: for some, power and control define their relationships, rape myths and scripts are prevalent, and they, in tandem with societal and historical traumas as well as social and cultural norms, fuel the underreporting of sexual assault. The lie of entitlement can overwhelm us with devastating assumptions about what interpersonal violence and sexual assault really mean and do. As you consider your communication around the tragedy and trauma of interpersonal and sexual violence, ask yourself the following questions:

1. In what ways might my own communication, or the communication I hear and see around me, do any of the following: insult, humiliate, criticize, or destroy someone's self-esteem; threaten, intimidate, or cause fear; control someone's behaviors or deny them permission to do something; display extreme jealousy and insecurity? What does this communicate about the lies that entitlement perpetuates?
2. Where have I encountered narratives that subscribe to rape myths and scripts? Did I hear them from a person I was speaking with, or the media I watched, or someplace else? What can these myths and scripts tell me about our cultural understanding of sexual violence?
3. What might communication about sexual and interpersonal violence look like if it were more aware and respectful of societal and historical traumas?
4. Have I seen the male emotional funnel system or the lie of entitlement in media, in conversations with friends and family, or in other places? How might I talk with the people I know, whether old or young, about the male emotional funnel system, the lie of entitlement, and the damage they do? What might those conversations look like, and with whom would I talk?

Senior worker entitlement. First World entitlement. Religious entitlement. And so on."[73] We must, Hernández-Avila concludes,

> imagine a world without rape. But I cannot imagine a world without rape, a world without misogyny, without imagining a world without racism, classism, sexism, homophobia, ageism, historical amnesia, and other forms and manifestations of violence directed against those communities that are seen to be asking for it. Even the earth is presumably asking for it, as are all the endangered species. So are the children, the disabled, anyone who is different. Different from what? What scale are we using to determine who is normal, who is rational? We are pitted against each other. Why? Whose interests are being served by our mistrusting each other, fearing each other, despising each other, and even sometimes mounting holy wars against each other?[74]

The Cheyenne say that "A nation is not conquered until the hearts of its women are on the ground. Then it is done, no matter how strong the weapons, or how brave the warriors." Hernández-Avila asks how might "all of us as women ensure that our hearts do not hit the ground? What strategies might we as women use to remind ourselves to hold our heads and hearts high?"[75] Moving outside the binary presentation of women and men, as intersectional communicators must move, we recognize that all of us must do the work of holding heads and hearts high, across the range of our complex identities. We must all do this work as we all relearn to value and respect one another as human beings.

Resources

Suzanne Marie Enck and Blake A. McDaniel, "Playing with Fire: Cycles of Domestic Violence in Eminem and Rihanna's 'Love the Way You Lie,'" *Communication, Culture and Critique* 5, no. 4 (December 2012): 618–644, https://doi.org/10.1111/j.1753–9137.2012.01147.x.

Suzanne Enck Wanzer, "All's Fair in Love and Sport: Black Masculinity and Domestic Violence in the News," *Communication and Critical/Cultural Studies* 6, no. 1 (2009): 1–18, doi: 10.1080/14791420802632087.

Jessica Ladd, "The Reporting System that Sexual Assault Survivors Want," filmed February 2016 in Vancouver, British Columbia, TED2016 video, 5:53, https://www.ted.com/talks/jessica_ladd_the_reporting_system_that_sexual_assault_survivors_want.

Men Stopping Violence, http://menstoppingviolence.org.

"Post-Traumatic Stress Disorder (PTSD)," Mayo Clinic, https://www.mayoclinic.org/diseases-conditions/post-traumatic-stress-disorder/symptoms-causes/syc-20355967.

"Power and Control Wheel," Domestic Abuse Intervention Programs, Duluth, MN, and "Understanding the Power and Control Wheel," YouTube video, 2:18, May 2, 2016, https://www.theduluthmodel.org/wheels/.

Notes

1. Inés Hernández-Avila, "In Praise of Insubordination, or, What Makes a Good Woman Go Bad?" in *Transforming a Rape Culture*, ed. Emilie Buchwald, Pamela R. Fletcher, and Martha Roth, rev. ed. (Minneapolis: Milkweed Editions, 2005), 328.
2. Hernández-Avila, "In Praise of Insubordination," 327.
3. Alison Rutherford, Anthony B. Zwi, Natalie J. Grove, and Alexander Butchart, "Violence: A Glossary," *Journal of Epidemiology and Community Health* 61, no. 8 (August 2007): 678–680, doi: 10.1136/jech.2005.043711. See also Katie M. Edwards, Kateryna M. Sylaska, Johanna E. Barry, Mary M. Moynihan, Victoria L. Banyard, Ellen S. Cohn, Wendy A. Walsh, and Sally K. Ward, "Physical Dating Violence, Sexual Violence, and Unwanted Pursuit Victimization: A Comparison of Incidence Rates Among Sexual-Minority and Heterosexual College Students," *Journal of Interpersonal Violence* 30, no. 4 (February 2015): 581, doi: 10.1177/0886260514535260.
4. Etienne G. Drug, Linda L. Dahlberg, James A. Mercy, Anthony B. Zwi, and Rafael Lozano, eds., "World Report on Violence and Health" (Geneva: World Health Organization, 2002), 89, https://apps.who.int/iris/bitstream/handle/10665/42495/9241545615_eng.pdf.
5. World Health Organization, "Violence Against Women, Key Facts," November 29, 2017, https://www.who.int/news-room/fact-sheets/detail/violence-against-women.
6. "About Sexual Violence," RAINN25years, Sexual Violence, accessed August 3, 2019, https://www.rainn.org/about-sexual-assault; World Health Organization, "Violence Against Women, Key Facts."
7. "Violence Prevention, Preventing Sexual Violence," Centers for Disease Control and Prevention, National Center for Disease Prevention and Control, Division of Violence Prevention, page last reviewed March 12, 2019, https://www.cdc.gov/violenceprevention/sexualviolence/definitions.html.
8. Compiled from "Facts About Domestic Violence and Physical Abuse," National Coalition Against Domestic Violence, 2015, https://assets.speakcdn.com/assets/2497/domestic_violence_and_physical_abuse_ncadv.pdf; Natalie Sokolff and Ida Dupont, "Domestic Violence at the Intersections of Race, Class, and Gender: Challenges and Contributions to Understanding Violence Against Marginalized Women in Diverse Communities," *Violence Against Women* 11, no. 1 (February 2005): 43, https://doi.org/10.1177/107780120427147644; Douglas A. Brownridge, "Partner Violence Against Women with Disabilities: Prevalence, Risk, and Explanations,"

Violence Against Women 12 (2006): 805–822; Edwards et al., "Physical Dating Violence," 591; Mikel L. Walters, Jieru Chen, and Matthew J. Breiding, The National Intimate Partner and Sexual Violence Survey (NISVS): 2010 Findings on Victimization by Sexual Orientation," January 2013, https://www.cdc.gov/violenceprevention /pdf/nisvs_sofindings.pdf; Peggy Orenstein, *Girls and Sex: Navigating the Complicated New Landscape* (New York: Harper Collins, 2016), 171; Tarana Burke, "Me Too Is a Movement, Not a Moment," TEDWomen, 2018, https://www.ted.com/talks/tarana_burke_me_too_is_a_movement_not_a_moment/transcript.

9. Kae Greenberg, "Still Hidden in the Closet: Trans Women and Domestic Violence," *Berkeley Journal of Gender, Law and Justice* 27, no. 2 (2012): 198–251; World Health Organization, "Key Facts"; Sonja Elks, "Murders of Transgender People Rising World-Wide—Activists," Thomson Reuters Foundation, November 20, 2018, http://news.trust.org/item/20181120075803–0k6vn/.
10. Edwards et al., "Physical Dating Violence," 591.
11. Suzanne Enck Wanzer, "All's Fair in Love and Sport: Black Masculinity and Domestic Violence in the News," *Communication and Critical/Cultural Studies* 6, no. 1 (2009): 1–18.
12. Marc T. Swogger, Zach Walsh, and David S. Kosson, "Domestic Violence and Psychopathic Traits: Distinguishing the Antisocial Batterer from Other Antisocial Offenders," *Aggressive Behavior* 33, no. 3 (2007): 253–260.
13. World Health Organization, "Violence Against Women, Key Facts."
14. UN Women, "Facts and Figures: Ending Violence Against Women," November, 2018, https://www.u1–18 .nwomen.org/en/what-we-do/ending-violence-against-women/facts-and-figures.
15. Catherine Loh, Christine A. Gidyca, Tracy R. Lobo, Rohini Luthra, "A Prospective Analysis of Sexual Assault Perpetration: Risk Factors Related to Perpetrator Characteristics," *Journal of Interpersonal Violence* 20, no. 10 (2005): 1342, doi: 10.1177/0886260505278528.
16. Loh et al., "A Prospective Analysis," 1343.
17. Rutgers: Office for Violence Prevention and Victim Assistance, "Why Does Sexual Violence Occur?" 2017, accessed April 5, 2017, http://vpva.rutgers.edu/sexual-violence/why-does-sexual-violence-occur/; Center for Sex Offender Management, "Section 3: Common Characteristics of Sex Offenders," Office of Justice Programs, U.S. Department of Justice, accessed April 5, 2017, http://csom.org/train/etiology/3/3_1.htm.
18. Ryan McKelley, "Unmasking Masculinity—Helping Boys Become Connected Men," TEDxUWLaCrosse, 8:50, November 26, 2013, https://www.youtube.com/watch?v=LBdnjqEoiXA. See also Kate Lockwood Harris, "Yes Means Yes and No Means No, But Both These Mantras Need to Go: Communication Myths in Consent Education and Anti-Rape Activism," *Journal of Applied Communication Research* 46, no. 2 (2018): 155–178.
19. Sokolff and Dupont, "Domestic Violence at the Intersections," 43.
20. Ann Burnett, Jody L. Matern, Liliana L. Herakova, David H. Kahl, Jr., Cloy Tobola, and Susan E. Bornsen, "Communicating/Muting Date Rape: A Co-Cultural Theoretical Analysis of Communication Factors Related to Rape Culture on a College Campus," *Journal of Applied Communication Research* 37, no. 4 (2009): 465–485, https://doi.org/10.1080/00909880903233150.
21. Adapted from Diana L. Payne, Kimberly A. Lonsway, and Louise F. Fitzgerald, "Rape Myth Acceptance: Exploration of its Structure and Its Measurement Using the Illinois Rape Myth Acceptance Scale," *Journal of Research in Personality* 33, no. 1 (March 1999): 27–68, https://doi.org/10.1006/jrpe.1998.2238.
22. Payne, Lonsway, and Fitzgerald, "Rape Myth Acceptance," 29.
23. Heather L. Littleton and Julia C. Dodd, "Violent Attacks and Damaged Victims: An Exploration of the Rape Scripts of European American and African American U.S. College Women," *Violence Against Women* 22, no. 14 (February 2016): 1726, doi: 10.1177/1077801216631438.
24. Zoe D. Peterson and Charlene L. Muehlenhard, "Was It Rape? The Function of Women's Rape Myth Acceptance and Definitions of Sex in Labeling Their Own Experiences," *Sex Roles* 51, no. 3–4 (August 2004): 142, doi: 10.1023/B:SERS.0000037758.95376.00.
25. Kate Lockwood Harris, "The Next Problem with No Name: The Politics and Pragmatics of the Word Rape," *Women's Studies in Communication* 34, no. 1 (May 2011): 52, doi: 10.1080/07491409.2011.566533. See also Littleton and Dodd, "Violent Attacks," 1725; and UK Center for Research on Violence Against Women, "Top Ten Series," December 2011, accessed March 21, 2017, https://opsvaw.as.uky.edu/sites/default/files /07_Rape_Prosecution.pdf.
26. Lockwood Harris, "Next Problem with No Name," 50.
27. Lockwood Harris, "Next Problem with No Name," 53.
28. Lockwood Harris, "Next Problem with No Name," 52.
29. Lockwood Harris, "Next Problem with No Name," 50.
30. Lockwood Harris, "Next Problem with No Name," 52.
31. Lockwood Harris, "Next Problem with No Name," 53, 58.
32. Thema Bryant-Davis, Heewoon Chung, and Shaquita Tillman, "From the Margins to the Center: Ethnic Minority Women and the Mental Health Effects of Sexual Assault," *Trauma, Violence, and Abuse* 10, no. 4 (October 2009): 331.
33. Littleton and Dodd, "Violent Attacks," 1729.
34. Shaquita Tillman, Thema Bryant-Davis, Kimberly Smith, and Alison Marks, "Shattering Silence: Exploring Barriers to Disclosure for African American Sexual Assault Survivors," *Trauma, Violence, and Abuse* 11, no. 2 (April 2010): 60, doi: 10.1177/1524838010363717.

35. Tillman et al., "Shattering Silence," 60.
36. Tillman et al., "Shattering Silence," 60.
37. Ann Cotton, Melissa Farley, and Robert Baron, "Attitudes toward Prostitution and Acceptance of Rape Myths," *Journal of Applied Social Psychology* 32, no. 9 (2002): 1790–1796.
38. Eric Sprankle, Katie Bloomquist, Cody Butcher, Neil Gleason, and Zoe Schaefer, "The Role of Sex Work Stigma in Victim Blaming and Empathy of Sexual Assault Survivors," *Sex Research and Social Policy* 15, no. 3 (September 2018): 242–248.
39. "Outrage as Comedian Damon Wayans Calls the Women Who Accused Bill Cosby of Drugging and Raping Them 'B**ches' Who Were 'Unrapeable,'" *Daily Mail,* October 6, 2019, https://www.dailymail.co.uk/news/article-3224457/Damon-Wayans-fire-branding-Bill-Cosby-rape-accusers-bitches-unrapeable.html.
40. Sabrina Nelson, "Slut-Shaming and Rape Culture," HuffPost, July 15, 2013, https://www.huffpost.com/entry/rape-culture.
41. Bryant-Davis et al., "From the Margins," 331.
42. Bryant-Davis et al., "From the Margins," 343.
43. Roe Bubar and Pamela Jumper Thurman, "Violence Against Native Women," *Social Justice* 31, no. 4 (2004): 72.
44. Bonnie Duran, Eduardo Duran, and Maria Yellow Horse Brave Heart, "Native Americans and the Trauma of History," in *Studying Native America: Problems and Prospects,* ed. Russell Thornton (Madison: University of Wisconsin Press, 1998), 63.
45. Teresa Evans-Campbell, "Historical Trauma in American Indian/Native Alaska Communities: Multilevel Framework for Exploring Impacts on Individuals, Families, and Communities," *Journal of Interpersonal Violence* 23, no. 3 (2008): 316.
46. Evans-Campbell, "Historical Trauma," 321.
47. Evans-Campbell, "Historical Trauma," 322.
48. Evans-Campbell, "Historical Trauma," 322.
49. Bubar and Thurman, "Violence Against Native Women," 75, 76.
50. Tillman et al., "Shattering Silence," 64.
51. Bryant-Davis et al., "From the Margins," 335–336.
52. Bryant-Davis et al., "From the Margins," 336, 337.
53. Bryant-Davis et al., "From the Margins," 342, 343. See also Lambda Legal, "FAQ About Trans Gender Parenting," https://www.lambdalegal.org/know-your-rights/article/trans-parenting-faq.
54. Domestic Abuse Shelter, Inc., http://www.domesticabuseshelter.org/infodomesticviolence.htm.
55. Indian Law Resource Center, "Ending Violence Against Native Women," accessed November 20, 2019, https://indianlaw.org/issue/ending-violence-against-native-women.
56. Janice L. Ristock, ed., *Intimate Partner Violence in LGBTQ Lives* (New York: Routledge, 2001).
57. Stephanie Huston Grey, "Wounds Not Easily Healed: Exploring Trauma in Communication Studies," *Communication Yearbook* 31, no. 1 (2007): 176, https://doi.org/10.1080/23808985.2007.11679067.
58. Huston Grey, "Wounds," 177. See also Suzanne Marie Enck and Blake A. McDaniel, "'I Want Something Better for My Life': Personal Narratives of Incarcerated Women and Performances of Agency," *Text and Performance Quarterly* 35, no. 1 (2015): 43–61.
59. Terrance Crowley, "The Lie of Entitlement," in *Transforming a Rape Culture,* ed. Emilie Buchwald, Pamela R. Fletcher, and Martha Roth, rev. ed. (Minneapolis: Milkweed Editions, 2005), 307.
60. W.J. Musa Moore-Foster, "Up from Brutality: Freeing Black Communities from Sexual Violence," in *Transforming a Rape Culture,* ed. Emilie Buchwald, Pamela R. Fletcher, and Martha Roth, rev. ed. (Minneapolis: Milkweed Editions, 2005), 352.
61. Crowley, "Lie of Entitlement," 307.
62. Crowley, "Lie of Entitlement," 307.
63. Crowley, "Lie of Entitlement," 308.
64. Crowley, "Lie of Entitlement," 308.
65. Haki R. Madhubuti, "On Becoming Antirapist," in *Transforming a Rape Culture,* ed. Emilie Buchwald, Pamela R. Fletcher, and Martha Roth, rev. ed. (Minneapolis: Milkweed Editions, 2005), 174, 175.
66. Moore-Foster, "Up from Brutality," 348.
67. Alexa Dodge, "Digitizing Rape Culture: Online Sexual Violence and the Power of the Digital Photograph," *Crime Media Culture* 12, no. 1 (2016): 71.
68. Hernández-Avila, "In Praise of Insubordination," 326.
69. Moore-Foster, "Up from Brutality," 354.
70. Moore-Foster, "Up from Brutality," 353.
71. Moore-Foster, "Up from Brutality," 352.
72. Hernández-Avila, "In Praise of Insubordination," 330.
73. Hernández-Avila, "In Praise of Insubordination," 331.
74. Hernández-Avila, "In Praise of Insubordination," 337.
75. Hernández-Avila, "In Praise of Insubordination," 339.

CHAPTER

7

Intersectional Discourses for Talking about Sexual Violence

IN THIS CHAPTER, YOU WILL FIND . . .

KEY TERMS AND CONCEPTS

- aura of non-responsibility
- burden of ability
- burden of credibility
- burden of performance
- burden of silence
- *feminicidios*
- grammar of non-agency
- *maquiladoras*
- rape culture
- response-ability
- *testimonio*
- trigger warnings

DISCOURSES OF PUBLIC CRUELTY

To talk about sexual violence from an intersectional orientation is to engage "the cruelty of sexual harassment and assault and the discursive regimes that keep that cruelty in place." Michelle Rodino-Colocino describes this cruelty as public. Public cruelty, Rodino-Colocino explains, is "the deliberate infliction of physical, and secondarily emotional, pain upon a weaker person or group by stronger ones in order to achieve some end, tangible or intangible." Public cruelty is "made possible by differences in public power," and it is essential to those systems and structures of power that rely on hierarchy and privilege.[1] Even when they admit to or are accused of harassment, assault and violence, those with public power are allowed to make policies, recruit, appoint, hire, reward, or conversely, discipline and fire. But what is the pain that such public cruelty inflicts and are there ways to counter it? In the sections that follow, we explore particular discourses of cruelty that place unequal burdens on the victims-survivors of sexual violence as compared to the perpetrators. The chapter concludes with stories that encourage us to change the ways we think about sexual violence and the ways in which we can respond to it.

COMMUNICATION AND THE BURDEN OF PERFORMANCE

In the United States, the members of a jury in courtroom proceedings come from its citizens. For this reason, legal proceedings, particularly in courtrooms with juries, are an excellent case study with which to expose the expectations of the common person surrounding sexual violence, the narratives that inform those expectations, and the language used to legitimize violence and discredit its victims-survivors.[2] Corey Rayburn, professor of law at the University of Kansas and a scholar of the language surrounding sexual assault and legal decisions, describes what is called the **burden of performance** that is placed on victims-survivors by juries in any sexual assault trial. This "burden of performance" names the "difficulty witnesses have in persuading a jury by the force of their testimony" that a rape was, indeed, a rape.

In a courtroom, Rayburn explains, the "persuasion that takes place is not based on logic or reason." Rather, it depends on the ability of witnesses to define their "character role and provide a cogent story" that "appeals to a juror's sense of reality. To successfully overcome the burden of performance the narrative must fit within the script of the trial and the larger rape meta-narratives" present in any culture.[3] Even when the facts are true, this truth doesn't hold much persuasive power. Rayburn explains that although the facts may be presented, when "a rape is recounted through oral testimony, with limited physical evidence, it is likely to underwhelm a jury."[4] For cisgender women, here's why:

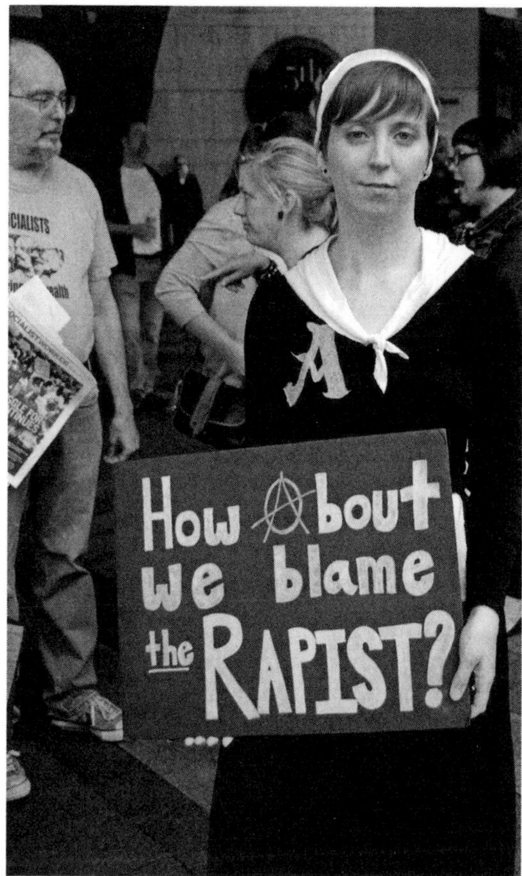

Figure 7.1 The culture of cruelty includes blaming victims, instead of perpetrators, for sexual violence. This protestor is challenging this discursive regime of cruelty by holding the perpetrators responsible for their crimes. (Source: iStock. Credit: 400tmax)

> A person who is on the witness stand telling her story of rape does not just have to convince that jury she is telling the truth. Instead . . . she has to compete with every movie, television program, book, magazine, newspaper and website depicting rape or consensual sex that any of the twelve jurors has ever seen. If her story does not measure up to the jury's high standards as constructed by years of mass media inculcation of rape imagery, then the defendant will walk free. . . . The images of the especially graphic and shocking rapes in mass media create a standard that is too high for most accusers to meet in front of a jury already confronted with conflicting accounts of an alleged rape event. . . . The jurors have heard it all before, but with more shocking details, more horrifying tidbits, and, if through movie or television, with an accompanying audio/video record.[5]

The "fact that television or movie rapes may have been fictional does not mean a jury's conception of rape is not actively shaped by them," just as most people's conceptions of rape have been shaped.[6] This is because, in "a world where rape and violence are constantly represented and re-represented, there can be no blank slate from which to educate a juror [or anyone else, for that matter] about sexual violence."[7]

Rayburn notes that not only have our conceptions of "real rape" been overly constructed and force-fed to us, but our notions of "normal sex" have as well. There is a "common cultural belief" that "holds that 'playing hard to get' is 'normal sex,'" and "a strong belief" that "forceful seduction" leads to great sex and happy endings. Compounded with the reality of "significant gender gaps in determining what constitutes a threat of force," Rayburn concludes that there is no person who is an "empty vessel" regarding ideas of rape.[8] The degree to which any person's views of rape have been constructed for them "is astounding."[9]

Our views, it seems, are not actually our own views. Our views are influenced by and filtered through rape myths and scripts. Media present voyeuristic stories and dramas that romanticize, legitimize, and valorize sexual violence. We watch images and consume stories not of our own making. We watch stories that teach us that resistance is a normal precursor to sex, violence and force are natural and stimulating, and that if sex happened, then it must have been consensual. Maureen Ryan, writing for *Variety,* explains, "rape is one of our media's "most frequently used dramatic devises." Writers think it adds "edge" to a story and "depth" to a female character. Rape has "become shorthand for backstory and drama. . . . Everyone knows rape is awful and a horrific violation, so it's easy for an audience to grasp."[10]

But, Ryan explains, "the sheer amount of competition" for viewer attention "has created an arms race—the shortcut to standing out from the pack is to up the ante." How to top last week's horrific display of violence? Throw in another, even more violent, rape.[11] As feminist and media studies scholars Lisa Cuklanz, Sujata Moorti, and Sarah Projansky reveal, sexual violence is ubiquitous in our media—it is ever present and omnipresent.[12] The result is that common citizens watch these stories, serve on our juries, and filter the horrifying events through very distorted and harmful narratives. The burden of proof falls not on the facts, but on the ways facts align with Hollywood myths and lies. If survivors of sexual violence cannot tell the familiar story, their experiences are deemed illegitimate.

COMMUNICATION AND THE BURDEN OF CREDIBILITY

Irena Lieberman, the director of Legal Services at the Tahirih Justice Center, is an attorney as well as the daughter of a refugee who fled her country because of ethnic and religious persecution. Lieberman offers the story of "any woman," a woman she calls "Maya," to illustrate the "unspeakable human rights abuses" women incur when they escape such physical abuses as "torture, imprisonment, rape, [interpersonal] violence, forced marriage, stoning, and numerous other atrocities—all for the simple reason that they were women,"

> Maya is an Afghan woman living in Afghanistan. An Afghan man rapes Maya. She tells no one. In her culture, she will be blamed for the rape. "People in her community will believe she provoked it—invited it—and she will be punished accordingly." She may be put in jail, her husband and family and even strangers could hurt her. "She may be ostracized, taunted, harassed, shunned, beaten, mutilated—all because of the action of another." She cannot tell the police, they may tell her husband, not believe her, imprison her, laugh at her, tell her she deserved it, or rape her. "A police officer may have been her rapist, and he knows where she lives and when she is home."[13] She is traumatized, yet she can tell no one because it is "shameful and inappropriate to speak to anyone about sexual matters" and unspeakable to share the rape with a stranger, especially a male.
>
> Maya's husband, who worked for the former government, has been killed and she must flee the country. Terrified her attacker will find her, she manages to flee to the United States, thanks to "generous family friends who are able to procure a passport and visa for her."[14] She is emotionally exhausted, she has PTS from the rape, she is grieving her husband's murder. She is afraid she will be questioned as she enters this new country, and she is facing intense language and cultural barriers. She arrives after a long and stressful flight, and is allowed to enter the country.
>
> Maya wants to apply for asylum, she wants legal protection and to stay in the United States. She has very little money, and her friends tell her that a lawyer is unnecessary: she can apply on her own. She knows she will have to tell of the rape, and "alone and unassisted" she applies with the Immigration and Naturalization Service (INS) for political asylum. "Her case is denied." The INS says that "she has provided insufficient detail about the events in her home country and no evidence to support her claim of rape." She also must show that she was "persecuted on account of her race, religion, nationality, membership in a particular social group, or political opinion"; gender is not seen as a legitimate legal category for asylum.[15]
>
> She now must present her case in front of a male judge. Her culture has taught her never to look a man directly in the eye or to speak of intimate things. The judge wants details: describe what happened, the dates, times, places, what he said, how she responded, and "*why* was she raped?" Maya is humiliated, confused, she is sobbing. She does not understand the question, "*why* was she raped?" The judge wants to know if it was because of her "political opinion, her social group, her religion, her nationality, her race? She doesn't know." The judge wants to know why she told no one, why she has no evidence, why there is no police report, no medical records, no witnesses. How does she know she won't be safe in another city? Did she ever try to get to another city? "Did her attacker follow her? Why didn't she flee if she was no longer safe?" In asylum cases such as Maya's her "only evidence is her word." Maya must prove, on her own and without help, that she is credible.[16]

Communication scholar Sara McKinnon's work on gender and asylum focuses on the "particularly precarious group of asylum applicants: women whose claims to asylum involve gender-based forms of persecution." McKinnon explains that gender "is not legally recognized as an identity for which one can be politically persecuted," even as women are persecuted on the basis of their gender.[17] Moreover, immigration judges, because of the Real ID Act of 2005, have the ability to "deny asylum claims based on perceived inconsistencies in testimony," in short, they may deny a woman asylum because the judge does not see her testimony as credible.[18] A judge may perceive a woman as lacking credibility for a variety of ambiguous, culturally, gendered, and raced reasons. She may, for example and for reasons based on culture, religion, language, and post-traumatic stress, share only a portion of her story in a first interview, and then add information in a second interview, which a judge deems inconsistent and untrustworthy. Or, as in the example of Maya, she may fail to "perform" credibly, avoiding eye contact with a male judge, exhibiting displays of emotion such as crying or sobbing, or appearing unreliable as she sorts through confusing questions and language barriers. McKinnon explains that the standards for credibility "remain elusive; they are instituted by many through their own interpretations, but never definitively articulated."[19]

Similar to the burden of performance that victims of sexual violence within the United States face, refugees and asylum seekers face a **burden of credibility** when they fail to "match the judge's gendered expectations of emotion." McKinnon explains that "judges evaluate the claimant's speech against her vocal and corporeal cues, often without acknowledgment of different cultural norms regarding emotion and the challenges of performing [traumatizing] narratives in court." In one asylum case, McKinnon shares, the woman, a Togo citizen using a French translator, spoke too softly for the judge, causing the judge to stop her testimony and state, "You have to speak up so I can hear your voice. Today passiveness and demureness is not the regiment of the day. Today aggressiveness and loudness is the regiment of the day and you can even scream at the Court." The judge "is not concerned with the text of her performance," McKinnon notes, but rather with the performance itself.[20] McKinnon concludes that, as the audience for the testimony, the judge shapes "the possibility of access to citizenship in the United States," focusing on the perceived credibility of the woman, which is filtered through "the conventions of speaking well," rather than the truth of her testimony and the horrors she has endured.[21]

COMMUNICATION AND THE BURDEN OF SILENCE

If the victim-survivor of sexual assault is gender nonconforming—particularly transgender—the negative consequences of telling their story to anyone are profound—profound enough to keep most transgender people silent about the violence. Rebecca L. Stotzer explains that for transgender individuals, "despite the growing anecdotal knowledge that violence is a significant problem in the transgender community, data about this issue are not readily available."[22] Similar to cisgender survivors-victims, acquaintances and family members of the transgender person are the "most common perpetrators of sexual violence."[23] Additionally, over half of all transgender people self-report that they have been victims-survivors of sexual violence. However, the rates of reporting that vio-

Figure 7.2 The rates of reporting sexual violence for individuals who identify as gender nonconforming are far lower than the actual occurrence of that violence. Gender fundamentalism, which is part of a gender binary structure that recognizes only two genders and punishes those who are nonconforming by further victimization, explains some of the reasons for this low rate of reporting. (Source: iStock. Credit: FG Trade)

lence to authorities is less than 20 percent, and almost half of those assaulted do not tell anyone at all.[24] The reasons for this silence are simple, yet complex: transphobia explains one piece of this lack of communication about the violence, victimization and revictimization explain yet another. In a society that encourages gender conformity, those who "transgress gender roles" are targets for punishment and violence against them by people committed to "gender fundamentalism."[25]

Transgender individuals report that the motivations for the assault and violence on the part of the perpetrator are usually identity-based—the person who assaults is transphobic and sees enacting violence and discrimination as legitimate expressions of that transphobia. Transphobia is not limited to assailants or perpetrators of sexual violence, however. When gender nonconforming individuals share their identities with others, they regularly experience "discrimination and abuse at home, in school, in the public sphere, in the workplace, as well as with landlords, doctors, and public officials, including judges and police."[26] For transgender individuals, the discrimination and abuse are profound. "Despite having attended college or gained a college degree or higher at 1.74 times the rate of the general population (47 percent versus 27 percent)," transgender individuals experience "unemployment at twice the rate" and live in "extreme poverty ($10,000 annually or less) at four times the rate of the general population."[27]

The **burden of silence** reinforces the consequences of talking about sexual violence with anyone, particularly as a transgender person, where exposing one's identity risks the very real threat of further victimization and discrimination.

COMMUNICATION AND THE BURDEN OF ABILITY

We know that individuals with disabilities are at a higher risk for being the victims of interpersonal violence than their nondisabled peers, that women of color with physical disabilities are at a higher risk of sexual assault than their peers who are white and physically disabled, and that women with intellectual disabilities are four times more likely to be victims of interpersonal violence and sexual assault than their non-intellectually disabled peers.[28] But we rarely hear their stories. Douglas Brownridge, professor of Community Health Sciences, describes the "the paucity of research on women with disabilities who experience violence by an intimate partner." The scarcity of research stems, in part, because of the false assumption that women with physical disabilities are asexual. But it also hinges on low reporting rates. Women with physical disabilities may be reluctant to report violence, which usually is perpetrated by a caregiver, partner, or spouse, because they may fear that if they report the violence, they will lose not only the services of the caregiver or partner, but be forced to move into a less independent living situation.[29]

In one of the few studies available on interpersonal violence and women with disabilities, Bette Bottoms and her colleagues report that for individuals with intellectual disabilities, the **burden of ability** is particularly profound: "their claims are unlikely to be reported to authorities, acted on by authorities if reported, or prosecuted in court."[30] Women with intellectual disabilities often are "seen as easy targets." Perpetrators, usually family members and caregivers, assume that women with intellectual disabilities "will not complain and have less access to the criminal justice system than other women." When assaults are reported, "the accounts are often not believed, not fully investigated, or not prosecuted" because legal systems are not equipped to work with or represent women with intellectual disabilities.[31] When scholars investigated the ability of individuals to tell their stories, and the believability of those stories, however, via a mock-trial study, what they found was enlightening. Jurors were more likely to believe the testimony of a person labeled mildly intellectually disabled than when that same testimony was attributed to person labeled of average intelligence. They found the person labeled mildly intellectually disabled more credible, more believable, and decided in favor of the intellectually disabled person more often than the non-disabled person.

Janine Benedet and Isabel Grant, law professors at the University of British Columbia, report that women with intellectual disabilities "experience the same or very similar kinds of unfairness as sexual assault complainants as [do] all women. It is not only women with [intellectual] disabilities who find themselves being judged on the quality of their verbal or physical resistance when trying to establish the credibility of their claims of nonconsent." Women with intellectual disabilities do not necessarily need special provisions; they do, however, need to be heard, supported, and defended.[32] Regarding women with physical disabilities, Brownridge explains that, yes, attention to their particular forms of vulnerability is important, but "more attention should also be directed toward perpetrators. Efforts to reduce patriarchal dominating and male sexually proprietary behaviors in the general population will also help to reduce partner violence against women with disabilities."[33]

These constraints—the burdens of performance, credibility, silence, and ability—actively circulate in our discourse about sexual violence. They keep the focus of our attention on the victims-survivors and do help us understand how difficult talking about sexual violence as a victim-survivor can be. However, they also prevent us from focusing on the perpetrators of sexual violence and the discursive regimes at work in our communication, which we turn to next.

COMMUNICATION ABOUT THE PERPETRATORS: FORCES BEYOND THEIR CONTROL

In "Telling It Like It Isn't," Linda Coates and Alan Wade report that the "degree of responsibility" assigned to any sexual assault offender "depends only in part upon his or her actions. It hinges also on how both the offender's and the victim's actions are represented linguistically in police reports, legal arguments, testimony, related judgments, and more broadly in professional and public discourse." Coates and Wade reviewed seven years of Canadian judicial decisions (1986–1993) in cases in which the terms "sexual" and "assault" were included in the text (total of 64 judgments; all offenders were men; the victims were women, boys and girls—no other identity categories were recorded). Coates and Wade discovered that "judges characterized sexual assaults most frequently as erotic, romantic, or affectionate acts. For example, an offender forcing his tongue into the victim's mouth was reformulated as 'they French kissed,' rape was reformulated as 'intercourse' or 'unwanted sex,' and violating physical contact was reformulated as 'fondling.' None of these accounts reflect the unilateral nature of sexualized violence or the victim's experience of those acts."[34]

The judges in Coates and Wade's study also relied on what Susan Ehrlich calls the **grammar of non-agency,** which paints the offender with an **aura of non-responsibility,** a victim of forces beyond his own control.[35] Coates and Wade found judges used eight categories of non-agency to minimize the responsibility assigned to the offender (see table 7.1) Coates and Wade explain that the logic in none of these categories rings true. That is, the justifications for the violent behaviors do not logically match up with the actions.

Table 7.1 Categories of Non-Agency/Non-Responsibility

Category	Excuse	Why Invalid
Alcohol and drug abuse	His abuse eroded his inhibitions and made him act out of character.	When intoxicated or under the influence of drugs, the majority of men do not assault women sexually.
Sexual drive	His lack of sexual fulfillment was a precipitating factor.	Making sexualized assault synonymous with sexual activity conceals the violence, casts the act as mutual, and "is analogous" to the "idea that someone can fulfill his need for positive social affiliation by assaulting people."
Psychopathology	He was just reacting to a pre-existing psychological disorder.	Possessing a psychopathology minimizes the violence and casts the offender as "indulging his needs," suggesting a "biological requirement that must be met in order to survive"—like breathing.
Dysfunctional family upbringing	His damaged family background caused the assault.	A dysfunctional family explains the violence as inevitable and reduces the responsibility of the individual by placing the blame on his past rather than on him.
Trauma and stress	Family pressures, combat experiences, and external stresses caused behavior.	Using past trauma and stress as an explanation for the violence casts the acts as occurring because of prior trauma rather than something he did deliberately, even in light of a past trauma.
Character traits	The offender is a violent person, he had no choice but to behave violently.	Essentializing an offender as violent by nature requires that we ask the question, "Can a person act in a way contrary to his or her nature?" and answer it with "No, he cannot."
Emotion	His experience of overwhelming emotions, such as anger, caused the assault.	Ascribing overwhelming emotion as the cause of violence denies the deliberateness and seriousness of what are, in fact, premeditated assaults.
Loss of control	He didn't intend to hurt them, things just got out of hand.	Attributing violent behaviors to a loss of control or things "getting out of hand," even when the victim is a small child, denies the deliberateness and seriousness of the assault. "Difficulty controlling" one's own behavior becomes "he didn't intend to hurt them, but he just could not help himself."

SOURCE: Modified from Linda Coates and Allan Wade, "Telling It Like It Isn't: Obscuring Perpetrator Responsibility for Violent Crime," *Discourse and Society* 15, no. 5 (2004): 507–514.

Coates and Wade conclude that the discourse employed by the judges minimized not only the violence done to the victims but also the responsibility of the offender in perpetrating that violence. By portraying the men (judges relied on binary constructions of sex and gender) who committed the violence as non-agents "compelled by forces beyond their control (e.g. alcohol, sexual urges, pathology, emotion, stressful experiences, or past experiences)," judges reformulated the deliberate and violent actions by men as "non-deliberate and even non-autonomous."[36]

Outside the courtroom and in our popular press, the grammar of non-agency and non-responsibility also are present. When celebrity figures, such as William Kennedy Smith and Kobe Bryant, were charged with sexual assault, their defense attorneys described them as "respectable" professionals from "good" families and, as such, unlikely to engage in such violent behaviors (the jury found Smith not guilty and Bryant's case reached a settlement before going to trial). News reports often describe the victim, rather than the perpetrator, as deviant. Relying on rape scripts and myths, journalists regularly blame the victim for having engaged in actions deemed suspect or problematic.[37] This ignores the fact that empirical research shows that "men and women are similarly literate" in understanding refusals for sex, even complex ones, but that "to avoid culpability, rapists falsely claim they misunderstood whether the other person agreed to sexual activity."[38]

Similarly, even though employees of Harvey Weinstein, the media mogul who victims-survivors confronted about sexual abuse, reported that though his "mistreatment of women" was considered a "serial problem," there was a "culture of complicity . . . with numerous people throughout his companies fully aware of his behavior but either abetting it or looking the other way." Weinstein's advisor describes him as "an old dinosaur learning new ways" and as someone needing to understand that because of his power, some of his "words and behaviors can be perceived as inappropriate, even intimidating."[39] Bill Cosby, once considered to be "America's Dad" (but who now is a registered sex offender and sentenced to prison for his sexual violence), was said to be of no "risk to the community," especially since "there have been no new allegations of sexual abuse leveled at him since 2004."[40]

When sexual violence occurs within organizations, as it does on college and university campuses, for example, the grammar of non-agency and the aura of non-responsibility also are present. Although the majority of institutions of higher education in the United States officially report that sexual assault does not occur on their campuses, since 2012, Pennsylvania State University, Amherst College, University of California Berkeley, Dartmouth College, Occidental College, Otterbein University, Swarthmore College, University of Montana, University of North Carolina, University of Southern California, and Yale University "have all been criticized, investigated, or found liable for sexual violence on campus."[41] Spokespeople for these institutions explain the sexual violence that occurs at "officially sanctioned university activities," such as recruiting events for athletes, are the responsibility of the individuals involved. Despite the fact that these campus activities are officially approved, supported, and sanctioned and that dependence on "the presence of women as accessories" is well known and publicized ("potential team members are assigned female 'Ambassadors' to guide them during campus visits"), campus organizations take no responsibility for the cultures of sexual violence they create and support.[42] Instead, hegemonic notions of masculinity, including dominance over women and access to their bodies are valorized and accepted as the norm.

In the majority of these cases, the harms done to the person violated are rarely addressed; instead, news coverage focuses on "how [a] town or the rapists' families were themselves affected by the rape." In "Monsters, Playboys, Virgins, and Whores: Rape Myths in News Media's Coverage of Sexual Violence," Shannon O'Hara reports that coverage often "shifts accountability away from those responsible." One reporter wrote that the rape "left many residents in the working-class neighbourhood where the attack took place with unanswered questions. Among them is, if the allegations are proved, 'how could their young men have been drawn into such an act?'" Another wrote, "Many have been wondering how so many young males [19 of them] could stand accused of violating a sixth grade student."[43]

But it is not only the harms done to those assaulted that are ignored, it's their actual voices. Barbara Bowman, in "Bill Cosby Raped Me," shares that only after a male comedian's skit went viral did the accusations gain any credibility: "While I am grateful for the new attention to Cosby's crimes, I must ask my own questions: Why wasn't *I* believed? Why didn't *I* get the same reaction of shock and revulsion when I originally reported it? Why was *I*, a victim of sexual assault, further wronged by victim blaming when I came forward? The women victimized by Bill Cosby have been talking about his crimes for more than a decade. Why didn't *our* stories go viral?"[44]

COMMUNICATION FROM THE PERPETRATORS: "LEGITIMATE FORMS OF HUMILIATION"

Alexa Dodge, of Carleton University in Canada, explored the digital postings of photographs by the rapists of three young women, postings that led to their suicides. Dodge shares that the narrative of the passivity of the rapist is, in fact, a lie: here is why. Dodge explains that a photograph is "a kind of promise that the event will continue," a promise that the assault will continue to be viewed and will not only "haunt their victims in a very tangible way"[45] but also celebrate and commend the actions of the rapists. The photographs taken during the rapes were "taken unobstructed. The field of vision is clear. No one is seen lunging in front of the camera to intercept the view." No one is preventing the photographer from capturing the image. "This is torture in plain view" and it occurs in a "safety zone that surrounds and supports the persecutors" in the scene.[46]

Dodge explains that the photographer, as well as the rapists, "do not recognize themselves as morally corrupt"; one of the rapists, who was assaulting the young woman from behind, "does not even attempt to hide his identity, but rather turns toward the camera, smiling and posing with a thumbs-up gesture."[47] The photographs are to be read as entertainment, as "legitimate forms of humiliation," and are "so widely shared, it seems, that there was hardly a thought that something might be amiss here."[48] There is no passivity or "unusual behavior" on the part of these young men, they are actively engaged in sexual assault and actively documenting the images, even as they assault,

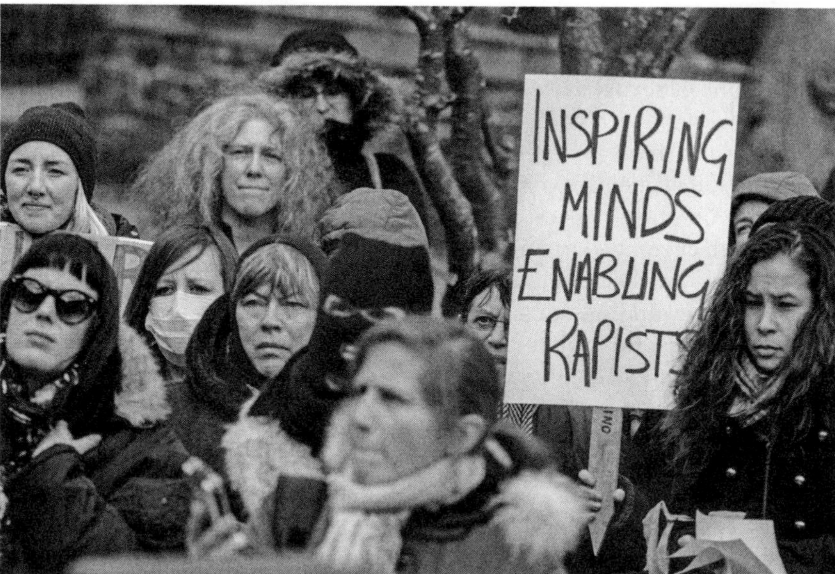

Figure 7.3 These protestors are responding to the discovery of a Facebook group operated by thirteen male dentistry students at Dalhousie University. On Facebook, the group advocated drugging and raping their female classmates as well as having "hate" sex with them. Because posting misogynistic messages on Facebook is not considered a crime, officials allowed the women targeted to decide how to deal with the violent postings. The women choose restorative justice, a process in which victims and perpetrators come together to consider what and why something happened and how to respond to and fix it. (Source: iStock. Credit: shauni)

so the images can be distributed later on Facebook pages and other social media sites.

Many who saw these photos interpreted the images through the lens of a rape culture. **Rape culture**—a culture that sympathizes more with the perpetrators than with the victims-survivors—comprises "a complex set of beliefs that encourage male sexual aggression and support violence against women. It is a society where violence is seen as sexy and sexuality as violent. In rape culture women perceive a continuum of threatened violence that ranges from sexual remarks to sexual touching to rape itself. A rape culture condones physical and emotional terrorism as the norm."[49] In a rape culture, these photographs are read as though the young women are "sluts," deserving of violence and violation. The images of the young men, in a rape culture, are dismissed as "boys being boys."

These are not passive acts, however, nor are they "legitimate" forms of humiliation. They are conscious and preplanned, they are deliberate and deliberately humiliating, and they are recorded and distributed. Lockwood Harris explains that these photographs are not misunderstandings in communication, but instead are acts of malice.[50] Their recording and distribution speak volumes about the agency and intentionality of the act: "The online dissemination of photographs of sexual assault not only extends the experience of the sexual assault, but can be seen as an act of sexual violence in and of itself, the impact of which is sometimes described as even more traumatic than the original assault."[51] The women are continually victimized and the men are continually rapists.

Although current communication about and from the perpetrators of sexual violence overwhelmingly denies their culpability and remorse, individuals are speaking out and speaking back to this erasure of accountability. In the section that follows, we explore the communication that resists this erasure of perpetrator guilt and liability and engage the communication that is working to create private and public spaces that are free from sexual violence.

STORIES OF RESILIENCE AND RESISTANCE

As we work to hold the perpetrators of sexual violence responsible for that violence, we must change the discourses that grant those with power and privilege the right to behave violently toward others and then to describe that violence through their own lenses. Victims, survivors, and their allies are speaking back to the common narratives of sexual violence and harassment, holding the perpetrators responsible for that violence and revealing the devastating consequences of that violence. To better share these narratives of resilience and resistance, alternative forms and outlets are often created for them, circumventing the structures of power and privilege that wish to keep victims-survivors and their allies silenced.

On the Streets

Kelly Oliver, feminist philosopher and novelist, defines **response-ability** as "the capacity to collectively respond to sexual violence and its cultures of racial, gendered and sexuality harassment."[52] For Oliver, and those who are response-able, the "capacity to respond and be responded to" is an ethical obligation: "the response-able witness is someone positioned proximately to document harassment, catcalls and rape jokes, among other communicative signifiers of rape culture," and to use "the tools of mobile phone video, audio recording and Google mapping techniques," as well as YouTube videos, blogs, tweets, Instagram, and other social media outlets to talk back to violence.[53]

The tone of this response-ability can be an in-your-face humor or a brutal honesty that challenges the "victim-blaming rhetoric" so prevalent in discussions of and assumptions about sexual assault and violence. The posts "place responsibility for sexual [and other] violence on those who perpetrate and support it" while the documentation reveals the harsh reality of sexual violence and assault in public places. Posts often contain **trigger warnings** that give users and viewers advance notice of "graphic topics" that may be upsetting and cover the range of "the various ways in which our culture excuses, normalizes, and sometimes condones rape, sexual assault," racism, homophobia, transphobia, ableism and the violence accompanying these isms and phobias.[54]

Examples of this witnessing and mapping can be found at stfurapeculture.tumblr.com, fanmail.wordpress.com/streetharassment, twitter.com/iHollaback, harassmap.org, globalcitizen.org, sexual assault and the LGBTQ community, violence against trans and nonbinary people, transrespect.org, Trans Murder Monitoring project (TMM), and more. Carrie Rentschler, feminist media studies scholar, shares that these "responses to rape culture" take charge of the discourse that reinforces rape culture and responds to it.[55] The responses "hold accountable those who are responsible for its practices when mainstream news media, police and school authorities do not." Rentschler explains that social media can connect "the dots from Penn State to India to Steubenville. . . . If instances of teenage girls being sexually assaulted and cyberbullied are so common that they rarely make the news . . . social media are increasingly understood as a key platform of communicative response-ability for anti-rape activists and feminist critics."[56] Those working with and for the Trans Murder Monitoring project explain that "the members of the TvT team wish that such research was unnecessary (because no trans and/or gender-diverse people were murdered)" but it is, because "the data prove, in vividly graphic form, that murders of trans and/or gender-diverse people do occur in all six world regions."[57] The communication coming from these uses of social media and mapping are challenging victim blaming rhetoric inherent in rape culture "in order to place responsibility for sexual violence on those who perpetrate and support it."[58]

On College Campuses

Two high-profile rape cases, one at Stanford University and the other at Columbia University, also are part of widespread efforts on the part of those who have been assaulted to change the ways we speak and think about rape. Emily Doe (a pseudonym) and Emma Sulkowicz responded to the failure on the part of legal and campus officials to prosecute the men who raped them by speaking out in ways rarely heard in popular media or legal proceedings. Both engaged in public performances that spoke against the erasure of women's experiences of sexual assault by engaging an alternative narrative. Dow, in her victim impact statement to the courtroom at the trial, addressed her rapist directly, by using her own words to describe her experience. In this excerpt, she addresses her supporters:

> When I was told to be prepared in case we didn't win, I said, I can't prepare for that. He was guilty the minute I woke up. No one can talk me out of the hurt he caused

> me. . . . He has been found guilty of three serious felonies and it is time for him to accept the consequences of his actions. . . . To conclude [this statement], I want to say thank you. . . . Thank you to girls across the nation that wrote cards to my DA to give to me, so many strangers who cared for me. And finally, to girls everywhere, I am with you. On nights when you feel alone, I am with you. When people doubt you or dismiss you, I am with you. I fought every day for you. So never stop fighting, I believe you. As the author Anne Lamott once wrote, "Lighthouses don't go running all over an island looking for boats to save; they just stand there shining."[59]

The statement also reached a larger audience than just those in the courtroom when it was published online.

Sulkowicz also changed the narrative around sexual violence in two performance pieces, *Mattress Performance* (*Carry That Weight*) and *Ceci n'est pas un viol* (*This Is Not a Rape).* In *Mattress Performance,* Sulkowicz carried a 50-pound mattress everywhere they[60] went thought their final semester at Columbia University. In *Ceci n'est pas un viol,* Sulkowicz uses both written language and visual images "to undo public assumptions about the experience of a rape by redirecting the discomfort" of the rape away from theirself as the victim and instead "onto audiences."[61]

By giving voice to their experiences in ways that challenge commonly held assumptions about sexual violence, Doe and Sulkowicz showcase the ways that institutional approaches to sexual assault and violence "access violence through a male perspective," ignore female bodies, and "continually fail to deliver justice to women who experience sexual violence."[62] Giving voice to their experiences in their own words and through their own performances, Doe and Sulkowicz share with their listeners the physical, emotional, and material realities of sexual assault and violence.

The result of these alternative discourses, Stephanie Larson explains, is a visceral engagement of sexual violence. This visceral engagement "exposes an orientation to and violence felt within the body's deep insides," creating an alternative discursive framework for understanding rape.[63] This discursive framing moves listeners away from "hearing about pain," which can lead to doubt or suspicion about that pain, and into an emotional, gut-level engagement of that pain. Larson shares, "if audiences feel discomfort while listening and watching, then such tactics are rhetorically successful."[64]

In Social Settings

The mobile phone app Circle of 6 is designed to intervene—to disrupt an interaction before the violence happens. Circle of 6 is a "survivor-led and queer-led initiative" that draws "from the experiences of sexual assault survivors, youth health experts and LGBTQ users." Described as a "tool to support friends in potentially dangerous situations" as well as to encourage bystander intervention, software developer Christine Corbett and her team designed the app to "feel like a lifestyle app and to be discreet." Recognizing that young women and men often find themselves in unsafe situations as they explore their sexuality, experiment with alcohol, and establish their identities and independence, the Circle of 6 app links one individual with six trusted friends or adults. Users can tap several messages: a "Come and get me. I need help getting home safely" icon, with GPS coordinates of their location; a "Call and pretend you need me. I need an interruption" icon, if they are feeling unsafe but unsure of how to exit a situation; an "I need to talk" icon, when they are confused about a situation or relationship; as well as icons that link them directly "to information about sexuality, relationships, and safety" and hotlines.[65]

Circle of 6 is used by over 350,000 individuals in thirty-six countries and has as its motto "I won't let violence happen in my circle." Corbett shares that youth often are "unsafe with a friend" or someone they thought was a friend, so "getting out of a situation that makes you uncomfortable" can be confusing and tricky. Communication is central to the success of Circle of 6, as users have already discussed with their "circle that these are issues," that sexual assault is wrong and a problem we can solve. "They've had conversations beforehand, discussed a plan," and established mechanisms for safety. Circle of 6 also "brings young men and boys into the conversation." They are a part of preventing the problem because they can respond, tap for help if a friend is behaving badly, and even get answers to their own questions and help getting out of unsafe situations. Corbett reminds us that it is "positive to be able to look out for friends and have friends look out for you."[66]

In Communities

Founded by Tarana Burke in 2006, the "me too" movement (the phrase was not originally capitalized) caught the attention of the media when #MeToo went viral. Focused on helping "survivors of sexual violence, particularly Black women and girls, and other young women of color from low wealth communities, find pathways to healing," Burke's goal was to bring together survivors of sexual assault, providing resources for them to heal, and to create a "community of advocates, driven by survivors, who will be at the forefront of creating solutions to interrupt sexual violence in their communities." Alyssa Milano initiated the tweet that brought #MeToo into the public eye, but when black women saw it, they feared another coopting of the work of black women, and so they spoke out about Burke's work and the legacy of white women erasing that work. Milano apologized for not knowing of Burke's work, offered to collaborate with her, and publicly credited Burke for her work founding the "me too" movement.[67]

Although Burke had kept her work with survivors of sexual violence out of the public eye, as a way to protect the privacy of the survivors, when #MeToo went viral, Burke states that a "vital conversation about sexual violence" was "thrust into the national dialogue."[68] Milano's tweet, and the decade of work by

Burke that was unknown to many white feminists, reminds those who are willing to listen of "a great lack of intersectionality across these various movements." But also, Burke explains, Me Too is "bigger than just one person. . . . It's bigger than me and bigger than Alyssa Milano. Neither one of us should be centered in this work. This is about survivors."[69]

Burke has a vision for a particular kind of world. Not the #MeToo world trivialized or mocked by media but rather, a world "where sexual violence and the behaviors that contribute to normalizing it are stigmatized." Burke "recalls hearing somebody compare the normalization of sexual violence with the normalization of smoking: 'When you see someone smoking these days, you're kind of like, really? Smoking is definitely not cool anymore, and the folks who have worked against that have done a great job.' What if we could do that for rape?" She adds, "We could actually live in a time where sexual violence and sexual harassment, which is a gateway to more severe forms of sexual violence, [would be uncool]. We could live in a time where guys are going to be like 'Really, dude? Are you really catcalling? We don't do that anymore. We don't touch a girl's butt.'"[70]

To that end, in 2017 Burke and her movement joined Girls for Gender Equity (founded by Joanne Smith in 2000). Girls for Gender Equity focuses on building a movement that is designed to "eliminate gender-based violence within school systems" and communities. To accomplish this goal, Girls for Gender Equity clearly defines what sexual harassment in schools is, decriminalizes schools and creates safe learning environments, and supports the "free expression of gender and sexuality through research and policy." Girls for Gender Equity also created a Young Women's Advisory Council, designed to center the voices of "cis and trans young women and gender nonconforming young people of color ages 12–24" in their governing process, as well as Sisters in Strength, a group of youth organizers who engage in "community organizing around gender-based violence . . . [confronting] the multiple layers of individual and institutional discrimination that threaten the safety of girls and women."[71]

Smith and Burke explain that they want to expand the conversation about sexual violence so that it speaks to the "needs of a broader spectrum of survivors including young people, queer, trans, and disabled folks, black women and girls, and all communities of color." Smith and Burke are seeking accountability, "long term and sustainable change, and attention to the systemic and global nature of the problem of sexual violence." They report, "Our work continues to focus on helping those who need it find entry points for individual healing" while also disrupting "the systems that allow for the global proliferation of sexual violence."[72]

In Free Trade Zones

Situated in northern Mexico, Cuidad Juárez shares borders with both New Mexico and Texas. Cuidad Juárez is home to more multinational corporations than any other country, the result of NAFTA's (North American Free Trade Agreement) creation of tariff-free manufacturing zones between Canada, the United States, and Mexico. Cuidad Juárez, however, is perhaps better known as the "site of disappeared and murdered women and girls."[73] Explanations for these murders and disappearances are both complex and appalling simple. NAFTA gave rise to ***maquiladoras,*** factories that manufacture goods specifically for export and make their profits, in large part, by paying their workers less than they would be paid in factories outside Mexico. Women comprise more than half of these workers, and because they cannot afford childcare, they often work at night. Moreover, the *maquila* worker rarely can afford to live near the *maquiladora* so she must travel long distances to and from work, alone, making her an easy target for men to violate and even murder. The *maquila* worker also is viewed as disposable: "If a woman disappears" on her way to or from work "the *maquiladora* owners can simply replace her with another laboring body."[74] The USMCA (United States–Mexico–Canada Agreement, sometimes called NAFTA 2.0) that replaced NAFTA would increase Mexican wages slightly in *maquiladora* factories in exchange for continued free trade zone status, but the situation for women would remain unchanged.

Mexico's government has failed to respond to these murders and disappearances: "currently, on average, seven women are killed every day—their bodies often showing evidence of mutilation, torture, and sexual abuse."[75] Moreover, thousands of girls and women have gone missing—their bodies have never been found.[76] Communication scholar Michelle Holling asks not just why these girls and women have been murdered or gone missing—a profound question in itself—but why these girls and women are being killed in the ways they are. The brutality of the murders and assaults is evident, and from those bodies found, and the stories told by those who have survived, we learn of "unadulterated hatred and hostility toward the poor brown female body."[77] The murders are known as ***feminicidios,*** because the term reveals not only the tragedy of those murdered or disappeared but also the extreme sexual and physical violence, unadulterated misogyny, and blatant sexism embedded in the acts.

Survivors and their families are engaging in what scholars call *testimonio.* Teresa Maria Linda Scholz explains that ***testimonio*** refers to a collective story, typically told by a single individual who belongs to a disenfranchised group. *Testimonio* gives voice to—explains to others—the histories and experiences not only of those who cannot be heard, but also those who have been silenced by power and privilege. Unlike the simple sharing of a story, however, *testimonios* "occupy" the listener such that the audience bearing witness to the *testimonio* may be called to action.[78] Holling explains that this is because the *feminicidio testimonio* positions "listeners as witnesses." In the telling, "listeners are gathered in the flesh as witnesses" to the atrocities. The space in which a *testimonio* is shared, the events leading up to the listeners arriving at that space, the way the *testimonio* is delivered (in the first person and in a circular

Figure 7.4 Cuidad Juárez, population 1.3 million, is situated on the Rio Grande, just south of El Paso, Texas. Juárez is home to *maquiladoras,* factories that manufacture goods for export, and also *feminicidios,* the murder and disappearance of women and girls in extremely violent ways. (Source: iStock. Credit: Denis Tangney, Jr.)

or nonlinear pattern of organization), the firsthand experience of the violence, and the recounting of that "hyper(gendered) violence" function to bring the murder and disappearance of girls and women "close to home for listeners": it becomes real, personal, and material.[79]

Holling and several students traveled to Cuidad Juárez to educate themselves, listen, and bear witness to one *testimonialista,* Alma. As Alma delivered her *feminicidio testimonio,* in which she described seven cases of violence and death, she mapped out a range of "sexual, physical and emotional abuse, verbal threats, and intimidation, all of which intend to harm, maim or kill" girls and women. The last case she spoke about was her sister's, Corazón, who "fought her attackers, was assaulted sexually and physically, and escaped (as reported by eyewitnesses)." Corazón "was later kidnapped by 'several men' who took 'her to a car and beat and raped her for about three hours.' Eyewitnesses reported the crime to police," but they never arrived nor do their records show evidence of any report. As Alma brought her *feminicidio testimonio* to a close, she shared the death threats she and other women were receiving, and also the "fear of attack, the fear of not being able to freely walk in the streets, the fear of what would happen to my children if something were to happen to me. . . . And so the only thing left for me to do as a mother and a family member here in this city is every time I leave my house, I say goodbye to my family as though it's going to be the last time."[80]

Holling explains that *feminicidio testimonios* are discursive acts of resistance—they are a refusal to be silenced, regardless of the danger in speaking out. Turning listeners into witnesses, *feminicidio testimonios* and the *testimonialistas* communicate that girls and women are willing to continue "to live and move forward in a struggle for justice amidst" horrific violence and death threats.[81] Communication scholar Nina Lozano-Reich shares that because "the impunity surrounding these crimes continues," new activist groups are "working side by side with earlier waves of activist groups to denounce the Mexican government's rhetoric that the *feminicidios* are merely 'a dark legend.'" Lozano-Reich continues, "only when the deadly material conditions within the free trade zones of the Juárez border change locally," and economic systems that put profits ahead of human rights and safety change globally, "will the phenomenon of *feminicidio* cease."[82] Bearing witness to the *feminicidio testimonios* that are coming from the women and girls in Cuidad Juárez is a step toward changing those deadly economic structures.

THE POWER OF COMMUNITY

Ione Wells, a student studying for her exams at Oxford University in 2015, wrote a letter to the person who violently attacked her as she made her way home from a social gathering in London. Wells wrote, "I cannot address this letter to you, because I do not know your name. I only know that you have been charged with serious sexual assault and prolonged attack of a violent nature. And I have only one question." When you attacked me, Wells asked, "did you ever think of the people in your life?" Wells wrote, "I am a daughter, I am a friend, I am a girlfriend, I am a pupil, I am a cousin, I am a niece, I am a neighbor, I am the employee who served everyone down the road coffee in the café under the railway." These people are her community, she explained, and the man who attacked her attacked every one of them.

Explaining that there are "infinitely more good people in the world than bad," Wells said people could never underestimate the power of community. Wells reminded the man who attached her of the response to the July 7, 2005 terrorist bombings in London: "the terrorists did not win, because the whole community of London got back on the Tube the next day. You've carried out your attack, but now I'm getting back on my Tube." Like the *testimonialistas*, those using social media and mapping, and those creating apps and organizations that empower young people, Wells and her community refused to let the attacker set the terms by which they would live their lives. They would take the Tube after dark, walk on their streets alone, move about in public, "because we

7.1. GUIDE TO COMMUNICATION

Sexual Violence and Intersectional Literacy

Developing an intersectional vocabulary around the topic of sexual violence can feel quite challenging. To assist you in developing this new vocabulary, try the following:

1. Over several weeks, explore how fluent are you in the intersectional language of sexual violence. To do this, listen for the non-intersectional language of burden, credibility, silence, and ability in media, group or interpersonal conversations, and even in your own language. Record the specific words and phrases that make this discourse about sexual violence non-intersectional. If you wanted to speak intersectionally about sexual violence, how might you reframe these conversations?
2. Consider the approaches to resistance you have learned about in this chapter (telling stories of successful resistance, stigmatizing sexual violence, engaging bystanders, reporting and responding, building community, sharing histories, and educating people). Do you already engage in some of these acts of resistance? Are there others you would like to participate in? To whom do you or would you direct your messages—who is or would be your audience? What is your message? Are there other forms of resistance you have seen, or would like to engage, as you tell an intersectional story about sexual violence?

will not ingrain or submit to the idea that we are putting ourselves in danger in doing so."

Wells published her letter to the attacker in her school newspaper, asking those who wanted to join in the conversation to reply to the hashtag "NotGuilty . . . to show that we could all stand up against sexual assault."[83] Almost overnight, the letter went viral, and Wells began receiving letters and tweets from women and men around the world. She explains that her letter and the campaign that followed gave real people, not journalists and news broadcasters, "what they needed and had previously lacked: a platform to speak out, the reassurance they weren't alone or to blame for what happened to them, and open discussions that would help to reduce stigma around the issue." Citing Nelson Mandela, Wells says, "you must never allow the enemy to determine the grounds for battle." We cannot, she adds, fight prejudice with prejudice or injustice with more injustice. Use the internet, share your story, in order to "network, to have signal, to connect—all these terms that imply bringing people together" so we can hear our voices and stories and support rather than divide.[84]

Resources

Tarana Burke, "Me Too Is a Movement, Not a Moment," filmed November 2018 in Palm Springs, CA, TEDWomen video, 16:02, https://www.ted.com/talks/tarana_burke_me_too_is_a_movement_not_a_moment#t-942137.

Kirby Dick, director and writer, *The Hunting Ground* (Park City, UT: Sundance Film Festival; Chain Camera Pictures, 2015).

Kirby Dick, director and writer, *The Invisible War* (Park City, UT: Sundance Film Festival; Chain Camera Pictures, 2012).

Kate Lockwood Harris, "Yes Means Yes and No Means No, But Both These Mantras Need to Go: Communication Myths in Consent Education and Anti-Rape Activism," *Journal of Applied Communication Research* 46, no. 2 (2018): 155–178.

Ione Wells, "How We Talk about Sexual Assault Online," filmed June 2016 in Banff, Alberta, TEDSummit video, 14:02, https://www.ted.com/talks/ione_wells_how_we_talk_about_sexual_assault_online.

Notes

1. Michelle Rodino-Colocino, "Forum: Me Too, #MeToo: Countering Cruelty with Empathy," *Communication and Critical/Cultural Studies* 15, no. 1 (2018): 96.
2. Because the term "victim" holds power for some individuals but is disempowering for others, and the term "survivor" empowers some yet feels like an erasure of experience to others, I use the two together throughout this chapter.
3. Corey Rayburn, "To Catch a Sex Thief: The Burden of Performance in Rape and Sexual Assault Trials," *Journal of Gender and Law* 15 (2006): 446, 460.
4. Rayburn, "To Catch a Sex Thief," 473.
5. Rayburn, "To Catch a Sex Thief," 472.
6. Rayburn, "To Catch a Sex Thief," 473.
7. Rayburn, "To Catch a Sex Thief," 466.
8. Rayburn, "To Catch a Sex Thief," 462.
9. Rayburn, "To Catch a Sex Thief," 467.
10. Maureen Ryan, "The Progress and Pitfalls of Television's Treatment of Rape," *Variety,* December 6, 2016, http://variety.com/2016/tv/features/rape-tv-television-sweet-vicious-jessica-jones-game-of-thrones-1201934910/.
11. Ryan, "Progress and Pitfalls."
12. Lisa M. Cuklanz and Sujata Moorti, "Television's 'New' Feminism: Prime-Time Representations of Women and Victimization," *Critical Studies in Media Communication* 23, no. 4 (October 2006): 302–321; Sarah Projansky, "Rihanna's Closed Eyes," *The Velvet Light Trap,* no. 65 (Spring 2010): 71–73; Sarah Projansky, "The Elusive/Ubiquitous Representation of Rape: A Historical Survey of Rape in U.S. Film, 1903–1972," *Cinema Journal* 41, no. 1 (Fall 2001): 63–90, doi: 10.1353/cj.2001.0023; Sarah Projansky, *Watching Rape: Film and Television in Postfeminist Culture* (New York: New York University Press, 2001).
13. Irena Lieberman, "I Hope This Letter Will Reach You," in *Women for Afghan Women: Shattering Myths and Claiming the Future,* ed. Sunita Mehta (New York: Palgrave Macmillan, 2002), 168.
14. Lieberman, "I Hope This Letter Will Reach You," 171.
15. Lieberman, "I Hope This Letter Will Reach You," 171.
16. Lieberman, "I Hope This Letter Will Reach You," 172.
17. Sara L. McKinnon, "Citizenship and the Performance of Credibility: Audiencing Gender-based Asylum Seekers in the U.S. Immigration Courts," *Text and Performance Quarterly* 29, no. 3 (2009): 207.
18. McKinnon, "Citizenship and Credibility," 210.
19. McKinnon, "Citizenship and Credibility," 210.
20. McKinnon, "Citizenship and Credibility," 215.
21. McKinnon, "Citizenship and Credibility," 218.
22. Rebecca L. Stotzer, "Violence Against Transgender People: A Review of United States Data," *Aggression and Violent Behavior* 14, no. 3 (2009): 171.
23. Stotzer, "Violence," 172–173.
24. Stotzer, "Violence," 173.
25. Emilia L. Lombardi, Riki Anne Wilchins, Diana Priesing, and Diana Malouf, "Gender Violence: Transgender Experiences of Violence and Discrimination," *Journal of Homosexuality* 42, no. 1 (2001): 90–91.
26. Jack Harrison, Jamie Grant, and Jody L. Herman, "A Gender Not Listed Here: Genderqueers, Gender Rebels, and OtherWise in the National Transgender Discriminatory Survey," *LGBTQ Public Policy Journal at the Harvard Kennedy School,* 2 (2011–2012): 13.
27. Harrison et al., "A Gender Not Listed Here," 13.
28. Bette Bottoms, Kari L. Nysse-Carris, Twana Harris, and Kimberly Tyda, "Jurors' Perceptions of Adolescent Sexual Assault Victims Who Have Intellectual Disabilities," *Law and Human Behavior* 27, no. 2 (2003):

205–227. See also Sandra Martin, Neepa Ray, Daniela Sotres-Alvarez, Lawrence L. Kupper, Kathryn E. Moracco, Pamela A. Dickens, Donna Scandlin, and Ziya Gizlice, "Physical and Sexual Assault of Women with Disabilities," *Violence Against Women* 12, no. 9 (2006): 823–837; and Ann I. Alriksson-Schmidt, Brian S. Armor, and Judy K. Thibadeau, "Are Adolescent Girls with Physical Disability at Risk for Sexual Violence?" *Journal of School Health* 80, no. 7 (2010): 361–367. No data regarding sexuality or queer identities and disability were available at the time of publication.

29. Douglas A. Brownridge, "Partner Violence Against Women with Disabilities: Prevalence, Risk and Explanations," *Violence Against Women* 12, no. 9 (2006): 806.
30. Bottoms et al., "Jurors' Perceptions of Adolescent Sexual Assault Victims," 206.
31. Janine Benedet and Isabel Grant, "Hearing the Sexual Assault Complaints of Women with Mental Disabilities: Consent, Capacity and Mistaken Belief," *McGill Law Journal* 52, no. 2 (2002): 257.
32. Benedet and Grant, "Hearing the Sexual Assault Complaints," 288.
33. Brownridge, "Partner Violence Against Women with Disabilities," 820.
34. Linda Coates and Allan Wade, "Telling It Like It Isn't: Obscuring Perpetrator Responsibility for Violent Crime," *Discourse and Society* 15, no. 5 (2004): 500–501.
35. Susan Ehrlich, quoted in Rayburn, "To Catch a Sex Thief," 462.
36. Coates and Wade, "Telling It Like It Isn't," 514.
37. Suzanne Enck-Wanzer and Scott A. Murray, "'How to Hook a Hottie': Teenage Boys, Hegemonic Masculinity, and *CosmoGirl!* Magazine," *Mediated Boyhoods: Boys, Teens and Young Men in Popular Media and Culture* (2011): 57–77; Projansky, *Watching Rape;* Marian Meyers, *News Coverage of Violence Against Women: Engendering Blame* (Thousand Oaks, CA: Sage, 1997).
38. Kate Lockwood Harris, "Yes Means Yes and No Means No, But Both These Mantras Need to Go: Communication Myths in Consent Education and Anti-Rape Activism," *Journal of Applied Communication Research* 46, no. 2 (2018): 160.
39. Ronan Farrow, "Harvey Weinstein's Accusers Tell Their Stories," *New Yorker,* October 13, 2017, https://www.newyorker.com/news/news-desk/from-aggressive-overtures-to-sexual-assault-harvey-weinsteins-accusers-tell-their-stories; Jodi Kantor and Megan Twohey, "Harvey Weinstein Paid Off Sexual Harassment Accusers for Decades," *New York Times,* October 5, 2017.https://www.nytimes.com/2017/10/05/us/harvey-weinstein-harassment-allegations.html.
40. Grahm Bowley and Joe Coscarelli, "Bill Cosby, Once a Model of Fatherhood, Is Sentenced to Prison," *New York Times,* September 25, 2018, https://www.nytimes.com/2018/09/25/arts/television/bill-cosby-sentencing.html.
41. Kate Lockwood Harris, "Show Them a Good Time: Organizing the Intersections of Sexual Violence," *Management Communication Quarterly* 27, no. 4 (2013): 572.
42. Lockwood Harris, "Show Them a Good Time," 571.
43. Shannon O'Hara, "Monsters, Playboys, Virgins, and Whores: Rape Myths in News Media's Coverage of Sexual Violence," *Language and Literature* (July 24, 2012): 254, https://doi.org/10.1177/0963947012444217.
44. Barbara Bowman, "Bill Cosby Raped Me. Why Did it Take 30 Years for People to Believe My Story?" *Washington Post,* November 13, 2014, https://www.washingtonpost.com/posteverything/wp/2014/11/13/bill-cosby-raped-me-why-did-it-take-30-years-for-people-to-believe-my-story/?noredirect=on&utm_term=.ea2ea8e4f1ea.
45. Alexa Dodge, "Digitizing Rape Culture: Online Sexual Violence and the Power of the Digital Photograph," *Crime Media Culture* 12, no. 1 (2016): 68.
46. Dodge, "Digitizing Rape Culture," 72.
47. Dodge, "Digitizing Rape Culture," 72.
48. Dodge, "Digitizing Rape Culture," 71.
49. Carrie A. Rentschler, "Rape Culture and the Feminist Politics of Social Media," *Girlhood Studies* 7, no. 1 (2014): 66.
50. Lockwood Harris, "Yes Means Yes," 160.
51. Dodge, "Digitizing Rape Culture," 69.
52. Rentschler, "Rape Culture," 68.
53. Rentschler, "Rape Culture," 69.
54. http://stfurapeculture.tumblr.com; http://photos.orlandoweekly.com/27-pulse-survivors-family-members-first-responders-share-stories/?slide=1&dear-world-orlando-pulse-series-daymon-gardner-for-dear-world-17.
55. Rentschler, "Rape Culture," 66.
56. Rentschler, "Rape Culture," 67.
57. TvT Research Project (2016); Trans Murder Monitoring, "Transrespect versus Transphobia Worldwide" (TvT) project website: www.transrespect.org/en/research/trans-murder-monitoring/.
58. Rentschler, "Rape Culture," 70.
59. Katie J.M. Baker, "Here's the Powerful Letter the Stanford Victim Read to Her Attacker," BuzzFeed News, June 3, 2016, https://www.buzzfeednews.com/article/katiejmbaker/heres-the-powerful-letter-the-stanford-victim-read-to-her-ra#.rgr32oDQz.
60. Sulkowicz's preferred pronouns are they/them.

61. Stephanie R. Larson, "'Everything Inside of Me Was Silenced: (Re)defining Rape Through Visceral Counterpublicity," *Quarterly Journal of Speech*, 104, no. 2 (2018): 135. Emma Sulkowicz's *Ceci n'est pas un viol* is available at http://www.emmasulkowicz.com/video.
62. Larson, "'Everything Inside of Me," 124.
63. Larson, "Everything Inside of Me," 127.
64. Larson, "Everything Inside of Me," 128.
65. "Circle of 6" (2011), https://www.circleof6app.com.
66. Christine Corbett, "An App to Help Prevent Sexual Violence," filmed March 2015 in Adliswill, TEDxYouth@Adliswil, YouTube video, 15:55, https://www.youtube.com/watch?v=s-HrNTJKO28.
67. Nicole A. Spigner, "In the Crawlspace: Hill, Franken, and #MeToo Pain," *The A-Line Journal of Progressive Thought* (February 6, 2018), https://alinejournal.com/arts-and-culture/crawlspace-hill-franken-metoo-pain/; and "The Woman Who Created #MeToo Long Before Hashtags," October 10, 2017, https://www.nytimes.com/2017/10/20/us/me-too-movement-tarana-burke.html.
68. "About," metoo, https://metoomvmt.org/about/.
69. "#MeToo Before Hashtags," https://www.nytimes.com/2017/10/20/us/me-too-movement-tarana-burke.html.
70. Vera Papisova, "Tarana Burke Is Launching a Social Platform: She Shares Her Plans with Teen Vogue," May 11, 2018, https://www.teenvogue.com/story/tarana-burke-is-launching-a-social-platform.
71. "Sisters in Strength," Girls for Gender Equity, https://www.ggenyc.org/programs/sisters-in-strength/.
72. GGENYC, "The Me Too Movement Lives at Girls for Gender Equity: A Joint Letter," May 18, 2017, https://medium.com/girls-for-gender-equity/the-me-too-movement-lives-at-girls-for-gender-equity-a-joint-letter-c60007bc2ff2.
73. Nina Maria Lozano-Reich, "Reconceptualizing *Feminicidio:* Border Materiality in Cuidad Juárez," *Women's Studies in Communication* 41, no. 2 (2018): 104.
74. Lozano-Reich, "Reconceptualizing *Feminicidio,*" 105.
75. Lozano-Reich, "Reconceptualizing *Feminicidio,*" 104.
76. Michelle A. Holling, "'So, My Name Is Alma, and I Am the Sister of . . .': A *Feminicidio Testimonio* of Violence and Violent Identifications," *Women's Studies in Communication,* 37 no. 3 (2014): 313.
77. Holling, "So, My Name Is Alma," 313–314.
78. Teresa Maria Linda Scholz, "The Rhetorical Power of *Testimonio* and *Ocupación:* Creating a Conceptual Framework for Analyzing Subaltern Rhetorical Agency," PhD diss., University of Colorado, 2007; Teresa Maria Linda Scholz, "Hablando Por (Nos) Otros, Speaking for Ourselves: Exploring the Possibilities of 'Speaking Por' Family and Pueblo in the Bolivian *Testimonio* 'Si Me Permiten Hablar,'" in *Latina/o Discourse in Vernacular Spaces: Somos du Una Voz?* ed. Michelle A. Holling and Bernadette M. Calafell (Lanham, MD: Lexington Books, 2011), 203–222.
79. Holling and Calafell, *Latina/o Discourse,* 332; see also 331–333.
80. Holling and Calafell, *Latina/o Discourse,* 331.
81. Holling and Calafell, *Latina/o Discourse,* 331.
82. Lozano-Reich, "Reconceptualizing *Feminicidio,*" 107.
83. Ione Wells, "How We Talk about Sexual Assault Online," filmed June 2016 in Banff, Alberta, TEDSummit video, 14:02, transcript, https://www.ted.com/talks/ione_wells_how_we_talk_about_sexual_assault_online/; and "About," #NotGuilty, http://notguiltycampaign.co.uk/about/
84. Wells, "How We Talk."

CHAPTER

8

Intersectional Approaches to Spaces for Learning

IN THIS CHAPTER, YOU WILL FIND . . .

KEY TERMS AND CONCEPTS

- bullying
- cultural homophobia
- cyberbullying
- hermeneutical injustice
- homophobic sexism
- microaggressions
- public mass murder

THE RIGHT TO SAFETY IN OUR SCHOOLS

Questions and disputes over how students learn, who should teach, and what should be taught have challenged communities, teachers, and politicians for more than two centuries.[1] Should our classrooms be sites of political debate and argument, from which a single truth prevails; spaces in which students learn to understand and engage differences, coming to appreciate multiple perspectives and approaches rather than a single truth; some combination of the two or even something entirely different? As challenging as these questions are, we also are faced with equally challenging questions of safety, and the lack of safety, for many students in our schools.

When students feel unsafe, their learning is profoundly affected; when they are unsafe, it's halted. This chapter takes an intersectional approach to school safety, addressing not just the physical and mental safety of our students, but the discourses that perpetuate a lack of safety, as well as those that provide students with agency and security. We begin this chapter by exploring bullying in our schools—in real time and online. We then turn to how bullying can escalate to deadly violence and the ways we frame that violence. Next, we explore matters of curriculum, define and unpack microaggressions, and consider non-binary pronouns. Finally, we turn to Title IX, the Civil Rights Act of 1964, and the Americans with Disabilities Act, which provide many students voice, access, and the structural support to advocate for change.

BULLYING

Defined as repetitive "abusive conduct that is threatening, humiliating, or intimidating," **bullying** in our schools takes the form of threats, "efforts to harm the reputation or relationships of a targeted youth," and damage to property. In schools, bullying threats are often accompanied by physical attacks, such as being shoved into a locker or toilet. Some bullying also falls "into criminal categories, such as harassment, hazing or assault."[2] Because of its prevalence—between one in three and one in four students report bullying at school—school officials are scrambling to address not just face-to-face bullying, but online stalking, online bulling, and the other ways technology facilitates the violation of a person's privacy and the defamation of their character. Bullying strategies are both discursive—the use of hostile and threatening language—and physical, and they can be difficult to spot and address. Educators and parents sometimes struggle with the differences between good-natured teasing and bullying, as well as the enormous damage done by the bullying discourses directed at certain students.

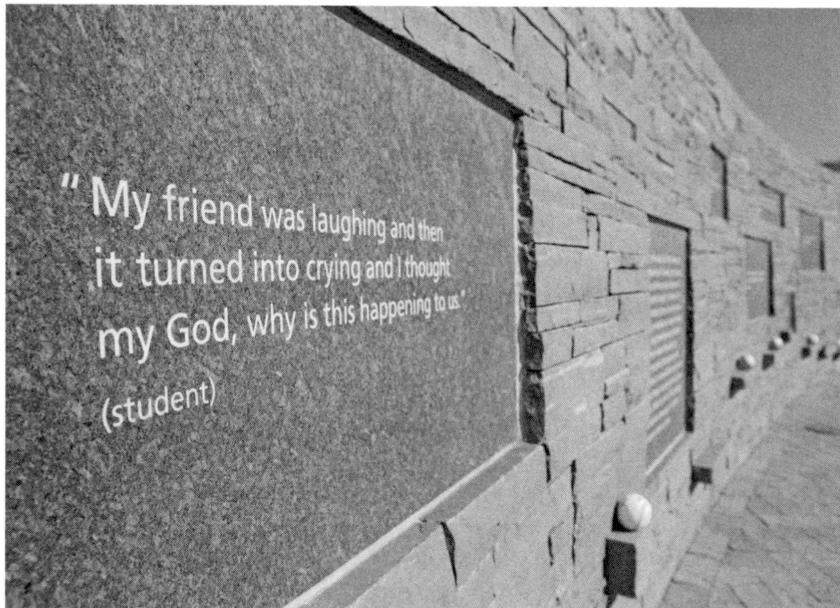

Figure 8.1 Although schools should be known as sites of education, Columbine High School is recognized as the site of one of the deadliest massacres perpetrated by two white male students on school grounds. This section of the Massacre Memorial Wall captures the danger present for students in many schools today. (Source: iStock. Credit: Banks Photos)

Who Bullies and Who Gets Bullied?

At schools, bullies target anyone perceived as different.[3] This obviously casts a wide net on potential targets for a bully because "different" includes just about everybody: youth who may be socially awkward, youth with disabilities, youth with religious differences, youth with high body mass indices, LGBTQ youth, youth who do not conform to stereotypical norms for gender, youth who mature early or late, youth who are high achievers academically, and those who are not doing well.[4] Bonnie Carter and Victor Spencer note that among this list of potential targets, students with both visible and non-visible disabilities are the most likely to experience "name-calling, teasing, physical attacks, severe verbal bullying, verbal aggressions, threats, taking belongings, imitating," and being made fun of.[5]

Weight-based victimization also poses serious threats to a student's sense of safety. Rebecca Puhl, a nationally recognized expert in the field of weight-based bullying, and her colleagues Jamie Lee Peterson and Joerg Luedicke, suggest that students who are obese or have high body mass indices are more vulnerable to teasing and the teasing is "more harmful, frequent, and upsetting" than it is for their non-overweight peers. Bullying of overweight children can lead to an increase in unhealthy behaviors such as binge eating, unhealthy weight control measures, and avoidance of healthy activities in favor of sedentary pastimes. Bullying also can lead to social isolation, decreased self-esteem, skipping school, and decreased academic performance.[6]

Lesbian, gay, bisexual, transgender, queer, and questioning youth are also at a very high risk of being bullied and experience twice as much bullying as their straight counterparts. LGBTQQ youth hear, on average, eight homophobic slurs daily, and one high profile case in Canada captures the essence of the bullying LGBTQQ students endure. Over a five-year period, a gay student suffered "repeated harassment, homophobic name calling, threats of being dipped in acid, and overt physical assault by other students that included being spit upon, kicked, punched, having his shirt lit on fire, his tent urinated on during a school field trip, and nails and grapes thrown at him."[7] As troubling as this case is, LGBTQQ students usually do not report bullying. One transgender ninth grader explains, "They wouldn't do anything because it's part of the school's environment. People in my town actually think it's funny when someone harasses and assaults people for being different. If you're different it's seen as your fault for whatever happens to you."[8]

In what is described as **homophobic sexism,** LGBTQQ students also report that male bullies use physical assault to teach gay youth "what it's like to be a man," while they use sexual harassment and sexual assault to "teach lesbian youth that they should be attracted to men."[9] Sorting out the gendered, homophobic, and racist aspects of bulling for LGBTQQ youth can be confusing: "You got bashed because you're queer. No, no, no; it happened because I'm Black . . . it's never that clear."[10]

Cultural norms can also complicate the experience of being bullied for all students. Students whose expression of religion differs from the mainstream, such as the wearing of hijabs (head scarves), patkas or dastaars (turbans), or yarmulkes, "report being targeted because of these visible symbols of their religions."[11] For LGBTQQ youth who come from minority groups, the term **cultural homophobia** names the experience. As one young lesbian woman explains, "when you're brown you can't be lesbian. You can't be gay. My culture has no word for you. You cannot be both. You have to choose . . . either you choose the sexuality or you choose the race." A black queer youth adds that there is a kind of betrayal associated with being black and queer, with bullies saying "that's what white people are like; we're not. So what are you doing?" The charge to "not be white" is regularly accompanied by the very real likelihood of "being beaten up fairly badly" by your cultural peer group—much worse than a "LGBT white, middle class youth" might be. Troubling, too, is that support may be absent, regardless of race, ethnicity, or economic upbringing. As bullying and victimization occur, LGBTQQ youth may face "familial homophobia," which "is just feeling like they could just never, ever, ever, ever, ever turn to their family."[12]

Transgender youth are among the most vulnerable members of this group. Although they may be able to "fit in" outside their home communities, the "'public' nature of transitioning often garners severe bullying." Violence is a very real issue, and in early 2017, "a trans girl was shot with a BB gun by fellow pupils in Greater Manchester." Although unharmed by the pellet, prior to the attack the young girl had been "physically assaulted several times as well as verbally abused and insulted." The girl's mother told *The Telegraph,* "Our child came home to us in December and said she couldn't take any more and was going to throw herself off a bridge."[13]

The violence and fear are compounded for transgender immigrants who stand in the "intersections between racism, xenophobia, classism, and homophobia." If "you have that big, huge, layer of insecurity because of your legal status . . . because otherwise you're going to be sent to your country where you could be killed . . . you feel you have to comply with people, attitudes towards you . . . to really be safe and not stand up for yourself because you don't want to get yourself in trouble." This transgender immigrant shares, "The more 'isms' you have to deal with, the harder it is."[14]

Race and ethnicity also can affect who gets bullied. In schools where racial and ethnic differences are accompanied by power imbalances, students who fall into the minority category experience higher levels of bullying than do those where those imbalances are not present.[15] Language differences, cultural traditions that influence what students eat and how they dress, economic resources, as well as religion, all play a factor—as do gender identity, sexuality, physical appearance and ability, and more—in bullying patterns. In their study of the desegregation of schools in South Africa, Everard Weber, Mokubung Nkomo, and Christina Amsterdam suggest that "schools are the social barometers of the nation."[16] They help mold society and history, both within the United States and internationally.

Bullying: Real Time and Online Patterns

In real time, bullies often work in groups, with individuals supporting the main bully in bullying others. **Cyberbullying,** the bullying that occurs online, through social media, and on our cell phones, can change that pattern. Individuals who cyberbully often work alone or in small groups, can do so anonymously, and at any time of the day or night. With cyberbullying, the abuse can be particularly traumatic as not only can it happen around the clock and be incessant, but images and messages can go viral quickly and be impossible to remove, and it often is done anonymously. Little formal research has been done on cyberbullying in our schools, and what has been done has been framed within a binary logic. What scholars have begun to find suggests that girls are more often the victims, and the "fear, discomfort, threat, anger and sadness" that is experienced by the victims tends to be worse for girls and younger adolescents than for males.

Stopbullying.gov reports that "kids who are being cyberbullied often are bullied in person, as well. Additionally, kids who are cyberbullied have a harder time getting away from the behavior."[17] This is because "the information revolution," however many positive options it has added to our lives, "has vastly increased the scope of technologies of intrusion."[18] Research suggests a "double-involvement" that warrants further exploration, with victims sometimes also assuming the role of the "aggressors . . . with the aim of revenge or to retrieve the dominant position of the cycle of violence."[19] Little is known about this "double-involvement" and scholars are working to explain whether it is a real phenomenon, a means of defending oneself rather than actual bullying, or whether the idea of double-involvement is actually the product of different research methodologies scholars use to investigate bullying.

Confounding this already complex phenomenon is that most bullying in schools and online is perpetrated by someone the victim knows. This means that "relationship familiarity may actually exacerbate cyber-victim hazards, as these relationships are more trusted," causing the victim to dismiss the bullying and to be less likely to acknowledge their victimization, or seek help from an adult.[20] Binary gendered societal scripts for femininity play a role, too. Girls, in general, tend to go "behind the scenes and in more subtle ways," while boys, in general, tend to follow the more overt and physically aggressive masculine script for bullying. And, because of this, boys are more likely to be caught.[21]

Bullying causes enormous damage to our learning environments, yet our language is only beginning to name and help us explore that damage fully. When the bullying goes unreported or is ignored by authorities, perpetrators continue to bully without consequence. Suicide as a result of bullying also is a topic that school personnel avoid, but it is very real. Studies show that approximately 4,400 students commit suicide every year as a result of real time or online bullying. This is the tip of the iceberg, however. For every completed suicide, there are one hundred suicide attempts by bullied students, every year.[22] This translates to 440,000 attempted suicides annually, from bullying, almost half a million students every year. Some students, however, are pushed beyond their ability to cope with the unceasing hostility. Rather than report the bullying, they retaliate.

Mass Shootings: Yesterday and Today

Today, we would describe a **public mass murder** as "the killing of at least three victims during a single episode at one or more closely related locations."[23] These murders occur in public places such as hotels, theatres, malls, churches, stores, and roadways, and are perpetrated by one or two individuals. This type of violence captures extensive and extended media attention. But Grant Duwe, in *A History of*

Sand Creek Massacre by U.S. Army Troops, 1887

Figure 8.2 The Sand Creek massacre in 1864, in which 675 men of the Third Colorado Cavalry killed or mutilated an estimated 500 Cheyenne and Arapaho men, women and children, speaks to the reality that mass murders are not unusual in the history of the United States. (Source: iStock. Credit: bauhaus1000)

Mass Murder in the United States, shares that mass murders have been with us since the late 1700s.[24] So, to understand mass murders in our schools today, we need to take a quick historical journey of mass murders outside our schools.

Between 1775 and 1890, for example, the American Indian Wars thinly disguised wholesale massacres of entire populations of indigenous people on the part of settlers, soldiers, and miners. These mass murders are typified by what Duwe describes as "the so-called battle" that occurred at Wounded Knee in South Dakota. In the Wounded Knee Massacre of the Lakota in 1890, several hundred old men, women of all ages, and children died. The U.S. Cavalry had moved the Lakota to an area near Wounded Knee Creek where the Lakota made camp. The Lakota were surrounded when army officers mistook a religious Ghost Dance ritual for a call to arms and opened fire. Congress later passed a resolution of "deep regret" for the incident. Such massacres were not unusual during the American Indian Wars. Prior to Wounded Knee, for example, there was the "Sand Creek massacre of 150 Cheyenne," again mostly women and children. But because indigenous peoples were considered no better than "dogs by many, the mass murder of groups of Indigenous individuals by white men went, largely, unrecorded."[25]

Similarly, African Americans have also been the targets of mass murder. In New Orleans, for example, in the late 1800s, "nearly fifty African Americans were slaughtered and more than a hundred injured for meeting to discuss voting." And after the Civil War, the South "descended into nothing less than an age of violence and terror" for African Americans. Another "gory bloodbath" took place in the Memphis riots of 1866 when racial tension erupted into three days of violence: 46 African Americans died; 75 were injured; 100 were robbed; 5 black women were raped; and every black church and school was burned to the ground, along with 91 homes. Two white individuals lost their lives.[26] Perhaps more well known, the Ku Klux Klan during this time—and well beyond—was given free rein to murder, either individually or collectively, recently freed slaves and basically any individual with dark skin. Although many are reluctant to admit this, mass murders are a part of U.S history.

Contrary to popular belief, Duwe argues that school shootings and mass murder are not on the rise. Duwe reports that between 1900 and 1999, "909 mass killings" occurred, which translates to slightly more than nine per year.[27] Duwe is not alone. James Fox and Monica DeLateur's study of "Mass Shootings in America: Moving Beyond Newtown" imply that the frequency of mass murder has not increased. Instead, what has increased, they suggest, is the media coverage of these atrocities.[28] Fox and DeLateur claim that the 1966 mass murder of 16 people at the University of Texas, Austin, did not find its way into our televisions, computers, and cell phones in the same way that the news coverage of the 2012 mass murder of 26 children, staff, and teachers at Sandy Hook elementary school did. In 1966, "there were no 24-hour news stations or fleets of satellite trucks to relay images of the tragedy" as it unfolded.[29]

Some scholars do argue, however, that the frequency and scope of mass murders is, indeed, increasing. Their research and statistics support their analysis. J. Pete Blair and M. Hunter Martaindale note that between "2000 and 2010, 84 total [active shooter] events occurred: one in 2000, steadily rising over the next seven years, increasing to sixteen in 2009, and twenty-one in 2010." Blair and Martaindale also report that their "tracking [indicates] an increased number of attacks" in 2011 and 2012 (their research was published in 2013).[30] The Campus Safety Project concurs with this steady increase. In 2018, 82 active shooter events took place in K-12 schools[31] and CNN reports that by June of 2019, 22 more events had occurred.[32] Between 2010 and 2019, 188 mass shootings occurred—the equivalent of ten shootings per year. Even more striking, however, is that in the one and a half years between January of 2018 and June of 2019, the number of shootings increased to a rate of 17 per month, or 52 shootings per year. What has changed, it would appear, is the frequency of mass shootings. The perpetrators of these violent acts, however, also have changed: mass murders by single shooters are increasingly common in comparison to the mass murders conducted by groups of soldiers or KKK members prior to the mid 1900s.

We are drawn to these tragedies largely because of their seemingly senselessness and public nature. As a result of our desire to understand these killings, we have learned that the perpetrators are by far male, and white males are substantially more likely to be responsible for mass murders:

94 percent of perpetrators are male

63 percent of perpetrators are white

19 percent of perpetrators are Asian

9 percent of perpetrators are Latino

6 percent of perpetrators are black[33]

Mass murderers who are white kill larger numbers of people in their public killings than do their minority counterparts, something we will take up in the next section in this chapter through an intersectional lens.

Although we have a history of considering deadly violence in schools as an exception, it is far from exceptional. Additionally, the links between bullying and deadly school violence now are being acknowledged. We even have a phrase to capture this link: "pull a Columbine." According to Michael Kimmel, professor of sociology and gender studies, the phrase refers to "two seniors" who "walked calmly through the halls of Columbine High School, opening fire, seemingly randomly, on their fellow students. By the time the carnage was over, twelve students and one teacher lay dead, alongside the two troubled teenagers who had pulled the triggers." An additional twenty-four students were physically injured, and countless other students, teachers, and staff were traumatized. In the aftermath of the Columbine massacre, what we now know is that virtually every young man or boy who has murdered his fellow students, and some teachers, suffered from endless and extreme bullying.[34]

Those who have studied the adult perpetrators in recent mass murders identify several factors that are common among these predominately white men:

- the loss of privilege and the entitlement that accompanies that privilege
- blaming others for problems or losses
- extreme harassment and bullying in younger years
- a desire for revenge and to prove oneself

How does this list help us understand mass murder in our schools? The profile of the school-age mass murderer is remarkably similar to the adult profile:

- The school shooter describes his school days as "a relentless gauntlet of bullying, gay-baiting epithets, physical assault, and harassment until they 'snapped.'"
- The school shooter is "desperate" to prove his masculinity and prove those who have tormented him wrong.
- The school shooter sees violence against others as a viable way to redeem a shattered self-esteem.
- The school shooter commits "suicide by mass murder," taking as many of "them" as he can before he takes his own life.[35]

On the heels of relentless and excessively harsh bullying comes the need, at least for some white men, to enact murderous revenge as a way to prove one's masculinity, once and for all.

Violence Is Synonymous with Masculinity

In "Triple Entitlement and Homicidal Anger," Eric Madifs explains that in the United States, violence "operates 'as a signifier of masculinity.'" Violence, Madifs reasons, "is a masculine act; the more violently men behave, the more manly they are viewed." In both legal and criminal institutions, the most violent man is "the most capable, the most skilled, and the most worthy of a leadership position":

> The military soldiers who engage in the most combat (such as Marines and Navy Seals) are widely considered to be the toughest and manliest of their kind, as are the police officers who work the most dangerous beats, the sports stars whose bodies suffer the most debilitating injuries, and the gang members who commit the most violent crimes.[36]

Violence "is synonymous with masculinity," and it should come as no surprise, Madifs reasons, that when viewed through a male/female binary, "men commit more than their share of violence."[37] In our schools, this translates to violent bullying and, sadly, dramatic increases in shooting rampages on school grounds.

But the perpetrators of this violence are not only male, they are overwhelmingly white as well. Certainly, those young white men who are mass murderers in our schools have serious psychological disorders; certainly, adults failed to recognize these disorders; certainly, fellow students lacked the power and agency to get adults to recognize the problems, or ignored them, themselves. However, if we are to communicate effectively about mass school shootings, our discourse must be intersectionally oriented. Our conversations need to include discussions of race and ethnicity, gender and sex, sexuality and homophobia. Our discussions need to address the mostly white and mostly male administrations that sanction bullying by ignoring its presence and denying its severity. When we think and communicate about school violence, we need to assess, through an intersectional lens, our conceptualizations of heterosexual and white masculinity, entitlement, privilege, and the male emotional funnel system we continue to ignore.

MICROAGGRESSIONS

In the 1970s, Harvard medical school professor Chester Pierce, the first African American to become a professor at Massachusetts General Hospital, coined the term *microaggressions* "to refer to the everyday subtle and often automatic 'put-downs' and insults directed toward Black Americans." Pierce, an MD and professor in three departments at Harvard University, "specialized in how people react to extreme environments and racial relations" and felt that the everyday interactions between blacks and whites "were a model for understanding oppression in all its forms." These interactions, he knew, could shed light on how "the dominant white group sought to control the time, space, mobility, and energy of the nondominant black group."[38] Since the 1970s, the use of microaggressions to control the behaviors of nondominant groups has been explored across the range of identities.

In this section, we define and discuss microaggressions as they affect a range of identities and reflect a strong commitment to binary thinking. Although they are not limited to our schools, exploring them here helps us understand questions of safety and the freedom to learn. Schools are places in which we gather together, interact with one another, and explore our identities. As such, they are a venue in which we find microaggressions, which can be described as words that over time, feel like a hundred thousand paper cuts.[39]

Defining Microaggressions

Derald Wing Sue, professor of psychology at Columbia University, explains that "it is clear that microaggressions can be expressed toward any marginalized group in our society; they can be gender-based, sexual orientation-based, class-based, or disability-based." Described as "brief and commonplace," Sue shares that **microaggressions** are "daily verbal, behavioral and environmental indignities, whether intentional or unintentional, that communicate hostile, derogatory, or negative racial, gender, sexual-orientation, and religious slights and insults to the target person or group." Significantly, "perpetrators are usually unaware that they have engaged in an exchange that demeans" someone.[40] Microaggressions differ from the acts of incivility that many people who occupy identities of privilege may experience because "they are constant, continual and cumulative. They occur from the moment of birth until the day that person dies. As a result, any one microaggression in isolation may represent the feather that breaks a camel's back."[41]

Microagressions differ from outright bigotry or hate in that they are unconscious and unintentional. They can be verbal, such as comments or remarks that involve or focus on someone's appearance, language, religion country of origin, or culture.

Appearance: describing someone as exotic or different, attempting to guess a person's race or ethnicity, sharing that you don't think of that person as black (or Asian, disabled, gay, or the like), asking to touch someone's hair, and/or commenting on the strangeness of a person's clothing, piercings, hair, or makeup

Language: commenting on someone's level of proficiency in English, describing an accent as sweet or endearing, making fun of an accent, asking someone who looks Asian if they can read Japanese or Chinese characters,

Figure 8.3 Religions, and religious texts, often are the targets of outright bigotry and hate, but also the target of microaggressions. Recall some of the microaggressions you may have heard directed at the Quran, the central religious text of Islam and the Muslim faith. (Source: iStock. Credit: Hussein Aziz)

referring to people within an ethnic or racial grouping as "those people" or "you people"

Religion: commenting on religious artifacts, making jokes about a holy text, and mocking religious traditions

Country of origin: asking someone where they are really from, asking where someone's home country or country of origin is, asking how long someone has been in this country

Culture: questioning the relevance of, mocking, or making light of historical events, and/or cultural traditions and practices; making jokes about, ignoring, or mocking and minimizing societal and historical traumas; criticizing, mocking, or making jokes about food types, food rituals, and food ingredients specific to a culture

Microaggressions also can also be nonverbal, involving physical displays that suggest dislike, dismissal, or even discomfort. These nonverbal microaggressions include, for example,

- crossing to the other side of a street
- making extended hostile eye contact

- avoiding eye contact
- delaying or refusing service
- failing to include someone in a discussion, conversation, or project
- rolling your eyes, sighing, or fidgeting when someone is talking

Microaggressions can also be communicated visually and occur when media rely on images that directly or indirectly communicate stereotypes and put-downs, or simply do not include marginalized individuals in the representation at all.[42]

Examples of Microaggressions

Because research on microaggressions began with race, our examples begin there. From a series of YouTube videos titled "Sh*t People Say," examples of common microaggressions focused on race include:

"Why isn't there a White Entertainment Television?"

"The Jews were slaves too. You don't hear us complaining about it all the time."

"My best friend was black. I mean, she's still black. But we're not really friends anymore."

"That's so ghetto!"[43]

"Like, where were you born!?"

"You're so dark! Do you go tanning?!?"

"Can you, like, say 'Taco' in English?"

"I love Mexico. I've been to Cancun, like, 5 times."[44]

"You're really pretty . . . for an Asian."

"You kind of remind me of Jackie Chan."

"I don't even see you like, Asian-Asian, you're like, just not Asian."

"It's in Chinese, can you read this?"[45]

"Oh, I never asked, do you have a green card?"

"So, how did you get over the border? Did you hide in the trunk?"

"Hey, do you know any drug dealers?"

"My housekeeper's Mexican, you should talk to her in Mexican, I mean, Spanish!"

"#All Lives Matter."[46]

But race is not the only identity category that is a target of microaggressions. The StanfordPush project shares the microaggressions able-body people regularly say to disabled people. The list includes

"What happened to you?"

"But you're so pretty!"

"Yeah, it's totally accessible, there's just a single step."

"I totally understand you, I get so frustrated when the elevator's broken."

"Jesus will heal you, if you keep praying for it."

"So, you work!?!"

"Don't you feel embarrassed when you are out in public?"

"Beats walking, huh?"

"Oh My God, you are SUCH an inspiration . . . I don't know how I could get myself up in the morning."

"I wake up feeling rotten about my life, and then I think of you."[47]

Sexuality also is a frequent identity category for microaggressions. In "Sh*t Straight People Say to Gay Guys," AlrightHey shares what he's heard:

"I know you're both guys, but which one's the man of the relationship?"

"This is just so amazing, I've always wanted a gay best friend."

"I just don't understand like, how do you know if you're gay if you've never slept with a girl."

"Oh My God, when you want to have kids I will totally be your surrogate."

"That is so gay!"[48]

Transgender men and women also are the targets of microaggressions:

"You will *Never* be a REAL WOMAN!"

"You are so beautiful for a Trans Girl!"

"So when are you gonna REALLY transition?"

"Cool! You're my first trans friend."

"Did you transition because you thought you were an ugly girl?"

"Wow! I would never have known you used to be a girl."

"Did you have *The* surgery?"

"There's no way that's real. Can I touch?"[49]

The power of microaggressions to belittle and ostracize individuals cannot be underestimated. Sue explains,

> In my day-to-day interactions with people, they would say things or do things that appeared to be compliments but that left me feeling insulted, invalidated and hurt. One example I like to give to people is that I'm often complimented for speaking good English. To the person saying it, it's perceived as a compliment, but it happens to me so often, as an Asian-American, that the underlying, hidden message is that "You are a not a true American. You are a perpetual alien in your own country."[50]

NON-BINARY PRONOUNS

One way we can begin to move beyond these binary constructions of people and their identities is through the pronouns we use to refer to someone. The novelist Sassafras Lowrey shares how her gender identity continues to evolve from when she came out as gender queer to today:

> I came out as genderqueer when I was 17 years old, and now at 33 I've now spent almost half my life as an out genderqueer person! For me being genderqueer means that I'm not a man or a woman, and that regardless of my presentation, my gender identity exists outside the binary of female or male. . . . Over the years my gender presentation has been fluid from: butch to transgender man, to bearded lady, to queer femme. The only constancy to my gender identity over the years has been genderqueer and my nonbinary pronouns: ze/hir.[51]

Lowrey explains that identities, like language, are always evolving. Ze shares, "I understand that using non-binary pronouns might be challenging, but when someone says my pronouns are 'too hard' for them to remember, what I hear is that you don't value our friendship, the work that I'm doing in the world, or me as a person."

There are solutions, however, and for students interested in intersectional communication, Lowrey and others suggest using non–binary pronouns and sharing our own preferred pronouns in meetings and in our emails. When we are working or socializing with others we ask everyone in the room for their preferred pronouns, and "not just the person you think might be trans or non-binary." For those who identify as cisgender, she/her/hers and he/him/his are the most common choices. For those who do not identify with the gender binary construction, pronoun options appear in Table 8.1.

Campuses across the country are beginning to acknowledge the importance of non-binary pronouns for students. At orientations, students are "asked to introduce themselves with their name, hometown, and preferred gender pronoun (sometimes abbreviated PGP)." At the University of Vermont, although the list is limited, students can indicate their preferred pronouns in the computer system, selecting from "he," "she," "they," "ze," or "none." Keith Williams, the university's registrar, explains that this procedure maximizes the student's ability to control their identity and, as such, is an important part of their college experience. To date, 3,200 students have entered their preferred gender pronouns at the university, while at Harvard, which followed Vermont's approach, 10,000 have indicated their PGPs.[52]

Adjusting and identifying preferred pronoun use is not new. Linguists note that non-binary pronoun suggestions occurred in the nineteenth century, with "ip" a term so unfamiliar that it did not remind speakers of "he" or "she," "nis" which replaced the "h" in "his" with a gender neutral "n," and "hisr," a blend of "his" and "her."[53] Although none of these suggestions survived, the push for non-binary pronouns continues. Students at Cambridge launched a "Make No Assumptions" campaign, and professors there are described as largely open to non-binary pronouns. At Ohio University, in contrast, faculty "thought 'they' was a typo on their student rosters" when students selected that pronoun as the preferred one to use. "They" can be tricky, Emrys Travis, a student at Cambridge shares, but even their (Travis's) trans friends "mess up—repeatedly, often. . . . As long as I think they're trying, it doesn't bother me."[54]

Table 8.1 Preferred Gender Identity Pronoun (PGP)

Preferred Gender Identity Pronoun (PGP)	Example Sentences
she/her/hers; he/him/his	She wants you to use her pronouns. She went to her favorite store.
e/ey/em/eir/eirs	E wants you to use ey pronouns. E went to eir favorite store.
ze/hir	Ze wants you to use hir pronouns. Ze went to hir favorite store.
they/them/their/theirs	They want you to use their pronouns. They went to their favorite store.
co/cos	Co wants you to use cos pronouns. Co went to cos favorite store.
xe/sem/xyr	Xe wants you to use xyr pronouns. Xe went to xyr favorite store.
hy/hym/hys	Hy wants you to use hys pronouns. Hy went to hys favorite store; did you see hym there?
per/pers	Per wants you to use pers pronouns. Per went to pers favorite store.
no pronoun: use the person's name instead of a pronoun	Sassafras wants you to use Sassafras's pronouns. Sassafras went to Sassafras's favorite store.

SOURCE: Compiled from Sassafras Lowrey, "A Guide to Non-Binary Pronouns and Why They Matter," Huffpost, November 8, 2017, https://www.huffingtonpost.com/entry/non-binary-pronouns-why-they-matter_us_5a03107be4b0230facb8419a; and Avinash Chak, "Beyond 'He' and 'She': The Rise of Non-Binary Pronouns," BBC News, December 7, 2015, https://www.bbc.com/news/magazine-34901704.

In *Gender Diversity and Non-Binary Inclusion in the Workplace,* Sarah Gibson and J. Fernandez explain that "when we have a few billion humans each with a few trillion cells in their bodies, things tend to be a little more messy" than the simple XX and XY chromosome pairings we learned in school. Our chromosomes can line up as "XX, XY" they explain, but also as "XXY, XO and many more." Our sex hormones "get similarly complicated, with different kinds and different levels as well as how receptive we are to each of them, as does the structure and function of our reproductive organs."[55]

Determining a person's sex or gender through hormones and chromosomes, and through biological traits and physical characteristics, is a profoundly inexact and often incorrect approach. Rather, Gibson and Fernandez explain, we should determine a person's gender and sex identities by their own experiences of themselves and by "how they interact with the world."[56] Gibson and Fernandez share that

> Non-binary people are simply people trying to get along with their lives in a way that makes them happy. What makes someone non-binary is easier to understand

> than some people would have you believe, with many wanting to challenge their validity through an incomplete understanding of biological or social variations. What makes someone non-binary is the same as what makes someone a man or a woman—it is simply what suits that person best.[57]

Binary language fails all of us because it rejects the diversity of our experiences of being human and our need to have words and labels that resonate with our complex identities. S. Bear Bergman shares, "I got into my first argument with a university professor about the validity of gender-nonspecific pronouns."[58] Tiny words, these pronouns, yet when they deny someone's identity, assign them to a category with which they do not identify, or prevent them from even naming that identity, we commit "hermeneutical injustice." Bergman explains that **hermeneutical injustice** happens when "a person has no way to describe their experience because the conceptual framework doesn't exist yet due to their stigmatized or disempowered identity."[59]

Anthropologist John J. Gumpertz suggests that "to understand issues of identity . . . we need to gain insights into the communicative processes" by which these issues arise. "We must focus on what communication does: how it constrains evaluation and decision making."[60] Because, as Kelly Oliver, feminist philosopher and novelist reminds us, "There is an intimate and necessary correspondence between how we conceive of others and how we treat them."[61]

THE RIGHT TO LEARN

At its best, education teaches individuals to be citizens and "members of political communities." It urges us to consider "how one may live," what constitutes a "virtuous good life," the differences in people we should honor, and the very "nuances" and complexities of our identities and our humanity. Because of education, "adults and children, teachers and students, come together for the purpose of transmitting the basic ideas and ideals of [a] culture and nurturing the development of its members."[62] In our schools, students may know how to bully and harass one another, but they also need the opportunity to learn how to "live together in the face of social division and conflict." Our schools could be places in which young people learn about citizenship, ethics, and the histories of the ideas that inform our world.[63] Talking openly and honestly about our identities, and their complexities, could help us make schools safer places in which to learn.

Title IX, Civil Rights Act, and Americans with Disabilities Act: No Exclusions

Passed in 1972, Title IX states that "No person in the United States shall, on the basis of sex, be excluded from participation in, be denied the benefits of, or be subjected to discrimination under any program or activity receiving Federal financial assistance."[64] The Department of Education's Office for Civil Rights "enforces, among other statues, Title IX." But what does Title IX have to do with safety in our schools, and what does it mean for those institutions that receive federal financial assistance—and who are they? Let's take the last question first. The educational institutions that receive federal financial assistance are the majority of our elementary and secondary schools, the majority of our state-funded colleges and universities, and many privately owned schools, colleges, and universities. They also are most charter schools, many for-profit schools, and most libraries, museums, and vocational rehabilitation agencies. If the institution or agency is involved in education, it likely receives financial assistance from the Education Department (ED) of our federal government. If an agency or institution receives what is known as ED financial support then it cannot, legally, discriminate.

But in what ways is it legally bound to not discriminate? The answer is that it cannot discriminate in the recruitment and admission of students, counseling opportunities, ways it distributes financial assistance, how athletics are organized and supported, when sex-based harassment occurs, in its treatment of pregnant students or students who are parents, how it disciplines students, how it manages sex education, as well has who and how it employs. And if a student files a complaint, the institution or agency may not retaliate against that person.

As you can see, the scope of Title IX is enormous. Title IX applies to sexual assault, harassment, sexual violence, and gender-based violence. It applies to athletic opportunities, hostile environments, harassment and bullying, biases in the treatment of students on the basis of their gender or sex identities, faculty and student relationships, and the language used by employees of the agency or institution.[65] Title IX, in sum, gives an incredible number of students a powerful sense of agency denied them for decades. Because of Title IX, students have a legal avenue through which they can name the discrimination and harassment they experience. They can stand up to inequities with the backing of a federal statute that supports them.

Beyond Title IX, however, the Equal Employment Opportunity Council (EEOC), "the division of the federal government that enforces laws making it illegal to discriminate against an employee on the basis of their sex, race, age, etc.," recently decided that the Civil Rights Act of 1964 protects transgender people. "The term 'gender,'" the EEOC stated, "encompasses not just a person's biological sex but also the cultural and social aspects associated with masculinity and femininity." This "expanded the reach of Title IX protections, making sex discrimination based on gender identity a violation of the law."[66] In 1990, congress passed another act, the Americans with Disabilities Act (ADA), making it illegal to discriminate against someone on the basis of disability. This act went one step further, however, requiring employers and schools

Figure 8.4 Because of the Americans with Disabilities Act, public educational institutions are required to provide reasonable accommodations for their students with disabilities. These accommodations include not only physical alterations, such as curb cuts, ramps, elevators, parking spaces, and the like, but also accommodations in classrooms, such as sign language interpreters, note takers, modifications to test taking procedures, and more. (Source: iStock. Credit: Tashi-Delek)

to provide "reasonable accommodations" for their disabled employees and students.

These statutes and acts are rarely discussed and often are unknown by students. Yet Title IX, the Civil Rights Act of 1964, which "ended segregation in public places and banned discrimination on the basis of race, color, religion, sex or national origin," and the American's with Disabilities Act, provide students with the legal grounds with which to speak out against discrimination.[67] Because of these three laws, students can file complaints, grievances, and lawsuits if the schools they attend discriminate on the basis of gender, sex, race, age, sexuality, ability, and transgender and queer-identified identities.

Curriculum Matters

Who decides what content belongs in our classrooms? What aspects of history, math, geography, literature, music, or even athletics do we engage as we attend school? Who, and what, do we learn about? In the 1970s, feminists began to discuss what they called the "hidden curriculum" in education. This hidden curriculum reinforced a non-intersectional presentation of not just course content—what students' learned in their classes—but also who they should learn from and what they should learn about themselves.[68] Nearly fifty years of research focused on the content and presentation of educational materials indicates that many segments of our overall community are missing from the curriculum:

- Women of all races and ethnicities are underrepresented in educational materials.
- Minorities of all races and ethnicities are underrepresented in educational materials.
- People with disabilities are underrepresented in educational materials.
- People who aren't heterosexual or cisgender are underrepresented in educational materials.
- People who are not Christian are underrepresented in educational materials.

Books written by people with any of these underrepresented identities are rarely used in our educational systems. When people with any of the identities are included in educational materials they usually are presented in highly stereotypical ways.

Surveying almost one hundred years of Caldecott Book Awards, one of the most prestigious awards a book written for children can receive, Melanie Koss, Nancy Johnson, and Miriam Martinez's research confirms this assessment. The books that received the award between 1938 and 2017 are overwhelmingly authored and illustrated by white people (86 percent). Not only are the main characters overwhelmingly white (70 percent), but the "corpus of Caldecott books does not reflect our multiethnic world, signifying that White representation dominates the Caldecott Landscape, and racism is present."[69]

The content of our educational materials creates a narrative that white, cisgender, heterosexual, able-body, Christian males are more important, more active, more productive, and more worthy of study than other people.[70] What we learn in our schools is that the contributions of this narrow group of individuals are the most important to study. If you doubt this is true, see if you can accomplish any of the following:

- Name ten famous women of any identity, no longer living, who weren't also entertainers.
- Name ten famous men of any non-white identity, no longer living, who weren't also entertainers or sports figures.
- Name ten famous, LGBTQI and/or queer-identified individuals, who are not or were not entertainers.
- Name ten famous people with disabilities.
- Name the U.S. presidents who had or have disabilities.

Of course, this list of naming could go on and on. Are you aware, for example, that the Tuskegee Airmen of World War II were the first black pilots in the U.S. Army and that their heroism and success paved the way for a new branch of the military, the U.S. Air Force? Did you know that the first woman to run for president of the United States was the Equal Rights Party candidate Victoria Woodhull, who ran in 1872, before women had the right to vote? Her running mate was the abolitionist and former slave Frederick Douglass. In this vein, consider whether you can name any queer-identified or minority authors, playwrights, or intellectuals? If your answers are "I can't name any" or "I can only think of a few" or "I know of none," then your education has presented you with a very narrow understanding of human accomplishments, struggles, and progress.

Beyond the actual content of our educational materials, who stands in front of a classroom matters as well. The Center for American Progress reports that although "students of color make up more than 40 percent of the school-age population" in our elementary and secondary schools, teachers of color are only "17 percent of the teaching force."[71] Our elementary and high school teachers are largely female (approximately 75 percent) and our teachers at institutions of higher education are overwhelmingly male (70–77 percent).[72] In higher education, 77 percent of the teachers are white. Even though "22 percent of the general population has disabilities," only 1.5–4 percent of our teachers do.[73] Statistics for the percentage of LGBTQI and/or queer-identified teachers at any level are not being gathered at this time and so are unavailable.

The content of our curriculum and the identities of our teachers do not reflect the demographics of our student populations in schools. The National Center for Educational Statistics reports that in elementary and secondary schools, 51 percent of our students are white, while the remaining 49 percent are Hispanic/Latinx, black, Asian/Pacific Islander, American Indian/Alaskan Native, or two or more races.[74] In higher education, 60 percent of students identify as white while 40 percent identify as students of color. In our public schools, 13 percent of students identify as having a disability, while in higher education, between 11 and 22 percent of our students do, depending on age and veteran status. Again, data for LGBTQI and/or queer-identified students are not available or are not being collected at this time.

How are we to communicate effectively about the history of ideas, inventions, and accomplishments if we have not learned the full story? How are we to learn in the most productive ways when identities are grossly underrepresented or presented stereotypically? How is it that only a select group of identities are in the front of our classroom as teachers? Recall Chimamanda Adiche's caution in chapter 1 about the danger of a single story. When we learn only one story, our understanding of the world is quite narrow. As we increase the diversity of the stories we hear, study, explore, and come to understand, our understanding of the human experience is vastly improved. This deeper and broader understanding of the human experience informs our communication as well as our ability to engage one another productively as we think about the complex issues we face in our world today.

With regard to education, our students feel safer when their identities are made visible, respected, and appreciated. If they can learn from people who share their same identities, as well as from those they see as different from themselves, their understanding of the world around them expands. And, as the content of any classroom changes to reflect the diversity of contributions made by a diversity of identities, we all come to understand the world as a world of multiple stories, one that cannot be explained by just a single story.

REJECTING DISCOURSES OF SUPREMACY

Zeus Leonardo, at the University of California, Berkeley, explains that our discourse often reflects privilege: it reveals assumptions about ourselves, other people, and the places we occupy on the hierarchies of value that are at work. When our discourse reflects privilege, it "comes with the unfortunate consequence of masking history," concealing the agents of domination, and "removing the acts that make it clear who is doing what to whom."[75] That is, it attempts to erase the uneven distribution of power and agency that benefit some at the expense of others. Bullying, biased curriculum, microaggressions, and non-binary pronouns all are rooted in discourses of privilege. They are grounded in the belief that we do not need to be careful about the words we use, the wounds they cause, or the epistemic injustices that result from our use of them. Although non-intersectional approaches to communicating with others hurts as bad as the sticks or stones we might throw at them, we pretend that they do not.

Leonardo suggests that there is a supremacy that is taught to us as children in our schools, churches, and homes: "it is pedagogical." Leonardo calls this a "hidden curriculum" that saturates everyday life and explains that "one of the first steps to articulating its feature is coming to terms with its specific modes of discourse."[76] This supremacy gives those who have power and privilege the license to say insulting things and to excuse their discourse as not really insulting. Supremacy teaches us that microaggressions are just simple and benign curiosity, that non-binary pronouns are awkward and too odd sounding to be of use, and that biased curriculum is what is most important to learn. Discourses of supremacy tell us that bullying teaches kids to toughen up, and teachers who are white, cisgender, heterosexual and able-body can be the primary role models for all children.

Those with privileged identities, Leonardo suggests, "enjoy privileges largely because they have created a system of domination under which they can thrive as a group." The enactment of those privileges "is quite simple: set up a system that benefits the [privileged] group," then "mystify the system," making it hard to identify and talk about. Next, remove or erase the actual identities of the agents of domination "from discourse, and when interrogated about it, stifle

Communication Checklist for Inclusive Language

- ✓ *Put people first.* Focus on the person, not their characteristics: for example, instead of "a blind woman" or "a woman salesperson," use "a woman who is blind" or "a woman on our sales team."
- ✓ *Use gender neutral language.* Using "guys" to address all people is gendered language that may insinuate that men are preferred. Instead, use inclusive words such as *friends, folks, people, you all, y'all,* and *team,* and avoid terms that connote gender or are condescending, such as *man* (*man hours, man power*), and *girls, ladies, gals, females* (which could feel condescending: use *women*).
- ✓ *Use last names.* Women are often referred to by their first names when the male counterpart is addressed by his last name, preceding by "Mr." Be neutral in presentations or in written work and use last names to refer to both women and men.
- ✓ *Ask about preferred pronouns.* It's simple: "What pronouns do you prefer?" PGPs include *he/she, they, ze, per* and many others.
- ✓ *Be aware of stigmatizing or shaming phrases.*
  - ✓ Mental disability/handicap—Focus instead on the person ("Jeremiah has autism") rather than the handicap ("Jeremiah has a mental disability" *or* "is autistic" *or* "is handicapped").
  - ✓ "Bossy"—a condescending term when referring to a woman; use *powerful, assertive, take-charge.*
  - ✓ "Ghetto"—a bigoted term unflatteringly connoting nonwhite.
  - ✓ "Gypped"—a racial slur, from "gypsy," a slur for Romany people.
  - ✓ "Fat"—a negative term that can feel shaming; use body-positive descriptors that are neutral like *large, big, robust.*
- ✓ *Avoid triggering language.* Avoid using violent terms to describe a nonviolent experience. Replace "that test raped me" with "that test was awful, I think I failed" and "we killed that team" with "our team has never played so well before," for example.

Source: Modified from Courtney Seiter's "Principles of Inclusive Language," in Nehemiah Green, "Diversity Together," July 31, 2018, https://medium.com/diversity-together/70-inclusive-language-principles-that-will-make-you-a-more-successful-recruiter-part-1–79b7342a0923. Seiter is director of people at Buffer and co-founder of Girls to the Moon and the college career network Handshake.

the discussion with insane comments about the 'reality' of the charges being made," the absurdity of the request, or the overly sensitive nature of the target of the discourse.[77]

Alice McIntyre, the author of *Making Meaning of Whiteness,* explains that what is so "striking about whites talking to whites is the infinite ways we

8.1. GUIDE TO COMMUNICATION

Discourses of Value

Reflect on the following possibilities for an invitational (defined in Chapter 1) approach to difference:

1. Watch the 2011 Documentary *Bully.* Consider how you could communicate invitationally with the school officials in this documentary. Are there ways you could invite their perspectives and also share your own respectfully and without demonizing anyone?
2. If you are curious about someone's identities or want others to be more respectful of your own, how might your questions or comments sound if they came from a non-hierarchical frame of mind?
3. Considering the "Sh*t People Say" YouTube videos, have you been the target of similar microaggressions or perpetuated microaggressions unknowingly on others? What are some examples of ways to avoid microaggressions through respectful communication using an intersectional lens?
4. What are your preferred pronouns? Consider how you can avoid microaggressions when asking other people about their own preferred pronouns or revealing your PGP as you get to know them or work with them.
5. Do your own intersectional identities reveal areas of privilege that might inhibit your recognition of the injustices other people experience? Do your intersectional identities reveal experiences of injustice that contribute to you listening to, and being outraged by, bullying and violence? How might you use your own privilege and experience of injustice to avoid discourses of supremacy in your communication with other people?

manage to 'talk ourselves out of' being responsible for racism." We can extend this claim to any of the identities under discussion: heterosexual people do not take responsibility for homophobic laws, practices, and assumptions; able-body individuals do not acknowledge their centrality in the creation of barriers faced by disabled individuals, bullies do not take responsibility for the damage done to the people they bully, and so on and so on. McIntyre explains that those with privilege control the conversation and discourse such that they never have to take responsibility for the inequities that are a part of "our society *today.*" All too often, those with privilege dismiss inequities and tragedies as things of the past. "It was worse then, but it's so much better now," they claim.[78]

Leonardo explains, "If racist [sexist, homophobic, transphobic, ableist, classist, xenophobic, and the like] relations were created only by people in the past, then racism [sexism, homophobia, transphobia, ableism, classism, xenophobia, and the like] would not be as formidable as [they are] today. It [they] could be regarded as part of the historical dustbin and a relic of a cruel society."[79] But they are not, and these inequities are reflected in the educational practices of today.

People in positions of privilege rarely talk about inequities with any sense of outrage.[80] McIntyre shares that people with privilege fear being thought of as having privilege, "yet at the same time usually do not experience the outrage at [injustices] that would move us to act differently." If people with privilege were not so privileged, they would be outraged at the unjust treatment they could be subject to. Individuals with privilege come to a "tacit acceptance" of inequities and their discourse reveals this acceptance.[81] Exploring the discourse of domination reveals "a collection of everyday [discursive] strategies" that mask privilege and oppression and the ways that masking of privilege and oppression are embedded in language.[82]

Leonardo explains that privileged individuals often tolerate "only small, incremental doses" of confrontation about their privilege.[83] Conversations must not get too emotional, those who have been insulted must not ask too much, traditions must not be upset, change takes time, but most of all, we must always be polite to those with privilege when they say or do something offensive. Asking a person to be polite to you if you have insulted them only once may be a reasonable request. Asking a person to be polite to you when you, and others before you, have insulted them for centuries is an entirely different request.

Resources

Sebastian Bortnik, "The Conversation We Are Not Having about Digital Child Abuse," filmed October 2016 in Buenos Aries, TedxRiodelaPlata video, 13:39, https://www.ted.com/talks/sebastian_bortnik_the_conversation_we_re_not_having_about_digital_child_abuse.

Ashley Judd, "How Online Abuse of Women Has Spiraled Out of Control," filmed October 2016 in San Francisco, CA, TEDWomen 2016 video, 16:03, https://www.ted.com/talks/ashley_judd_how_online_abuse_of_women_has_spiraled_out_of_control.

R. J. Palacio, *Wonder* (New York: Alfred A. Knopf, 2012).

Jodi Picoult, *Nineteen Minutes* (New York: Washington Square Press, 2007).

Alex Stapleton and Chelsea Handler, "Hello Privilege, It's Me Chelsea," 2019, Netflix Official Site, www.netflix.com.

Notes

1. Dianne Gereluk, "Citizenship and Ethics," *Oxford Research Encyclopedia of Education* (New York: Oxford University Press, published online April 2017), accessed November 15, 2019, doi: 10.1093/acrefore/9780190264093.013.15.
2. Compiled from Gary Namie, "2014 WBI U.S. Workplace Bullying Survey," February 2014, http://www.workplacebullying.org/wbiresearch/wbi-2014-us-survey/; Workplace Bullying Institute, "Who Gets Targeted," http://www.workplacebullying.org/individuals/problem/who-gets-targeted/; and "Facts About Bullying," October 14, 2014, accessed June 1, 2017, https://www.stopbullying.gov/media/facts/index.html#listing.
3. Adrianne Dessel, "Prejudice in Schools: Promotion of an Inclusive Culture and Climate," *Education and Urban Society* 20, no. 10 (2010): 1–23.
4. "Who Is at Risk," stopbullying.gov, accessed June 1, 2017, https://www.stopbullying.gov/at-risk/index.html.
5. Bonnie Bell Carter and Victor G. Spencer, "The Fear Factor: Bullying and Students with Disabilities," *International Journal of Special Education* 21, no. 1 (2006): 21; see also Faye Mishna, "Learning Disabilities and Bullying: Double Jeopardy," *Journal of Learning Disabilities* 36, no. 4 (2003): 336–347. See also Chad A. Rose, Lisa E. Monda-Amaya, and Dorothy L. Espelage, "Bullying Perpetration and Victimization in Special Education: A Review of the Literature," *Remedial and Special Education* 32, no. 2 (2011): 120.

6. Rebecca Puhl, Jamie Lee Peterson, and Joerg Luedicke, "Weight Based Victimization: Bullying Experiences of Weight Loss Treatment-Seeking Youth," *Pediatrics* 131, no. 1 (2013): 1–9.
7. Andrea Daley, Steven Solomon, Peter A. Newman, and Faye Mishna, "Traversing the Margins: Intersectionalities in the Bullying of Lesbian, Gay, Bisexual, and Transgender Youth," *Journal of Gay and Lesbian Social Services* 19, no. 304 (2007): 11.
8. Joseph G. Kosciw, Emily A. Greytak, Mark J. Bartkiewicz, Madelyn J. Boesen, and Neal A. Palmer, *The 2011 National School Climate Survey: The Experiences of Lesbian, Gay, Bisexual, and Transgender Youth in Our Nation's Schools* (New York: GLSEN, 2012), http://files.eric.ed.gov/fulltext/ED535177.pdf.
9. Daley et al., "Traversing the Margins," 17.
10. Daley et al., "Traversing the Margins," 19.
11. "Considerations for Specific Groups," stopbullying.gov, accessed June 1, 2017, https://www.stopbullying.gov/at-risk/groups/#religion.
12. Daley et al., "Traversing the Margins," 20.
13. Camilla Turner, "Transgender 11-Year-Old Shot at School, as Mother Says Teachers Are Failing to Combat Bullying," *Telegraph*, February 9, 2017, accessed June 1, 2017, http://www.telegraph.co.uk/education/2017/02/09/transgender-11-year-old-shot-school-mother-says-teachers-failing/.
14. Daley et al., "Traversing the Margins," 22.
15. Dessel, "Prejudice in Schools"; Orhan Agridag, Janick Demanet, Mieke Van Houtte, Piet Van Avermaet, "Ethnic School Composition and Peer Victimization: A Focus on Interethnic School Climate," *International Journal of Intercultural Relations* 35, no. 4 (2011): 465–473.
16. Everard Weber, Mokubung Nkomo, and Christina Amsterdam, "Diversity, Unity, and National Development: Findings from Desegregated Gauteng Schools," *Perspectives in Education* 27, no. 4 (2009): 349.
17. "What Is Cyberbullying," stopbullying.gov, May 2018, last reviewed May 30, 2019, https://www.stopbullying.gov/cyberbullying/what-is-it/index.html.
18. Brian H. Spitzberg and Gregory Hoobler, "Cyberstalking and the Technologies of Interpersonal Terrorism," *New Media and Society* 4, no. 1 (2002): 72.
19. Filipa Pereira, Brian H. Spitzberg, and Marlene Matos, "Cyber-Harassment Victimization in Portugal: Prevalence, Fear, and of Help-Seeking Among Adolescents," *Computers in Human Behavior* 62 (2016): 137, https://www.researchgate.net/profile/Filipa_Pereira6/publication/299626065_Cyber-harassment_victimization_in_Portugal_Prevalence_fear_and_help-seeking_among_adolescents/links/5703661b08aeade57a2476fc.pdf.
20. Pereira et al., "Cyber-Harassment," 142.
21. "Brutal Boys vs. Mean Girls: Male Bullying vs. Female Bullying," Just Say Yes: Youth Equipped to Succeed, May 5, 2019, https://www.justsayyes.org/bullying/brutal-boys-vs-mean-girls/.
22. "Bullying and Suicide," Bullying Statistics, http://www.bullyingstatistics.org/content/bullying-and-suicide.html.
23. Eric Madifs, "Triple Entitlement and Homicidal Anger: An Exploration of the Intersectional Identities of American Mass Murderers," *Men and Masculinities* 17, no.1 (2014): 67.
24. Grant Duwe, *A History of Mass Murder in the United States* (Jefferson, NC: McFarland and Co., 2007), 22.
25. Russell Thornton, *American Indian Holocaust and Survival: A Population History Since 1942* (Norman: University of Oklahoma Press, 1987), 49.
26. Carol Anderson, *White Rage: The Unspoken Truth of Our Racial Divide* (New York: Bloomsbury, 2016), 31, 32.
27. Duwe, *A History of Mass Murder,* 22.
28. James Alan Fox and Monica J. DeLateur, "Mass Shootings in America: Moving Beyond Newton," *Homicide Studies* 30, no. 1 (2013): 1–21.
29. Fox and DeLateur, "Mass Shootings," 6.
30. J. Pete Blair and M. Hunter Martaindale, "United States Active Shooter Events from 2000–2010: Training and Equipment Implications," Texas State University, 2013, http://www.acphd.org/media/372742/activeshooterevents.pdf.
31. "School Shootings: The K-12 School Shooting Statistics Everyone Should Know," Campus Safety, https://www.campussafetymagazine.com/safety/k-12-school-shooting-statistics-everyone-should-know/.
32. Michelle Lou and Christina Walker, "There Have Been 22 Shootings This Year," CNN, https://www.cnn.com/2019/05/08/us/school-shootings-us-2019-trnd/index.html.
33. Adam Lankford, "Race and Mass Murder in the United States: A Social and Behavioral Analysis," *Current Sociology* 64, no. 3 (2016): 482.
34. Michael S. Kimmel, *Angry White Men: American Masculinity at the End of an Era* (New York: Nation Institute, 2017), 69.
35. Kimmel, *Angry White Men,* 73, 77.
36. Madifs, "Triple Entitlement and Homicidal Anger," 78.
37. Madifs, "Triple Entitlement and Homicidal Anger," 78.
38. Ezra E. H. Griffith, "Chester Middlebrook Pierce, M.D.: A Life that Mattered," *Psychiatric News,* American Psychiatry Association, October 28, 2016, http://psychnews.psychiatryonline.org/, https://doi.org/10.1176/appi.pn.2016.11a27.
39. Unknown student, personal conversation, Colorado State University, 2008.

40. Derald Wing Sue, *Microaggressions in Everyday Life: Race, Gender, and Sexual Orientation* (Hoboken, NJ: John Wiley and Sons, 2010), 5.
41. Derald Wing Sue, interview by Charlayne Hunter-Gault, "Derald Sue Talks with PBS about Microaggressions on Campuses," November 20, 2015, http://www.tc.columbia.edu/articles/2015/november/derald-sue-talks-with-pbs-about-microaggressions-on-campuses/.
42. Adapted from Lindsay Pérez Huber and Daniel G. Solórzano, "Microaggressions: What They Are, What They Are Not, and Why They Matter," *Latino Policy and Issues Brief,* UCLA Chicano Studies Research Center, no. 30 (November 2015), http://www.chicano.ucla.edu/files/PB30.pdf.
43. chescaleigh [Franchesca Ramsey], "Shit White Girls Say . . . to Black Girls," YouTube video, 2:36, January 4, 2012, https://www.youtube.com/watch?v=ylPUzxpIBe0.
44. Christina Igaraividez, "Shit White Girls Say to Latinas," YouTube video, 3:23, January 24, 2012, https://www.youtube.com/watch?v=ZcQSLJHpwCA.
45. Dominique Amor, "Shit White Girls Say to Asian Girls," https://www.youtube.com/watch?v=cKd70bMBxmQ.
46. Itsmepaty, "Shit White Girls Say to Mexicans," YouTube video, 4:20, January 21, 2012, https://www.youtube.com/watch?v=XX8qnHJwhW8.
47. The StanfordPushProject, "Shit People Say to People with Disabilities," YouTube video, 3:23, February 23, 2012, https://www.youtube.com/watch?v=DNoVSusaAVE.
48. AlrightHey, "Shit Straight People Say to Gay Guys," YouTube video, 2:23, February 27, 2017, https://www.youtube.com/watch?v=hlBr0Tn9wpQ.
49. Dani Heffernan, "GLAAD Launches Trans Microaggressions Photo Project #transwk," GLAAD, November 14, 2015, https://www.glaad.org/blog/glaad-launches-trans-microaggressions-photo-project-transwk.
50. Derald Wing Sue, interview by Sarah Hamson, "Derald Wing Sue on Microaggression, the Implicit Racism Minorities Endure," *The Globe and Mail,* July 8, 2016, http://www.theglobeandmail.com/life/relationships/derald-wing-sue-on-microaggressions-racism/article30821500/.
51. Sassafras Lowrey, "A Guide to Non-Binary Pronouns and Why They Matter," Huffpost, November 8, 2017, https://www.huffingtonpost.com/entry/non-binary-pronouns-why-they-matter_us_5a03107be4b0230facb8419a.
52. Avinash Chak, "Beyond 'He' and 'She': The Rise of Non-Binary Pronouns," BBC News, December 7, 2015, https://www.bbc.com/news/magazine-34901704.
53. Dennis Baron, *What's Your Pronoun: Beyond He and She* (New York: Liveright Publishing, 2020).
54. Chak, "Beyond 'He' and 'She.'"
55. Sarah Gibson and J. Fernandez, *Gender Diversity and Non-Binary Inclusion in the Workplace: The Essential Guide for Employers* (Philadelphia: Jessica Kingsley, 2017), 17.
56. Gibson and Fernandez, *Gender Diversity,* 18.
57. Gibson and Fernandez, *Gender Diversity,* 19.
58. S. Bear Bergman, "Non-Binary Activism," in *Genderqueer and Nonbinary Genders,* ed. Christina Richards, Walter Pierre Bouman, and Meg-John Barker (New York: Palgrave Macmillan, 2017), 39.
59. Bergman, "Non-Binary Activism," 41; Miranda Fricker, *Epistemic Injustice: Power and the Ethics of Knowing* (Oxford: Oxford University Press, 2007).
60. John J. Gumpertz, ed., *Language and Social Identity* (Cambridge: Cambridge University Press, 1982), 1.
61. Kelly Oliver, *Witnessing: Beyond Recognition* (Minneapolis: University of Minnesota Press, 2001), 3.
62. Lauren Bialystok, "Authenticity in Education," *Oxford Research Encyclopedia of Education* (New York: Oxford University Press, published online September 2017), accessed November 15, 2019, doi: 10.1093/acrefore/9780190264093.013.168.
63. Gereluk, "Citizenship and Ethics."
64. U.S. Department of Education, Office for Civil Rights, Title IX and Sex Discrimination, 2015, https://www2.ed.gov/about/offices/list/ocr/docs/tix_dis.html?exp=0.
65. Compiled from "Title IX," End Rape on Campus, http://endrapeoncampus.org/title-ix/; "Title IX: Gender Equity in Education," ACLU, https://www.aclu.org/title-ix-gender-equity-education; "Title IX Protections for Transgender Students," FindLaw, 2018, https://education.findlaw.com/discrimination-harassment-at-school/title-ix-protections-for-transgender-students.html.
66. Katie Barnes, "How Title IX Expanded to Protect LGBT Students," ABC News, January 17, 2017, https://abcnews.go.com/Sports/title-ix-expanded-protect-lgbt-students/story?id=44832919.
67. "Civil Rights Act of 1964," History, updated June 6, 2019, https://www.history.com/topics/black-history/civil-rights-act.
68. Maggie Humm, *The Dictionary of Feminist Theory* (Columbus: Ohio University Press, 1990), 95–96.
69. Melanie D. Koss, Nancy J. Johnson, and Miriam Martinez, "Mapping the Diversity in Caldecott Books from 1938 to 2017: The Changing Topography," *Journal of Children's Literature* 44, no. 1 (2018): 13.
70. Rae Lesser Blumberg, "The Invisible Obstacle to Educational Equality: Gender Bias in Textbooks," *Prospects: Comparative Journal of Curriculum, Learning, and Assessment* 38, no. 3 (September 2008): 345–361, https://doi.org/10.1007/s11125–009–9086–1.
71. Ulrich Boser, "Teacher Diversity Revisited: A State-by-State Analysis," Center for American Progress, May 2014, 1, https://files.eric.ed.gov/fulltext/ED564608.pdf.

72. Ben Meyers, "Where Are the Minority Professors?" *Chronicle of Higher Education,* February 14, 2018, https://www.chronicle.com/interactives/where-are-the-minority-professors.
73. Joseph Grigely, "The Neglected Demographic: Faculty Members with Disabilities," *Chronicle of Higher Education,* June 27, 2017, https://www.chronicle.com/article/The-Neglected-Demographic-/240439.
74. Melanie Koss, Miriam G. Martinez, and Nancy J. Johnson, "Where Are the Latinxs? Diversity in Caldecott Winner and Honor Books," *The Bilingual Review* 33, no. 5 (2017): 50–62.
75. Zeus Leonardo, "The Color of Supremacy: Beyond the Discourse of 'White Privilege,'" *Educational Philosophy and Theory* 36, no. 2 (2004): 138.
76. Leonardo, "Color of Supremacy," 144.
77. Leonardo, "Color of Supremacy," 149.
78. Alice McIntyre, *Making Meaning Out of Whiteness: Exploring Racial Identity with White Teachers* (Albany: State University of New York Press, 1997), 45.
79. Leonardo, "Color of Supremacy," 143.
80. Christine E. Sleeter, Foreword, in McIntyre, *Making Meaning Out of Whiteness,* x.
81. Christine E. Sleeter, Foreword, in McIntyre, *Making Meaning Out of Whiteness,* xi.
82. Zeus Leonardo, "The Souls of White Folk: Critical Pedagogy, Whiteness Studies, and Globalization Discourse," *Race, Ethnicity and Education* 5, no. 1 (2002): 32.
83. Leonardo, "Souls of White Folk," 39.

CHAPTER

9

Intersectional Approaches to Workplace Injustices

IN THIS CHAPTER, YOU WILL FIND . . .

KEY TERMS AND CONCEPTS

- epistemic injustice
- exclusionary discourse
- gender harassment
- hostile work environment
- ideology of affluence
- principle of equality
- quid pro quo
- racial and ethnic harassment
- self-determination
- sexual harassment
- strategic ambiguity
- structural violence
- sweatshops
- taken-for-granted discourse
- wage gap
- workplace bullying
- workplace harassment

A DIFFERENT STORY OF POOR COMMUNITIES

"I'm tired," shares Mia Birdsong, family justice advocate and co-director of Family Story; "I'm tired of the story we tell that hard work leads to success, because that story allows those of us who make it to believe we deserve it, and by implication, those who don't make it don't deserve it."[1] I'm tired, she says, of the story that tells us that poor people are lazy freeloaders, of the story that wants us to believe that the poor are helpless and had "neglectful parents that didn't read to them enough." Those stories are based on lies and a lack of information. Sure, Birdsong acknowledges, there are some bad apples, but for every negative myth we tell, "I've got 50 [examples] that tell a different story about the same people showing up every day and doing their best."[2] Our poor communities are "full of smart, talented people, hustling and working and innovating, just like our most revered and most rewarded CEOs." The difference, Birdsong points out, is that we reward the CEOs and not those in poor or impoverished communities. The difference is that we tell one story of the hard work and innovation that comes with being over-resourced and a far different, and untrue, story about those grossly under-resourced.[3]

In this chapter, we take up issues related to poverty and fairness in the workplace. We begin by looking at how consumer culture creates workplaces housed outside the United States that are unfair and unjust for the workers that produce the clothing we wear. We then turn our focus to the United States, addressing questions of wage gaps, myths about poverty, and workplace harassment. Throughout this chapter, we take an intersectional approach in order to understand how our complex identities affect our views—and thus our discourses—of fairness, equity, and productive work environments. The chapter concludes with an exploration of how to listen carefully to narratives about workplace injustices, and how we might create workplaces that are fair to the individual as well as the employer.

FAST FASHION: POVERTY WAGES AND DREADFUL WORKING CONDITIONS

If you've ever heard of "fast fashion," or "ready to wear clothing," you've likely heard of Tazreen Fashions or Rana Plaza or Dhaka or Bangladesh. If you've ever purchased inexpensive clothing from H&M, Walmart, Gap, C&A, Sears, Dickies, Disney, Edinburgh Woolen, Mills, Enyce, or Soffee/Delta Apparel, then you've been a "fast fashion" consumer. You may not know, however, one of the reasons those garments are so inexpensive: unsafe working conditions. According to the International Labor Rights Forum, millions of women, and some men, too, work in "apparel factories" also known as **sweatshops.** To save costs and make the least expensive clothing possible, factory owners ignore

Figure 9.1 Sweatshop fires do not just destroy buildings. Thousands of workers have been killed or maimed because they were forced to work in unsafe conditions. (Source: iStock. Credit: Baloncici)

dilapidated buildings, building codes, inadequate fire-fighting tools, absent or inefficient emergency exits, broken fire alarms, and even the functioning alarm when it sounds.

Which is exactly what happened in 2012 at the Tazreen Fashions factory, in Bangladesh: Fire alarms alerted people to a fire, but owners told the workers to ignore them and continue sewing. Doors and gates were locked, fire extinguishers did not work, and 112 people were killed as the fire swept through the building.[4] In 2013, cost cutting measures went awry at the Rana Plaza garment factory—also in Bangladesh, built on swamp land, and in serious violation of building codes. The factory collapsed, killing 1,135 people and injuring approximately 2,500 others. Owners of the building "forced workers to enter the building despite their unwillingness" just one day after the building developed major cracks.[5]

Bangladesh's 5,000 garment factories employ over four million people—no small number. Eighty-five percent of the workers are women, fewer than 300 factories allow unions, and workers are regularly instructed on how to lie to inspectors. Expected to meet high production quotas that necessitate 60 to 140 hours of overtime a week, workers do not receive their minimum wage-paychecks in a timely way and are discriminated against should they become part of a union.[6] Garment workers are engaged in efforts to change these oppressive working conditions, however. In 2019, approximately 50,000 workers protested and staged strikes in Dhaka, in response to their low wages (8,000 takas a month, which equals $96), while thousands of workers throughout Bangladesh demonstrated over low wages, causing dozens of factories to close. Workers often are fired because of their involvement in the protests (in 2019, management fired over 11,000 garment workers from Bangladesh's garment factories) and are injured in clashes with police during protests. Rabeya, who uses only her first name to protect her identity, reports that she began to protest in the streets of Dhaka in January of 2019, and was fired shortly after. "I was vocal in defending our rights," she says, "we work hard day in and day out. Suddenly, our bosses come up to us and tell us to go home."[7]

The conditions are similar for garment workers worldwide, regardless of the country in which they work. Garment workers "are working for poverty wages, under dreadful conditions" as they make clothes for many of the most profitable companies in the world, explains Emilie Schultze, in "Exploitation or Emancipation? Women in the Garment Industry." Schultze reports that in a "labour-intensive industry such as garment," profits are achieved by "paying lower salaries," pushing for longer hours, and reducing environmental and building standards. Additionally, women "tend to earn significantly less than men, they face systematic discrimination, and they are only able to access the lowest paid jobs with very poor prospects for promotion."[8]

In stark contrast to these conditions and salaries, however, CleanClothes.org reports that in 2014, women's wear was worth $621 billion, men's wear worth $402 billion, and children's wear worth $186 billion.[9] A quick trip to one's own closet, dresser, or credit card statement will inform each of us about our own contribution to these profits and more than dangerous working conditions, and perhaps prompt us to ask, "Is this fair?"

Inexpensive Clothing: At What Cost?

What drives our desire for inexpensive clothing, and so much of it, and what would a safe and fair working environment look like? The second question is easier to answer. Made by Women offers a prescription for safe and fair working environments that includes material dignity, such as a living wage and timely payment, as well as emotional dignity, such as being spoken to with respect by supervisors and freedom from verbal and physical harassment. Their prescription includes

- a contract to work
- a living wage
- timely payment
- medical care
- maternity leave

- a pension
- the right to organize
- freedom from forced overtime
- the ability to advocate for safe working conditions[10]

None of these components sound outrageous yet for workers in the garment industry, they are extremely rare.

The first question—what drives the desire for so many inexpensive items of clothing, produced under unsafe and unfair working conditions—is harder to answer. Consumer cultures, and the United States is a consumer culture, are profit and media driven. To survive, consumer cultures need consumers to consume—and media help promote and glorify an ideology of consumption. Rather than identifying fast fashion (cheap clothing and lots of it) as unethical, unsustainable, and harmful to garment workers (as well as our environment), consumers are bombarded with messages that tell them how much they can have for so little. The number of items in one's closet takes precedent over human safety and dignity: what is fair to others is less important than our desire for a lot of inexpensive clothing. So much so that we forget to ask ourselves, "Is this outfit worth more than another human's safety and dignity?"

Dangerous Conditions: Profits Not Safety

The disregard for worker safety is not exclusive to the garment industry or to workplaces in foreign countries. The United States displays a similar trend with regard to those who work at low-paying jobs. These include meat and poultry processing plants; itinerant farm labor; lumber, fishing, and fracking industries; mining, quarrying, and gas extraction; garment industries, and more. Individuals in the lowest socioeconomic strata in the United States and other countries, epidemiologists share, are prone to "precarious" and "contingent" employment. These individuals tend to be women, of all races and ethnicities, but also disproportionately black and Hispanic men. In fact, "being a minority in any way increased workers' chance of being exposed to hazards." Their jobs are more likely to be insecure, temporary, disempowering, low wage, without rights or benefits, and without unions. This means that workers have no control over the pace of the work, which is often repetitive, and they "are not protected by laws designed to ensure proper pay and safe, healthful and nondiscriminatory workplaces, and many are not covered by workers compensation."[11]

Although many occupations are classified as dangerous, many of those also have extensive safety measures in place. For example, although police work and firefighting are dangerous, there are equipment, clothing, tools and technologies, policies, and protocols to protect those who work in these industries. Other occupations do not receive this same level of investment in ensuring safe working conditions; instead, they mirror the conditions and disregard for safety present in the garment industry.

As difficult as it is to acknowledge, consumers play a role in sustaining unsafe working conditions. The drive to secure profits at the expense of safety is powerful. The discourses that surround us tell us that placing profits over safety is good and fair. Capitalism thrives on competition, we are told, and those who can cut costs are the winners in this competition. These discourses often are legitimized by our own tight bank accounts and our desire to "get the best deal" possible. When combined, these narratives can make it easy to ignore unsafe working conditions. When our conversations about our clothes, food, energy, homes, cars, and electronics do not include discussion of workplace conditions, we may be participating in discourses of exploitation and unfairness. We are told that the cheaper an item, the happier we may be—ignoring that this comes at someone else's expense, who is working in very unfair and unsafe conditions.

WAGE GAPS: THE DIFFERENCES IN IDENTITIES

The **wage gap** is defined as the "relative difference in gross hourly earnings" of individuals when identities such as gender, race, sexuality, disability, and the like are calculated. But what does this mean? A helpful analogy is to think of a loaf of bread. If that loaf has 100 slices of bread, then here is what this gap looks like in the United States:

> Hispanic women are paid 57 slices of bread an hour when white men are paid 100 slices an hour—for the same jobs.
>
> Native women are paid 58 slices of bread an hour when white men are paid 100 slices an hour—for the same jobs.
>
> Black women are paid 62.5 slices of bread an hour when white men are paid 100 slices an hour—for the same jobs.
>
> Asian women are paid 78 slices of bread an hour when white men are paid 100 slices an hour—for the same jobs.
>
> White women are paid 79.5 slices of bread an hour when white men are paid 100 slices an hour—for the same jobs.[12]
>
> The birth of a child correlates to 9–18 fewer slices of bread for mothers and an increase of 9 slices for fathers.[13]
>
> States that are more religious have a larger gender pay gap then those less religious.[14]

When we move beyond the gender binary, however, we get yet another view of the wage gap:

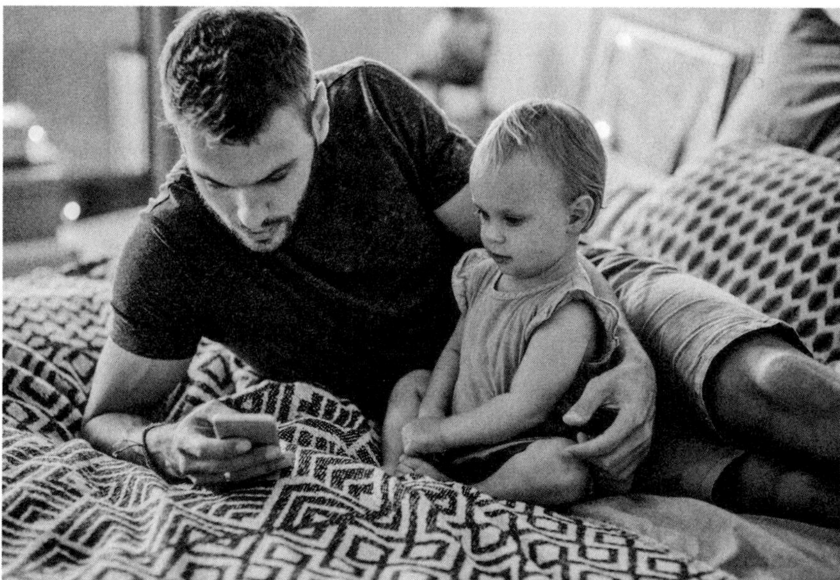

Figure 9.2 The birth of a child affects fathers and mothers differently. Men see an increase in their hourly earnings after a child is born, while women see a decrease in their hourly earnings. (Source: iStock. Credit: svetlkd)

> White men who are gay or bisexual are paid between 90 and 68 slices of bread compared to the 100 slices white heterosexual men are paid—for the same jobs.
>
> Black men are paid 70 slices of bread as compared to the 100 slices their white male counterparts earn—for the same jobs.
>
> Hispanic men are paid 67 slices of bread as compared to the 100 slices their white male counterparts earn—for the same jobs.
>
> Individuals who have disabilities are paid 63 slices of bread as compared to the 100 slices their able body colleagues earn—for the same jobs. Approximately 75 percent of those with disabilities are unemployed, however.[15]
>
> White women who are lesbian are paid slightly more slices of bread than their female heterosexual counterparts, but fewer slices than their white heterosexual male counterparts.[16]

These wage gaps are more evident in jobs in which salaries are higher. Studies show that our "highest paid occupations have the biggest [wage] gaps and the lowest paid occupations have the smallest gaps."[17] This means that as we move away from minimum wage jobs and into salaried work, certain groups of individuals are earning much more than others.

Compounding these differences is the grouping, sorting, and funneling of individuals with certain identities into particular kinds of jobs: women, and individuals who identify as female, tend to dominate teaching and nursing occupations; racial and ethnic minorities tend to dominate low-skill and low paying occupations; and white men tend to dominate high-skill and high paying occupations.[18] Highly educated black women are far less likely to work in high paying jobs than their highly educated white women peers, and the same is true for highly educated Hispanic women.[19] Additionally, women "are more likely to work in occupations with other women, irrespective of their race, than they are to work with men of their own race or ethnicity." Finally, "the level of occupational segregation between White men and men of other racial/ethnic groups is larger" than for all other groups, "a compounding of advantage for White men when compared to all other groups, male or female."[20]

How do we explain these wage gaps and the segregation of our workplaces? Scholars and researchers around the world have offered a dizzying array of possibilities, ranging from worker qualifications and motivation, wage negotiation and job networking strategies, family leave choices and differential responsibilities in the home, and even worker expectations for wages and advancement. None of the explanations hold true, however, and they put the burden of responsibility on the employee and not the employer.[21] They blame the individual rather than larger systemic practices of hiring, promoting, retaining, and rewarding employees. Regardless of our identities, all of us are variously skilled, motivated, and engaged in family responsibilities. Yet, the gender binary narrative tells us that men are more motivated and talented professionally, while women are less driven and usually only work to supplement the family income. White men are especially gifted, we've been told, and while that may hold true for a few individuals and their higher earnings, it does not explain the very real differences in wages across all identities. When the range of identities we bring to a workplace is accounted for, and earnings and job segregation are included in our research and conversations, harsh inequities are revealed.

When viewed intersectionally, a new narrative emerges:

> High wage employers employ "female workers less frequently than male workers" and they pay them less.
>
> High wage employers employ white, able body, cisgender, heterosexual men far more than their nonwhite, disabled, homosexual or transgender or gender queer counterparts, regardless of their maleness or femaleness.
>
> Low wage employers employ far more individuals who are racial and ethnic minorities then they do individuals from racial and ethnic majorities.
>
> The majority of jobs in any workplace are segregated by identities, and even though there are exceptions, most of us work with individuals who share our same racial and gender identities.[22]

After a single hour of work doing the same job, a white male will have the equivalent of 100 slices of bread, while heterosexual Hispanic, black, Native, Asian men, or gay or bisexual men, or white women, or coworkers who have disabilities will have between 57 and 90 slices. If they have families, or live in states that are religious, they may have even less.

Wage inequities communicate a strong message: some workers are valued more than others on the basis of their identities, not their contributions. Certain identities make many employers uncomfortable in certain situations, and so we explain their underrepresentation in our occupations as a lack of motivation and skill on their part rather than a phobia on the part of the employer. Studies long have shown that resumes presenting identical qualifications often are evaluated differently by hiring committees, depending on the name and the job being applied for. Our names, it seems, tell prospective employers something important about our ability to do a job, regardless of our qualifications.[23]

Beyond discrimination, however, understanding the wage gap helps us understand poverty in important ways. Ariane Hegewisch and her colleagues from the Institute for Women's Policy Research share that "equal pay would cut poverty" among working people and their families "by more than half and add $513 billion to the national economy."[24] In "medium skill occupations," equal pay would mean an increase of "$3,555 per year in predominately female dominated occupations . . . $6,999 in predominately male dominated occupations," and "$9,380 in integrated occupations." At the highest level of skill, incomes would increase by as much as $17,451.[25] Wage discrepancies, and the identities that undergird them, inform our discussions of poverty and wealth, employment and underemployment, and fairness in powerful ways.

THE MYTHS OF POVERTY

Michelle Alexander, author of *The New Jim Crow,* explains that even though we repeatedly hear "that anyone, with the proper discipline and drive, can move from a lower class to a higher class" if they just try hard enough, the reality is that they cannot.[26] What is rarely discussed when conversations about upward mobility and the proverbial idea of "pulling yourself up by the bootstraps" are engaged is the forces of institutional, structural, and systemic racism and classism. It's not as simple as individuals who "lack opportunities" or drive, Alexander explains, it's that they can be "barred by law," entangled in deceptive myths of laziness, and confronted daily by what anti-racist educator Tim Wise calls the "culture of cruelty": all of these prevent them from advancing. In this section, we explore those barriers and myths and the discourses that perpetuate them.

The Bootstrap Myth

In his book *Under the Affluence,* Tim Wise explains that the power of those with wealth and resources to define the narrative about economic injustices cannot be overstated. The **ideology of affluence,** the dogma that posits that "anyone can make it," has such a stronghold on our belief systems and our rhetoric that structural and systemic inequities have become normalized and rationalized as the fault of the individual and not of institutions and society. The end result, Wise shares, is that "the conditions of the impoverished, the underemployed and the struggling," regardless of their racial and ethnic identities, "are justified as the inevitable result of inadequate effort on their part, or of cultural flaws, while the wealth and success of the rich are likewise rationalized as owing to their superior talent or value systems."[27]

Discussions of poverty, which have to involve conversations about low wage jobs, underemployment, and unemployment; a lifetime of limited access to quality education; food insecurity; and cycles of homelessness, can be frightening. Far simpler is to engage the familiar narrative of laziness rather than untangle the web of intersecting factors that lead a person or family into poverty, or keep them there. Wise insists that poverty and underemployment are the result of the intersections of race, class, gender, sexuality, and ability. These intersections make our conversations about economic barriers and injustices frustratingly complex. And the fact that we have not addressed these intersections only strengthens the myths that encourage us to believe that we all can "make it on our own talents," we get what we work for, and that the wealthy are uniquely qualified to be rich. Unless we address these intersections, Wise notes, our "attempts to rectify" or to even understand "the current situation will likely fail."[28]

Let's consider employment first. Wise explains that when we hear that "if you want a job, you can get a job," we believe that the playing field is level and that the unemployed are out of work because they lack the motivation to secure employment. But these beliefs are misguided. Wise reports that there are twice as many people actively seeking employment than there are job openings. The competition for jobs, he states, can be more intense than the "competition to get into an Ivy League college." Here's an example:

- Walmart's Washington, D.C. store received 23,000 applications for 600 positions in 2013, giving those 23,000 individuals a 2.6 percent chance of securing a job.
- McDonald's hires about six out of every one hundred applicants.
- In June of 2014, 9.5 million unemployed individuals competed for 4.7 million job openings.

Wise notes that "no matter the work ethic of the unemployed and no matter their drive, determination, skills, values, sobriety, intelligence or anything else, half of all job seekers could not possibly find work."[29] Many individuals have given up and are not even represented in the numbers presented above; people of color are having an especially difficult time. "Latinos are about sixty percent more likely than whites to be unemployed (so much for the often heard phrase that they're 'taking all the good jobs') and African Americans are almost two and a half times as likely as whites to be out of work."[30]

When applicants possess the same degree of education, a high school diploma, for example, the facts are even more depressing. African Americans are twice as likely to be unemployed, and Latinos and Latinas "have an unemployment rate 20 percent higher than whites." When applicants have graduated from college, Latinos and Latinas are "50 percent more likely to be unemployed, than are whites," while African Americans are "70 percent more likely to be unemployed" than their white peers.[31] Despite the common claim that Affirmative Action policies created "reverse discrimination" by promoting hiring irrespective of race, religion, or national origin, white job applicants are far more likely to receive an offer than their minority counterparts. It is hard, Wise explains, to underestimate just "how effective the conservative narrative has been in terms of its impact on the national consciousness," however cruel and untrue that narrative is.[32] That narrative wants us to believe that it is the people in poverty who are the problem when, in fact, it is the system perpetuating that poverty that is the culprit and not the individuals so heavily impacted by it.[33]

What happens if you are one of the lucky Walmart or McDonald's hires? Although the majority of Walmart employees are hired half time, not full time, if you do land that full time job, what might your income be?

- A person working full-time at a minimum wage job in 2018 would receive an annual gross income (before taxes and with no time off) of $19,872.
- Two people working minimum wage jobs would gross $39,744.

If you do even a quick calculation of your own financial needs, you can see that it is very difficult to make ends meet on two minimum wage jobs, let alone one. So, what do you do? Working full time on that income, you could decide to apply for government assistance, rather than starve or lose your home. But, Wise asks, are you now joining the "culture of poverty" we so often hear about? Aren't you headed down a road of dependence, deceit, and sloth? Wise explains that the "only way that someone could really believe that social welfare programs in the United States encourage dependence is by knowing almost nothing about the nation's welfare apparatus." Given the "paltry nature of most program benefits and how few people actually receive them, becoming dependent on the benefits of those programs is virtually impossible."[34]

Here are the facts—a different story to tell—about government assistance programs: the majority of people living in poverty are *not* receiving government assistance. Of the 43.1 million people living in poverty in 2018, in the

United States, less than one in ten receive cash assistance.[35] Of those that do, the majority are children:

- About 3.6 million people received cash welfare under the TANF program (Temporary Assistance to Needy Families). That's a little less than 12 percent of the total population living in poverty.
- Of those 3.6 million people, 2.8 million are children (78 percent).
- Of those 2.8 million children, 75 percent are under the age of twelve.
- The percentage of adults receiving TANF is less than 0.5 percent of the total adult population in the United States and less than 1.5 percent of the total TANF population.[36]

For the almost three million children under the age of twelve living in poverty, getting temporary aid may make the difference between being homeless or not, having food to eat or not, and having heat in the home or not. One recipient explains that as a child whose family received assistance (her parents divorced and her father did not pay child support), the experience was humiliating yet crucial. Clothes were hand-me-downs, and there was no money for toys and gadgets, but "I would've starved some days if we didn't have that option [government assistance]. Many days there was only dry milk, bread, mayonnaise, and mustard in the refrigerator. More than once did my sisters and I eat mustard-and-mayonnaise sandwiches. One winter, our hot-water tank broke and we didn't have money to repair it. We live in Buffalo, New York—Buffalo with no hot water in January. Have you ever washed your hair in cold water?" Now an adult, this woman looks back on what was then called the AFDC (Aid to Families with Dependent Children) program and shares, "I do not know what would have become of my sisters and me" without it.[37]

The typical profile of a TANF family, in addition, is not what our media and politicians share:

- One in four recipients lives with a family who has at least one full-time worker.
- Four in ten live in a family with at least one part-time or full-time worker.
- Six in ten live in a family with someone who works or is actively looking for work.

This means, Wise explains, that 91 percent of TANF recipients "*do not fit* the image" of those receiving welfare: "Only nine out of every one hundred" TANF recipients "fits the description of 'doing nothing.'" The remaining ninety-one people in every hundred are either too young to secure employment (or too old) or modeling self-sufficient behaviors by either working or by looking for work.[38]

The actual dollar amounts that go to these individuals and families also are enlightening. On TANF, in 2015,

- A family of two received a maximum of $363 per month ($12.10 a day or $6.05 per person).
- A family of four received a maximum $611 per month ($20.37 a day or $5.01 per person).
- A family can only receive TANF support for 60 months (5 years).[39]
- A family waiting for Section 8 housing vouchers may be placed on a list that is "thousands of families long" and wait "three to six years" to receive a voucher.[40]

When enrolled in the SNAP program (Supplemental Nutrition Assistance Program)—which many college students, as well as people over the age of 65, are enrolled in—the facts, again, are enlightening:

- The average SNAP monthly benefit is $128 per person, which equals $4.27 per day, which equals $1.42 per meal.[41]
- With both TANF and SNAP in place, a family of two receives an extra $619 per month. This is the equivalent of $20.36 per day, or $10.32 per person per day.
- With both TANF and SNAP in place a family of four receives an extra $1,123 per month. This is the equivalent of $37.43 per day, or $9.35 per person.

Although this sounds like a lot of free money and a sweet deal, consider the average cost of renting a place to live in your area, and how much you, your friends, or your family spend on food per day. Then consider the average cost of childcare (remember, most people living in poverty are under the age of twelve, so if both parents are working, childcare is a necessity). Nationwide, childcare costs can range from $900 to $2,000 a month, per child, depending on location. Most families on government assistance have one or two children, but not more. At the lowest range, their childcare costs will be $1,800 a month.

One last fact adds an important bit to this alternative narrative regarding poverty. Recall from chapter 5 the discussion of crime myths and the criminalizing of normal behaviors that lead to the over-incarceration of minority men. With a felony record a person is denied the right to vote and to serve on juries, and "may be ineligible for many federally-funded health and welfare benefits, food stamps, public housing, and federal educational assistance." This person's "driver's license may be automatically suspended," making it hard to get to interviews and jobs. Certain professional licenses are unattainable, preventing individuals from securing gainful employment. The privilege of enlisting in the military, or securing any kind of federal security clearance, is denied. And these are the penalties for a crime for which a white person is rarely sentenced.[42]

The Stigmatization of Poverty

In her work on physical disability and cultural devaluation, Rosemarie Garland-Thomson shares that in any culture there is an assumption about who a normal individual is—what she labels a "normate"—and anyone who deviates from that norm is "infused with negative value." That negative value is stigmatizing, reflecting the cultural assumptions, social comparisons, and collective devaluation of some individuals but not others. Stigmatizing results in specific human traits being "deemed not only different, but deviant."[43] Garland Thomson's work on physical disability and the body resonates with the myth of the "culture of poverty" and the narrative that people need to pull harder on their own bootstraps rather than depend on government "handouts." When societies stigmatize particular traits—in this case not enough money, unemployment or underemployment, homelessness, in short, poverty—the trait takes over the entire person. Rather than a person out of work, the stigma of poverty consumes a society's conception of the person. The trait, poverty, becomes the whole person—who is defined as lazy, dependent, and dishonest, according to our current cultural myth. At the beginning of the chapter, Mia Birdsong shared the story she is tired of, that if someone would just work harder, they would not be poor. Rather than seeing Mia Birdsong's person living in poverty as hardworking, caring, and innovative, we see the myth we have been led to believe.

Traits are "sculpted by a social group attempting to define its own character and boundaries," Garland Thomson explains, as those in power "determine which differences are inferior" and then "perpetuate those judgments."[44] In the United States, the normal individual—the "ideal" individual—is closely linked to the "American Ideal." Garland Thomson shares that there are "four interrelated ideological principles" that inform this ideal: "self-government, self-determination, autonomy, and progress."[45] In a country such as the United States, Garland Thomson states, one saturated in "an individualist egalitarian" notion of democracy, each individual comes to be seen as a "microcosm of the nation as a whole." Each individual, on her or his own, represents the ideals of the nation. The problem, Garland Thomson explains, is that our ideas of self-determination are at odds with the reality of that condition. When people have **self-determination,** they have the *ability* to compete, succeed, and move forward. The "idea of self-determination places tremendous pressure on individuals to feel responsible for their own social stations, economic situations, and relations with others."[46] To succeed, however, self-determination relies on an egalitarian society, one in which everyone is equal and can truly be responsible for their stations, situations, and relations. The **principle of equality** "implies sameness of condition," which rarely is present.

Nirmala Erevelles, also a scholar in disability studies, notes that this "sameness of condition," this self-determination, is not present. What is present are "social structures—economic, political, legal, religious, and cultural—that stop individuals, groups, and societies, from reaching their full potential." Erevelles explains that this is "because they seem so ordinary, in our ways of understanding the world, they appear almost invisible. Disparate access to resources, political power, education, health care, and legal standing are just a few examples." Erevelles calls this **structural violence,** suggesting that the "idea of *structural violence* is linked very closely to social injustice and the social machinery of oppression."[47]

When we organize poverty as a failure to enact self-determination, a failure to take up opportunities that are said to be available to everyone, we engage in another flawed truth regime. When our discourses are centered on "equal access for all" but there are twice as many applicants as there are jobs, we are not speaking fairly about the reality of that equality. When we stigmatize whole sets of people based on a few traits, we deny the material inadequacies of our federal minimum wage in meeting the real costs of living. These are structural, systemic, and institutional inequities and cruelties (which are discussed more fully in chapters 10 and 11). They are the responsibility of societies and cultures, and not single individuals. When we refuse to acknowledge the systemic violence that is occurring in our conversations about poverty, we fail to see how we are complicit in perpetuating the bootstrap myth and the stigmatization of poverty.

What is the identity breakdown of the recipients of federal aid, those we would consider to be living in poverty? Aside from the fact that the overwhelming majority of them are children, of those enrolled in Temporary Aid to Needy Families, just over one third are black, just under one third are white, and just under one third are Hispanic. Of those enrolled in Supplemental Nutrition Assistance Program, 45 percent of recipients are white, 31 percent of the recipients are black, and 19 percent of recipients are Hispanic. The majority have only one or two children, and most have some kind of income from employment.

Poverty and Epistemic Justice

Miranda Fricker, a philosopher, writes about epistemic injustice.[48] **Epistemic injustice** can be defined as denying a person's way of knowing and experiencing the world. It disallows their experiences, views, and understandings of the way things work, how they work, and why they work the way they do. Epistemology refers to the study of knowledge—what we can know and what we consider "knowable." In short, it helps us think about what we have been told is true and real. For students of intersectional communication, understanding the ways we construct our narratives—the stories we tell—about those who live in poverty can lay a foundation for epistemic injustice but also for epistemic justice. Listening to new stories can make a space for new knowledge.

We commit epistemic injustice when we deny a person's lived experiences and the knowledge they gain from those lived experiences. With very little real information, we often make sweeping claims about poverty, work, wages, motivations, and even "hand-outs." We commit epistemic injustice when we fail to listen to alternative narratives, or to even seek them out. Epistemic justice, however, can occur when we use our intersectional communication skills and engage these new stories—these new ways of understanding the world—and

Figure 9.3 If you were committed to epistemic justice, how would you begin to gather knowledge about the person who owns this cart? (Source: iStock. Credit: ENTphotography)

make spaces for new knowledge. These new stories can re-energize our communication and our conversations. When we make spaces for new ways of knowing, informed by complex identities and situations, our communication comes alive.

Yes, there are "bad apples," as Mia Birdsong acknowledges in the opening paragraph of this chapter—at every level. If the "bad apples" become the definition of the entire crop of apples, we commit epistemic injustice. We cannot communicate meaningfully about any other type of apple. But, when we see the diversity of apples, seek out and listen to the range of stories—good, bad, in between—we create the possibility for epistemic justice. When we listen to those who are making concerted efforts to improve their situations, against some very real odds, our communication is informed in new, and just, ways.

WORKPLACE HARASSMENT: REAL TIME AND ONLINE

When we harass someone, we bother or attack them, repeatedly. Harassment is uninvited—that is, it is not welcomed by the person being harassed. The behavior directed at them is not perceived as a compliment or joke, nor it is seen as fun or funny, flirtatious, romantic, or even endearing. Between 30 and 50 percent of employees report being harassed in their workplaces, making this form of workplace discrimination a systemic problem. Workplace cultures can ignore, and thus legitimize, the harassing behavior, or they can take steps to stop it and prevent it all together. To understand how workplace harassment happens, and why it is so prevalent, we begin by defining this negative form of communicating with others. We then turn to the various identities that are the most common targets of harassment and address the intersectional nature of these identities. This is followed by an examination of two specific genres of harassment—sexual harassment and bullying.

Defining Workplace Harassment

Workplace harassment is defined as "ongoing exposure to negative acts that the target has difficulty defending against due to a real or perceived power imbalance between the parties." Workplace harassment creates a hostile environment for both the target of the harassment as well as those working with them.[49] It also is illegal, violating "Title VII of the Civil Rights Act of 1964, the Age Discrimination in Employment Act of 1967 (ADEA), and the Americans with Disabilities Act of 1990 (ADA)." According to the U.S. Equal Employment Opportunity Commission (EEOC), to qualify as workplace harassment, and not just annoying behavior, the harassing conduct must be focused on a person's "race, color, religion, sex (including pregnancy), national origin, age (40 or older), disability or genetic information." The EEOC sets two criteria for harassment to be considered illegal, "enduring the offensive conduct" must become a "condition of continued employment," or it must "create a work environment" that a "reasonable person would consider intimidating, hostile, or abusive."[50]

Workplace harassment often is a communication phenomenon: we harass others through our verbal and nonverbal messages. Verbally, a harasser might make offensive statements or tell hostile jokes, post offensive images in common spaces or online, spread innuendos or slurs about the person, engage in name-calling and insults, dismiss or discredit the target's work, and make threats or unreasonable demands of the person. All of these can happen either in public or private. Nonverbally, a harasser creates a hostile environment by communicating disapproval or even disgust of the target. This gets communicated when the harasser directs any of the following at the target: rolling their eyes when the person being harassed speaks, releasing heavy sighs when the person enters the room or tries to communicate, making gestures of dismissal before the person is finished communicating, fidgeting while that person is communicating, turning away from the person being harassed during conversation, and even "forgetting" to share important information with the person being harassed.

Harassers also engage in physically intimidating, hostile, or threatening actions like standing over a person, standing too close to someone, grabbing them, touching them without their permission, abruptly closing or slamming doors, and even stalking them. Nonverbal harassment might also include exclusion: not enough chairs, so the person remains standing; last minute invitations, so the person cannot make the event; improper log in and access codes, so they are late for meetings or cannot access the information they need to participate fully; and even unit or departmental rules for engagement that make it difficult for someone to participate in meetings or conversations. The harasser's communication with and about the person, in sum, creates an "intimidating, hostile, or offensive work environment."[51]

To successfully prosecute, the target of workplace harassment must be able to prove that the harassment was a result of one of their protected identities—gender, race, age, religion, ethnicity, or disability, for example—which can be difficult to do. Comments are often delivered without any witnesses, the target's identities are never mentioned overtly, rumors are spread anonymously, and isolation is explained away as the fault of the target and not the perpetrators. Because it is so hard to prove, employers are reluctant to pursue cases, and harassment largely goes unreported and unaddressed. This means that "a significant portion of workers are harassed to the point that they become ill or leave the organization."[52]

Identities and Workplace Harassment

Using an intersectional orientation helps us see that workplace harassment, once thought to be exclusively sexual in nature, can "be based on various identity group characteristics" such as "race, gender, disability, religion, national origin, sexual orientation" and more. We also know that the targets "often experience multiple forms of mistreatment."[53] When one kind of harassment is present, for example, racial harassment, then sexual harassment or bullying likely are present as well. In this section, we examine the intersecting identities that are most frequently the targets of workplace harassment.

Because the problem is so severe, in 2007 the EEOC established E-RACE (Eradicating Racism and Colorism from Employment) to address harassment targeted at a person's racial and ethnic identities. **Racial and ethnic harassment** is defined as "unwelcome conduct" focused on a person's race or ethnicity "that unreasonably interferes with an individual's work performance or creates an intimidating, hostile, or offensive work environment." Racial and ethnic harassment are the most pervasive form of workplace harassment with "40–76 percent of ethnic minorities" reporting "at least one unwanted race-based behavior" in their workplaces.[54]

Antonio Lino, a United Parcel Service worker in Maumee, Ohio, is one of a group of African American employees who filed suit against UPS for racial harassment. Lino describes one incident where "I walked into work, I set up like I normally do, and I just happened to look over my shoulder and it was a noose handing over my workspace first thing Monday morning." Lino believed this was a threat to his life, so he took a photo "because they'll say it didn't happen . . . you've got to have proof." When he talked to management about the threat, he was told to delete the photograph and the situation would be taken care of. Doubtful, Antonio posted the photo online. The physical noose was not the only event, however. The word "noose" circulated through group texts, and a white worker stated, "I'm late for a Klan meeting." Another worker involved in the lawsuit shares, "You're fighting just to exist."[55] Harassment isn't always this explicit, however. Unwanted communication also includes "offensive jokes, slurs, epithets or name-calling, physical assaults or threats, intimidation, ridicule or mockery, insults or put-downs, offensive objects or pictures, and interference with work performance."[56]

Racial and ethnic harassment in the workplace communicate an ideology of racial superiority. This harassment can come through a harasser's verbal communication, in the form of insulting names that mock a person's race, ethnicity, or culture; ridicule for mispronouncing words; making jokes about someone's clothing or hair; racial slurs and slogans; and hostile language or comments, such as "those people" or "If I had my way, I'd gas them . . . like Hitler did." Racial and ethnic harassment also include nonverbal communication: offensive images such as swastikas and gorillas, insulting gestures such as "mimicking martial arts movements" or pulling "eyes back with [your] fingers to mock Asian appearance."

Racial and ethnic harassment also are communicated physically. This physically harassing communication includes throwing items at a person that reinforce stereotypes and mock a person's racial or ethnic history, and even physically grabbing or shoving someone, as when an ethnic minority salesperson's "white manager grabbed him by the collar and dragged him through the dealership."[57] It also can include not doing or allowing certain things, such as refusing to give individuals time off for religious holidays, disallowing head scarves or other items of clothing associated with race, ethnicity, or religion, or insisting that individuals do not speak their native languages in the workplace.[58]

A second form of identity-based harassment, labeled gender harassment, has no legal protection. It does, however, have serious and negative outcomes for employees. **Gender harassment** refers to "experiences of disparaging conduct not intended to elicit sexual cooperation; rather these are crude, verbal, physical, and symbolic behaviors that convey hostile and offensive attitudes about members of one gender" or those who do not conform to gender norms. Gender harassment "appears to be motivated by hostility toward individuals who violate gender ideals" rather than a desire for sexual favors. It encompasses a wide range of behaviors and is largely directed at individuals who do not conform to society's expectations of gender. This form of harassment includes

Figure 9.4 Workers who challenge identity stereotypes frequently are targets of workplace harassment. Reporting can be complicated because harassers often leave very little concrete evidence of their hostility. (Source: iStock. Credit: AnandaBGD)

"anti-female jokes, comments that women do not belong in management, and crude terms of address."[59] It involves homophobic and transphobic slanders and slurs, as well as offensive jokes, inappropriate and/or invasive comments, and insulting a person's gender queer or gender fluid identities. It also is communicated through wage gaps, the failure to promote qualified individuals because of their gender nonconformity, and even passing over qualified individuals for important assignments.[60]

Forty-two percent of heterosexual women and "35 percent of gay and bisexual people who are out at work suffer from harassment." As many "58 percent of LGBT people have heard derogatory comments about sexual orientation or gender identity in the workplace."[61] The goal of gender harassment is to insult rather than seek sexual behaviors and to make individuals feel unwelcome and denigrated because they do not conform to gender norms.

Using an intersectional lens, we can also see how race and ethnicity, ability, economic status, and citizenship are factors in workplace harassment. In their work on Canadian women, citizenship, and domestic labor, Sandy Welsh and her colleagues describe gender harassment as "like a mix. It's a Mix action. You don't know if that person is doing it to you because of the color of your skin and the type of job that you have," your citizenship status, or other reasons, "you don't know if it is harassment or sexual harassment."[62] Because there are no laws to protect individuals from gender harassment, it remains largely unreported (the occupations with the highest levels of reporting are women in military and legal professions). However, its consequences can be severe; among these negative impacts are "decreased psychological well-being," "symptoms of psychological trauma," "greater anger, anxiety, and depression," "decreased job satisfaction," and "loss of productivity."[63]

Sam Hall, a gay man, worked in the coal mines in West Virginia. He tells of his experience with his "locker broken into . . . a screwdriver taken to a brand new Explorer." Coworkers would say in front of the team they "wish all faggots would die . . . and then look at me." Hall describes how he "would cut and load his own coal . . . to make sure it was safe." He remarks, "I've heard this before: underground, accidents happen every day. I wasn't going to be an accident. That was not going to happen, not to me." He complained to his supervisor to no avail. He complained to a federal inspector and was told, "You have no protection." He explains, "They just didn't care. . . . It was painful." He finally quit and is now a store manager. Hall says, "I make a point to outdo people at my job just to show them because I'm gay, it ain't no handicap."[64] Rather than drawing a person into sexual relationships, gender harassment "*rejects* [that person] and attempts to drive them out of jobs where they are seen to have no place."[65]

Sexual Harassment

Charlotte, who worked in a London pub, described the workplace situation this way: "groped . . . while carrying plates of food," tipped £20 "while being asked to go to a hotel"; the sexual harassment was "continuous." Charlotte explains, "It made me feel unsafe and miserable. . . . I broke down and had to go home to my parents for two weeks because I just couldn't take it anymore." However, she did not complain because she feared "making too much fuss would reduce my hours when I was struggling to support myself."[66] With the #MeToo campaign, the epidemic of sexual harassment in the workplace finally took center stage. After decades of being ignored, dismissed, and discredited, the conversation about sexual harassment began to hold perpetrators accountable for their actions. Portrayed in our media as "overtly aggressive" and easy to spot, sexual harassment in the workplace often is far more subtle than our media claim. The #MeToo campaign, as well as the sexually harassing actions of high profile celebrities, discussed in chapter 7, exposed not just its prevalence, but also its covert complexity. The decades of damage done to women and their careers cannot be overestimated. Yet, with these high profile campaigns and cases, we may now be able to begin to truly understand what sexual harassment is, the damage done to the people harassed, and the immense power the harassers possess, and bring these insights into our conversations.

Defined as "unwelcome sexual advances or conduct of a sexual nature which unreasonably interferes with the performance of a person's job," **sexual harassment** "creates an intimidating, hostile, or offensive work environment."[67] The research, to date, is largely done from a gender-binary perspective. Those who report sexual harassment describe a "no-filter, say-anything workplace" with eight out of every ten sharing that the sexual harassment involves saying something out loud (a male Tinder executive called the then marketing vice president from Tinder a "whore" in front of her coworkers at a company party). But inappropriate touching (a lingering hug or adjusting a woman's collar or necklace) and sexual advances make up 40 percent of the harassment women experience (a male customer informed a Houston bartender that he knew "where to get some really good coke if you want to do a line off my dick"). One in four women harassed sexually receive lewd texts or emails (a New York tech entrepreneur received the following email from a male co-worker, late at night: "Take off your underwear, put it in a bag, and leave it on my desk").[68]

Sexual comments or jokes, inappropriate touching or nonverbal signals, and insinuating language in an email or text, "a link to a porn video that pops up on Gchat," or "a comment about how hot you look," often leave their recipients confused and uncertain as to what is going on.[69] David Low, an employment attorney in San Francisco, shares that with the "advent of social media, there is a much more casual relationship between coworkers and supervisors, and that absolutely creates more opportunity for people to cross the line between professional and unprofessional conduct." Statistics suggest that 48 percent of women of any age report being sexually harassed at work. Ninety percent of Asian American women report being both sexually and racially harassed.[70] Forty-one percent of men say that have witnessed sexual harassment in their workplaces, and the EEOC reports that men file 15 percent of the commission's sexual harassment cases.

Although it is the high profile cases in our media and entertainment industries that catch our attention, the worst occupations for sexual harassment are the restaurant industry (42 percent of women say they've been harassed), retail (36 percent of women say they've been harassed), science and technology as well as arts and entertainment (31 percent of women say they've been harassed), legal fields (30 percent women say they've been harassed), and the military (25 percent of women say they've faced severe sexual harassment, but 81 percent of victims also did not report the harassment or ensuing assault). The underreporting of sexual harassment in the military mirrors the underreporting in the majority of sexual harassment cases overall (70–80 percent of cases are not reported).

Reporting can be complicated because many harassers are careful to make comments when no one else is around. Too often, the target of the harassment is accused of taking things too seriously and harassers are quick to point out they were only making a joke, trying to be friendly, or "building new, more egalitarian" working environment through socializing and relaxing together.[71] Retaliation is also a huge problem, not just in sexual harassment cases, but also racial and ethnic harassment situations. Although it is illegal to retaliate, the EEOC reports that of the total number of cases of harassment filed with them, almost half of them were for the retaliation of employers against their employee.[72]

When women do report sexual harassment in the workplace, there are laws (in the United States) that recognize just two types of sexual harassment: quid pro quo and hostile work environment.

quid pro quo: Translated as "this for that," quid pro quo harassment occurs when a person in a position of authority demands that sexual harassment be tolerated in return for keeping one's job, getting a promotion or assignment, or a raise. This can include kissing, touching, and sexual activities. A single incident is enough to press charges.

hostile work environment: Hostile work environments occur when the conduct of supervisors or coworkers is unwelcome, based on sex, and severe or pervasive enough to create an abusive or offensive work environment. This includes comments, noises, and physical or visual displays. To press charges, the behavior must be frequent, offensive, or hostile, and judged to be such by a reasonable person.

Significantly, these two categories can also be used for filing and prosecuting racial and ethnic harassment claims. When a person in a position of authority demands that the employee tolerate the harassment or hostile work environment as a condition of employment, the employee can claim racial and ethnic quid pro quo and file hostile work environment charges against that person.

Bullying

In *When You Work for a Bully,* Susan Futterman says, "Up until I met him, I was confident in my ability to do my job, believed I had reasonably good people skills and was a conscientious, responsible and valuable employee." Her performance evaluations were good and her letters of recommendation were strong. In her new job, however, Futterman states, "in less than six months, I was a wreck. I was working 12 hour days, with an increasing number of those hours devoted to responding to the continuing barrage of memos, emails, and voice-mails" that came from her new boss telling her that her performance was far below expectations and she was not doing her job. Panic attacks became a regular part of her life, she shares, as did sick days and doctors. Eventually, Futterman explains, the experience was so horrible and unsustainable that she quit her job, which she used to love.[73]

Bullying is not limited to our schools. Workplace bullying is "shockingly common and enormously destructive." Estimates suggest that between 30 and 37 percent of U.S. workers are bullied over the course of their work careers, approximately one-third of the people in any workplace. Bullying harms not only the individuals who are targeted but can have a "serious negative impact on" co-workers as well, who fear they might also become targets. It also damages workplace morale and productivity.

Defined as "repeated, health-harming mistreatment," **workplace bullying** includes "verbal abuse; offensive conduct and behaviors . . . that are threatening, humiliating, or intimidating; or work interference and sabotage that prevent work from getting done."[74] When employees are excluded from meetings, become the recipient of "persistent and unwarranted criticism," are subjected to condescending and patronizing discourse, have their responsibilities and authority undercut, and/or have information withheld—information they need to do their jobs—they "are being bullied."[75] When a boss "bombards you with memos and telephone calls, focused on the minutiae" or conversely, refuses to return emails, texts, and phone calls, abruptly changes your schedule without consulting you, constantly interrupts you, and denigrates you to co-workers or clients, "you can again be pretty certain that you've been targeted by a bully."[76] "Constructive criticism," Futterman explains, "is a necessary part of any workplace—it is how we improve." Bullying, in contrast to constructive criticism, is hostile, petty, destructive, "often obnoxious" and "frequently cruel."[77]

The most common type of bullying is a supervisor bullying a supervisee, as in Futterman's case, but colleagues also can "gang up" on other colleagues, sometimes called "mobbing"; subordinates may even occasionally engage in "bullying up," to abuse a higher-level organizational member. As our research on workplace bullying has become more intersectional, we have learned that where people are located with regard to power best explains the bully/bullied profile: managers, supervisors, and those in upper level positions make up 60 to 80 percent of the bullies. "In a nationally representative survey . . . 72 percent of reported bullies were managers, some of whom had the sponsorship and support of executives, managerial peers, and human resources."[78] If a person is inclined to bully, occupying positions of power seems to be more of a determining factor than sex, gender, race, sexuality, or the like.

Even though most workplaces know bullying happens, organizations and the people who work in them frequently deny its existence. If forced to address complaints of bullying, people in organizations regularly dismiss its severity. They often explain away the bullying behavior as a supervisor's personality or quirk and not actually bullying. Organizations also focus their energies on discrediting the complainant rather than addressing the culture that fosters bullying behaviors and communication. Bullying organizational culture, that is, workplaces in which bullying occurs frequently often are highly competitive and lacking in resources, opportunities for advancement, or promotions. They tend to be organizations in which the pressures to produce more and reduce costs are intense, and where there is long-term chaos, job insecurity, and/or a lack of privacy.[79]

The targets of bullies are more likely to be someone with less power than to possess any specific characteristic or trait. Some studies describe the people who are bullied as independent, high in emotional intelligence, respected, ethical, and honest (almost every whistleblower is a target of bullying), more technically skilled than their bosses, and nonconfrontive. But they also have been described as shy and submissive, unsophisticated, suspicious of others, or, conversely, overachievers. The most consistent finding in this confusing array of traits is that "low-status workers are simply more vulnerable"—power matters in the bullying hierarchy.[80]

Creuza Oliviera became a domestic worker in Brazil when she was ten years old. Her employers bullied her—calling her names like "lazy," "monkey," and other racial slurs—if she broke something or her work wasn't considered up to their standards. In addition, her payment consisted of food, clothing, and shelter, and Oliviera did not receive any financial compensation for her work until she was twenty-one. Today she is president of the National Federation of Domestic Workers in Brazil, having heard about the organization on the radio, and a spokesperson for the more than nine million Brazilian domestic workers, most of whom are black. "Domestic work in my country still carries the legacy of slavery," she says, "almost half a million domestic workers in Brazil are children and teenagers between 5 and 17 years of age, working without compensation, as slaves. . . ."[81]

It is also difficult to pinpoint the motives behind the bully. People who bully are sometimes described as threatened by or jealous of the person they target, as pursuing a vendetta, or as just being who they are. With respect to the targets of bullying, heterosexual women experience "campaigns of hatred and intimidation" from bullies, while lesbian women report more "homophobic bullying," which takes an "indirect" approach and includes "repeated failed attempts to secure employment, threats of job loss, and repeatedly being treated badly or excluded in the workplace as a result of being 'out.'"[82] Race also influences bullying, with individuals from Asian (33.3 percent), African American (33 percent) and Hispanic (32.5 percent) backgrounds being targeted more than whites (24.1 percent).[83]

The effects of bullying are serious and, for organizations, include loss of productivity, high turnover, and difficulty recruiting new employees. For workers, the effects include "low self-esteem, concentration difficulties, anger, lower life satisfaction, frustration, burnout, reduced productivity, increased absenteeism, and greater intentions to quit their jobs." Studies also have linked the stress of bullying to "depression, sleep problems, symptoms of PTSD, and physician diagnosis of psychiatric" illness.[84] As with workplace harassment, those who attempt to "make a case against" a bully "may find that the bullying only gets worse." Retaliation is a real issue and those who do make claims against a bully often have to either "find different employment" or make the best of an untenable situation.[85]

Listening to Subordinates Rather Than Supervisors

Organizational Communication scholar Robin Clair explains that bureaucracies control the discourse we use to understand injustices. Bureaucracies,

9.1. GUIDE TO COMMUNICATION

Talking Back to Systems of Workplace Harassment

In order to explore ways we can change the discourse around bullying and harassment, consider the following steps:

1. *Understand human rights violations.* According to the United Nations, "Human rights are rights inherent to all human beings, regardless of race, sex, nationality, ethnicity, language, religion, or any other status. Human rights include the right to life and liberty, freedom from slavery and torture, freedom of opinion and expression, the right to work and education, and many more. Everyone is entitled to these rights, without discrimination." How true is this for the places you work as well as the places in which the items you buy are manufactured?
2. *Develop an intersectional vocabulary.* In "Transforming Resistance," communication scholars Shiv Ganesh, Heather Zoller, and George Cheney ask "to what degree do resistance efforts address multiple forms of inequality and difference, such as gender, ethnicity, nationality, class, religion, and sexuality?" Rather than hold individuals wholly responsible for workplace inequities, explore the organizational discourses in the places you work and assess who is being held accountable, and which identities are clearly named as central to the inequities that may be occurring.
3. *Expand your own narrative.* Following Robin Clair's research, examine the taken-for-granted, strategically ambiguous, and exclusionary discourses in your own communication about workplace inequities. Whose experiences are being valued and sanctioned? Whose experiences are being concealed and devalued?

Source: "Human Rights," United Nations, 2018, http://www.un.org/en/sections/issues-depth/human-rights/, and Shiv Ganesh, Heather Zoller, and George Cheney, "Transforming Resistance, Broadening Our Boundaries: Critical Organizational Communication Meets Globalization from Below," Communication Monographs 72, no. 2 (2005), 181.

through their policies for addressing injustices, dictate the terms of engagement, the language those who are bullied can and cannot use, and the procedures they must follow to file a grievance. Rather than listening to those who are the targets of the injustice, Clair says, we listen to those in power. Organizational structures and traditions "disguise power imbalances," in effect, silencing those who are being harassed. Clair states that organizations use three communicative practices to silence those who attempt to speak out about injustices: taken-for-granted discourse, strategic ambiguity, and exclusionary discourse.

Taken-for-granted discourses reinforce an injustice as "the norm": It's just how things are, how they have always been, and how they always will be. In terms of intersectional workplace injustices, this form of discourse says harassment will always be present in organizations—or so we are supposed to believe. **Strategic ambiguity** "is the use of discourse to foster multiple interpretations" of policies as well as events. This allows diverse groups within any organization to "interpret a message (e.g., policy or formalized procedures) based on their own viewpoint." The language is vague enough that workplace harassment becomes "a supervisor's personality" rather than actual harassment, sexual harassment is interpreted as "flirtation" and misunderstandings, and gender and racial/ethnic harassment "just a joke" on the part of the harassers and oversensitivity on the part of the targets.

Exclusionary discourse rests heavily "upon concealment versus disclosure." Policies limit the nature, amount, and kind of information that can be shared, sometimes stating a target must report the abuse within a particular time frame of the actual events. The use of the passive voice is ubiquitous ("he was harassed," rather than "his boss harassed him"), gag orders are pronounced in order to "protect the identities" of the harassers, and, although targets are told to report offenses, retaliation is a very real obstacle to that reporting, effectively functioning to keep the harassment concealed.[86]

Discourse creates and maintains our meaning systems, and these systems are never neutral. "Discourse has the ability to oppress as well as emancipate people." It can create, enact, and reproduce power structures, or it can dismantle them.[87] Whether it be the clothing we buy, the conditions of a workplace, or the cultures that sanction harassing behaviors, our discourse—the narratives we tell and listen to—have the power to expose and address inequities. We simply need to unleash and listen to them.

Resources

Gretchen Carlson, "How We Can End Sexual Harassment at Work," filmed November 2017 in New Orleans, LA, TEDWomen 2017 video, 14:37; https://www.ted.com/talks/gretchen_carlson_how_we_can_end_sexual_harassment_at_work#t-84989.

Sir Ken Robinson, "Do Schools Kill Creativity?" filmed February 2006 in Monterey, CA, Ted2006 video, 19:13, https://www.ted.com/talks/ken_robinson_says_schools_kill_creativity.

Notes

1. Mia Birdsong, "The Story We Tell About Poverty Isn't True," filmed May 2015 in Monterey, CA, TEDWomen video, 15:09, https://www.ted.com/talks/mia_birdsong_the_story_we_tell_about_poverty_isn_t_true/transcript, 9:14–10:11.
2. Birdsong, "Story We Tell About Poverty," 9:33.
3. Birdsong, "Story We Tell About Poverty," 8:06.
4. "Sweatshop Fires in Bangladesh," Bangladesh Fire Safety, International Labor Rights Forum, http://old.laborrights.org/sweatshop-fires-in-bangladesh, accessed April 2017.
5. "Rana Plaza Collapse: Dozens Charged with Murder," *Guardian*, June 1, 2015, https://www.theguardian.com/world/2015/jun/01/rana-plaza-collapse-dozens-charged-with-murder-bangladesh, accessed April 13, 2017.
6. Sarah Butler, "Bangladesh Garment Workers Still Vulnerable a Year after Rana Plaza," *Guardian*, April, 24, 2014. https://www.theguardian.com/world/2014/apr/24/bangladesh-garment-workers-rights-rana-plaza-disaster, accessed April 13, 2017.

7. Arun Devnath and Lain Marlow, "Thousands Fired from $30 Billion Bangladesh Garment Sector," *Bloomberg*, February 15, 2019, https://qz.com/1540275/5000-garment-workers-in-bangladesh-were-fired-after-protesting-low-wages/; Marc Bain, "5,000 Workers Protesting Low Wages in Bangladeshi Garment Factories Have Been Fired," *Quartz*, February 1, 2019, https://qz.com/1540275/5000-garment-workers-in-bangladesh-were-fired-after-protesting-low-wages/; "Bangladesh Strikes: Thousands of Garment Workers Clash with Police Over Poor Pay," *Guardian*, January 13, 2019, https://www.theguardian.com/world/2019/jan/14/bangladesh-strikes-thousands-of-garment-workers-clash-with-police-over-poor-pay.
8. Emilie Schultze, "Exploitation or Emancipation? Women Workers in the Garment Industry," *European Year for Development*, March 24, 2015. https://europa.eu/eyd2015/en/fashion-revolution/posts/exploitation-or-emancipation-women-workers-garment-industry, accessed April 13, 2017.
9. Lina Stotz and Gillian Kane, "The Global Garment Industry," Global Garment Industry Factsheet, accessed April 13, 2017, https://cleanclothes.org/resources/publications/factsheets/general-factsheet-garment-industry-february-2015.pdf.
10. Nina Ascoly, "Introduction: Why Gender Is Important," *Made by Women: Gender, the Global Garment Industry, and the Movement for Women Worker's Rights*, eds. Nina Ascoly and Chantal Finney (Clean Clothes Campaign, 2005), 6–7, accessed April 13, 2017, http://digitalcommons.ilr.cornell.edu/cgi/viewcontent.cgi?article=1164&context=globaldocs.
11. Paul A. Landsbergis, Joseph G. Grzywacz, and Anthony D. La Montagne, "Work Organization, Job Insecurity, and Occupational Health Disparities," Eliminating Health and Safety Disparities at Work Conference, September 14 and 15, 2011, revised November 15, 2011, http://www.aoe cdata.org/conferences/healthdisparities/whitepapers/work-organization.pdf.
12. Compiled from "Resource: The Wage Gap by State for Native Women," National Women's Law Center, December 28, 2018, https://nwlc.org/resources/equal-pay-for-native-women/; "Fact Sheet, The Gender Wage Gap 2016 by Occupation, Race, and Ethnicity," Institute for Women's Policy Research, April 2017, https://iwpr.org/wp-content/uploads/2017/04/C456.pdf; Mary C. Daly, Bart Hobijn, and Joseph H. Pedtke, "Disappointing Facts about the Black-White Wage Gap," Federal Reserve Bank of San Francisco, Economic Letter, September 2016, https://www.frbsf.org/economic-research/publications/economic-letter/2017/september/disappointing-facts-about-black-white-wage-gap/; "The Wage Gap by Gender and Race," Infoplease, https://www.infoplease.com/us/wage-gap/wage-gap-gender-and-race.
13. Shelly Lundberg and Elaina Rose, "Parenthood and the Earnings of Married Women," *Labour Economics* 7, no. 6 (November 2000): 690.
14. Philip Perry, "Do Religious States Have a Wider or Narrower Gender Pay Gap?" Big Think, November 2, 2016, https://bigthink.com/philip-perry/gender-pay-gap-in-the-us-affected-by-a-states-religiosity; Snoman Seth, "The Level of Religiousness Has Huge Effects on How Much Men and Women Are Paid," *Business Insider*, October 24, 2016, https://www.businessinsider.com/gender-pay-gap-affected-by-religiousness-of-state-2016-10.
15. Compiled from "The Simple Truth about Gender Pay Gap," AAUW, 2019, https://www.aauw.org/research/the-simple-truth-about-the-gender-pay-gap/; "Fact Sheet, Gender Wage Gap 2016"; "AIR Index: The Pay Gap for Workers with Disabilities," American Institutes for Research, 2015, https://www.air.org/resource/air-index-pay-gap-workers-disabilities.
16. Heather Antecol, Anneke Jong, and Michael Steinberger, "Sexual Orientation Wage Gap: The Role of Occupational Sorting and Human Capital," *Industrial Labor and Relations Review* 61, no. 4 (July 2008): 515–543.
17. "Fact Sheet, Gender Wage Gap 2016."
18. Angela Byars-Winston, Nadya Fouad, and Yao Wen, "Race/Ethnicity and Sex in U.S. Occupations, 1970–2010: Implications for Research, Practice, and Policy," *Journal of Vocational Behavior* 87 (April 2015): 54–70.
19. Ariane Hegewisch and Heidi Hartmann, "Occupational Segregation and the Gender Gap: A Job Half Done," Institute for Women's Policy Research, January 23, 2014, 1–23, https://iwpr.org/publications/occupational-segregation-and-the-gender-gap-a-job-half-done.
20. Hegewisch and Hartmann, "Occupational Segregation," 10.
21. Louis N. Christofides, Alexandros Polycarpou, and Konstantinos Vrachimis, "Gender Wage Gaps, 'Sticky Floors' and 'Glass Ceilings,'" Working Paper, Department of Economics, University of Cyprus, February 2013.
22. Ana Rute Cardoso, Paulo Guimaraes, and Pedro Portugal, "What Drives the Gender Wage Gap? A Look at the Role of Firm and Job-Title Heterogeneity," *Oxford Economic Papers* 68, no. 2 (April 2016): 11, https://doi.org/10.1093/oep/gpv069.
23. Eden B. King, Saaid A. Mendoza, Juan M. Madera, Mikki R. Hebl, and Jennifer L. Knight, "What's in a Name? A Multiracial Investigation of the Role of Occupational Stereotypes in Selection Decisions," *Journal of Applied Social Psychology* 36 (April 21, 2006): 1145–1159; Sonja K. Kang, Katerine A. DeCelles, András Tilcsik, and Sora Jun, "Whitened Résumés: Race and Self-Presentation in the Labor Market," *Administrative Science Quarterly* 61, no. 3 (September 1, 2016; published online March 17, 2016): 1–34; Shelby McIntyre, Dennis J. Moberg, and Barry Z. Posner, "Preferential Treatment in Preselection Decisions According to Sex and Race," *Academy of Management Journal* 23, no. 4 (1980; published online November 30, 2017), doi: 10.5465/255560.

24. Ariane Hegewisch and Emma Williams-Baron, "The Gender Wage Gap by Occupation 2016: and by Race and Ethnicity," Institute for Women's Policy Research, accessed April 4, 2017, https://iwpr.org/issue/employment-education-economic-change/pay-equity-discrimination/.
25. Hegewisch and Williams-Baron, "Gender Wage Gap," 19.
26. Michelle Alexander, *The New Jim Crow: Incarceration in an Age of Colorblindness* (New York: New Press, 2010), 13.
27. Tim J. Wise, *Under the Affluence: Shaming the Poor, Praising the Rich and Sacrificing the Future of America* (San Francisco: City Lights Books, Open Media Series, 2015), 10.
28. Wise, *Under the Affluence*, 13.
29. Wise, *Under the Affluence*, 159.
30. Wise, *Under the Affluence*, 35.
31. Wise, *Under the Affluence*, 35, 36.
32. Wise, *Under the Affluence*, 93.
33. Wise, *Under the Affluence*, 96.
34. Wise, *Under the Affluence*, 139.
35. "What Is the Current Poverty Rate in the United States," Center for Poverty Research, University of California, Davis, updated October 15, 2018, https://poverty.ucdavis.edu/faq/what-current-poverty-rate-united-states.
36. Wise, *Under the Affluence*, 139.
37. Rosa Inocencio Smith, "I Am a Welfare Success Story," *Atlantic*, August 24, 2016, https://www.theatlantic.com/notes/2016/08/i-am-the-product-of-afdc/497192/.
38. Wise, *Under the Affluence*, 140.
39. Wise, *Under the Affluence*, 140, 142.
40. "Section 9 (housing), Wikipedia, https://en.wikipedia.org/wiki/Section_8_(housing); see also "Housing Choice Vouchers Fact Sheet," HUD.gov, U.S. Department of Housing and Urban Development, https://www.hud.gov/topics/housing_choice_voucher_program_section_8.
41. Wise, *Under the Affluence*, 142.
42. Alexander, *New Jim Crow*, 142–143.
43. Rosemarie Garland Thomson, *Extraordinary Bodies: Figuring Physical Disability in American Culture and Literature* (New York: Columbia University Press, 1997), 31.
44. Garland Thomson, *Extraordinary Bodies*, 31.
45. Garland Thomson, *Extraordinary Bodies*, 41.
46. Garland Thomson, *Extraordinary Bodies*, 43.
47. Nirmala Erevelles, *Disability and Difference in Global Contexts: Enabling a Transformative Body Politic* (New York: Palgrave Macmillan, 2011), 16.
48. Miranda Fricker, *Epistemic Injustice: Power and the Ethics of Knowing* (Oxford: Oxford University Press, 2007).
49. Mats Glambek, Anders Skogstad, and Ståle Einarsen, "Workplace Bullying, the Development of Job Insecurity and the Role of Laissez-Faire Leadership: A Two-Wave Moderation Mediation Study," *International Journal of Work, Health and Organizations* 32, no. 3 (January 2018): 297.
50. U.S. Equal Employment Opportunity Commission, "Harassment," https://www.eeoc.gov/laws/types/harassment.cfm.
51. Jana L. Raver and Lisa H. Nishii, "Once, Twice, Three Times as Harmful? Ethnic Harassment, Gender Harassment, and Generalized Workplace Harassment," *Journal of Applied Psychology* 95, no. 2 (March 2010): 237.
52. Jagdish Khubchandani and James H. Price, "Workplace Harassment and Morbidity among US Adults: Results from National Health Interview Survey," *Community Health* 40, no. 3 (June 2015): 555–563.
53. Raver and Nishii, "Once, Twice, Three Times as Harmful," 236.
54. NiCole T. Buchanan and Louise F. Fitzgerald, "Effects of Racial and Sexual Harassment on Work and Psychological Well-Being of African American Women," *Journal of Occupational Health Psychology* 13, no. 2 (2008): 138.
55. Mallory Simon and Sara Sidner, "Black Workers Describe Details of 'Living Hell' at UPS Center in Ohio," CNN, updated March 15, 2019, https://www.cnn.com/2019/03/14/us/ohio-black-workers-sue-ups/index.html.
56. Brenda J. Allen, "Racial Harassment in the Workplace," in *Destructive Organizational Communication: Processes, Consequences, and Constructive Ways of Organizing*, ed. Pamela Lutgen-Sandvik and Beverly Davenport Sypher (New York: Routledge, 2009), 173.
57. Allen, "Racial Harassment," 173–174.
58. Marcia Pledger, "Workplace Religious Discrimination Complaints Double over 10 Years," Religion News Science, HuffPost, November 25, 2011, updated November 26, 2011, https://www.huffingtonpost.com/2011/11/25/workplace-religious-discrimination_n_1112313.html.
59. Sandy Lim and Lilia M. Cortina, "Interpersonal Mistreatment in the Workplace: The Interface and Impact of General Incivility and Sexual Harassment," *Journal of Applied Psychology* 90, no. 3 (2005): 483.

60. Kim Parker and Cary Funk, "Gender Discrimination Comes in Many Forms for Today's Working Women," Pew Research Center, December 14, 2017.
61. Mark Joseph Stern, "Harassment Is Still a Massive Problem in the American Workplace," *Slate*, June 20, 2016, http://www.slate.com/blogs/outward/2016/06/20/harassment_in_the_workplace_eeoc_shows_it_remains_a_problem.html.
62. Sandy Welsh, Jacquie Carr, Barbara MacQuarrie, and Audrey Huntley, "'I'm Not Thinking of It as Sexual Harassment': Understanding Harassment across Race and Citizenship," *Gender and Society* 20, no. 1 (2006): 96.
63. Stern, "Harassment."
64. Preston Mitchum, "5 LGBT Workers Who Experience Legal Workplace Discrimination," Think Progress, August 7, 2013, https://thinkprogress.org/5-lgbt-workers-who-experienced-legal-workplace-discrimination-da98ddff6396/.
65. Emily A. Leskinen, Lilia M. Cortina, and Dana B. Kabat, "Gender Harassment: Broadening Our Understanding of Sex-Based Harassment at Work," *Law and Human Behavior* 35, no. 1 (February 2011), 27, doi: 10.1007/s10979–010–9241–5.
66. "'I Wasn't Protected at All': Why Women Are Made Vulnerable by Zero-Hour Contracts," *Guardian*, March 19, 2018, https://www.theguardian.com/lifeandstyle/2018/mar/19/women-made-vulnerable-zero-hours-contracts-sexual-harassment-work.
67. "Sexual Harassment at Work," FindLaw, accessed April 26, 2017, http://employment.findlaw.com/employment-discrimination/sexual-harassment-at-work.html.
68. Michelle Ruiz, "What Sexual Harassment at Work Really Looks Like," *Cosmopolitan*, February 16, 2015, accessed April 26, 2017, http://www.cosmopolitan.com/career/a36462/sexual-harassment-at-work/.
69. Lauren Ahn and Michelle Ruiz, "Survey: 1 in 3 Women Has Been Sexually Harassed at Work," *Cosmopolitan*, February 6, 2015, accessed April 26, 2017, http://www.cosmopolitan.com/career/news/a36453/cosmopolitan-sexual-harassment-survey/?dom=fb_hp&src=social&mag=cos.
70. Buchanan et al., "Effects of Racial and Sexual Harassment," 10.
71. Ruiz, "What Sexual Harassment at Work Really Looks Like."
72. Bryan E. Kuhn, "EEOC Statistics Suggest Retaliation and Harassment Areas of Concern," https://www.bryankuhnlaw.com/Articles/EEOC-statistics-suggest-retaliation-and-harassment-areas-of-concern.shtml; Michael Brewer, "EEOC FY 2017 Statistics Recap: Retaliation Claims Charge Ahead," *The Employer Report: Navigating US and Global Employment Law*, February 1, 2018, https://www.theemployerreport.com/2018/02/eeoc-fy-2017-statistics-recap-retaliation-claims-charge-ahead/.
73. Susan Futterman, *When You Work for a Bully: Assessing Your Options and Taking Action* (Leona: Croce Publishing, 2004), 10.
74. Pamela Lutgen-Sandvik, Gary Namie, and Ruth Namie, "Workplace Bullying: Causes, Consequences, and Corrections," in *Destructive Organizational Communication: Processes, Consequences, and Constructive Ways of Organizing*, ed. Pamela Lutgen-Sandvik and Beverly Davenport Sypher (New York: Routledge, 2009), 29; "Do You Have Workplace Bullies at Your Job," Bullying Statistics, http://www.bullyingstatistics.org/content/workplace-bullying.html.
75. Futterman, *When You Work for a Bully*, 11.
76. Futterman, *When You Work for a Bully*, 12.
77. Futterman, *When You Work for a Bully*, 13
78. Lutgen-Sandvik et al., "Workplace Bullying," 33.
79. Compiled from *Destructive Organizational Communication*; Christine Comaford, "75 Percent of Workers Are Affected by Bullying—Here's What to Do About It," *Forbes*, August 27, 2016, https://www.forbes.com/sites/christinecomaford/2016/08/27/the-enormous-toll-workplace-bullying-takes-on-your-bottom-line/#2f83d97b5595; Rebecca Koenig, "Battling Bullying in the Workplace," *USNews*, 2017, https://money.usnews.com/money/careers/company-culture/articles/battling-bullying-in-the-workplace; and "Do You Have Workplace Bullies at Your Job," Bullying Statistics.
80. Lutgen-Sandvik et al., "Workplace Bullying," 33.
81. "Real Life Stories: Creuza Oliviera, a Domestic Worker in Brazil," More Than Meets the Eye: Let's Fight Racism, United Nations, https://www.un.org/en/letsfightracism/oliveira.shtml.
82. Andrea Daley, Steven Solomon, Peter A. Newman, and Faye Mishna, "Traversing the Margins: Intersectionalities in the Bullying of Lesbian, Gay, Bisexual, and Transgender Youth," *Journal of Gay and Lesbian Social Services* 19, no. 3–4 (2007): 11.
83. Compiled from "Workplace Bullying: Race, Ideology, and the U.S. Bullying Experience," Workplace Bullying Institute, May 12, 2014, accessed June 1, 2017, http://www.workplacebullying.org/2014-race/.
84. Khubchandani and Price, "Workplace Harassment," 555–563.
85. "Do You Have Workplace Bullies at Your Job," Bullying Statistics.
86. Robin P. Clair, *Organizing Silence: A World of Possibilities* (Albany: University of New York Press, 1998), 99–118.
87. Clair, *Organizing Silence*, 101.

PART

INTERSECTIONALITY AND STRUCTURES OF POWER

CHAPTER

10

Hegemony and Structures of Power

The most obvious, important realities are often the ones that are hardest to see and talk about. Stated as an English sentence, of course, this is just a banal platitude, but the fact is that in the day to day trenches of adult existence, banal platitudes can have a life or death importance.

—David Foster Wallace

IN THIS CHAPTER, YOU WILL FIND . . .

KEY TERMS AND CONCEPTS

- dominant ideologies
- hegemonic discourses
- hegemony
- institutional bias
- institutions
- manufacturing of consent
- structural racism
- structures of inequality
- system
- systems of privilege

How are we to understand the larger structures of power and privilege that exist outside any single person's sphere of influence? While we might recognize that there are injustices around us, we often feel as though they happen without our input or direction. They occur even as we try to "do good" in the world: bad things happen without our conscious consent. In his comment about "important realities," David Foster Wallace is referring to these structures of power and privilege—the larger but often invisible frameworks that organize our understandings of the world. He is calling our attention to these structures of power and privilege because, although they may not be obvious to us, they make up the overarching frameworks that inform our day-to-day activities and our communicative practices.

To explore these larger structures and the ways they influence our communication, we begin this chapter by introducing a process known as hegemony. Once we begin to understand just what hegemony is, and how it operates, we can assess the ways hegemony influences the institutions and the systems that shape the world around us. Although the words *hegemony, institutions,* and *systems* can seem intimidating, coming to understand them is enormously helpful for students of communication and intersectional identities. Understanding larger forces of control and privilege, those that exist outside our individual spheres of influence, gives us additional tools with which to engage other people, and the dilemmas we often face, through the lens of intersectionality.

HEGEMONY AND THE MANUFACTURING OF CONSENT

Many of us consider ourselves smart people: we go to school, watch and read the news, stay up on current events, discuss issues with friends and family, and even explore on our own those dilemmas and problems that are of interest to us. So how do some truth regimes come to be dominant while others do not? How do some discourses ascend to power and others don't? How do binaries, color-blind logics, phobias, even discourses of outrage become the dominant views of a time? How it is that these discourses are present yet also may seem invisible to us? How is it that they seem so "normal" that we hardly pay attention to them? Hegemony explains this process.

Defining Hegemony

Hegemony refers to the ways in which something comes to be considered common sense, common knowledge, human nature, and even normal. Hegemony helps explain how those conceptualizations of what is deemed "common" and "normal" become dominant in a society. Hegemony helps us understand how "one concept of reality [defined as normal] is diffused throughout society."[1] It explains how individuals in a society "variously identify with, resist,

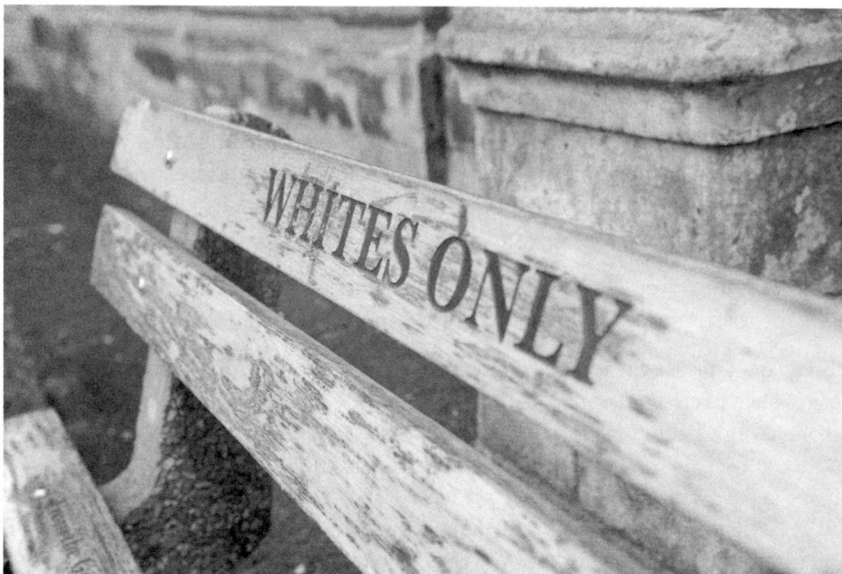

Figure 10.1 Common sense once dictated that places to sit in public should be segregated by race. The inappropriateness of this "common sense" ordinance seems obvious to most people today, but its appropriateness was hegemonic for centuries. (Source: iStock. Credit: brazzo)

and transform the systems of meaning that structure their experiences of the world."[2] Although hegemony feels invisible, it dictates such everyday behaviors as how and when we get dressed and the types of clothing we wear, how and when we go to school or work, and what we do while we are there, and even how and when we stand in line, order food, beg for food, share our food, and eat our food. Hegemony—what seems "just normal"—shapes the structure of our lives. Consider, for example, what we think of as the "correct" side of the road on which we should drive our cars. This is a relatively benign practice—as long as drivers are all on the same page regarding the right or left side, it really doesn't matter which side drivers use. Because of hegemonic notions of proper sides, however, we often see one side as normal and correct and the other side as wrong or odd.

For students of communication, hegemony can be fascinating, because it is our communication that makes something become hegemonic, that is "common sense" or "common knowledge." Our communication encourages specific ways of thinking about what is "real" and "normal." We use what are called **hegemonic discourses,** ways of talking about things that normalize them, making them seem natural and like they are a part of human nature. Hegemonic discourses, those familiar ways of communicating about the world around us, tell us what is "right" or "wrong" and thus we come to see certain things as right or wrong. These ways of talking are more than just the words and phrases—as driving on the "correct" side of the road illustrates. Hegemonic practices often are more morally or ethically laden than the practice of driving on the left or right side of a road. Recall discourses such as the "pull yourself up by your bootstraps" myth or the "ideology of affluence" from the previous chapter or consider the hegemonic discourses discussed in chapter 4, which justified seeing people within a hierarchy of humanness, including discourses that

- enslaved people,
- kept certain people from voting or owning property, and
- made it feel unnatural for some women to work outside the home.

Today, hegemonic discourses can cause us to feel uncomfortable with certain terms, such as *cisgender* or *zir,* as well as the identities of people deemed deviant or wrong or not fully human. They encourage us to believe in crime and poverty myths, subscribe to rape myths and cultures, and hold the victims at fault rather than the perpetrators. Hegemony teaches us that violence is normal and injustices always will be with us. It fuels our phobias of people who look, act, worship, speak, and move through the world in ways that we have come to see as abnormal.

Hegemonic practices and belief systems reflect **dominant ideologies.** Brenda J. Allen, professor of communication, describes "*ideology* as a 'set of assumptions and beliefs that comprise a system of thought.' Ideology has powerful, intricate influences on all of us."[3] Consider, for example, the ideology of patriarchy discussed in chapter 2, or the ideology of heterosexism discussed in chapter 3, or the ideology of eugenics discussed in chapter 4. Communication scholars Lee Artz and Bren Ortega Murphy concur: "Ideologies thrive, change, or disappear as a result of human practices corresponding to social interests, social power, and political struggle. . . . Ideologies have serious consequences because they organize human practices." Rather than true or false, "they are *legitimate* to the extent that they are active in everyday life."[4]

When hegemonic discourses are doing their work, defining things as normal or abnormal, we rarely recognize that they are at work at all—and that invisibility is what makes them so powerful. Hegemonic discourses, as Wallace suggests in this chapter's opening quotation, and as Artz and Murphy explain, are often the hardest to see and the most difficult to talk about. Underpinning Allen's discussion of ideology is the premise that "hegemony operates everywhere in a society," lubricating the wheels of daily life, reinforcing the rightness of familiar routines and practices, all the while keeping our attention diverted from its very existence.[5]

How Ideas Become Hegemonic

How do hegemonic assumptions come to be hegemonic? We learn what to believe is real and normal from families, friends, schools, and places of

Figure 10.2 Hegemonic ideas regarding aristocratic fashion are apparent in this 17th century image. Ruffles, heels, and flowery adornments were considered normal attire for aristocratic Dutch men and remained unchallenged for quite some time. (Source: iStock. Credit: ZU_09)

worship. We learn from social media, news posts and broadcasts, television, movies, and books. We learn from politics and politicians, and from legal decisions, codes, and norms. Ideas become hegemonic in the ways they are presented in music, architecture, art, and fashion. When the majority of these entities portray an idea or a practice as "good" or "bad," or somewhere in between, often enough and long enough, we come to accept that idea or practice as true. As we explore in chapter 1, the discourses of science, religion, medicine, education, health, economics, identity, citizenship, and rights provide frameworks for the structures of power and privilege we believe to be true. For example, for centuries, hegemonic discourses convinced people that the world was flat and that if someone walked to the edge, they would fall off into oblivion. That discourse of science remained unexamined and unquestioned for quite a while—it was common sense. Similarly, "common sense" prior to the late 1800s had people of the upper class in Europe believing that if women received a formal education their uteruses would atrophy and that they were prone to fainting because of weak constitutions (rather than their corsets, which severely restricted breathing). Common sense at this time also held that men of the upper classes wore wigs, high heels, and ruffles, and that solving disputes by dueling with pistols was a legitimate approach to conflict resolution.

When we communicate in a certain way about a certain thing across enough platforms (family, school, media, and so on), for enough time, ideas and practices become hegemonic. But how do hegemonic notions remain invisible? Over time, if the majority of people and information with whom a person comes in contact present something as common sense, that thing comes to be known as common sense. If an idea or belief system is reinforced as "normal" long enough, people often do not question its accuracy or foundation—as in the "world is flat" example. But a hegemonic discourse is not a "forever" discourse—our "common sense" can be questioned and made visible. For example, when enough people began to challenge the assumption of flatness and disseminate a discourse of roundness, people came to accept a different hegemonic discourse about the earth. Today, a hegemonic discourse of roundness has the active consent of most people and this discourse is so much common sense now that people rarely think about the shape of the earth at all. Similarly, contemporary beliefs about education, styles of clothing, and approaches to conflict resolution have changed significantly, and the discourses we engage to negotiate these aspects of our lives have evolved to reflect this change.

Although individuals in every culture subscribe to hegemonic notions of what is real and normal, we also know that people do and can resist. This is because, as philosopher Linda Martín Alcoff explains in chapter 3, what is described as human nature is not, in fact, human nature at all. It is hegemony at work. Hegemony is the **manufacturing of consent.** That is, whether it is to our benefit or not, we subscribe to certain sets of ideas about what is normal, about people and privilege, and about identities and the choices people have. Although hegemonic discourses often go unrecognized and unacknowledged in the ways we organize our daily lives and private worlds, they powerfully influence our institutions, public policies, and even our media and entertainment venues.

HEGEMONY AND INSTITUTIONAL PRIVILEGE AND BIAS

Although hegemonic discourses are at work in our own communication, to be sure, they also exist at levels beyond our own individual conversations and decisions. Hegemonic discourses infuse the larger structures of power and privilege that we encounter on a daily basis. Understanding how hegemonic discourses operate at this macro level helps us identify the ways power and privilege operate outside our own spheres of influence. Exploring hegemonic discourses in larger structures helps explain how we may try to do good things, but often our efforts seem to go awry, regardless of our best intentions. Exploring how hegemonic discourses are at work in institutions can help us understand how our individual efforts to effect change are tangled up in larger structures of power and privilege.

Understanding Institutional Privilege and Bias

Institutions are more than just buildings with people working inside them. Intersectionally, **institutions** can be understood in three ways. First, institutions are comprised of highly organized practices and patterns of operation. The people working within, or affected by, an institution adhere to these practices and patterns of operation. They understand them and, even if they do not agree with them, if they want to be a member of the institution, they abide by them. If people resist, they often are disciplined, encouraged to change their views and attitudes, or even asked to leave. Institutions usually have long histories and can be identified and understood not just by their ideologies and belief systems, but also by their enduring traditions. Although there are thousands of institutions operating in our world, and we are strongly influenced by most of them, two examples help clarify this complex entity: the Catholic church and funerals.

The Catholic church has been a powerful institution for centuries, and members of the church as well as those who are not members know its longstanding traditions. As an institution, the Catholic church defines the correctness and incorrectness of such practices as attending mass, getting married, using birth control, or becoming a priest or nun. It appoints key spokespeople, such as the pope, and determines who can perform marriages or say mass. It prescribes the proper dress code for various occasions as well as when to stand, sit, or kneel during these events. It even dictates the proper method of educating children. As an institution, the Catholic church holds considerable power.

So too with the institution of the funeral. Even if you have never attended a funeral, when filtered through your own religious or spiritual affiliations, you understand the norms, values, and customs for laying someone to rest. The traditional patterns of operation for a funeral inform decisions about who, what, where, when, and how people pay respects to someone who has died, and great care is taken to ensure they are "done right."

Second, institutions—including the Catholic church, the funeral, and others—operate at both the micro level (small, intimate, mundane) as well as the macro level (reaching across and affecting other institutions and practices).[6] We can easily think of religious as well as educational, political, legal, and medical institutions as fitting these criteria: they are well established, they are enduring, they have rules and patterns that dictate behavior and practices, they influence other institutions by sharing similar practices or norms. Taking the medical institution as an example, we see that within this institution, patient and doctor communication is meant to be private. Yet, should we need educational assistance (we have a learning disability, for example) or legal assistance for something related to our medical condition (we have been denied access to an educational system because of our disability, for example), we share our private medical information with other institutions. When others need that same information, our private communication, in collaboration with the patient/doctor/educators/lawyers we have worked with, is shared with other institutions. Employers make accommodations, politicians lobby for access, even public transportation begins to change. Institutions, in sum, collaborate with regard to the needs and desires of individuals.

Third, institutions are not neutral. Just like the individuals who work for them, institutions are biased—they have preferences and they privilege specific norms of behavior. Institutions favor certain ideologies, practices, and traditions over others. The Catholic church, for example, favors ideologies about birth control and marriage that are quite different from those of the Unitarian church. Catholic holiday traditions are quite different from pagan holiday rituals and traditions, which are different from Jewish holiday traditions, which are different from Muslim holiday traditions. The Catholic church keeps records that are quite different from those kept in a medical institution, or for a political party, or even for advertisers on Facebook. Institutions have preferences.

Even though institutional bias is common, it can be quite harmful. Negative and harmful **institutional bias** can be defined as "those established laws, customs, and practices which systematically reflect and produce group-based inequities in any society."[7] Obvious historical examples of institutional biases that have produced negative group-based inequities include slavery and segregation, anti-gay and anti-female military service legislation, and the institutionalization of individuals with disabilities. These biases produced longstanding inequities for the groups they were biased against: we have yet to recover from slavery and segregation, our military still is anti-gay and anti-female, and individuals who have disabilities and their allies continue to identify and remedy the stigmatizing harms done by institutionalization.

Because they may be well established, enduring, and respected, institutional biases often get described as business as usual. But as Terry Moe, professor of political science at Stanford University, explains, whoever controls the agenda controls the power, and institutions wield an important brand of power.[8] Not only do institutions define rules and norms for behavior, they can enforce compliance through rewards, as well as through discipline, surveillance, and even shaming.[9] This institutional power and privilege works hegemonically, that is, "through routine, ongoing practices to advantage particular groups without those groups necessarily establishing or maintaining those practices."[10] Those being advantaged, in sum, often fail to recognize the bias that works in their favor.

Examples of Institutional Privilege and Bias

Two examples of institutional privilege and bias help clarify the power an institution can exert over groups of people. This power results in advantages going to some groups of people while disadvantages go to other groups of people.

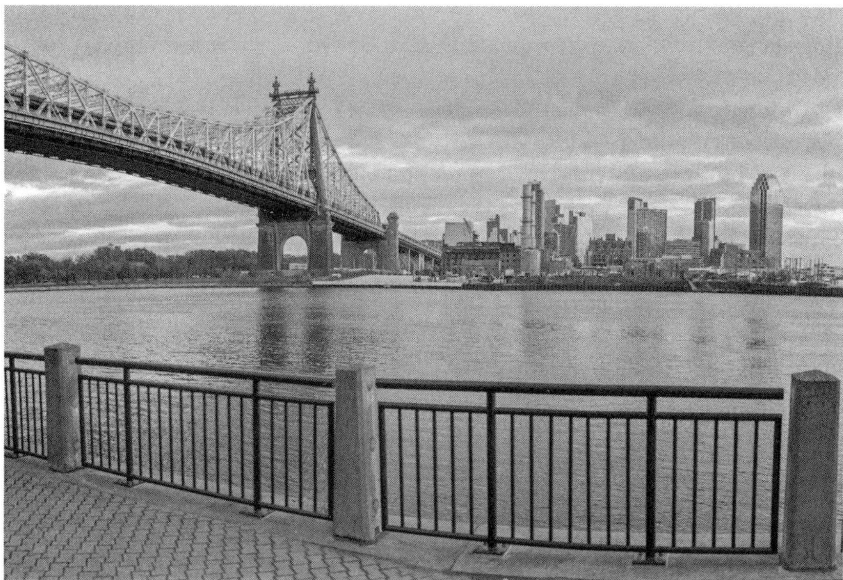

Figure 10.3 The Queensboro Bridge links Long Island City (in the borough of Queens) with the Upper East Side of Manhattan. Built in 1909, the bridge is tall enough to carry buses to and from Long Island City and Manhattan. Once on Long Island, however, bus drivers are likely to encounter the obstacles designed by Robert Moses: numerous too-low overpasses. (Source: iStock. Credit: Joaquín Camejo Disego)

This privilege and bias often are described as "just the way things are," and the result is that many individuals have difficulty seeing the long-standing practices and ways of organizing things that created the privilege and bias. Consider the institution of public transportation in New York during the period from the 1920s to the 1970s:

> Chief architect of New York's Public Works, Robert Moses, oversaw the design of the overpasses on Long Island from 1920–1970. The numerous overpasses, "which are so low that they do not permit 12-foot high public buses to use the parkways over which those overpasses go" were "not happenstance." Rather, they were "an intentional control strategy" on the part of Moses, designed to keep "poor people and blacks, who normally used public transit . . . off the roads because the twelve-foot tall buses could not handle the overpasses." Moses, and New York's Public Works sought to, among other things, deny poor and black people access to the beautiful Jones Beach, which was "Moses' widely acclaimed public park."[11]

Those low overpasses, entrenched in racist and classist ideologies, not only controlled the movement of people fifty years ago, they still exist today, continuing to control the ease with which certain individuals can travel to and from Long Island, or not. Moses's bias, in short, found its way into the institution of transportation in New York, privileging white, able body, economically well-off individuals with their own cars, and disadvantaging poor individuals of a range of identities: an institutional bias that continues to permeate those roads today.

A more recent example also clarifies the power of hegemonic processes in institutions and the ways it masks privilege. Consider the institution of computer programming and information technologies. Joy Buolamwini, a graduate student at MIT, describes what she calls "the coded gaze" or "algorithmic bias" present in face-recognition technologies. Buolamwini, who is African American, works with social robots and the technology that enables cameras to recognize faces. She explains that technicians use algorithms (problem-solving procedures) to develop software that can teach computers "this is a face. This is a face. This is a face. This is not a face. And, over time, you can teach a computer how to recognize other faces. However, if the training sets aren't really that diverse, any face that deviates too much from the established norm will be harder to detect."

When her own face is in front of the camera, computers often don't recognize Buolamwini. But when she puts on a white mask, or uses a photograph of her white roommate instead of her own, they do. Computer programming industries and generic facial recognition software, it seems, do not see the inclusion of black faces into their algorithm training programs as important. The "this is a face, this is a face, this is not a face" problem-solving pattern communicates the message, perhaps unintended: a black or brown face is not a face worth recognizing.

In contrast to the unrecognizability of the black or brown face, however, Buolamwini discusses just the opposite kind of algorithmic bias that targets minority faces. She describes research that detects "widespread, mysterious and destructive algorithms" that are being used to determine the length of prison sentences, who is hired or fired, who is eligible for a loan or insurance, college acceptance, and even whether or not "you and I pay the same price for the same product purchased on the same platform." Buolamwini concludes that computer programming's algorithmic bias "doesn't necessarily always lead to fair outcomes. . . . Who codes matters, how we code matters, and why we code matters."[12] Institutional biases in everyday algorithmic traditions and standards, in short, matter greatly to our institutional practices and procedures of facial recognition, incarceration practices, insurance policies, college acceptance rates, and even the prices we pay when we shop.

Institutions are everywhere: we work and play within and around them almost constantly. They are not just benign buildings or neutral practices: institutions are informed by the hegemonic discourses of their times. They are slow to change and their reach is far and wide: religion, transportation, and the algorithms for facial recognition are but the tip of the iceberg of institutional breadth and influence. Institutional biases, and the privileges they grant and deny as a result, also seep into the systems and structures of our lives.

HEGEMONY AND SYSTEMS OF PRIVILEGE AND BIAS

Institutional privilege and bias are intimately connected to the systems that organize our ways of thinking and acting. Hegemonic discourses exist that legitimize particular systems of doing and thinking and discourage other systems for doing and thinking about things. Understanding how hegemonic discourses operate at a systemic level helps us continue to identify the ways power and privilege operate outside our own spheres of influence. Exploring the hegemonic discourses that legitimize systems helps explain how privilege and bias often go undetected—until we resist those systems.

Understanding Systems of Privilege and Bias

A **system** is an organized set of principles that classifies, arranges, assembles, and coordinates efforts and processes. Systems are designed to facilitate the movement or functioning of processes and efforts and to eliminate irregularities so that the system can run smoothly. Systems work with institutions, but they are not the same thing. Institutions are larger than systems, and systems usually work under the umbrella of an organization. But, like institutions, they are infused with privilege and bias. Examples of systems help clarify the power in institutions and their systems.

The institution of education has systems that dictate the principles by which we grade students' work and classify them into grade levels, but also how we rank their achievement. Understanding the difference between an A as opposed to a B grade, for example, requires a system of ranking. Identifying the categories of undergraduate and graduate student, for example, or kindergartener and middle-school student, requires systems of arrangement. Both are housed within the educational institution, yet both are systems of arrangement and classification. Systems are all around us: within our educational institutions, they dictate how to learn, how to study, how to schedule classes, and more. Systems are a part of every institution we can name. The systems keep those institutions running, rewarding some, punishing others, privileging certain behaviors and discouraging others.

Although we have learned to not think about systems (except when you get a B grade rather than an A and decide to talk with your instructor about why, for example), they are infused with power. Who decides the criteria for an A, or the best way to study, or schedule classes? There are many ways to organize, arrange, and assemble systems, but hegemonic discourses dictate "the best" way in each of these categories. An A grade privileges certain skill sets over others (good at multiple choice, as compared to essays, or good at memorizing rather than critical thinking, for example), or good in large and heated class discussions rather than small-group or one-on-one discussions. Exploring the range and power of systems helps us see that there are particular systems of privilege, dominance, and discipline in place all around us—many of them invisible until they don't work for us, or someone we care about, and then we may call them into question.

Systems exert their power by "'knowing' the population" they are attempting to control. One of the ways a system "learns" about the population it wants to control is by gathering statistics and numbers about that population. Jonathan Simon, professor of law at the University of California, Berkeley, describes this gathering of data as "so familiar and banal that it is difficult to notice" at all. And when we don't notice the gathering of data, we struggle to see it as a form of control over us—like hegemonic processes, it "just is." Yet, mirroring Buolamwini's examination of biased algorithms, systems influence "hiring, admitting, campaigning, selling, sentencing," educating, and much more.[13]

But how is this information gathered? Every time we log into our computers and the internet, data are being gathered about us. Each "app" we download on our phones, game we play, or YouTube clip we watch allows companies and institutions to record information about us. Credit card purchases, discount cards, gift cards, and the like, all make available what we do, when we do that thing, and how often we do it. Even our test scores, from elementary school to college, are entered into data banks designed to measure and assess systems for the "best" learning and achievement practices and standards.

Systems of privilege work by constructing "an image of the 'normal' subject in any defined social space." Those who fit this "normal" image are rewarded. Those who do not fit that image are encouraged to do so, and when they cannot they often are punished or removed from the social space.[14] Children's education is an excellent example of this process. In schools, standardized tests determine the "normal" child. Although there might be a range of "normal," children who do not fall within this range are placed into special classrooms or programs. The test as an accurate measure of "normal" is never called into question, nor is the actual structure of the educational system. Rather, the child is considered the problem, because, if they differ from the hegemonic ideas of normal, they do not and cannot fit into the traditional educational systems. The result, as Simon explains, is that individuals who may have no concept of themselves as members of a "special" group before this testing are "striped of a certain quality of belongingness to others" as a result of the test—they are no longer "normal."[15]

Systems Are Not Neutral

Our systems of counting and measuring, grouping and ordering, are not simply neutral forms of knowledge gathering. Notions of "different," "special," and "normal" are ideological constructs, that is, they are infused with power, privilege, and hierarchy. Our systems determine who has power, who does not have power, and who should not have power. Systems "allow the exercise of power to be targeted quite precisely" and they "play a central role in a proliferating set of social practices."[16] To be sure, our identities "develop in constant interaction with powerful institutions [and systems] that sometimes subtly but often overtly 'teach' actors patterns of thought, feeling and action."[17] We can, and often do, resist those identities and patterns. However, we often are unaware of the influence of those systems on our identities—or unable to resist them because of negative repercussions. When individuals find themselves constantly in the "normal" grouping, this is because the counting and measuring practices of a system have privileged that person's identities. However, when people find themselves in the "abnormal" grouping, we can be sure a system has defined them as such. We can be sure we are being influenced and defined by hegemonic discourses that tell us what is "real," "natural," and "good."

When we consider systems intersectionally, we ask such questions as What invisible system of privilege is at work here? How is this individual being labeled, and what are the implications of that labeling? Where and from whom is this labeling coming, and what is motivating this labeling? and How might this system of counting and labeling advantage some and disadvantage others?

The systems through which we travel are set into motion by the gathering of statistics, by counting things, and sped up by the current practices of data mining so common on our own computers. Systems establish practices that are called "appropriate," "efficient," and "orderly." Systems, however, are arbitrary forms of organizing ideas, practices, and people. They may have come to feel smooth, natural and right, for some, but for others, they are cumbersome, unjust, and limiting.

HEGEMONY AND STRUCTURAL INEQUALITY

The members of the Aspen Institute, located in Washington, D.C., pose several questions that help us understand the importance of looking at systems and institutions in tandem. When we put the two together, we expose the larger structures Wallace mentions in the quote that opens this chapter. We also reveal the role of hegemonic discourses, institutional bias, and systems of privilege in perpetuating **structures of inequality**—structures we may want to see changed but have difficulty figuring out just how to do so. Focusing on race, the Aspen Institute roundtable members ask:

> How is it that a nation committed to equal opportunity for all—regardless of race, national origin, or gender—continually reproduces patterns of inequality?
>
> Why, in the world's wealthiest country, is there such enduring poverty among people of color?

> How is it that in our open participatory democracy, racial minorities are still underrepresented in positions of power and decision making?[18]

The answers, they suggest, lie in structural racism.

The term **structural racism** (sometimes termed *institutional* or *systemic racism*) refers to the ways that our "public policies, institutional practices, cultural representations, and other norms work in various, often reinforcing, ways to perpetuate racial group identity."[19] The Aspen Institute scholars explain that many "of the contours of opportunity for individuals and groups in the United States are defined—or 'structured'—by race and racism." This is because "beginning with the expropriation of Native American lands, a racialized system of power and privilege developed and white dominance became the national common sense, opening the door to the enslavement of Africans, the taking of Mexican lands [when the United States annexed northern Mexico after the Mexican-American War in the mid-nineteenth century], and the limits set on Asian immigrants [beginning with the increase in Asian immigration during the California Gold Rush, and enacted in various immigration policies since then]."[20] White dominance, in sum, became hegemonic. Everyone is implicated by and in this hegemonic structure of white dominance, because "structural racism is a system for allocating social privilege" and "whiteness" functions as the "default setting," for race in the United States—the norm and standard by which all else is measured in our institutions as well as our systems.[21]

Manning Marabel, professor of Public Affairs, History, and African-American Studies at Columbia University, shares that most white Americans are in a "'deep fog' about the character, construction, and reproduction of white racism as a social system."[22] He explains,

> Millions of Americans still think and talk about race in terms of fixed biological or genetic categories. A strikingly different way to view the concept of "race" is as an unequal relationship between social groups based on the privileged access to power and resources by one group over another. Race is historically and socially constructed, created (and recreated) by how people are treated in the normal actions of everyday life.[23]

Marabel describes how, despite changes, our "collective histories . . . have been largely defined around a series of oppressive institutions and practices." Institutions and systems perpetuate these oppressive practices. These oppressive practices are referred to as *deep structures of inequality.* Throughout this book, we have discussed the ways many of these came to be. Marabel describes the deep structures in American democracy that perpetuate racialized minorities:

> Although laws regarding the treatment of racialized minorities have changed over the years, *the deep structure of white prejudice, power, and privilege forming the undemocratic foundation of most human interactions has not fundamentally been altered.* In order for American democracy finally to become a reality for all of our

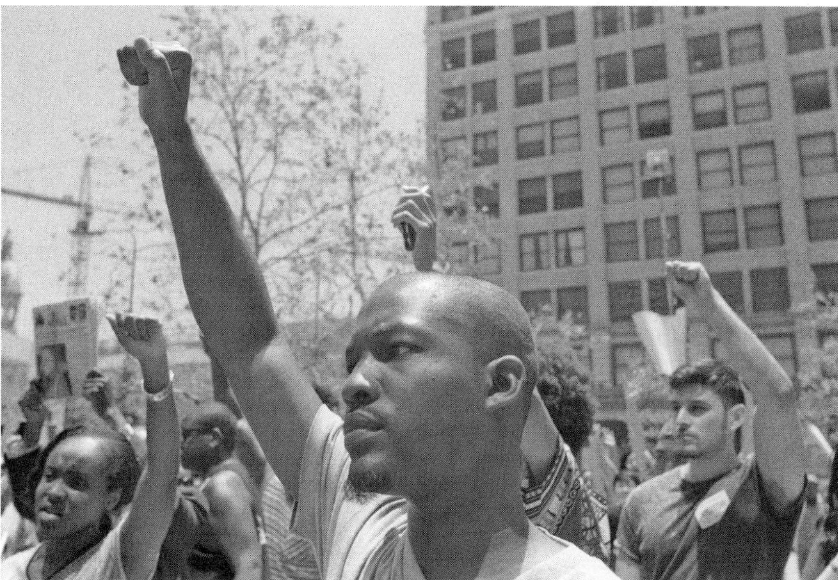

Figure 10.4 Black Lives Matter protestors across the country are challenging the structures of racism in U.S. society. They are asking white people to step out of the deep fog of denial and to recognize the continued presence of structural racism in our institutions, structures, and systems. (Source: iStock. Credit: br-photo)

> citizens, we must, first, understand historically how and why these deep structures of racial inequality came into being, and how they continue to be decisively expressed in the daily lives and life chances of racialized minorities and whites alike.[24]

Acknowledging that the deep structures of racism, classism, sexism, ableism, heterosexism, anti-Semitism, ethnocentrism, homophobia, Islamophobia, transphobia, queer phobia, xenophobia—in sum, human disqualification—are embedded in our institutions and systems is a necessary first step. Inequality is not "just the way things are," neither is it solely individually created. Inequality is a structural phenomenon that is obscured by the hegemonic discourses present in our institutions and systems. These hegemonic discourses can make it very difficult to name the important realities of human disqualification, phobia, and bias.

Obviously, race is not the only structural inequality we must face. We can extend our awareness of structural racism to other marginalized groups: they, too, are subject to institutional and systemic biases. We can begin to face structural classism (the unaffordability of healthy food, clean and safe living environments, the scarcity of employment, and the absence of a decent education, for example), structural ableism (the inaccessibility of buildings, recreational facilities, transportation, and homes, as well as the stigmatization of

Communication Checklist for Acknowledging Privilege

- ✓ Acknowledge the harmful and oppressive legacies of our past.
- ✓ Acknowledge how these legacies persist in our "national policies, institutional practices and cultural representations."
- ✓ Acknowledge how these legacies of oppression are transmitted, amplified, or mitigated through our private, public, and community institutions.
- ✓ Acknowledge the ways individuals internalize and respond to these oppressive structures.

Source: Keith Lawrence, Stacey Sutton, Anne Kubish, Gretchen Susi, and Karen Fulbright-Anderson, "Structural Racism and Community Building," Aspen Institute Roundtable on Community Change, 2004 (Washington, D.C.: The Aspen Institute, 2004), 3, https://assets.aspeninstitute.org/content/uploads/files/content/docs/rcc/aspen_structural_racism2.pdf.

disabilities that leads to underemployment and unemployment), structural sexism (misogyny, wage gaps and ceilings, and the normalization of violence), structural homophobia (hate crimes, housing and employment discrimination, parental rights, and legal injustices), because all (and more) are present in our institutions and systems.

Just how might one acknowledge this "deep fog"? Communication scholars Lee Artz and Bren Ortega Murphy remind us that knowledge isn't inherently scientific, factual, and objective. Instead, knowledge is produced, developed, negotiated, altered, or cemented by individuals and practices as they exist in their political, cultural, social, and economic contexts. Knowledge does not exist before humans, but rather, in "the process of living, doing, and making our world, we come to know." Artz and Murphy suggest that in order to understand hegemonic consensus and its relationship to power and privilege, we need to consider the relationships between knowledge and practice. They explain that what we know, we know through practice: "'practice is a process of knowledge'. . . . We do what we know. We also learn through doing."[25]

Structural "isms" perpetuate the hierarchical policies and practices that are embedded in our institutions and systems, and these policies and practices privilege some at the expense of others. When we attend to the structural isms in institutions and systems, we step out of the "deep fog" of structural racism, classism, sexism, ableism, heterosexism, anti-Semitism, ethnocentrism, homophobia, Islamophobia, transphobia, queer phobia, xenophobia—in sum, the human disqualifications that are embedded in our institutions and systems.

10.1. GUIDE TO COMMUNICATION

The Language of Hegemony

To help you explore the complex but very real institutions, systems, and structures hegemonic discourses put into motion, and to increase your ability to communicate effectively when faced with hegemonic notions of "right" and "wrong," consider the following questions:

1. What is being presented as "normal" or "common sense"?
2. Who is telling me that this is "normal"—what are their identities and how full is their invisible knapsack?
3. Can I begin to identify the institutional, systemic, and structural privileges that are operating in this situation?
4. What type of consent is being manufactured—what am I being encouraged to think or believe or discouraged from thinking or believing?
5. Using the ideas presented by the Aspen Institute, create a "Deep Fog of Privilege" checklist to help you become more aware of structural inequities. Your checklist should name the ways people can get themselves out of this "deep fog." Now apply this checklist to one of the following structures of power covered in this book: racism, classism, ableism, sexism, homophobia, transphobia, Islamophobia, xenophobia, or the like. What steps would you need to take to get out of these "deep fogs" of unawareness?

INTERSECTIONALITY AND STRUCTURES OF POWER

The concepts explored in this chapter are a bit slippery and, indeed, complex. They also are intimately interconnected, which makes them intersectional by their very nature. To help sort out these complex concepts and the ways they intersect, a brief summary may be useful. Recall that hegemony helps explain the ways in which what people call common sense, common knowledge, human nature, and normal are actually human constructs and not facts of science or nature. Hegemonic discourses refer to the familiar ways groups of people communicate about the world around them, identifying for them the accepted ideas of "right" or "wrong." Hegemony encourages humans to move through the world with particular assumptions about how things should and do work.

These assumptions about how things "should" work—hegemonic understandings of the world—inform the institutions that comprise any society. These assumptions reflect the dominant ideologies we have as humans working and living in patterned and organized ways. Recall that institutions consist of highly organized practices and patterns of organization that influence the small and everyday functioning of an organization as well as much larger levels of functioning: institutions organize other institutions—they work in relationships to one another. And, just like the individuals who work for them, institutions are not neutral: they are biased. They confer power and privilege on some and make access to that power and privilege very difficult for others. In our intersectional world, then, hegemony is constantly intersecting with institutions.

And hegemony and institutions also are intersecting with systems. Remember that a system works within an institution, helping individuals classify, arrange, assemble, and coordinate efforts and processes. Systems, which are a part of every institution we can name, keep institutions running. Systems reward, punish, privilege, and disadvantage according to a hegemonic and institutional image of normal. At this point, we have individuals, following hegemonic discourses, functioning within and across institutions, classifying, arranging, assembling, and coordinating ideas and people so that they can be rewarded and punished, privileged and disadvantaged.

Finally, in our intersectional summary, we see that hegemony, institutions, and systems create and perpetuate the larger structures of inequity that many of us have difficulty seeing and acknowledging. We may choose, however, to step out of the "deep fog" that fuels our refusal to see these important realities. In doing so, we reject the banal platitudes that have informed our communication for far too long. We embrace intersectional approaches to communicating about the deep structures of inequity that hegemonic discourses present to us as normal, natural, and common sense, all the while inviting others to do the same.

Resources

Human Flow, a movie by Ai Weiwei, Venice (Italy) Film Festival, Amazon, 2017, www.humanflow.com.

Finn Lutzow-Holm Myrstad, "How Tech Companies Deceive You into Giving Up Your Data and Privacy," filmed September 2018 in New York, NY, TEDsalon video, 12:04, https://www.ted.com/talks/finn_myrstad_how_tech_companies_deceive_you_into_giving_up_your_data_and_privacy#t-607446.

Kelly Richmand-Pope, "How Whistle-Blowers Shape History," filmed April 2017 in Chicago, IL, TEDXDePaulUniversity video, 11:53, https://www.ted.com/talks/kelly_richmond_pope_how_whistle_blowers_shape_history#t-47128.

Notes

1. Geoff Eley, "Nations, Publics, and Political Cultures: Placing Habermas in the Nineteenth Century," in *Habermas and the Public Sphere,* ed. Craig Calhoun (Cambridge, MA: MIT Press, 1993), 322.
2. Dennis K. Mumby, "The Problem of Hegemony: Rereading Gramsci for Organizational Communication Studies," *Western Journal of Communication* 61, no. 4 (1997): 345.
3. Brenda J. Allen, *Difference Matters: Communicating Social Identity,* 2nd ed. (Long Grove, IL: Waveland Press, 2011/2014), 32–33.
4. Lee Artz and Bren Ortega Murphy, *Cultural Hegemony in the United States* (Thousand Oaks, CA: Sage, 2000), 12.
5. Allen, *Difference Matters,* 30–31.
6. John C. Lammers and Joshua B. Barbour, "An Institutional Theory of Organizational Communication," *Communication Theory* 16, no. 3 (2006): 357.

7. P. J. Henry, "Institutional Bias," in *The Sage Handbook of Prejudice, Stereotyping and Discrimination*, ed. John F. Dovidio, Miles Hewstone, Peter Glick, and Victoria M. Esses (Thousand Oaks, CA: Sage, 2010), 426.
8. Terry M. Moe, "Power and Political Institutions," Articles 3 (2005): 216, https://files-politicalscience-stanford-edu.s3.amazonaws.com/s3fs-public/powerpoliticalinstitutions.pdf.
9. Thomas B. Lawrence, "Power, Institutions and Organization," in *Sage Handbook of Organizational Institutionalism*, ed. Royston Greenwood, Christie Oliver, Kerstin Sahlin, and Roy Suddaby (Thousand Oaks, CA: Sage, 2008), 172, https://thomaslawrence.files.wordpress.com/2008/08/lawrence-2008-power-institutions-and-organizations.pdf.
10. Lawrence, "Power," 174.
11. Lawrence, "Power," 178.
12. Joy Buolamwini, "How I'm Fighting Bias in Algorithms," filmed November 2016 in Brookline, Massachusetts, TEDxBeaconStreet video, 7:39, https://www.ted.com/talks/joy_buolamwini_how_i_m_fighting_bias_in_algorithms/transcript?language=en.
13. Jonathan Simon, "The Ideological Effects of Actuarial Practices," *Law and Society Review*, 22 (1988): 771, http://scholarship.law.berkeley.edu/facpubs/498.
14. Lawrence, "Power," 178.
15. Simon, "Ideological Effects," 774.
16. Simon, "Ideological Effects," 772–774.
17. David Wicks, "Institutional Bases of Identity Construction and Reproduction: The Case of Underground Coal Mining," *Gender, Work and Organization* 9, no. 3 (June 2002): 310.
18. Keith Lawrence, Stacey Sutton, Anne Kubish, Gretchen Susi, and Karen Fulbright-Anderson, "Structural Racism and Community Building," Aspen Institute Roundtable on Community Change, 2004 (Washington, D.C.: The Aspen Institute, 2004), 3, https://assets.aspeninstitute.org/content/uploads/files/content/docs/rcc/aspen_structural_racism2.pdf.
19. Lawrence et al., "Structural Racism,"11.
20. Lawrence et al., "Structural Racism," 8.
21. Lawrence et al., "Structural Racism," 11.
22. Manning Marabel, *The Great Wells of Democracy: The Meaning of Race in American Life* (New York: Basic Civitas Books, 2002), 320.
23. Marabel, *Great Wells of Democracy*, 322.
24. Marabel, *Great Wells of Democracy*, 322; emphasis in original.
25. Artz and Murphy, *Cultural Hegemony*, 12.

CHAPTER

11

Discourses of Colonialism and Colonization

IN THIS CHAPTER, YOU WILL FIND . . .

KEY TERMS AND CONCEPTS

- aesthetic imperialism
- colonization
- colonialism
- gendercide
- identity fragility
- identity politics
- indigenous
- objectified
- self-objectification
- voyeurism
- white fragility

NO ONE IS PURELY ONE THING

Palestinian American Edward Said, one of the founders of the academic field we now call "postcolonial studies," explains that, "No one today is purely *one* thing. Labels like Indian, or woman, or Muslim, or American are not more than starting-points" around which we exist for only a moment. The "worst and most paradoxical gift" of the hegemonic thinking that created this myth of singularity "was to allow people to believe that they were only, mainly, exclusively, white, or Black, or Western, or Oriental." Humans do make their own histories, cultures, and ethnic identities, Said states, and no one "can deny the persisting continuities of long traditions, sustained habitations, national languages, and cultural geographies." Even so, "there seems no reason except fear and prejudice to keep insisting on their separation and distinctiveness, as if that was all human life was about. Survival in fact is about the connections between things," Said offers. "It is more rewarding—and more difficult—to think concretely and sympathetically" about other people and not just about our own selves. And thinking in this way requires that we try not to rule others, or "to classify them or put them in hierarchies, above all, not constantly reiterating how 'our' culture or country is number one (or not number one, for that matter)."[1]

Yet, two of the most powerful but often invisible discourses circulating in our past and present truth regimes—the discourses of colonialism and colonization—encourage us to do just this, to place cultures and countries and the people who live in them in hierarchical rankings. As Said states, fear and prejudice insist on separation and distinctiveness, even though labels are fleeting and assumptions about those to whom we ascribe those labels ill-informed. Even though the terms might sound foreign to you, colonialism and colonization hold tremendous power over our thinking and our assumptions about people, progress, and advancement. Because colonizing discourses guide our thinking away from intersectionality and make conversations about complexity and intersections difficult, they are worth careful exploration.

In what follows, we take up Said's call to unpack our focus on seeing people, cultures, and countries as "only one thing." We reconsider Adiche's call from chapter 1 that we attend to the single story we might have accepted as true about people and cultures. To do so, we begin by exploring the definitions of colonialism and colonization and the ways they work discursively, that is, how they are present in our communication. Because colonialism and colonization are complex concepts and processes, we consider four examples of colonizing discourses and their material consequences. In the first two examples, we examine ideas of colonial masculinity and how they overtook, and attempted to destroy, ideas of indigenous masculinities. In the third example of colonizing discourses, we explore the discursive manipulation of the burqa after the September 11, 2001 attacks on the World Trade Center and the Pentagon and the ways U.S. citizens were encouraged to understand this item of clothing.

Figure 11.1 To colonize is to settle in a place or form a new community without regard for the people and customs of those already living in that place. These wind turbines dominating what once were Alberta First Nation tribal lands speak to the devastating consequences of colonization. (Source: iStock. Credit: wwing)

Finally, we turn our attention to media and popular culture, exploring the colonizing gaze through which we view most of our media.

DEFINING COLONIALISM AND COLONIZATION

If you look in a dictionary for a definition of *colonialism* or *colonization,* you likely will find a fairly simple definition: *to colonize* will be defined as settling in a new country or forming a new community in a new place. Absent will be any mention of individuals already living in this "new" country or of communities already existing in this new place. The story we are asked to believe is that there were and still are places in which groups of people don't already live, love, and work. Even if people are present, our colonizing story tells us that we can settle there and bring the inhabitants a better way of life. In order to mask the disruption to the people already living in these countries and places, we use a particular kind of language. We tell a story about the people living in these places, labeling the country as *underdeveloped* and the people as *third-world* and *backward.* We say that they need someone to come in and help them, someone who can bring them into the current century.

When viewed through the lens of intersectionality, however, the definition of colonization changes dramatically. An intersectional definition exposes the power dynamics at play in attempts by nonnatives to settle in a new place. Defined intersectionally, **colonization** and **colonialism** involve "the conquest of other people's land and goods." Viewed intersectionally, the focus is on those who already inhabit the land. To colonize, in this context, is to take control of the land, seas, rivers, roads, and airways that belonged to other people. It is to control their means of production and their lives—what people eat, where they live, how they dress, how they learn, how they worship, earn a living, and even travel from place to place. When we view colonization intersectionally, the ideas of progress and advancement are exposed as the exertion of power and control over groups of people who live differently from us, or who have resources we want. Through an intersectional lens, our country's progress and advancement, in truth, is another country's devastation.

When viewed through intersectional and feminist lenses, **colonization** is considered "one of the most complex and traumatic relationships in human history." This is because the "process of 'forming a new community' in the new land necessarily meant *un-forming* or *re-forming* the communities that existed there already." This un-forming and re-forming "involved a wide range of practices including trade, settlement, plunder, negotiation, warfare, genocide, and enslavement.[2] In order to "un-form" and "re-form," colonizers "readily resorted to violence wherever necessary" so that they might "secure both occupation and trading 'rights.'"[3] Motivated "by a desire to create and control opportunities to generate wealth" and to establish international markets, colonizing nations quickly realized that "colonialism was big business" and profits were "unimaginable."[4]

As difficult as it might be to accept, colonization almost always includes and relies on the massacre and displacement of the Indigenous people who live in an area. To be **indigenous** is to be the original occupant of a place and because of this originality to have strong historical ties to that place. Indigenous peoples have a cultural "distinctiveness" when compared to a colonizing population—they existed "pre-invasion." Indigenous people maintain close ties to their land, cultures, and economic practices and because of these factors are "particularly vulnerable to exploitation, marginalization and oppression" by those with more power and resources.[5] When we colonize, we destroy indigenous ways of living and replace them with the ways of the colonizer.

If we think colonization is rare, consider the following historical examples:

- The Spanish colonization of the Americas
- The Portuguese colonization of Africa, Brazil, and Indonesia
- The Russian colonization of Siberia
- The French colonization of Northeast Africa, the Sudan, and Southeast Asia
- The British colonization of the Caribbean, North America, New Zealand, Australia, Tasmania, the Solomon Islands, East Africa, India, and parts of the Middle East
- The German colonization of Southwest Africa
- The Belgium colonization of the Congo

- The colonization by the United States, after the British, of the eastern seaboard of North America, and then the western territories from the Great Plains to the Pacific Ocean as well as what was originally northern Mexico

Colonization continues today in the following places, enacted by governments, corporations, and drug cartels: the Baltic states, Bangladesh, Brazil, Colombia, the Democratic Republic of Congo, East Timor, Guatemala, Irian Jaya/West Papua, Myanmar, Paraguay, and Tibet.

The impact of colonization for Indigenous people is devastation: the loss of land, the loss of income, and the loss of control over agriculture, manufacturing, education, language, spirituality, politics, and cultures. Colonizing discourses, however, attempt to erase this impact. Authors, editors, and activists Daisy Hernández and Bushra Rehman explain that contrary to the benign dictionary definition in which "to colonize means to create a settlement" in reality, "to colonize is 'to strip people of their culture, language, land, family structure, and identity as a person and as a people.'"[6]

EXAMPLES OF DISCOURSES OF COLONIALISM AND COLONIZATION

Colonization happens when the desire to accumulate land and profits, regardless of the damage done, outstrips any ethical or moral obligation to treat other humans with respect and dignity. But what does this have to do with intersectional communication and our understanding of the complexities of our identities? How might communication be a part of this colonizing devastation? Canadian linguist Susan Ehrlich explains that "language is the primary vehicle through which cultural and institutional ideologies are transmitted." Ehrlich adds that "language is not neutral and not all speakers are served equally in any given discourse."[7] Although not many of us have a physical role in taking over countries and the people who live in those spaces, many of us do have an active role in advancing the language of colonization, "an elaborate network of discursive practices used to misrepresent 'others' as deficient and therefore as in need of assistance from proficient authorities."[8] Our language, in short, often actively supports this colonization.

Exposing colonial discourses helps us think about power in two ways—as the ability of individuals to establish power over others, but also as "global power" and the ways it establishes, maintains, and normalizes its rightness. Through communication, colonial discourses legitimize the power one nation imposes on another nation, describing the imposition of that order as "serving the best and widest interests of humanity," all the while "whitewashing" the "destructive histories of modern empires."[9] But it also erases the ways that individuals exert power over other people. Colonizing discourses can make the way people look at something, and then respond to it, seem "so right" and "so real" that they forget that communication is creating the narrative. Colonizing discourses confer power on some, but not others, and make that hierarchical arrangement seem normal.

The discourse of colonization is apparent in obvious places, as well as places we might never think of. Four examples help us think about colonizing discourses and the practices that follow as a result of that discourse: colonial masculinity, indigenous masculinities, the stigmatization of the burqa after the September 11, 2001 terrorist attacks, and the gaze with which we view our media.

Colonial Masculinity

Historians interested in masculinity state the obvious: masculinity is an invention. Adapting French feminist Simone de Beauvoir's famous assertion, "one is not born but becomes a woman," scholars begin their explorations of masculinity with the time-tested adage: one is not born a man, instead, one is trained to become one.[10] Social norms and codes teach cisgender versions of masculinity and cisgender masculine styles of behaving. But nothing about masculinity is inherent—that is, masculinity is not pre-embedded in the DNA of those born biologically male or those who identify as male and masculine. Because any version of masculinity is an invention, it changes over time, adapting to shifting social norms and expectations. Those interested in intersectionality ask, From where do our contemporary ideas of "proper" masculinity come?

Historians find that as white settlers arrived on the shores of North America they brought sixteenth- and seventeenth-century versions of European masculinity with them. At that time "manhood was reserved to some" but not others; it could be "denied" according to "markers of status or age." In Europe, masculinity meant land ownership—it was paramount to this identity—as was being cisgender, heterosexual, married, able-body, wealthy, and between the ages of thirty and fifty. If a man was older than fifty, at this time, he was considered a child again.[11] Not all men could succeed in accomplishing all of these markers of the male identity, however. Young or working-class men as well as clergy and poor men found themselves in a precarious position. Their masculinity could be denied: it was "tenuous" rather than certain and it had to be proved because it was not a given. Similar to today, the performance of masculinity was "policed" and carefully scrutinized to be sure it did not fail "to achieve its status." Manhood was an accomplishment, considered "scarce goods," "insecure or perishable": in short, one could be "unmanned."[12]

Masculinity's tenuousness caused alternative logics for the performance of manhood to develop during this time. For those unable to achieve these markers of land ownership, marriage, wealth, and age, "male bonding" or "youthful exploits" became the standard by which to measure manhood. This performance of masculinity took the form of "nightwalking," which involved "smashing glass, pulling up poles, breaking window lattices and demolishing men's work stalls," excessive drinking, waking those asleep, "rioting and swaggering" in the town, shouting sexual insults, and engaging in sexual assault and physical violence. For many young men, cisgender or not, the "humiliation of others" became a way to achieve the status of "man," and refusing to participate in such actions could cause the so-called fraternity of brothers to turn against those not willing to participate and inflict the same humiliation upon them.[13]

These markers of status and codes of humiliation were well entrenched in notions of European manhood by the time white settlers "arrived on Indigenous lands." Scott Morgensen, at the Department of Gender Studies at Queen's University, notes that with these norms firmly in place in Europe, how could white men not bring their "European modes of manhood" with them?[14] If masculinity "required achievement" in one's homeland—whether in the form of wealth and land ownership or the humiliation and degradation of others—why would it suddenly involve other factors after a trip across the Atlantic ocean? Indeed, white settlers brought their norms and practices of masculinity with them and, because European views of masculinity were so vastly different from indigenous views, they turned their views of manhood into colonial violence manifested in "methods of settler rule."[15]

Colonizing Indigenous Gender Systems

Morgensen shares that "Indigenous gender systems appeared to Europeans to be ambiguous or aberrant," that is, they failed to match the preconceived notions held by white settlers. Indigenous gender systems embraced a "complex complementarity of indigenous women's and men's authority and leadership" and settlers saw this as "a threat to heteropatriarchal rule." Unlike European women, Indigenous women held considerable "autonomy over desire, partnership, and marriage" and indigenous views of identity and sexuality fell far outside "European ideas of binary sex/gender." Indigenous people recognized a person's identity could be "neither fully male nor fully female . . . but a unique blend of characteristics resulting in a third or other gender." In addition, "sexual partnership between two of the same sex" was recognized as normal, natural, and positive.[16] In the views of white Europeans, "Indigenous men had failed to achieve European standards for manhood." Rather than facilitate a reframing of European notions of masculinity, this "failure" was fuel for a framing of indigenous practices as unmanly, degraded, and in "need of conquest for the sake of nature, church, or civilization."[17]

Deborah Miranda, Native American writer and poet, shares that "manhood became central to colonial violence when Indigenous gender or sexual diversity exceeded what Europeans deemed permissible."[18] Thus began what is known as

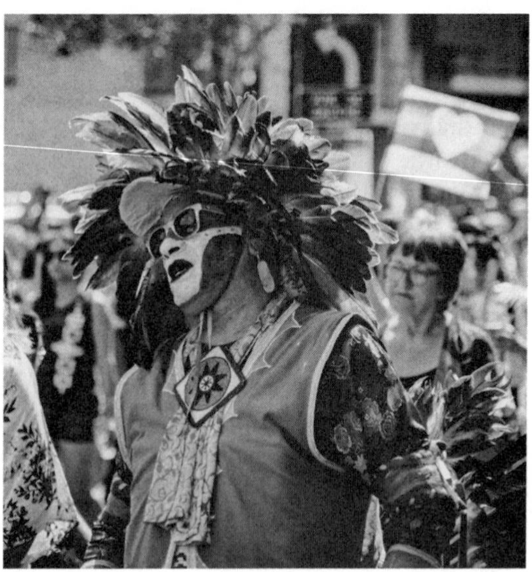

Figure 11.2 Indigenous gender systems threatened many European settlers' ideas of manhood and led to gendercide: the systematic targeting, punishment, and attempted elimination of traditional gender roles that Indigenous people recognized as perfectly normal and perfectly acceptable. Today, we see those fluid and perfectly normal and acceptable gender systems displayed in places like this Montreal Gay Pride event. (Source: iStock. Credit: Thomas HALBERG)

gendercide: "the systematic targeting, punishment, and attempted elimination of traditional gender roles that Indigenous people recognized" as perfectly normal and perfectly acceptable.[19] Morgensen and Miranda note that gender was defined in such a wide variety of ways "across the diversity of Indigenous societies" that white settlers felt so threatened and confused that they used these different ways of organizing gender and identity as one of several rationales for violence. This confusion and desire for conformity to European notions of masculinity legitimized horrific sexual violence. Not only against Indigenous women but also extreme and unreasonable violence against Indigenous men as well as "persons whom they read as gender-variant men," attacking "not only those individuals but also the communities that had accepted and embraced them." Morgensen states that the "capacity of this violence to illuminate colonial perceptions of manhood," and Indigenous peoples' threat to it, cannot be underestimated.[20]

Because the norms for gender and sexuality among Indigenous men were "at odds" with the invaders' sense of European morality, white settlers reframed indigenous practices as "unmanly" and "degraded." These fluid notions of sexuality and identity, as well as the collaborative and communal styles of leadership, were labeled not just as problematic but also as dangerous and "in need of conquest for the sake of nature, church, or civilization." This intense need to humiliate Indigenous men into adopting European codes for acceptable masculinity, Morgensen suggests, may reflect more than just a strict adherence to social codes and norms. It also spoke to white settlers' desire to prove that such "perversion" was "being overcome among or *within* themselves."[21] The violence against Indigenous men and women, the historical record proves, was excessive, brutal, and unrestrained. Was this violence "self-interested: informed by European men's fears of a capacity within their own manhood for self-betrayal or loss?" If one could be degraded because he might, at any moment, fail to meet his culture's dominant expectations for masculinity, then does the degradation of others take precedence over everything else?

The violence against Indigenous men and women continued, says Morgensen, "because colonization itself is violence." Colonization requires "modes of policing, reeducation, and assimilation." Colonizers must eliminate anyone or anything perceived to be a threat.[22] Colonial masculinity, in all its violence, led to an "institutional containment" of Indigenous people. Certain spaces became off-limits to Indigenous individuals. Canadian and U.S. military forcibly removed Indigenous populations from spaces and lands they had lived on for centuries. Officials created new "Indian Territories" that included reservations, preserves, and agencies. This violent removal of Indigenous populations resulted in what is considered the first "concentration camp" as "resistant Dakota" people were interned "under the sights of Fort Snelling" in 1862.[23] The establishment of Indian Territories made many of their familiar spaces off-limits to Indigenous people. Colonizers considered "Indigenous people who crossed into (white settler) 'public' spaces as out-of-place" in white territory, and, as such, subject to violence.[24]

Framed as "education," boarding schools also became an Indian-only space. American Indian children were sent to Indian boarding schools that were little more than prisons, torn from their families and kept from siblings and family members because of a strict sex/gender binary. Those who did not identify as cisgender were denied those identities, and colonizers forced these children to live as either male or female and to follow colonizer rules and expectations. Cherokee journalist Jan Deerinwater, who identifies as "two-spirit," explains, "Kinship ties were destroyed, and many children died or disappeared as colonizers forced their views of identity upon others."[25]

The gendercide, perpetrated by white colonial men, and supported by white colonial women, was an attempt to bolster a strict belief in a sex/gender binary. Fueled by the fear that the binary could be breached at any moment, colonization prevailed. Confronted with alternative views of sex and gender, which encouraged alternative views of identity and community, colonizers responded with violence. Colonial notions of masculinity, in sum, created a particularly violent discursive regime. Morgensen suggests that when colonial ideas of proper masculinity are threatened, this discursive regime

- acts violently to prove that it is untainted by that to which it is opposed;
- focuses on annihilating what it perceives to be a threat;
- targets a perceived threat for containment, surveillance, and policing;

- links masculinity with sexual violence;
- calls upon any institution, relationship, or story to incite or support these acts.[26]

The discursive regime of European, white, cisgender, heterosexual masculinity, in sum, perpetuated discourses that cast Indigenous people as a threat to all that was good and pure. These discourses, and the individuals who engaged in them, convinced enough other white, cisgender, heterosexual, European women and men that it was imperative that this threat be contained or annihilated. The narratives—the discursive regime—emphasized the necessity of using horrific violence in order to destroy or contain the threat.

If colonization could be understood just by exploring the violent response to the perceived threats to colonial masculinity, we could end our examination here. We might even be relieved that, while its presence dominated several centuries of our history, it is a travesty of the past. But colonization and colonizing discourses continue to exist today. As Morgensen suggests, if Europeans brought these discursive regimes with them, would they simply disappear after the annihilation of Indigenous people? In fact, they have not. The over-incarceration of Indigenous men and the over-representation of murdered, raped, and/or kidnapped Indigenous women and girls remain a crisis that is with us to this day.[27] Colonizing actions and discourses are present today, perhaps in a slightly different form than colonial-era notions of European masculinity, but they continue to dominate our conversations, casting some people as lower on the hierarchy of humanness, in need of salvation and even elimination.

Colonizing the Burqa

In the months immediately following the 2001 attacks on the World Trade Center and the Pentagon, then president George W. Bush labeled Muslim women in Afghanistan "our sister 'women of cover.'" Bush urged Americans to support a "War on Terror" in order to "save and liberate" these "sisters," these "women of cover." Laura Bush added to this colonizing depiction of Muslim women as in need of protection, calling on "civilized people throughout the world" to save these women and children by supporting the war against the "Taliban-and-the-terrorists, the cultural monsters who want to . . . 'impose their World on the rest of us.'"[28] This discourse circulated widely in popular press, news reports, classrooms, churches, and communities. Saving Muslim women became synonymous with supporting the War on Terror, American freedom, and the push for democracy everywhere. Many U.S. citizens believed in this colonizing depiction of a sister-woman-of-cover, failing to unpack or even explore the events that led to the attacks, the Muslim faith, or the burqa and its complex history.

Anthropologist Lila Abu-Lughod explains that as U.S and allied forces began to reduce the number of their troops in Afghanistan, these colonizing descriptions left many in the United States confused and surprised. Why was it "that even though Afghanistan [seemed to have] been liberated from the Taliban, women do not seem to be throwing off their burqas"?[29] Abu-Lughod shares important details that had been erased in the colonizing stories circulating about Muslim women and their need for U.S. liberation. First, Abu-Lughod explains, "the Taliban did not invent the burqa" or other forms of covering. Various forms of covering, including the burqa, have been in existence for centuries, for both men and women. This includes the *chadri,* which covers the entire face except for a small opening around the eyes, which existed in pre-Islamic times. Colonizing discourses erased the fact that both Muslim women and non-Muslim women, at times throughout history, wore the chadri.

Second, "the burqa is one of many forms of covering in the subcontinent and Southwest Asia." In addition to the burqa, which covers the full body leaving only a small cloth grill in the hood for the eyes, these various forms include the *niquab,* which covers the full body, including the face but not the eyes; the *hijab,* a headscarf covering the head and wrapped around the chin; and the traditional Tajik headscarf, which covers the head but not the eyes, and ties behind the head. Colonizing discourses erased the existence of these diverse forms of covering. Third, pre-Taliban, the burqa often symbolized "women's modesty and respectability." Pre-Taliban, a woman's own interpretation of modesty, in combination with her culture's interpretation, determined the covering she wore—yet another fact erased by the language of colonization.

Fourth, the burqa, and other forms of covering, mark "the symbolic separation of men's and women's spheres" and is part of "the general association of women with family and home, not with public space where strangers mingled." The burqa acts as a kind of "portable seclusion" for women. The burqa can signify "belonging to a particular community and participating in a moral way of life in which families are paramount in the organization of communities and the home is associated with the sanctity of women."[30] Pre-Taliban, for Muslim women who wore a burqa, their choice was a mixture of cultural expectations related to respect, honoring traditions, and a desire for privacy and control over one's own body. Modesty, and the choice to be modest, were not a part of the colonizing discourses circulating at that time.

Adopting a de-colonized understanding of head coverings and burqas, regardless of whether or not people "approve" of them, Abu-Lughold asks two compelling questions. As troops began to withdraw, "Why would women suddenly become immodest? Why would they suddenly throw off the markers of their respectability?" Using what Abu-Lughold offers as an imperfect analogy, she asks, "Why are we surprised that Afghan women do not throw off their burqas when we know perfectly well that it would not be appropriate to wear shorts to the opera?" She concludes, "I have done field work in Egypt over more than 20 years and I cannot think of a single woman I know, from the poorest rural to the most educated cosmopolitan, who has ever expressed envy of U.S.

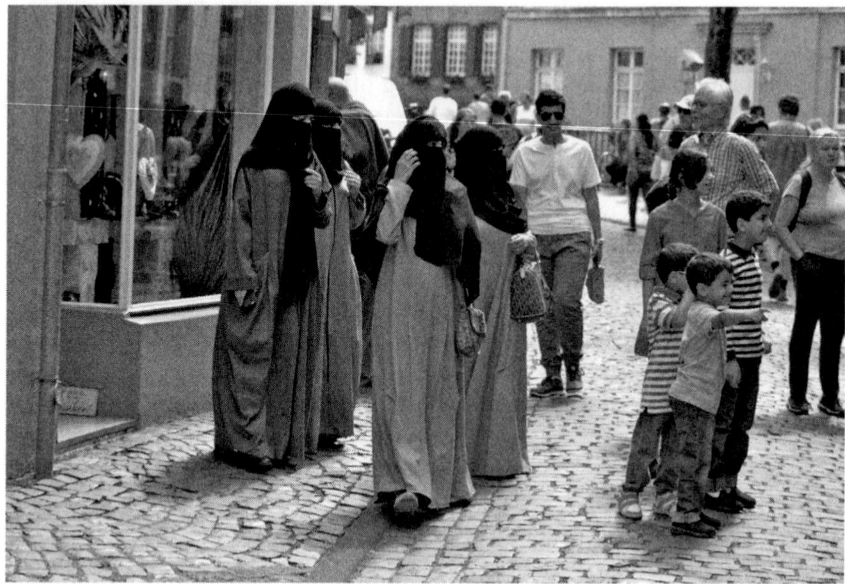

Figure 11.3 Lila Abu-Lughold asks us to consider why would Muslim women throw off their burqas to become more like U.S. women, whom they do not necessarily envy or wish to be like? (Source: iStock. Credit: Rklfoto)

women, women they tend to perceive as bereft of community, vulnerable to sexual violence and social anomie, driven by individual success rather than morality, or strangely disrespectful of God."[31]

As postcolonial and transnational feminist theorist Chandra Talpade Mohanty explains, women are not the same "across classes and cultures"—there is no "homogeneity of women as a group."[32] When we take white feminism in the United States as the point of entry and the standard for "normal" and "valuable," not only are binaries reinscribed—with white women at the center/women of color outside—but we also perpetuate discourses of hierarchy and colonization. Homi Bhabha, critical theorist and professor of humanities at Harvard University, reminds us that the language of colonization involves "the recognition and disavowal of racial/cultural/historical differences."[33] The discourse of colonization posits a "singular, monolithic notion of patriarchy or male dominance," resulting in the belief in a universal experience of oppression that should be engaged in and responded to in similar ways—regardless of person, time, or place. If the diversity of identities, practices, cultures, and people is to be understood in any meaningful way, we cannot take as our point of entry, and as our standard for what is normal and valuable the efforts, practices, belief systems, and ways of living of the dominant group.[34]

Bushra Rehman and Daisy Hernández share that like "many other women of color, the two of us first learned the language of feminism in college through a white, middle-class perspective, one form of colonization." Feminism, they explain, should have brought them "closer to our mothers and sisters and to our aunties in the Third World. Instead it took us further away."[35] This feminism did not teach them "how to talk with the women in our families about why they stayed with alcoholic husbands or chose to veil." The rejection, erasure, and misrepresentation of "their life choices as women" resulted in the loss of a "part of our selves and our own history."[36] When we engage in the language of colonizing, we tell a single story, engage in color-blind thinking, and we cast women, or any group of people we think can or should be grouped, as a unified and homogenous group. We fall into the trap of thinking that any group of people can be understood through the experiences of a very select group: the group with the most power.

In Rehman and Hernández's example, all women are subsumed under the category of cisgender, white, and comfortably mainstream women. The result is the silencing and erasing of the lived experiences, realities, efforts, and contributions of the range of identities: people of color; bisexual, lesbian, queer, transgender, and questioning people; bi or multi-cultural and bi or multi-lingual people; people with disabilities; and immigrant and refugee human beings. We ignore the impact of nations, cultures, and families; religions and spiritualties; as well as issues of security—food, housing, and income—and safety, safety at home, when out in public, and in social settings. When "truth" is presented from the perspective of a colonizing truth regime, the histories, stories, ways of living and thinking, and the efforts of individuals at resisting the colonizers are erased and misrepresented.

Colonizing Our Gaze

In 1975, Laura Mulvey introduced the idea of "the male gaze" into film studies. The male gaze refers to ways we are asked, as viewers of film and other media, to view women as they are presented on screen. The male gaze depicts women from a particular lens or standpoint. That gaze reflects what is considered a masculine and heterosexual perspective that repeatedly presents women on screen (and other entertainment venues, for that matter) as sexual objects for the pleasure of the male viewer. In this gaze, women are **objectified,** presented as objects for viewing pleasure even if they may possess some small or large degree of agency. Even though Mulvey's depiction of the male gaze relied on cisgender and the binary male/female, heterosexual/homosexual constructions of our identities, her theory revolutionized the ways we understood the presentation and consumption of stories and images in films. Interested in "visual pleasure," or how we are told to enjoy a film, Mulvey reasoned that "film reflects, reveals and even plays on the straight, socially established interpretation of sexual difference." Films, she suggested, not only depend on a white, heterosexual, cisgender, able-body, male world-view to tell their story, but they reinscribe that perspective, teaching us how to see ourselves and others. This "male gaze" communicates like "magic," making it difficult to see the ideologies behind the narratives and the images.[37]

Its discursive magic is so powerful, Mulvey explains, that it does not just present a slanted or biased story, it tells us what we should appreciate and enjoy seeing. Mulvey states that the gaze communicates to us that "men look and women are looked at" and that this way of looking and seeing is normal and natural.[38] Far from objective or neutral, however, the male gaze informs almost every aspect of our consumption of media. Interested in women's presence in films, Mulvey and the scholars exploring the gaze in the 1970s and 1980s, suggest that women, regardless of how their identities intersect, serve a very narrow function in cinema: that of securing men's superiority over them, in every way possible. This is done through images, lighting, language, actions, and story lines that establish men—usually white and cisgender, but not always—as the actors and saviors in almost every drama. Viewers are taught to enjoy this version of the world because the storylines, visual strategies, even the music that accompanies this version of male/masculine superiority reinforce the correctness, and value, of this narrative.

Because we are so familiar with this form of male gaze, and because it has been the dominant frame for the vast majority of our media consumption, Mulvey reasons that even large or small moments of challenge to this gaze cannot undo its dominance. Women—again, performing or presenting a range of identities—might resist and display agency and self-determination, whether for the full film or for but a moment in the narrative, but the impact of this resistance is severely minimized by the decades of stories told through this gaze. So, although the gaze might be challenged, it rarely is undone because of the overwhelmingly dominant presence and power of its ideology.

If we engage Mulvey's notion of the male gaze intersectionally, we can see that the gaze—the discursive package—through which we view our entertainment is not just a male discursive package. Rather, the discursive package, the ideology of the gaze, reflects a very specific kind of male: a white, masculine, cisgender, able-body, heterosexual, economically secure, Christian gaze/discursive package. And it has colonized our thinking about identities, giving us a standard for "normal" and "natural" that reflects only a very narrow view of what it means to be human and to have agency in the world. Diverse identities may have interjected a different kind of gaze over the years but, as media scholars have discovered, their ability to disrupt the dominant gaze is hampered by decades of the "normalcy" of this first gaze in our entertainment venues.

Mulvey explains that understanding this colonizing gaze as a representational system is key to understanding the dominant ways information is communicated to us by media. Focusing on the systems of representation helps us to unpack the invisibility of these ways of presenting and seeing and to understand just how monolithic this communication of identities is.[39] Recall from chapter 10 that systems classify, arrange, assemble, and coordinate efforts and processes; their reach is comprehensive, that is, they address all the pieces of the thing being organized. In film and media, this includes the spaces in which we consume a story as well as the content and presentation of the story itself. With regard to space and film, when we watch a film we feel as though we are "looking in on a private world," a "hermetically sealed world which unwinds magically, indifferent to the presence of the audience."[40] In a theatre, for example, the room is darkened, separating us from other viewers; on our computers or phones, our ear buds are in, creating a sense of separation from others; in a small group, our bodies and eyes are facing forward, toward the unfolding story, creating a sense that we are alone in our watching.

Representational systems also organize what we watch and tell us how to feel about what we are watching. The gaze with which we are so familiar is designed to create a certain kind of pleasure in looking. Mulvey explains that films "focus on the human form. Scale, space, stories are all anthropomorphic. Here, curiosity and the wish to look intermingle with a fascination with likeness and recognition: the human face, the human body, the relationship between human form and its surroundings, the visible presence of a human in the world," all draw us in as we look for similarities and the familiar.[41] Films are created so that we enjoy what we are seeing, they teach us what to enjoy, and they lead us step by step to that enjoyment through visual and sound effects, as well as the story line, itself.

This comprehensive system of representation is true of other genres of media as well. When we watch or listen to the news, we often feel as though the journalists are speaking directly to us; with television, alone or with friends, we are engaged in a private or semi-private world of watching, comparing, cheering, celebrating, or lamenting; when we post or explore online, we are looking at others and ourselves, as we search for similarities, differences, rights, and wrongs. What does it mean to be human? Through whose eyes are we looking? Who is like me? What behaviors and choices are appropriate? Whose stories are being shared (or are we sharing), over and over again, such that they come to be seen as the "right" and "true" story of our places in the world? A very specific system of representation is continually guiding our thinking and influencing our understanding of the world around us.

Understanding "the male gaze," which also can be described as a "colonizing gaze," helps us unpack who is an active subject, who is a passive object, who is labeled powerful, and what is presented as good. An intersectional approach to understanding the colonizing gaze helps identify the quality of the "pleasure" we are said to be receiving as we consume media productions, the ideologies embedded in that pleasure, and to decide whether or not this so-called pleasure actually is gratifying at all. Black feminist theorist and cultural critic bell hooks says that "Movies make magic. They change things. They take the real and make it into something else right before our very eyes." What movies do not do, hooks explains, is portray the real. Instead, they give viewers "the reimagined, reinvented version of the real. It may look like something familiar, but in actuality it is a different universe from the world of the real."[42]

INTERNALIZED COLONIZATION

Our media—in the widest sense possible—are pedagogical. Hooks shares that "even though most folks will say they go to movies to be entertained, if the truth be told lots of us, myself included, go to movies to learn stuff."[43] Media teach us "about race, sex, and class, they provide a shared experience, a common starting point from which diverse audiences can dialogue about these charged issues." Whether intentional or not, media "provide a narrative for specific discourses of race, sex, and class," and many of us engage these discourses through a colonizing as well as a colonized gaze.[44] As stereotypes move across our screens, viewers internalize the stereotypes they see, learning to survey and monitor their own bodies. Bonnie Moradi and Yu-Ping Huang suggest that this internalization of stereotypes often leads to **self-objectification.** As a result of this ever-present stereotyping, many people—for Moradi and Huang, cisgender women specifically—learn to view themselves as "objects to be looked upon and evaluated based upon bodily appearance."[45] Moradi and Huang explain that cisgender women may feel anxious or shame when their bodies do not match the ideal that saturates our media—they have learned to turn the male gaze upon themselves.

Because of the colonizing power of this gaze, hooks urges viewers to explore a film's standpoint, that is, investigate the perspective of the storyteller in order to identify the systems of representation. There often are several standpoints, hooks says, and the standpoints in a film may conflict with one another. Regardless, when viewers investigate those standpoints they are asked to consider the question, From whose perspective are we being asked to view the characters in a film and the narrative that is unfolding? This means, hooks explains, that as people watch or consume media, they consider "from what political perspective do we dream, look, create, and take action?"[46]

Hooks explains that what is seen by many as progressive presentations of complex identities and ideologies—new ways of thinking about sex, race, class, ability, and sexuality—often is not very progressive at all. Audiences need to be careful that what they think of as progressive and alternative, what they consider to be edgy or innovative presentations and understandings of our complex identities, really are. Hooks urges viewers to ask, Is this film actually reinscribing familiar and colonizing stereotypes or is it truly re-imagining, recreating, and revising these old lies? Obviously, audiences are not passive receptacles of the films they watch. But, hooks shares, even though someone might view a film as a resistant spectator, the reality is that "no matter how sophisticated our strategies of critique and intervention," almost all of us are seduced by the images and the narrative presented on the screen. In "the darkness of the theatre, most audiences choose to give themselves over, if only for a time, to the images depicted and the imaginations that have created those images."[47]

Whether we realize it or not, media play a central role in our looking at others. In "Voyeur Nation?" Jonathan Metzl speculates on whether or not we have become a nation of voyeurs. **Voyeurism** is typically understood as the practice of spying on unsuspecting people, usually strangers, who are naked or engaged in intimate behaviors, such as undressing, sexual activities, or other actions usually considered to be private in nature.[48] In our media-saturated society, voyeurism has become a sanctioned way of seeing: a way in which we collectively peer into the private lives of others, with or without their consent. Metzl notes that watching others is "never value free" but instead "is a practice that is imbued with power," privilege, and a host of other social, political, economic, religious, and identity imbalances.[49] People pay a high price for this voyeurism, Metzl claims, because they have been taught that watching others in private actions is normal and natural—but more than this, that "watching others engaged in private actions *from a particular standpoint* is good."[50]

Maria Hueng explains that voyeurism in our media—the looking at objectified and damaging images of people without their real consent—actually is a form of **aesthetic imperialism.** She explains that even though a single individual, or even several individuals, may consent to the portrayal on screen, the majority of individuals with similar identities have had no say in the depiction. She notes that "the bodies of Asian women are idealized and judged according to Western standards of exotic beauty, in conformity to the edicts of" this imperialism. "Whether portrayed as objects of sexual conquest and seduction, casualties of war and mail-order items for sale, or reduced to exotic but interchangeable elements of the decorative landscape, the bodies of Asian women are palpably present in the mass media in the most physicalized and sexualized terms."[51] They have been colonized and viewers have learned that gazing at them from this particular standpoint is not only good, but also enjoyable.

Hooks shares Pratibha Parmar's observation that "control over images is central to the maintenance of any system of racial domination."[52] This is because images "play a crucial role in defining and controlling the political and social power to which both individuals and marginalized groups have access. The deeply ideological nature of imagery determines not only how other people think about us, but how we think about ourselves." Hooks continues,

> Many audiences in the United States resist the idea that images have an ideological intent. This is equally true of black audiences. Fierce critical interrogation is sometimes the only practice that can pierce the wall of denial consumers of images

> construct so as not to face that the real world of image-making is political—that politics of domination inform the way the vast majority of images we consume are constructed and marketed. . . . I ask that we consider the perspective from which we look, vigilantly asking ourselves who do we identify with, whose image do we love.[53]

Hooks explains that the images that contribute to colonizing, images that violate and degrade other people, should be painful to watch: "That is how it should be. It should hurt our eyes to see racial genocide perpetuated in black communities, whether fictional or real."[54] She asks, "What can the future hold if our present entertainment is the spectacle of contemporary colonization, dehumanization, and disempowerment where the image serves as a murder weapon."[55]

Hooks notes that regardless of the identity of the film maker, we must be tuned into what the "black subject [does], how does it act, how does it think politically? . . . being black isn't really good enough for me: I want to know what" the filmmaker's "cultural politics are."[56] Similarly, viewers must be tuned into what a subject's various identities are doing—is the representational system reinforcing the aesthetics of human disqualification or is it rejecting it? Maria Heung shares that the "power of the colonizer is fundamentally constituted by the power to speak for and to represent" groups of people as they see fit.[57] Heung explains that in its "most concrete manifestation, colonization consists of actual territorial conquest and occupation; however, the notion also pertains to how dominant systems of representation produce and reinforce mental structures and images to constrain, dehumanize, and disempower particular individuals and social groups in both First-and Third-World cultures."[58]

Heung says that our imagination has been colonized: "Not only does the general population accept stereotypes of Asian women," or any group of individuals projected on our screens through the male/colonizing gaze, but these stereotypes have been created "without our consent." Heung explains that the "history of marginalized peoples can be interpreted as one in which bodies are disappeared and erased from history." When they are present, they are objectified, sexualized, criminalized, in short, "decorative . . . or one-dimensional." Heung suggests that because of this colonizing representational system, most of our "stories have been left unwritten or forgotten in the annals of official history."[59]

Instead of a diversity of stories circulating throughout our contemporary media, we have a narrow story and a colonizing view of how people live in, and move about, the world. A colonized and colonizing gaze has been with us for so long that the "stereotypes infiltrate and transform the consciousness" of all of us. Heung speculates that the result of this colonization is "dire" with regard to how individuals view and experience themselves and other people. "Internalized colonization," she posits, "is one of the most insidious and destructive effects of colonialism."[60]

BEYOND COLONIZING DISCOURSES

In *White Fragility: Why It's So Hard for White People to Talk About Racism,* Robin Diangelo notes that the "identities of those sitting at the tables of power in this country have remained remarkably similar: white, male, middle and upper class, able-bodied." Those at the tables of power make decisions, Diangelo explains, that "affect the lives of those not at the tables. Exclusion by those at the table doesn't depend on willful intent: we don't have to intend to exclude for the results of our actions to be exclusion."[61] People cling to tradition and familiarity, they are forgetful, they often do not see what is right in front of them. Unintentional exclusion happens. But sometimes people do intend to exclude. Difference can make them uncomfortable. What seems strange can also seem threatening—a person may have no frame of reference with which to understand this strangeness. And so they retreat. They intentionally exclude to avoid discomfort.

Whether the exclusion is intentional or not, Diangelo defines this retreat and avoidance as white fragility. **White fragility** is the inability of white people to cope with any challenge to their racial worldview and to their "identities as good, moral people." She explains, "the smallest amount of racial stress is intolerable."[62] Racial stress triggers emotions such as anger and guilt. It causes white people to be defensive and argumentative. White people withdraw from the conversation, blaming other people for being too sensitive, for reading too much into a situation, for not taking responsibility for their own lives. But fragility can infect any of our privileged identities. The unwillingness to explore our discomfort is an **identity fragility**. People are sex and gender fragile, class fragile, body fragile, religion fragile, culture fragile, and more. When people cling to binaries, place value in hierarchies of humanness, fail to recognize the ways colonization affects not only other people, but themselves, they often cling to their privileges as though they were hard earned and theirs by right. When challenged, identities become fragile.

When people are confronted with difference, they also are confronted with the identity politics that accompany that difference. **Identity politics** refers to the unequal distribution of power and privilege in our society—regardless of our nation's founding narratives that promised this would not be so. When binaries are challenged and unearned privileges are called into question, people often get defensive: they blame others, they shut down, they deny culpability. Diangelo shares that when confronted with "any suggestion that we are complicit in racism," for example, or that we have been socialized into a system that not only ranks people by identity but also tries to mask that system of ranking, rather than thank the person for pointing that out, "rather than gratitude and relief (after all, now that we are informed, we won't do it again), we respond with anger and denial."[63] Diangelo asks people to reflect on why they retreat to this anger and denial rather than express gratitude and relief. Why,

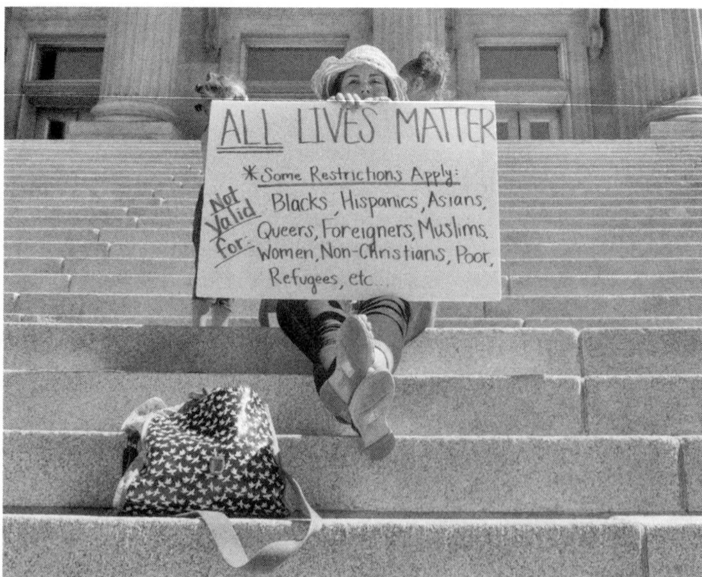

Figure 11.4 Identity politics refers to the unequal distribution of power and privilege in our society and helps people understand that although "all lives matter," restrictions do apply. When we acknowledge the very real unequal distributions of power that this protestor's sign calls out, we can avoid overly simplistic understandings of very complex issues related to our identities. (Source: iStock. Credit: txking)

she wonders, would someone repeatedly reject information that could be useful? When someone makes a mistake, why would they want to make it over and over again if it could be corrected?

Communication scholar Karma Chávez urges us to explore the "complicated and dynamic way in which identities, power, and systems of oppression intermesh, interlock, intersect, and thus interact." Rather than passively consume stories and images, Chávez suggests that we use our intersectional communication skills. She urges us to ask what are the "predictable ways oppression and power manifest in relation to and upon particular bodies"? Using an intersectional lens, we can consider how country and colonization interact. We can

> invite an understanding of how multiple oppressions (and privileges) deriving from systems such as race, class, gender, sexuality, and nation intermesh so that the experience of being a queer, working-class woman of color in the United States differs very much from being a queer, working-class white woman or any number of other women.

As we engage those questions intersectionally we might follow up with another, Chávez suggests: what are the "possibilities for creative and complicated responses to oppression"?[64]

11.1. GUIDE TO COMMUNICATION

Unpacking the Language of Colonization

To help you explore the complex concept of colonization and the ways it might be influencing your communication and your assumptions about individuals you see as different from you, consider the following questions:

1. What universal or homogenous identity is being advanced or accepted as right and normal in this description or exchange?
2. Whose identities are being erased or destroyed in this decision or approach to a problem or idea?
3. What do I really know about this culture, group of people, or individual?
4. What am I being encouraged to ignore or misunderstand of the history of this individual, culture, or group of people?

Resources

Ana Marie Cox, "With Friends Like These—'White Fragility 101,'" *Stitch,* August 24, 2018, 57:27, https://www.stitcher.com/podcast/cadence13/with-friends-like-these/e/55927773.

Robin Diangelo, *White Fragility: Why It's So Hard for White People to Talk About Racism* (Boston: Beacon Press, 2018).

"In Conversation with Laura Mulvey (Interview)," YouTube video, 8:09, "Another Gaze Journal," March 7, 2017, https://www.youtube.com/watch?v=vw-ps5mFQzA.

Jamila Lyiscott, "3 Ways to Speak English," filmed February 2014 in New York, NY, TEDSalon NY2014 video, 4:29, https://www.ted.com/talks/jamila_lyiscott_3_ways_to_speak_english#t-211337.

Elif Shafak, "The Revolutionary Power of Diverse Thought," filmed September 2017 in New York, NY, TEDGlobal>NYC video, 21:58, https://www.ted.com/talks/elif_shafak_the_revolutionary_power_of_diverse_thought#t-446810.

"Jill Soloway on the Female Gaze—Master Class—TIFF 2016," YouTube video, 57:48, "TIFF Talks," September 11, 2016, https://www.youtube.com/watch?v=pnBvppooD9I.

Notes

1. Edward Said, *Culture and Imperialism* (New York: Alfred A. Knopf, 1993), 336.
2. Ania Loomba, *Colonialism/Postcolonialism,* 3rd ed (New York: Routledge, 2015), 20.
3. Loomba, *Colonialism,* 25.
4. John McLeod, *Beginning Postcolonialism,* 2nd ed. (New York: Manchester University Press/Palgrave Macmillan, 2010), chapter 1.
5. Glenn Welker, Indigenous Peoples Literature, 2017, http://www.indigenouspeople.net.
6. Bushra Rehman and Daisy Hernández, "Introduction," in *Colonize This! Young Women of Color on Today's Feminism,* ed. Daisy Hernández and Bushra Rehman (New York: Seal Press, 2002), xxii.
7. Susan Ehrlich, *Representing Rape: Language and Sexual Consent* (New York: Routledge, 2001), 4.
8. Linda Coates and Allen Wade, "Language and Violence: An Analysis of Four Discursive Operations," *Journal of Family Violence* 22, no. 7 (2007): 512.
9. Loomba, *Colonialism,* 8.
10. Simone de Beauvoir, *The Second Sex,* trans. and ed. H.M. Parshley (1949, 1953; New York : Penquin, 1972), 249.
11. Alexandra Shepard, *Meanings of Manhood in Early Modern England* (Oxford: Oxford University Press, 2003), 267.
12. Scott L. Morgensen, "Cutting to the Roots of Colonial Masculinity," in *Indigenous Men and Masculinities: Legacies, Identities, Regeneration,* ed. Kim Anderson and Robert Alexander Innes (Winnipeg: University of Manitoba Press, 2015), 41.

13. Shepard, *Meanings of Manhood*, 97–99.
14. Morgensen, "Cutting to the Roots of Colonial Masculinity," 9.
15. Morgensen, "Cutting to the Roots of Colonial Masculinity," 39
16. Morgensen, "Cutting to the Roots of Colonial Masculinity," 42.
17. Morgensen, "Cutting to the Roots of Colonial Masculinity," 45.
18. Morgensen, "Cutting to the Roots of Colonial Masculinity," 43.
19. Morgensen, "Cutting to the Roots of Colonial Masculinity," 42.
20. Morgensen, "Cutting to the Roots of Colonial Masculinity," 43.
21. Morgensen, "Cutting to the Roots of Colonial Masculinity," 45.
22. Morgensen, "Cutting to the Roots of Colonial Masculinity," 45.
23. Morgensen, "Cutting to the Roots of Colonial Masculinity," 48.
24. Morgensen, "Cutting to the Roots of Colonial Masculinity," 49.
25. Morgensen, "Cutting to the Roots of Colonial Masculinity," 48–49.
26. Morgensen, "Cutting to the Roots of Colonial Masculinity," 55–56.
27. Pamela Palmater, "Shining Light on the Dark Places: Addressing Police Racism and Sexualized Violence Against Indigenous Women and Girls in the National Inquiry," *Canadian Journal of Women and the Law* 28, no. 2 (2016): 253–284; Sherene H. Razack, "Sexualized Violence and Colonialism: Reflections on the Inquiry into Missing and Murdered Indigenous Women," *Canadian Journal of Women and the Law* 28, no. 2 (2016): i-iv.
28. Lila Abu-Lughod, "Do Muslim Women Really Need Saving? Anthropological Reflections on Cultural Relativism and Its Others," *American Anthropologist* 104, no. 3 (January 7, 2008), https://doi.org/10.1525/aa.2002.104.3.783.
29. Abu-Lughod, "Do Muslim Women Really Need Saving?" 785.
30. Abu-Lughod, "Do Muslim Women Really Need Saving?" 785.
31. Abu-Lughod, "Do Muslim Women Really Need Saving?" 788
32. Chandra Talpade Mohanty, "Under Western Eyes: Feminist Scholars and Colonial Discourses," *Feminist Review*, no. 30 (Autumn 1988): 63.
33. Homi K. Bhabha, "The Other Question . . . Homi K. Bhabha Reconsiders the Stereotype and Colonial Discourse," *Screen* 24, no. 6 (November–December 1983): 23.
34. Mohanty, "Under Western Eyes," 65–66.
35. Rehman and Hernández, "Introduction," xxii.
36. Rehman and Hernández, "Introduction," xxii.
37. Laura Mulvey, "Visual Pleasure and Narrative Cinema," *Screen* 16, no. 3 (Autumn 1975): 6.
38. Anneke Smelik, "Gaze," *The Wiley Blackwell Encyclopedia of Gender and Sexuality Studies*, Wiley Online library, April 21, 2016, doi: 10:1002/9781118663219.wbegss157/full, http://onlinelibrary.wiley.com.ezproxy2.library.colostate.edu/.
39. Mulvey, "Visual Pleasure and Narrative Cinema," 6–18.
40. Mulvey, "Visual Pleasure and Narrative Cinema," 8. See also Robin R. Means Coleman and Emily Chivers Yochim, "The Symbolic Annihilation of Race: A Review of the 'Blackness' Literature," *African American Research Perspectives* 12 (2008): 1–10, http://hdl.handle.net/2027.42/60140.
41. Mulvey, "Visual Pleasure and Narrative Cinema," 8.
42. bell hooks, *Reel to Real: Race, Sex, and Class at the Movies* (New York: Routledge, 1996), 1.
43. hooks, *Reel to Real*, 2.
44. hooks, *Reel to Real*, 2.
45. Bonnie Moradi and Yu-Ping Huang, "Objectification Theory and Psychology of Women: A Decade of Advances and Future Directions," *Psychology of Women Quarterly* 32, no. 4 (2008): 377–378.
46. bell hooks, *Black Looks: Race and Representation* (Boston: South End Press, 1992), 4.
47. hooks, *Reel to Real*, 2.
48. Jonathan M. Metzl, "Voyeur Nation? Changing Definitions of Voyeurism, 1950–2004," *Harvard Review of Psychiatry* 12, no. 2 (2004): 127. See also "Voyeurism," Wikipedia, https://en.wikipedia.org/wiki/Voyeurism#cite_note-1.
49. Metzl, "Voyeur Nation?" 131.
50. Lemi Baruh, "Publicized Intimacies on Reality Television: An Analysis of Voyeuristic Content and Its Contribution to the Appeal of Reality Programming," *Journal of Broadcasting and Electronic Media* 53, no. 2 (2009): 191; emphasis in original.
51. Marina Heung, "Representing Ourselves: Films and Videos by Asian American/Canadian Women," in *Feminism, Multiculturalism, and the Media: Global Diversities*, ed. Angharad N. Valdivia (Thousand Oaks, CA: Sage, 1995): 90.
52. hooks, *Reel to Real*, 2.
53. hooks, *Reel to Real*, 5–6.
54. hooks, *Reel to Real*, 6.
55. hooks, *Reel to Real*, 7.
56. hooks, *Reel to Real*, 4.
57. Heung, "Representing Ourselves," 83.

58. Heung, "Representing Ourselves," 83.
59. Heung, "Representing Ourselves," 95.
60. Heung, "Representing Ourselves," 83–84.
61. Robin Diangelo, *White Fragility: Why It's So Hard for White People to Talk About Racism* (Boston: Beacon, 2018), 2.
62. Diangelo, *White Fragility,* 2.
63. Diangelo, *White Fragility,* 4.
64. Karma R. Chávez, *Queer Migration Politics: Activist Rhetoric and Coalitional Possibilities* (Urbana: University of Illinois Press, 2013), 57–59.

CHAPTER

12

Communicating through Feminist and Intersectional Lenses

IN THIS CHAPTER, YOU WILL FIND . . .

KEY TERMS AND CONCEPTS

- branding
- correct ourselves
- decolonize
- engage discomfort
- listen to difference
- medical/individual model
- paradigmatic
- pathology
- political/relational model
- rebellious bodies
- reject hierarchies of humanness
- relativism

THE REVOLUTIONARY POWER OF DIVERSE THOUGHT

While signing books at a literary festival, a teenage girl approached novelist Elif Shafak and asked, "Can you taste words?" The question caught Shafak by surprise but she responded yes, some people do taste words; it's an overlap in sensory abilities, she explained, and some people can "hear colors or see sounds, and many writers were fascinated by this subject," herself included. The young girl cut her off, saying, "Yeah, I know all of that. It's called synesthesia. We learned it at school. But my mom is reading your book, and she says there's lots of food and ingredients and a long dinner scene in it. She gets hungry at every page. So I was thinking, how come you don't get hungry when you write? And I thought maybe, maybe you could taste words. Does it make sense?"

Shafak shares that the girl's comments did make sense to her. But she was worried that if she offered a lengthy explanation about the ways "each letter in the alphabet has a different color, and colors bring me flavor," that "to this teenager, it might sound either too abstract or perhaps too weird, and there wasn't enough time anyhow, because people were waiting in the queue." It felt, Shafak explains, "like what I was trying to convey was more complicated and detailed than what the circumstances allowed me to say." And so she didn't try. She shut down and stopped talking: "I stopped talking because the truth was complicated, even though I knew deep within, that one should never, ever remain silent for fear of complexity." We often are so busy with facts and figures and analytics and algorithms that we forget that many things are difficult to measure and "perhaps impossible to cluster under statistical models."[1]

Shafak shares a second moment of complexity that occurred when she was living in Istanbul. In a conversation with a scholar from the United States, who studied women in the Middle East, the scholar said, "I understand why you're a feminist, because, you know, you live in Turkey." The comment troubled her, and Shafak replied, "I don't understand why you're not a feminist, because, you know, you live in America." This woman had divided the world into two parts, Shafak explains, the unstable and choppy East and the solid and stable West. But the whole world is choppy, she added: "our world is full of unprecedented challenges." These challenges come with backlash and a desire for stability and familiarity. When "things get too confusing, many people crave simplicity," Shafak notes. But simplicity can be dangerous because it causes the nuances to wither away—it destroys multiplicity. "I am an Istanbulite, but I'm also attached to the Balkans, the Aegean, the Mediterranean, the Middle East, the Levant. I am a European by birth, by choice, by the values that I hold. I have become a Londoner over the years. I have multiple attachments, just like all of us do. And multiple attachments mean multiple stories."[2]

Figure 12.1 Our identities can sometimes seem like this Pow Wow dancer's regalia: too complex and detailed to try to communicate or understand. We can't find the place where one of our identities begins and ends. We can, however, sense how that identity is in constant motion and interaction with other identities, and also how those identities can seem to pause for a moment before they move on again. We can learn to communicate effectively about our own identities, and attempt to understand the identities of others as they dance and swirl around us. (Source: iStock. Credit: ChristiLaLiberte)

INVITATIONAL STRATEGIES FOR INTERSECTIONAL COMMUNICATION

Learning to move beyond the gender binaries that have become so hegemonically familiar to many people and to communicate through an intersectional lens necessitates that we enter spaces rich with diversity. We open ourselves up to exploring Shafak's reminder that complexity and multiplicity are the fabric of our lives, even as we may feel rushed or crave simplicity. To get into multiplicity we must leave behind the binary systems of thinking we have learned so well: we have to engage with an enormous range of identities and experiences—we must seek out multiple stories—openly and honestly. Of course we can prepare ourselves for these experiences by doing research, and we should. We also can expose ourselves to new stories about how diverse our identities might be and explore how people make sense of their own lives. Indeed, these are necessary steps. But to learn to communicate through an intersectional lens, we must do more than this—we must engage with one another.

In this final chapter, we move beyond binary thinking by revisiting the intersectional, invitational, and feminist approaches to communication introduced to you in the opening chapters of this book. We build on these foundational discussions and explorations by focusing on four specific invitational strategies people can use to move beyond binary logics so that they might communicate through feminist and intersectional lenses. These strategies include being willing to listen to difference, reject hierarchies of humanness, engage discomfort, and correct ourselves.

Listen to Difference

To communicate through feminist and intersectional lenses, we must be willing to **listen to difference.** In "Why It's Worth Listening to People You Disagree With," student activist Zachary Wood explains that although listening to ideas he disagreed with or found blatantly offensive turned his stomach, "tuning out opposing viewpoints doesn't make them go away." People still hold those views. Wood shares that by "engaging with controversial and offensive ideas," we "can find common ground, if not with the speakers themselves, then with the audiences they may attract or indoctrinate. Through engaging, I believe that we can reach a better understanding, a deeper understanding, of our own beliefs and preserve the ability to solve problems, which we can't do if we don't talk to each other and make an effort to be good listeners."[3]

Recall from chapter 1 that when we communicate invitationally we do not need to agree with or adopt another person's views. If we listen, as Wood suggests, to better understand a position or perspective, we are listening *invitationally.* Although we might want to change their views, and may even attempt to do so later on, in the moment we are willing to listen to difference we have one goal: to explore that different perspective. But what does this really look like? Suppose you are passionate about hate speech. You might believe that hate speech does have a place in the public conversation, you might be absolutely opposed to hate speech, or you might take a position anywhere along the continuum. You may, for example, believe hate speech is a form of free speech, guaranteed by the First Amendment. On the other hand, you may believe hate speech is a form of verbal violence, and therefore a violation of a person's civil rights. Or you may find yourself in between these two views, supporting the constitutional right to say what we think and feel, but also keenly aware of the harms done to other people when someone expresses blatant verbal hatred.

How do you listen to these different views openly and honestly? Using an invitational framework, you begin by listening to the reasons a person presents for their views. If someone supports the right to deliver hate speech in public, for example, you would listen to the reasons they offer. Perhaps they believe that the constitutional right to say something hateful in public outweighs the harms done as a result of hate speech. For this person, it is more important to say something publicly than to tailor one's speech because of the potential harm it may do. Taking the opposite stance, if someone does not support hate

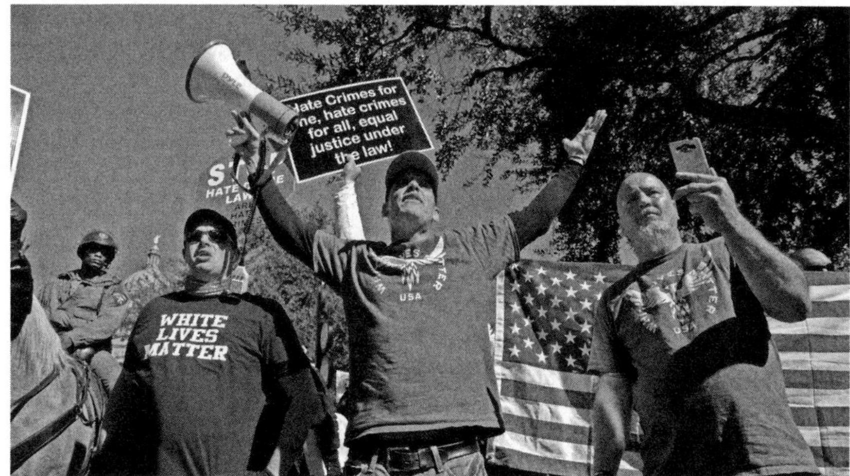

Figure 12.2 These protestors are advocating unrestrained free speech. The rally they are at is a protest of a hate crime law, passed in the state of Texas, that they believe is unfair to white people. (Source: iStock. Credit: Vichinterlang)

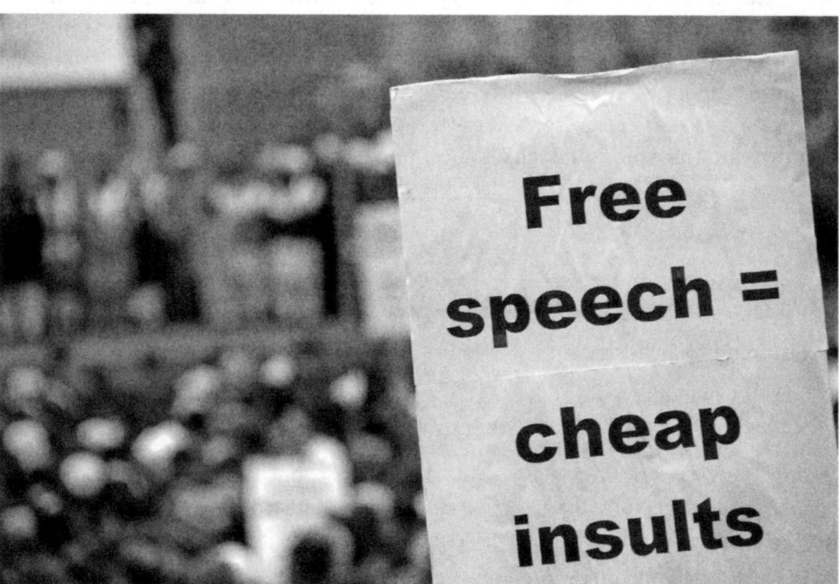

Figure 12.3 This sign is advocating restraints on free speech, suggesting that free speech often equals little more that cheap insults. How might you listen to these very different views presented in these two photos openly and honestly? (Source: iStock. Credit: Nikontiger)

speech, you would listen to those reasons. Perhaps this person believes that the constitutional right to free speech does not outweigh the harms done by hate speech. This person likely reasons that the harms done as a result of hate speech overpower the right to deliver such speech—people should curb their expressions in order to not do harm to another. But if someone is in the middle of these two views, how do you listen to this person? The person in the middle is likely attempting to make sense of a constitutional right and the ways it may conflict with a human right: a constitutional right (free speech) as it collides with a human right (safety in public places). This person likely reasons that there is some kind of balance to be found between these two forces.

These are differences that you are attempting to listen to. You are not looking to agree with them, necessarily, but you are seeking to recognize and to explore the ways they inform people's thinking, decisions, and actions. For some people, a constitutional right to speak out is the most important. For other people, a human right to be safe takes priority. For others, the answer lies somewhere in between. As Wood explains, listening to people with whom we disagree not only gives us important information but also informs the ways we approach issues and dilemmas. How do we juggle a constitutional right—the right to free speech—that is important to citizens of the United States with a basic human right such as right to move about safely in public spaces? If free speech is a foundation for democracy, and safety in public is a basic human right that also is protected by our constitution (the Fourteenth Amendment grants all U.S. citizens equal protection under the law), what value systems are colliding with one another? When we engage an invitational approach of openness and respect we listen to different views and try to unpack the reasons and value systems that are present. We attempt to understand one another through feminist and intersectional lenses.

12.1. GUIDE TO COMMUNICATION

Listening to Difference

To begin to work on the skills necessary to listen to difference, consider the reasons you offer to make your own case or advance your views.

1. Identify for yourself one or two topics or issues about which you feel passionate. Select one of those topics or issues for exploration.
2. Make a list of your own reasons for your views.
3. What values inform your position or view?
4. What underlying values might be at work in the views of those with whom you disagree?

Reject Hierarchies of Humanness

A second step in learning to communicate through feminist and intersectional lenses is to be willing to **reject hierarchies of humanness.** In chapter 4, we saw how certain truth regimes justified classifying people as not fully human (slavery, coverture, sterilization, Black Code laws, and laws of dispossession, for example). When we reject hierarchies of humanness, we reject the idea that some individuals are more valuable than others. We reject the truth regimes that tell us that sex, gender, sexuality, race, ethnicity, national origin, religion, education, profession, class, ability (physical and mental), or any other category, can be organized hierarchically. Such discourses have justified, among other wrongs, massacres, incarceration, the removal of children from families, and even eugenics (chapters 4 and 5). They have contributed to street harassment, rape culture, toxic masculinity, and bullying (chapters 5–9). They are a part of discourses of colonialism and colonization, including discourses of international development (chapter 11). It is not always easy to identify these discursive truth regimes because they thrive on hegemonic notions that normalize inequality and make that inequality seem natural. We are lulled into thinking that these inequities are a part of human nature (chapters 9 and 10). When we reject hierarchies of humanness, we become alert to how certain discourses communicate that some groups of people should be at the top of the hierarchy of humanness—they belong there—while others do not. When we reject these hierarchies, we explore these truth regimes and how the discourses imbedded in them tell us who is at the bottom, who is at the top, and why they are said to belong there.

When we hear, for example, a friend telling us that women athletes do not need to be paid the same as their male counterparts, because no one really wants to watch them play, even as more than a million people watched the 2019 Women's World Cup games, we are listening to a hierarchical truth regime. When we hear politicians tell us that the solution to unwanted immigration is to shoot the legs off of the people entering a country, even as they are attempting to secure a safe place to live, work, and raise families, we are listening to a hierarchical truth regime. When a friend wonders whether or not the proportionately small numbers of transgender individuals actually warrants the media attention and turmoil over their rights, we are listening to a hierarchy of human disqualification that tells us that the only rights we need concern ourselves with are those that affect enormous numbers of individuals. When we hear radio and television personalities refer to human beings as "ragheads," "sluts," "tranny," or "white trash," we are listening to a hierarchical arrangement of human beings, even though those to whom the labels are being ascribed are as fully human as every other human on the planet. Exposing and exploring these hierarchies uncovers discourses of disqualification. These discourses are based on little very real evidence or understanding of how some

12.2. GUIDE TO COMMUNICATION

Exploring Discursive Regimes

To help you begin to develop the skills you will need to reject hierarchies of humanness, consider what discourses of the past have been used to categorize individuals as "better" or "worse" humans. Explore whether and how such discursive regimes of "better" or "worse" are or are not possible today.

1. Make a list of the qualities you believe make someone human.
2. What discourses and reasons are you relying on to make your claims?
3. Now recount a narrative from history that tells us one person is more valuable than another (chapters 4–11 can help you identify these narratives).
4. What reasons, values, and assumptions are being used to create this narrative?

athletes have come to be paid less than others, why some individuals are forced to leave their homelands, why oppressing a thousand people because of their identities is as wrong as oppressing a million, and how name calling demonizes and denies people the complexity and multiplicity of their lives.

It is important to note that rejecting hierarchies does not mean that "it's all good" or that every choice made at any time in history was an "okay" choice because there are no hierarchies. That view, the "it's all good" view, is better known as **relativism,** or the view that every view is just as good as any other view. It is also a little like anarchy, which advocates the absence of any order or guiding principles. Rejecting hierarchies of humanness does not mean we take a relative or anarchic stance. Rather, it means that we explore the institutions, structures, and systems that put the hierarchies in place. We take time to learn how those at the top of the hierarchy of humanness arrived at the top and how those lower on that hierarchy struggle to be seen as equal human beings. We listen for the hegemonic discourses that reinforce those institutions, structures, and systems and make them mostly invisible to far too many of us. We ask questions and explore discursive regimes. Informed by Seyla Benhabib's principle of universal moral respect (chapter 4) we attend to hierarchical patterns of thinking. We use our communication skills to name these hierarchies and question their validity. We ask ourselves, Why is one person said to be more valuable than another?

Engage Discomfort

To communicate through feminist and intersectional lenses, we also must be willing to **engage discomfort.** Although some of our intersectional communication will be easy, a good deal of it will not be. As we learn new ways of thinking about sexes, genders, sexualities, queer and transgender identities, races, classes, religions and spiritualties, and bodies that represent the fullest spectrum of human existence, we may be uncomfortable. Once confident in our ability to see, hear, and know what is good or bad and right or wrong, or what is normal, when we reject identity binaries and adopt an intersectional approach, that confidence can be challenged every step of the way. Our uncertainty can make us uncomfortable. Rather than avoid that discomfort, to learn to communicate through feminist and intersectional lenses, we have to step into it. Discomfort can teach us important things. When we explore our discomfort because of an interaction with someone we see as different from our own self, we expose our own beliefs about what we thought was normal and just, but in fact may not be normal or just at all.

Consider, for example, whether you are uncomfortable during or after discussions of privilege. As the kaleidoscope of privileges available to individuals and groups of people align with our different avowed and ascribed identities, questions of who has what kind of benefits or disadvantages can be prickly. For example, you may identify as white and cisgender yet you may also have a disability or come from an economically insecure background. Because of these identities, you may have had to fight harder than other people to succeed in school or find work. Or, you might identify as transgender or queer, yet you grew up economically secure and attended excellent schools. Although you have an excellent education, employers have been reluctant to hire you, but you can rely on your family's resources to help you get by. Perhaps you grew up in a stable, loving, but also interracially or even internationally complex family. Because of this diversity, you are fluent in several languages, and this has served you well in your profession, yet these complex racial and ethnic identities have also been the source of much hostility and harassment from a wide range of people throughout your life—classmates, teachers, store clerks, law enforcement officers, and even strangers on the streets. This kaleidoscope of advantages and disadvantages can make individuals uneasy: how is it that individuals and societies can grant so much to some people, yet also deny so much from other people, because of their identities?

As we ponder the answers to these questions, we also are asked to engage the hierarchies, phobias, and human disqualifications discussed in chapter 3. We are asked to reflect on how we have bought into and/or rejected them. These reflections can trigger emotions that are uncomfortable. They ask us to be honest: honest about our own privileges and disadvantages; our fears about, and discomfort with, some identities as well as the fears and discomfort others have felt about our own identities; and the ways we have, unconsciously or consciously, ranked people by identity but also been ranked by others. As we reflect, emotions are brought to the surface and we may have trouble getting our footing. We might struggle to make sense of what we thought we knew was normal, true, and even right.

12.3. GUIDE TO COMMUNICATION

Engaging Discomfort

To begin to work on the skills you will need to engage discomfort, take some time to examine your own hierarchies, phobias, and tendencies to disqualify other humans. This will give you insight into what you have learned to see as "normal" and why you feel uncomfortable in some communication exchanges.

1. Return to chapter 3 and reconsider the various ways you are not only privileged because of some of your identities, but also disadvantaged because of others.
2. Try to identify the ways that discussing your own kaleidoscope of privilege (both the advantages and the disadvantages) might cause you to feel uneasy.
3. Now dig deeper into this discomfort and try to identify the source of this unease: what hierarchies, phobias, and disqualifying myths are being exposed and challenged?
4. Even as you are uncomfortable with this new information, consider the new insights you gain about the complexity of our identities and the ways you might begin to communicate about that complexity with other people.

Our discomfort is a source of powerful information, however. It reveals that in listening to difference, we expose the arbitrary system of ranking people by identities that has become hegemonic. We learn that we have been taught to fear some people and to disqualify them. When we engage discomfort, rather than ignore or reject it, we learn that identity is often the key factor in the inclusion or exclusion of people from opportunities and that there often is very little in the way of rational logic behind this exclusion and inclusion.

Correct Ourselves

Finally, we must be willing to **correct ourselves.** Beloved UCLA basketball coach John Wooden explained, "if you're not making mistakes, then you're not doing anything. I'm positive that a doer makes mistakes."[4] If we make a mistake in our communication, we can fix it. We can select a different strategy the next time—we can learn from our doing. And we must also be willing to be corrected. Correction is different from critique. When we critique someone, we are evaluating and ranking their performance and efforts. When we correct, we are helping a person learn a new way of doing something. Robin Diangelo shares that when someone corrects us, it's because they care enough to do so—they don't want us to make the same mistake again. Corrections can be a sign of value: they communicate the desire to have a relationship with the other person and the hope that the relationship can be built on respect rather than hierarchy and privilege.[5]

If someone cares enough to correct us, we can listen to the correction and thank them for it. An example helps illustrate how. Students in a classroom are discussing microaggressions and the talk turns to microaggressions in casual conversations. The majority of the students are white and cisgender, but a handful also identify as white and transgender, gender queer, gay, or lesbian. Only three students identify as racial minorities. Two identify as Latin@ and one as Asian American; all three are born and raised in the United States. When the three students who are racial minorities explain that being asked "Where are you from?" in casual conversations with white people they have just met often is a form of microaggression, the white students begin to resist and get defensive. They explain that they are never offended when asked where they are from, nor are they being anything but friendly when they ask others this question: "It's just a way to begin to get to know someone," they insist. The Asian American student tries to explain the difference, the white students swear they are correct, and the discussion begins to unravel and become unproductive.

The instructor, who is white and cisgender, steps in. She tells the students to stop arguing. She invites them to start listening to difference, to be open to being corrected, and to sit with their discomfort for a moment. She returns the floor to the Asian American student, asking her to continue to explain her views, if she feels comfortable doing so. The Asian American student declines, explaining with a shrug, "I'm over it." The instructor makes eye contact with the Latin@ students, and one is willing to try to offer the alternative read on the "just being nice" scenario. To the white students he shares that for minority individuals the question "Where are you from?" often is an attempt to place them as "not from here," rather than a friendly social query. This is because the answer to "Where are you from?" if it is "Nebraska" (or a similarly benign state) is almost always followed by "No, I'm mean, where are you *really* from?" If the answer still is "Nebraska," there is usually a second follow-up question, "Oh, then where is your *family* from?"

The class is quiet. Many students are looking down at their desks processing this new information. Several are still doubtful, but it is clear most are uncomfortable but also evaluating their previously unexamined assumptions and beliefs. Two students clearly refuse to accept there can be a difference—they roll their eyes, their arms are crossed—they are unreceptive to this new information. In this quiet moment, the instructor asks for a show of hands: "How many students get the follow-up 'Where are you *really* from?' question," she asks. The three minority students are the only students to raise their hands. "How many get the 'Where is your *family* from?' question." The three minority students are the only students to raise their hands, again. "How many have never been asked the follow-up 'Where are you *really* from?' question," she asks. All of the white students raise their hands.

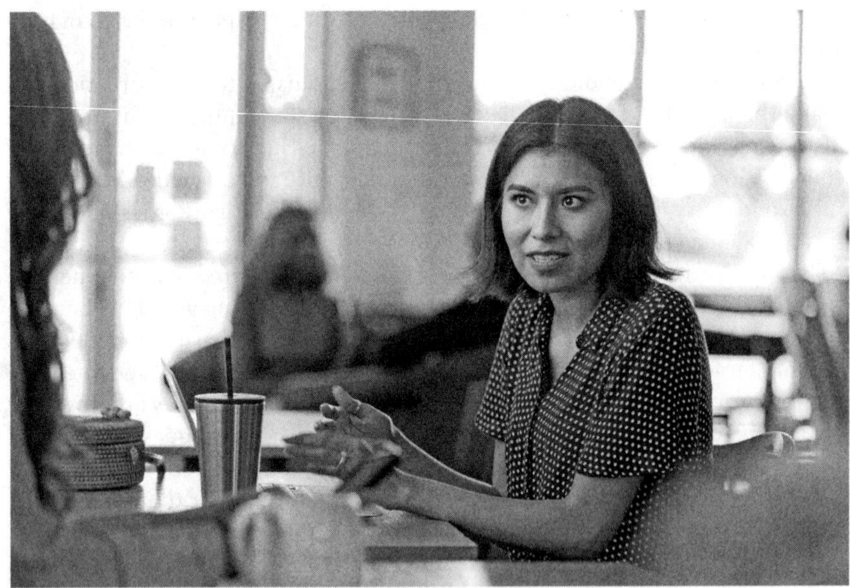

Figure 12.4 Microaggressions, such as the question "Where are you really from?" often occur in our casual conversations with other people. Correcting or pointing out microaggressions can be challenging because people often feel defensive and uncomfortable. It isn't fun to make mistakes, but we can learn to accept corrections with grace and humility. (Source: iStock. Credit: SDI Productions)

When we receive a correction from someone whose identities differ from our own, or who is an ally of those whose identities are seen as different, we can learn to put down our defensiveness, however uncomfortable this may feel initially. Of course, it isn't fun to make mistakes, and the students' resistance and defensiveness in the preceding example illustrate this. But we can learn from our honest interactions with others. We can make fewer and fewer mistakes as we communicate through feminist and intersectional lenses. Invitational communication can help accept these corrections and improve our communication, because it facilitates our learning about, rather than disagreement with, a nuanced world of intersectional identities.

To succeed at communicating through feminist and intersectional lenses, engaging difference—honestly meeting it and getting to know it—is a first step. To embrace the complexity of difference requires that we develop a new set of communication skills, including listening invitationally, being alert to and rejecting hierarchies of humanness, and becoming more comfortable with discomfort while welcoming correction. Our next move as feminist and intersectional communicators is to come to terms with just how much our understanding of the world and those who live in it has been colonized.

12.4. GUIDE TO COMMUNICATION

Welcoming Correction

Developing the skills we need to be open to correcting ourselves is not always easy. This is because discourses that support non-intersectional views are often invisible or difficult to spot. But welcoming correction is an important skill to develop because correction is part of growing in our intersectional understanding of ourselves and the world around us.

1. Take a moment and try to recall a time someone cared enough to point out a mistake you made during an exchange (as opposed to a hostile challenge to your views). They may have corrected a fact you presented, a line of reasoning you offered, an assumption you held as true and correct, or even the terms and phrases you used.
2. How did you receive this well-intentioned correction? Did you receive this correction with openness or did you bristle at the correction? Did you feel a bit embarrassed, or did you refuse to accept the correction at all?
3. Consider whether or not this mistake is one you are likely to make again and why this is so?
4. What value system or approach to communication informs your answer to that final question?

BEYOND GENDER BINARIES: DECOLONIZING OUR BODIES AND OUR DISCOURSE

Decolonizing our assumptions, theories, and communication practices is necessary if we are to truly communicate from an intersectional place. Recall from chapter 11 that to colonize is to create trauma, to take over not just material goods but also the ways people think: "to colonize is to strip a person of their culture, language, family structure, who they are as a person and as a people."[6] To **decolonize,** then, is to revolutionize the ways we live and think, to open up spaces for nondominant and nonbinary logics and discourses. When we decolonize, we not only allow a diversity of cultures, languages, family structures, and individual and group identities to exist simultaneously, but we also enjoy and appreciate that diversity. Decolonizing requires that we pay attention to power and that we are ever mindful of how power is defined, to whom it is granted, what a person must do or become to gain it, and what institutional, structural, and systemic practices support the power that is in place.

Decolonization involves questioning hegemonic notions of normal, at every turn, and continually investigating our assumptions about what we have been led to believe is normal and natural. Because our identities are so overtly linked to our bodies, beginning with efforts to decolonize our bodies is a first step. Attending to the ways we can decolonize our discourse is a second.

Decolonizing Our Bodies

In *Feminist, Queer, Crip,* Allison Kafer corrects many of our false assumptions about one another and shares two models for thinking about our bodies. Using what we consider the disabled body as her point of entry, Kafer shares one model that colonizes our thinking about the body and another that decolonizes. The first model, the **medical/individual model** of disability "frames atypical bodies and minds as deviant, pathological, and defective, best understood and addressed in medical terms." In this model, we "treat" the person in an attempt to "fix" them. "Solving the problem of disability, then, means correcting, normalizing, or eliminating the pathological individual."[7] Kafer shares that in this model the "category of 'disabled' can only be understood in relation to 'able-bodied' or 'able-minded,' a binary in which each term forms the borders of the other." A hierarchy is firmly in place, resources are distributed accordingly, and as disability studies scholar and activist Rosemarie Garland-Thomson shares, "an unequal distribution of resources, status, and power within a biased social and architectural environment" is legitimized.[8]

This medical/individual model of thinking about the body is not limited to ideas about disability, however. We can extend this insight to any body that does not fit the criteria for white, masculine, cisgender, heterosexual, and physically or mentally able. Almost every identity that does not fit these criteria can be managed under the medical/individual model. Even bodies that display religion and spirituality in ways that do not fit the "norm" in the United States can fall into this category. The medical/individual model is not exclusive to doctors' offices and hospitals: it is embedded into our institutions, structures, and systems. This is the environment that surrounds us and it has helped colonize our thinking about bodies and the people who inhabit them. It teaches us that we are too fat, too dark, too slow, too sensitive, too emotional, too lazy, too childlike, too active, too dangerous, too different, too ugly, too anything that deviates from our very narrow version of the norm. As you read in the opening chapters of this book, this is pretty much all of us at some time in our lives.

A second model, the political/relational model helps us decolonize our thinking about bodies. If we are willing to listen to this model, we can reduce our commitment to hierarchies of humanness and instead engage the principle of universal moral respect. In the **political/relational model,** the "problem" of disability "no longer resides in the minds or bodies of individuals but in built environments and social patterns that exclude or stigmatize particular kinds of bodies, minds and ways of being." Kafer notes that "under the

Figure 12.5 When we begin to decolonize the human body, we move beyond binaries and toward intersectional approaches to understanding our complex identities. This professional athlete serves as one model for decolonizing the human body. Engaging the political/relational model of understanding the body can help in the decolonizing and intersectional process. (Source: iStock. Credit: peepo)

medical/individual model, wheelchair users suffer from impairments that restrict their mobility. These impairments are best addressed through medical interventions and cures; failing that, individuals must make the best of a bad situation, relying on friends and family members to negotiate inaccessible spaces for them."[9]

The "problem" of these bodies is not solvable through medical intervention, "normalization," or erasure, however. The "problem" is not actually with these bodies, it is with the systems, structures, and institutions that have colonized them—and the ways we communicate about them so that they stay colonized. Kafer explains that the problem is not the disability. The problem is the "inaccessible buildings, discriminatory attitudes, and ideological systems that attribute normalcy and deviance to particular minds and bodies." "The problem of disability," the problem with our colonized view of the body, in reality, is solved not "through medical intervention or surgical normalization," Kafer explains, but instead "through social change and political transformation."[10]

We can extend this thinking to queer bodies, transgender bodies, intersex bodies, bodies of color, feminine bodies, old bodies, lesbian bodies, gay bodies, bisexual bodies, asexual bodies, and more. To decolonize our beliefs about bodies, and thus our discourse, we must investigate our assumptions, be willing to be uncomfortable as we learn new information, and be willing to examine how entrenched our binary thinking about individuals is. To do this, we may ask ourselves several questions:

Which bodies are described as good/bad?

Which bodies are seen as right/wrong, healthy/unhealthy, beautiful/ugly?

Which bodies are deemed acceptable/unacceptable, dangerous/safe?

Which bodies are labeled citizen/foreign?

Kafer urges us to see all models for understanding our bodies as political, as imbued with power and privilege. To decolonize our thinking about our bodies, we must bring an "increased recognition" of these politics, however strange or unfamiliar this new recognition may be. How we talk about bodies matters a good deal—to all of us. Writing about families living in poverty and a young boy he recently met, Jonathan Kozol shares the insights of the priest of the neighborhood church: "You have to remember . . . that for this little boy whom you have met, his life is just as important, to him, as your life is to you. No matter how insufficient or how shabby it may seem to some, it is the only one he has."[11]

Decolonizing Our Discourse

Throughout this book you have read that discourse refers to the collections of statements we make about particular events, phenomenon, identities, peoples, practices, and traditions. Discourse can be verbal as well as nonverbal, and it is present regardless of whether a single person makes a claim about the world or the statements emanate from larger structures and institutions. Because our discourse about disability is **paradigmatic**—that is, it serves as an excellent model for most of the colonizing discourses that circulate today—we continue with that identity as the entry point to our attempts to decolonize our discourse.

Disability scholar Roger Slee asks, "How do we come to know disability? The answer to this question for most of us is—*at a distance.*" We learn about disability from myths, Slee shares, and our myths are "outlandish," teaching us about exclusion and othering rather than universal moral respect.[12] Slee challenges the discursive regimes at work in our conceptualizations of disability. Bringing together multiple disciplines, these discursive regimes pathologize people's bodies and minds. A **pathology** is a disease or abnormality—and our pathologizing is not limited to physical disability. We pathologize anything that deviates from the "norm." The result is that, with the exception of those who hold the most privilege (chapter 3), most of us are pathologized during our lives—but many of us are pathologized far more often and for far longer, with devastating consequences.

We can easily be "seduced" by language, says Australian feminist and educator Dale Spender, thinking that the language or languages we use are free of bias and adequate to the job of naming and explaining reality. "Language is *not* neutral," Spender explains. Rather, it is a "shaper of ideas" and a program "for mental activity": the names for "reality" have been made for us and given to us, and they contain biases.[13] Certain principles have been coded into language, such as sexism, racism, classism, ableism, homophobia, transphobia, queer phobia, xenophobia and more. When these perspectives and practices are "culturally available" and dominant, our language mirrors them. Spender notes that a "language paradox" exists "for human beings: [language] is both a creative and an inhibiting vehicle," affording its users immense freedoms but also immense restrictions.[14]

To decolonize our discourse, we need to consider the power of this lack of neutrality and the ways we might control it, rather than naively allowing it to control us. Discourses name things, they influence how much agency we assign, and to whom, as well as how much value we believe those things hold. How we name, describe, and talk about something or someone is important because that collection of statements guides our thinking about that person. As Spender notes, we can be misled by discourse, and unless we are ever attentive, its colonizing influences can creep into our ways of seeing the world. To begin to decolonize our discourse, we may use two strategies. First, we can attempt to identify the branding that is present in a colonized discourse and the ways it preys on our emotions. Second, we can consider the ways a discursive regime promotes historical amnesia.

In *Rebellious Bodies: Stardom, Citizenship, and the New Body Politic,* Russell Meeuf discusses **branding** and the ways bodies that transgress "normal" are branded, that is, how they are carefully packaged and presented to viewers of media and popular culture. Meeuf defines **rebellious bodies** as bodies that challenge us to rethink our notions of acceptable. In the world of stardom, rebellious bodies might be celebrities who are considered fat or obese, very dark skinned, exotic because of their bi- or multi-racial heritages or cultural differences, or who are transgender or a drag queen. The dominant images of these bodies, and our discourses about them, do not objectively present these individuals who are seen to transgress; rather they focus our emotional attention on the "out-of-control" features of these bodies. These "rebellious bodies" are branded in particular ways that, Meeuf explains, "intensify anxiety about which bodies are accepted" and acceptable, and which are not.[15] Although these celebrities are presented as heroes and icons because they have transgressed the norm, they also are held to highly scripted, traditional, and binary notions of gender, sex, race, and sexuality. To succeed as transgressors, they must not make us too uncomfortable by transgressing too much. They are allowed to make us anxious about one aspect of their identities, or maybe two, but not much more. Our emotions regarding "normal" must not be overwhelmed.

Outside of stardom, the realm in which most of us live, transgressive or out-of-control bodies are colonized and branded in similar, yet also different ways. We tolerate a little bit of movement from the center, but not too much. When bodies transgress significantly, or are too out of control, they are branded through discourses that cast them as "sites of moral panic," "social and economic burdens," and "a drain on the U.S. welfare system." Discourses brand these bodies as inherently violent and dangerous, as lazy and asking for handouts, as alien and illegal, as a danger to our children or as modeling immoral behaviors, as engaging in abnormal or oppressive religious practices and traditions, and a host of other emotionally laden myths. When these bodies are discursively branded, our emotions are engaged. Meeuf shares that part "of the reason branding works" is because it "creates an object upon which the American public can focus their emotions." Branding and colonizing discourses turn people into objects and trigger our emotions, feeding us "cautionary tales of what to avoid, whom to fear, and who is outside the norm."[16]

We can decolonize these discourses if we are committed to doing several things. As students of intersectional communication, we can attend to the emotions triggered through branding using intersectional and feminist lenses. We can unpack the discourses and the emotions preyed on, before we accept the branding. If Slee is correct, if our experiences of "others" are largely from a distance, and are largely outlandishly mythological, then we can take responsibility for that disconnecting distance and those myths. In taking responsibility for them, we take control of the discourse and invite new terms and phrases into the conversation—those that dismantle binary thinking.

Communicators who engage intersectional approaches are uniquely equipped to decolonize discourse and to avoid binary thinking. Intersectional approaches to communication address the interconnected nature of the various parts of our identities and help us listen for the individual, institutional, structural, and systemic forces that constrain or privilege those identities. When people communicate through an intersectional lens, they notice hegemony and are willing to take the risk that comes with challenging it.

Today's struggles over citizenship and personhood, safety in public and private spaces, education, work, and even who is privileged, are intimately linked to the discursive regimes of our past. When we take a moment to explore those discursive regimes, although we may not like what we learn, we can recognize their affect on our struggles today. Words matter, discursive regimes matter, institutions and structures matter; they are at the heart and soul of our communication. Viewed through feminist and intersectional lenses, the discursive regimes of our past take on a new kind of power—a power that provides clarity and offers us more honest explanations for our world today.

POWER AND PRIVILEGE AS CONSTANT TRAVELING COMPANIONS

Whether we are marching in protest, posting to critique, blogging to inform, creating art to investigate, or simply talking and laughing with friends, we

12.5. GUIDE TO COMMUNICATION

Engaging Difference and Diversity Intersectionally

1. Consider the discursive regimes you take for granted and leave unexplored and unexamined. They might be related to religion, spirituality, food, exercise, education, medicine, clothing, entertainment, and more. What are the guiding principles for "normal" and "right" in these discursive regimes? What principles and practices might change if you decolonized those ideas of normal and right? How might your communication about these regimes change, as well?
2. If you are interested in exploring and getting to know ideas and people with whom you disagree, how might you begin to do so? Before you begin, consider how much discomfort you are willing to put yourself in. What information could this discomfort give you about who you are, your values, and the privileges you hold? How might you incorporate this information into your exposure to this difference? What would your goals be in engaging this difference?
3. Many of us want the world to be a "better place" and our communication often reflects this wish. One person's "better" can be another person's "worse," however. In your conversations with other people, when your "better" encounters another person's "better," and the two are at odds, what will you do? Consider the communication skills you have learned from this book and how you might use those skills to stand in the intersections with that person and explore colonization as well as decolonization.

make more sense when we are educated and informed. If we want to change something, we are better equipped to do so when we have enough information to understand the complexity of what we are talking about. Our personal experiences matter a great deal. But our communication about them has a more far-reaching affect when it is grounded in an understanding of our past. If we don't like a person's identity, rather than relying on the discourses of emotional branding, we can take time to learn about the history of that identity. If poverty bothers us, we can learn about poverty through feminist and intersectional lenses. If we are confused about gender, sexuality, and bodies, popular culture can only take us so far. We must do the work of educating ourselves intersectionally, so that we can communicate our own beliefs, values, and understandings to others in ways that invite conversation and don't engender hate.

Now again, imagine that you are traveling; you are on your way to something interesting or important. As you travel you arrive at a complex intersection. You realize that you do have tools to get you to your destination. You are able to see how many of the paths intersect with the others, how they connect yet also lead to additional and different paths. You recognize that power and privilege will be your constant traveling companions. You know that navigating this and other intersections will be challenging, yet you know that there are resources to help you. With your intersectional and feminist communication skills and awareness beside you, you step into the intersection and begin to make your way.

Resources

Justin Baldoni, "Why I'm Done Trying to Be 'Man Enough,'" filmed November 2017 in New Orleans, LA, 2017, TEDWomen 2017 video, 18:23, https://www.ted.com/talks/justin_baldoni_why_i_m_done_trying_to_be_man_enough.

Sabaah Folayan, director and producer, *Whose Streets?* Official Site, 2017, www.whosestreets.com.

Tiq Malin and Kim Katrin Malin, "A Queer Vision of Love and Marriage," filmed October 2016 in San Francisco, CA, TEDWomen 2016 video, 17:08, https://www.ted.com/talks/tiq_milan_and_kim_katrin_milan_a_queer_vision_of_love_and_marriage.

Zachary R. Wood, "Why It's Worth Listening to People You Disagree With," filmed April 2018 in Vancouver, British Columbia, TED2018 video, 11:23, https://www.ted.com/talks/zachary_r_wood_why_it_s_worth_listening_to_people_you_disagree_with/transcript.

Notes

1. Elif Shafak, "The Revolutionary Power of Diverse Thought," 2017, TEDGlobal>NYC, https://www.ted.com/talks/elif_shafak_the_revolutionary_power_of_diverse_thought.
2. Shafak, "Revolutionary Power."
3. Zachary R. Wood, "Why It's Worth Listening to People You Disagree With," filmed April 2018 in Vancouver, British Columbia, TED2018 video, 11:23, https://www.ted.com/talks/zachary_r_wood_why_it_s_worth_listening_to_people_you_disagree_with/transcript.
4. Robert John Wooden, https://www.brainyquote.com/quotes/john_wooden_386958.
5. Robin Diangelo, *White Fragility: Why It's So Hard for White People to Talk About Racism* (Boston: Beacon Press, 2018).
6. Bushra Rehman and Daisy Hernández, "Introduction," in *Colonize This! Young Women of Color on Today's Feminism*, ed. Daisy Hernández and Bushra Rehman (New York: Seal Press, 2002), xxii.
7. Alison Kafer, *Feminist, Queer, Crip* (Bloomington: University of Indiana Press, 2013), 5. See also Rosemarie Garland-Thomson, "Misfit: A Feminist Materialist Disability Concept," *Hypatia* 26, no. 3 (2011): 591–609.
8. Kafer, *Feminist, Queer, Crip*, 6.
9. Kafer, *Feminist, Queer, Crip*, 6.
10. Kafer, *Feminist, Queer, Crip*, 6.
11. Jonathan Kozol, *Amazing Grace: The Lives of Children and the Conscience of a Nation* (New York: Harper Perennial, 1995), 70.
12. Roger Slee, "Social Justice and the Changing Directions in Educational Research: The Case of Inclusive Education," *International Journal of Inclusive Education* 5, no. 2–3 (2001): 171.
13. Dale Spender, *Man Made Language* (London: Routledge and Kegan Paul, 1980), 139.
14. Spender, *Man Made Language*, 141.
15. Russell Meeuf, *Rebellious Bodies: Stardom, Citizenship, and the New Body Politic* (Austin: University of Texas Press, 2017), 6.
16. Meeuf, *Rebellious Bodies*, 5.

References

Abu-Lughod, Lila. "Do Muslim Women Really Need Saving? Anthropological Reflections on Cultural Relativism and Its Others." *American Anthropologist* 104, no. 3 (January 2008): 783–790.

Agridag, Orhan, Janick Demanet, Mieke Van Houtte, and Piet Van Avermaet. "Ethnic School Composition and Peer Victimization: A Focus on Interethnic School Climate." *International Journal of Intercultural Relations* 35, no. 4 (2011): 465–473.

Alcoff, Linda Martín. *Visible Identities: Race, Gender, and the Self.* New York: Oxford University Press, 2006.

Alexander, Michelle. *The New Jim Crow; Incarceration in the Age of Colorblindness.* New York: Free Press, 2010.

Allen, Brenda J. *Difference Matters: Communicating Social Identity.* 2nd ed. Long Grove, IL: Waveland Press, 2011/2014.

———. "Racial Harassment in the Workplace." In *Destructive Organizational Communication: Processes, Consequences, and Constructive Ways of Organizing,* edited by Pamela Lutgen-Sandvik and Beverly Davenport Sypher, 164–183. New York: Routledge, 2009.

Alriksson-Schmidt, Ann I., Brian S. Armor, and Judy K. Thibadeau. "Are Adolescent Girls with Physical Disability at Risk for Sexual Violence?" *Journal of School Health* 80, no. 7 (2010): 361–367.

Anderson, Carol. *White Rage: The Unspoken Truth of Our Racial Divide.* New York: Bloomsbury, 2016.

Anguiano, Claudia A. "Dropping the 'I-Word': A Critical Examination of Contemporary Immigration Labels." In *The Rhetorics of U.S. Immigration: Identity, Community, Otherness,* edited by E. Johanna Hartelius, 93–111. University Park: Pennsylvania State University Press, 2015.

Antecol, Heather, Anneke Jong, and Michael Steinberger. "Sexual Orientation Wage Gap: The Role of Occupational Sorting and Human Capital." *Industrial Labor and Relations Review* 61, no. 4 (July 2008): 515–543.

Artz, Lee, and Bren Ortega Murphy. *Cultural Hegemony in the United States.* Thousand Oaks, CA: Sage, 2000.

Bhabha, Homi K. "The Other Question . . . Homi K. Bhabha Reconsiders the Stereotype and Colonial Discourse." *Screen* 24, no. 6 (November–December 1983): 18–36.

Baruh, Lemi. "Publicized Intimacies on Reality Television: An Analysis of Voyeuristic Content and Its Contribution to the Appeal of Reality Programming." *Journal of Broadcasting and Electronic Media* 53, no. 2 (2009): 190–210.

Baron, Dennis. *What's Your Pronoun: Beyond He and She.* New York: Liveright Publishing, 2020.

Bates, Laura. *Everyday Sexism.* New York: Thomas Dunne Books/Saint Martin's Press, 2016.

Baumgardner, Jennifer, and Amy Richards. *Manifesta: Young Women, Feminism, and the Future.* New York: Farrar, Strauss, and Giroux, 2000.

Beale, Francis. "Double Jeopardy: To Be Black and Female." In *The Black Woman: An Anthology,* edited by Toni Cade Bambara, 109–122. 1970; New York: Washington Square Press, 2005.

Beauvoir, Simone de. *The Second Sex.* Translated and edited by H. M. Parshley. 1949, 1953; New York: Penguin, 1972.

Bell Carter, Bonnie, and Victor G. Spencer. "The Fear Factor: Bullying and Students with Disabilities." *International Journal of Special Education* 21, no. 1 (2006): 11–23.

Benedet, Janine, and Isabel Grant. "Hearing the Sexual Assault Complaints of Women with Mental Disabilities: Consent, Capacity and Mistaken Belief." *McGill Law Journal* 52, no. 2 (2002): 243–289.

Benhabib, Seyla. *Situating the Self: Gender, Community and Postmodernism in Contemporary Ethics.* New York: Routledge, 1992.

Bergman, S. Bear. "Non-Binary Activism." In *Genderqueer and Nonbinary Genders,* edited by Christina Richards, Walter Pierre Bouman, and Meg-John Barker, 31–51. New York: Palgrave Macmillan, 2017.

Bialystok, Lauren. "Authenticity in Education." In *Oxford Research Encyclopedia of Education.* New York: Oxford University Press, published online September 2017.

Blumberg, Rae Lesser. "The Invisible Obstacle to Educational Equality: Gender Bias in Textbooks," *Prospects: Comparative Journal of Curriculum, Learning, and Assessment* 38, no. 3 (September 2008): 345–361.

Bone, Jennifer Emerling, Cindy L. Griffin, and T. M. Linda Scholz. "Beyond Traditional Conceptualizations of Rhetoric: Invitational Rhetoric and a Move toward Civility." *Western Journal of Communication* 72, no. 4 (2008): 434–462.

Bottoms, Bette, Kari L. Nysse-Carris, Twana Harris, and Kimberly Tyda. "Jurors' Perceptions of Adolescent Sexual Assault Victims Who Have Intellectual Disabilities." *Law and Human Behavior* 27, no. 2 (2003): 205–227.

Brownridge, Douglas A. "Partner Violence Against Women with Disabilities: Prevalence, Risk, and Explanations." *Violence Against Women* 12 (2006): 805–822.

Bryant-Davis, Thema, Heewoon Chung, and Shaquita Tillman. "From the Margins to the Center: Ethnic Minority Women and the Mental Health Effects of Sexual Assault." *Trauma, Violence and Abuse* 10, no. 4 (October 2009): 330–357.

Bubar, Roe, and Pamela Jumper Thurman. "Violence Against Native Women." *Social Justice* 31, no. 4 (2004): 70–86.

Buchanan, NiCole T., and Louise F. Fitzgerald. "Effects of Racial and Sexual Harassment on Work and Psychological Well-Being of African American Women." *Journal of Occupational Health Psychology* 13, no. 2 (April 2008): 137–151.

Burnett, Ann, Jody L. Matern, Liliana L. Herakova, David H. Kahl, Jr., Cloy Tobola, and Susan E. Bornsen. "Communicating/Muting Date Rape: A Co-Cultural Theoretical Analysis of Communication Factors Related to Rape Culture on a College

Campus." *Journal of Applied Communication Research* 37, no. 4 (2009): 465–485.

Butler, Judith. *Bodies That Matter: On the Discursive Limits of Sex.* 1993; London: Routledge, 2011.

———. *Gender Trouble: Feminism and the Subversion of Identity.* New York: Routledge, 1990.

———. *Undoing Gender.* New York: Routledge, 2004.

Byars-Winston, Angela, Nadya Fouad, and Yao Wen. "Race/Ethnicity and Sex in U.S. Occupations, 1970–2010: Implications for Research, Practice, and Policy." *Journal of Vocational Behavior* 87 (April 2015): 54–70.

Calafell, Bernadette Marie. "Monstrous Femininity: Constructions of Women of Color in the Academy." *Journal of Communication Inquiry* 36, no. 2 (2012): 111–130.

Carrillo Rowe, Aimee. *Power Lines: On the Subject of Feminist Alliances.* Durham: Duke University Press, 2008.

Carter, Stephen L. *Civility: Manners, Morals and the Etiquette of Democracy.* New York: HarperPerennial, 1998.

Chávez, Karma R. *Queer Migration Politics: Activist Rhetoric and Coalitional Possibilities.* Urbana: University of Illinois Press, 2013.

Chavez, Leo R. *Covering Immigration: Popular Images and the Politics of the Nation.* Berkeley: University of California Press, 2001.

Chilton, Paul. *Analysing Political Discourse: Theory and Practice.* New York: Routledge, 2004.

Clair, Robin P. *Organizing Silence: A World of Possibilities.* Albany: University of New York Press, 1998.

Coates, Linda, and Allen Wade. "Language and Violence: An Analysis of Four Discursive Operations." *Journal of Family Violence* 22, no. 7 (October 2007): 511–522.

———. "Telling It Like It Isn't: Obscuring Perpetrator Responsibility for Violent Crime." *Discourse and Society* 15, no. 5 (2004): 499–526.

Combahee River Collective. "A Black Feminist Statement." In *This Bridge Called My Back: Writings by Radical Women of Color,* edited by Cherríe Moraga and Gloria Anzaldúa, 210–218. New York: Kitchen Table: Women of Color Press, 1983.

Cortese, Anthony. *Opposing Hate Speech.* Santa Barbara: Praeger, 2006.

Cotton, Ann, Melissa Farley, and Robert Baron. "Attitudes toward Prostitution and Acceptance of Rape Myths." *Journal of Applied Social Psychology* 32, no. 9 (2002): 1790–1796.

Crenshaw, Kimberlé. "Demarginalizing the Intersection of Race and Sex: A Black Feminist Critique of Antidiscrimination Doctrine, Feminist Theory and Antiracist Politics." *University of Chicago Legal Forum* (1989): 139–167.

———. "Mapping the Margins: Intersectionality Identity Politics and Violence against Women of Color." *Stanford Law Review,* 43, no. 6 (1991): 1241–1299.

Crowley, Terrance. "The Lie of Entitlement." In *Transforming a Rape Culture,* edited by Emilie Buchwald, Pamela R. Fletcher, and Martha Roth, 301–310, revised ed. Minneapolis: Milkweed Editions, 2005.

Cuklanz, Lisa M., and Sujata Moorti. "Television's 'New' Feminism: Prime-Time Representations of Women and Victimization." *Critical Studies in Media Communication* 23, no. 4 (October 2006): 302–321.

Daley, Andrea, Steven Solomon, Peter A. Newman, and Faye Mishna. "Traversing the Margins: Intersectionalities in the Bullying of Lesbian, Gay, Bisexual, and Transgender Youth." *Journal of Gay and Lesbian Social Services* 19, no. 304 (2007): 9–29.

Delgado, Richard, and Jean Stefancic. "Four Observations about Hate Speech." *Wake Forrest Law Review* 44 (2009): 353–370.

———. *Understanding Words that Wound.* Boulder: Westview Press, 2004.

Dessel, Adrianne. "Prejudice in Schools: Promotion of an Inclusive Culture and Climate." *Education and Urban Society* 20, no. 10 (2010): 1–23.

Dewing, Jan. "Personhood and Dementia: Revisiting Tom Kitwood's Ideas." *International Journal of Older People Nursing* 3 (2008): 3–13.

Diangelo, Robin. *White Fragility: Why It's So Hard for White People to Talk About Racism.* Boston: Beacon, 2018.

Dodge, Alexa. "Digitizing Rape Culture: Online Sexual Violence and the Power of the Digital Photograph." *Crime Media Culture* 12, no. 1 (2016): 65–82.

Duran, Bonnie, Eduardo Duran, and Maria Yellow Horse Brave Heart. "Native Americans and the Trauma of History." In *Studying Native America: Problems and Prospects,* edited by Russell Thornton, 60–78. Madison: University of Wisconsin Press, 1998.

Duwe, Grant. *A History of Mass Murder in the United States.* Jefferson, NC: McFarland and Co., 2007.

Edwards, Katie M., Kateryna M. Sylaska, Johanna E. Barry, Mary M. Moynihan, Victoria L. Banyard, Ellen S. Cohn, Wendy A. Walsh, and Sally K. Ward. "Physical Dating Violence, Sexual Violence, and Unwanted Pursuit Victimization: A Comparison of Incidence Rates Among Sexual-Minority and Heterosexual College Students." *Journal of Interpersonal Violence* 30, no. 4 (February 2015): 580–600.

Ehrlich, Susan. *Representing Rape: Language and Sexual Consent.* New York: Routledge, 2001.

Eley, Geoff. "Nations, Publics, and Political Cultures: Placing Habermas in the Nineteenth Century." In *Habermas and the Public Sphere,* edited by Craig Calhoun, 289–339. Cambridge, MA: MIT Press, 1993.

Ellis, Mark, and Richard Wright. "The Balkanization Metaphor in the Analysis of U.S. Immigration." *Annals of the Association of American Geographers* 88, no. 4 (1998): 686–698.

Enck, Suzanne Marie, and Blake A. McDaniel. "'I Want Something Better for My Life': Personal Narratives of Incarcerated Women and Performances of Agency." *Text and Performance Quarterly* 35, no. 1 (2015): 43–61.

Enck-Wanzer, Suzanne. "All's Fair in Love and Sport: Black Masculinity and Domestic Violence in the News." *Communication and Critical/Cultural Studies* 6, no. 1 (2009): 1–18.

Enck-Wanzer, Suzanne, and Scott A. Murray. "'How to Hook a Hottie': Teenage Boys, Hegemonic Masculinity, and *CosmoGirl!* Magazine," *Mediated Boyhoods: Boys, Tens and Young Men in Popular Media and Culture* (2011): 57–77.

Erevelles, Nirmala. *Disability and Difference in Global Contexts: Enabling a Transformative Body Politic.* New York: Palgrave Macmillan, 2011.

Evans, Sara M. *Born for Liberty: A History of Women in America.* New York: Free Press, 1989.

Evans-Campbell, Teresa. "Historical Trauma in American Indian/Native Alaska Communities: Multilevel Framework for Exploring Impacts on Individuals, Families, and Communities." *Journal of Interpersonal Violence* 23, no. 3 (2008): 316–338.

Few-Demo, April L., Julia Moore, and Shadee Abdi, "Intersectionality: (Re)Considering Family Communication from Within the Margins." In *Engaging Theories of Family Communication: Multiple Perspectives,* edited by Dawn O. Braithwaite, Elizabeth A. Suter, Kory Floyd, 175–186, 2nd ed. New York: Routledge, 2017.

Fogg-Davis, Hawley [Heath] G. "Theorizing Black Lesbians within Black Feminism: A Critique of Same-Race Street Harassment." *Politics and Gender* 2 (2006): 57–76.

Foss, Sonja K., and Cindy L. Griffin. "Beyond Persuasion: A Proposal for an Invitational Rhetoric." *Communication Monographs* 62, no. 1 (1995): 3–18.

Foucault, Michel. *The Archaeology of Knowledge.* Translated by A. M. Sheridan Smith. New York: Pantheon, 1972.

———. *The Order of Things: Archaeology of the Human Sciences.* New York: Pantheon, 1970.

Fox, James Alan, and Monica J. DeLateur. "Mass Shootings in America: Moving Beyond Newton." *Homicide Studies* 30, no. 1 (2013): 1–21.

Freire, Paolo. *Pedagogy of the Oppressed.* Translated by Myra Bergman Ramos. 1970; New York: Continuum, 2005.

Fricker, Miranda. *Epistemic Injustice: Power and the Ethics of Knowing.* Oxford: Oxford University Press, 2007.

Futterman, Susan. *When You Work for a Bully: Assessing Your Options and Taking Action.* Montvale, NJ: Croce Publishing, 2004.

Gandhi, Leela. *Postcolonial Theory: A Critical Introduction.* New York: Columbia University Press, 1998.

Garland Thomson, Rosemarie. *Extraordinary Bodies: Figuring Physical Disability in American Culture and Literature.* New York: Columbia University Press, 1997.

———. "Misfit: A Feminist Materialist Disability Concept." *Hypatia* 26, no. 3 (2011): 591–609.

Gereluk, Dianne. "Citizenship and Ethics." In *Oxford Research Encyclopedia of Education.* New York: Oxford University Press, published online April 2017.

Gibson, Sarah, and J. Fernandez. *Gender Diversity and Non-Binary Inclusion in the Workplace: The Essential Guide for Employers.* Philadelphia: Jessica Kingsley, 2017.

Gillman, Amanda B., Karl G. Hill, and J. David Hawkins. "Long-Term Consequences of Adolescent Gang Membership for Adult Functioning." *American Journal of Public Health* 104, no. 5 (2014): 938–945.

Glambek, Mats, Anders Skogstad, and Ståle Einarsen. "Workplace Bullying, the Development of Job Insecurity and the Role of Laissez-Faire Leadership: A Two-Wave Moderation Mediation Study." *International Journal of Work, Health and Organizations* 32, no. 3 (January 2018): 297–312.

Gordy, Eric. *Guilt, Responsibility and Denial: The Past at Stake in Post Milosevic Serbia.* Philadelphia: University of Pennsylvania Press, 2013.

Grant Bowman, Cynthia. "Street Harassment and the Informal Ghettoization of Women." *Harvard Law Review* 106, no. 3 (January 1993): 517–580.

Greenberg, Kae. "Still Hidden in the Closet: Trans Women and Domestic Violence." *Berkeley Journal of Gender, Law and Justice* 27, no. 2 (2012): 198–251.

Griffin, Cindy L. *Invitation to Public Speaking,* 6th ed. Boston: Cengage, 2018.

Gumpertz, John J., ed. *Language and Social Identity.* Cambridge: Cambridge University Press, 1982.

Hall, Stuart. "Cultural Identity and Diaspora." In *Identity: Community, Culture, Difference,* edited by Jonathan Rutherford, 222–237. London: Lawrence and Wishart, 1990.

Harrison, Jack, Jamie Grant, and Jody L. Herman. "A Gender Not Listed Here: Genderqueers, Gender Rebels, and OtherWise in the National Transgender Discriminatory Survey." *LGBTQ Public Policy Journal at the Harvard Kennedy School* 2 (2011–2012): 13–24.

Hartelius, E. Johanna, ed. *The Rhetorics of U.S. Immigration: Identity, Community, Otherness.* University Park: Pennsylvania State University Press, 2015.

Hegewisch, Ariane, and Emma Williams-Baron. "The Gender Wage Gap by Occupation 2016: and by Race and Ethnicity." Institute for Women's Policy Research, accessed April 4, 2017. https://iwpr.org/issue/employment-education-economic-change/pay-equity-discrimination/.

Hellman, Deborah. *When Is Discrimination Wrong?* Cambridge, MA: Harvard University Press, 2008.

Henry, P. J. "Institutional Bias." In *The Sage Handbook of Prejudice, Stereotyping and Discrimination,* edited by John F. Dovidio, Miles Hewstone, Peter Glick, and Victoria M. Esses, 426–440. Thousand Oaks, CA: Sage, 2010.

Hernández-Avila, Inés. "In Praise of Insubordination, or, What Makes a Good Woman Go Bad?" In *Transforming a Rape Culture,* edited by Emilie Buchwald, Pamela R. Fletcher, and Martha Roth, 323–342, revised ed. Minneapolis: Milkweed Editions, 2005.

Heung, Marina. "Representing Ourselves: Films and Videos by Asian American/Canadian Women." In *Feminism, Multiculturalism, and the Media: Global Diversities,* edited by Angharad N. Valdivia, 82–104. Thousand Oaks, CA: Sage, 1995.

Hill Collins, Patricia. *On Intellectual Activism.* Philadelphia: Temple University Press, 2013.

Hill Collins, Patricia, and Sirma Bilge. *Intersectionality.* Cambridge, MA: Polity Books, 2017.

hooks, bell. *Black Looks: Race and Representation.* Boston: South End Press, 1992.

———. *Feminism Is for Everybody: Passionate Politics.* New York: Routledge, 2017.

———. *Feminist Theory: From Margin to Center,* 2nd ed. Boston: South End Press, 2000.

———. *Reel to Real: Race, Sex, and Class at the Movies.* New York: Routledge, 1996.

———. *The Will to Change: Men, Masculinity, and Love.* New York: Washington Square Press, 2004.

Holling, Michelle A. "'So, My Name is Alma, and I Am the Sister of . . .': A *Feminicidio Testimonio* of Violence and Violent Identifications." *Women's Studies in Communication,* 37, no. 3 (2014): 313–338.

Holling, Michelle A., and Bernadette M. Calafell, eds. *Latina/o Discourse in Vernacular Spaces: Somos du Una Voz?* Lanham, MD: Lexington Books, 2011.

Humm, Maggie. *The Dictionary of Feminist Theory.* Columbus: Ohio University Press, 1990.

Huston Grey, Stephanie. "Wounds Not Easily Healed: Exploring Trauma in Communication Studies." *Communication Yearbook* 31, no. 1 (2007): 174–222.

Kafer, Alison. *Feminist, Queer, Crip.* Bloomington: University of Indiana Press, 2013.

Kang, Sonja K., Katerine A. DeCelles, András Tilcsik, and Sora Jun. "Whitened Résumés: Race and Self-Presentation in the Labor Market." *Administrative Science Quarterly* 61, no. 3 (September 1, 2016): 1–34.

Kappeler, Victor, and Gary Potter. *The Mythology of Crime and Criminal Justice,* 4th ed. Long Grove, IL: Waveland Press, 2010.

Kearl, Holly. *Stop Street Harassment: Making Public Places Safe for Women.* Santa Barbara: Praeger, 2010.

Keats Citron, Danielle. *Hate Crimes in Cyberspace.* Cambridge, MA: Harvard University Press, 2014.

Kennedy, George. "A Hoot in the Dark: The Evolution of General Rhetoric." *Philosophy and Rhetoric* 25, no. 1 (1992): 1–21.

Khubchandani, Jagdish, and James H. Price. "Workplace Harassment and Morbidity among US Adults: Results from National Health Interview Survey." *Community Health* 40, no. 3 (June 2015): 555–563.

Kimmel, Michael S. *Angry White Men: American Masculinity at the End of an Era.* New York: The Nation Institute, 2017.

———. "Toward a Pedagogy of the Oppressor." In *Privilege: A Reader,* edited by Michael S. Kimmel and Abby L. Ferber, 1–10, 2nd ed. Boulder: Westview Press, 2010.

King, Eden B., Saaid A. Mendoza, Juan M. Madera, Mikki R. Hebl, and Jennifer L. Knight. "What's in a Name? A Multiracial Investigation of the Role of Occupational Stereotypes in Selection Decisions." *Journal of Applied Social Psychology* 36 (April 21, 2006): 1145–1159.

Kinser, Amber. "Negotiating Spaces for/through Third-Wave Feminism." *NWSA Journal* 16, no. 3 (2004): 124–153.

Kosciw, Joseph G., Emily A. Greytak, Mark J. Bartkiewicz, Madelyn J. Boesen, and Neal A. Palmer. *The 2011 National School Climate Survey: The Experiences of Lesbian, Gay, Bisexual, and Transgender Youth in Our Nation's Schools.* New York: GLSEN, 2012. http://files.eric.ed.gov/fulltext/ED535177.pdf.

Koss, Melanie D., Miriam G. Martinez, and Nancy J. Johnson. "Where Are the Latinxs? Diversity in Caldecott Winner and Honor Books." *The Bilingual Review* 33, no. 5 (2017): 50–62.

Koss, Melanie D., Nancy J. Johnson, and Miriam Martinez. "Mapping the Diversity in Caldecott Books from 1938 to 2017: The Changing Topography," *Journal of Children's Literature* 44, no. 1 (2018): 4–20.

Kozol, Jonathan. *Amazing Grace: The Lives of Children and the Conscience of a Nation.* New York: Harper Perennial, 1995.

Lammers, John C., and Joshua B. Barbour. "An Institutional Theory of Organizational Communication." *Communication Theory* 16, no. 3 (August 2006): 356–377.

Lankford, Adam. "Race and Mass Murder in the United States: A Social and Behavioral Analysis." *Current Sociology* 64, no 3 (2016): 470–490.

Larson, Stephanie R. "'Everything Inside of Me Was Silenced: (Re) defining Rape Through Visceral Counterpublicity." *Quarterly Journal of Speech* 104, no. 2 (2018): 1223–1244.

Lawrence, Jane. "The Indian Health Services and the Sterilization of Native American Women." *The American Indian Quarterly* 24, no. 3 (Summer 2000): 400–419.

Lawrence, Keith, Stacey Sutton, Anne Kubish, Gretchen Susi, and Karen Fulbright-Anderson. "Structural Racism and Community Building." Aspen Institute Roundtable on Community Change, 2004. Washington, D.C.: The Aspen Institute, 2004.

Lawrence, Thomas B. "Power, Institutions and Organization." In *Sage Handbook of Organizational Institutionalism,* edited by Royston Greenwood, Christie Oliver, Kerstin Sahlin, and Roy Suddaby, 170–197. Thousand Oaks, CA: Sage, 2008.

Leonardo, Zeus. "The Color of Supremacy: Beyond the Discourse of 'White Privilege.'" *Educational Philosophy and Theory* 36, no. 2 (2004): 137–152.

———. "The Souls of White Folk: Critical Pedagogy, Whiteness Studies, and Globalization Discourse." *Race, Ethnicity and Education* 5, no. 1 (2002): 29–50.

Leskinen, Emily A., Lilia M. Cortina, and Dana B. Kabat. "Gender Harassment: Broadening Our Understanding of Sex-Based Harassment at Work." *Law and Human Behavior* 35, no. 1 (February 2011): 25–39.

Lesser Blumberg, Rae. "The Invisible Obstacle to Educational Equality: Gender Bias in Textbooks." *Prospects: Comparative Journal of Curriculum, Learning, and Assessment* 38, no. 3 (September 2008): 345–361.

Lieberman, Irena. "I Hope This Letter Will Reach You." In *Women for Afghan Women: Shattering Myths and Claiming the Future,* edited by Sunita Mehta, 166–175. New York: Palgrave Macmillan, 2002.

Lim, Sandy, and Lilia M. Cortina. "Interpersonal Mistreatment in the Workplace: The Interface and Impact of General Incivility and Sexual Harassment." *Journal of Applied Psychology* 90, no. 3 (2005): 483–496.

Littleton, Heather L., and Julia C. Dodd. "Violent Attacks and Damaged Victims: An Exploration of the Rape Scripts of European American and African American U.S. College Women." *Violence Against Women* 22, no. 14 (February 2016): 1725–1747.

Lockwood Harris, Kate. "The Next Problem with No Name: The Politics and Pragmatics of the Word Rape." *Women's Studies in Communication* 34, no. 1 (May 2011): 42–63.

———. "Show Them a Good Time: Organizing the Intersections of Sexual Violence." *Management Communication Quarterly* 27, no. 4 (2013): 568–595.

———. "Yes Means Yes and No Means No, But Both these Mantras Need to Go: Communication Myths in Consent Education and Anti-Rape Activism." *Journal of Applied Communication Research* 46, no. 2 (2018): 155–178.

Loh, Catherine, Christine A. Gidyca, Tracy R. Lobo, and Rohini Luthra. "A Prospective Analysis of Sexual Assault Perpetration: Risk Factors Related to Perpetrator Characteristics." *Journal of Interpersonal Violence* 20, no. 10 (2005): 1325–1348.

Lombardi, Emilia L., Riki Anne Wilchins, Diana Priesing, and Diana Malouf. "Gender Violence: Transgender Experiences of Violence and Discrimination." *Journal of Homosexuality* 42, no. 1 (2001): 89–101.

Loomba, Ania. *Colonialism/Postcolonialism,* 3rd ed. New York: Routledge, 2015.

Lozano-Reich, Nina Maria. "Reconceptualizing *Feminicidio:* Border Materiality in Cuidad Juárez." *Women's Studies in Communication* 41, no. 2 (2018): 104–107.

Lundberg, Shelly, and Elaina Rose. "Parenthood and the Earnings of Married Women." *Labour Economics* 7, no. 6 (November 2000): 689–710.

Lutgen-Sandvik, Pamela, Gary Namie, and Ruth Namie. "Workplace Bullying: Causes, Consequences, and Corrections." In *Destructive Organizational Communication: Processes, Consequences, and Constructive Ways of Organizing,* edited by Pamela Lutgen-Sandvik and Beverly Davenport Sypher, 27–52. New York: Routledge, 2009.

Madhubuti, Haki R. "On Becoming Antirapist." In *Transforming a Rape Culture,* edited by Emilie Buchwald, Pamela R. Fletcher, and Martha Roth, 173–188, revised ed. Minneapolis: Milkweed Editions, 2005.

Madifs, Eric. "Triple Entitlement and Homicidal Anger: An Exploration of the Intersectional Identities of American Mass Murderers." *Men and Masculinities* 17, no. 1 (2014): 67–86.

Marabel, Manning. *The Great Wells of Democracy: The Meaning of Race in American Life.* New York: Basic Civitas Books, 2002.

Mason, Lilliana. *Uncivil Agreement: How Politics Became Our Identity.* Chicago: University of Chicago Press, 2018.

Martin, Sandra, Neepa Ray, Daniela Sotres-Alvarez, Lawrence L. Kupper, Kathryn E. Moracco, Pamela A. Dickens, Donna Scandlin, and Ziya Gizlice. "Physical and Sexual Assault of Women with Disabilities." *Violence Against Women* 12, no. 9 (2006): 823–837.

McIntosh, Peggy. "White Privilege and Male Privilege: A Personal Account of Coming to See Correspondences Through Work in Women's Studies." In *Privilege: A Reader,* edited by Michael S. Kimmel and Abby L. Ferber, 13–26, 2nd ed. Boulder: Westview Press, 2010.

McIntyre, Alice. *Making Meaning Out of Whiteness: Exploring Racial Identity with White Teachers.* Albany: State University of New York Press, 1997.

McIntyre, Shelby, Dennis J. Moberg, and Barry Z. Posner. "Preferential Treatment in Preselection Decisions According to

Sex and Race." *Academy of Management Journal* 23, no. 4 (December 1980): 738–749.

McKinnon, Sara L. "Citizenship and the Performance of Credibility: Audiencing Gender-based Asylum Seekers in the U.S. Immigration Courts." *Text and Performance Quarterly* 29, no. 3 (2009): 205–221.

McLeod, John. *Beginning Postcolonialism.* New York: Palgrave, 2010.

Meeuf, Russell. *Rebellious Bodies: Stardom, Citizenship, and the New Body Politic.* Austin: University of Texas Press, 2017.

Mehta, Sunita, ed. *Women for Afghan Women: Shattering Myths and Claiming the Future.* New York: Palgrave Macmillan, 2002.

Metzl, Jonathan M. "Voyeur Nation? Changing Definitions of Voyeurism, 1950–2004." *Harvard Review of Psychiatry* 12, no. 2 (2004): 127–131.

Meyers, Marian. *News Coverage of Violence Against Women: Engendering Blame.* Thousand Oaks, CA: Sage, 1997.

Mishna, Faye. "Learning Disabilities and Bullying: Double Jeopardy." *Journal of Learning Disabilities* 36, no. 4 (2003): 336–347.

Mohanty, Chandra Talpade. "Under Western Eyes: Feminist Scholars and Colonial Discourses." *Feminist Review,* no. 30 (Autumn 1988): 61–88.

Moore-Foster, W. J. Musa. "Up from Brutality: Freeing Black Communities from Sexual Violence." In *Transforming a Rape Culture,* edited by Emilie Buchwald, Pamela R. Fletcher, and Martha Roth, 343–356, revised ed. Minneapolis: Milkweed Editions, 2005.

Moradi, Bonnie, and Yu-Ping Huang. "Objectification Theory and Psychology of Women: A Decade of Advances and Future Directions." *Psychology of Women Quarterly* 32, no. 4 (2008): 377–378.

Moraga, Cherríe. "La Güera." In *This Bridge Called My Back: Writings by Radical Women of Color,* edited by Cherríe Moraga and Gloria Anzaldúa, 22–29. New York: Kitchen Table: Women of Color Press, 1983.

Morgensen, Scott L. "Cutting to the Roots of Colonial Masculinity." In *Indigenous Men and Masculinities: Legacies, Identities, Regeneration,* edited by Kim Anderson and Robert Alexander Innes, 38–61. Winnipeg: University of Manitoba Press, 2015.

Mulvey, Laura. "Visual Pleasure and Narrative Cinema." *Screen* 16, no. 3 (Autumn 1975): 6–18.

Mumby, Dennis K. "The Problem of Hegemony: Rereading Gramsci for Organizational Communication Studies." *Western Journal of Communication* 61, no. 4 (1997): 343–375.

Muñiz, Ana. *Police, Power, and the Production of Racial Boundaries.* New Brunswick, NJ: Rutgers, 2015.

Namie, Gary. 2014 WBI U.S. Workplace Bullying Survey, February 2014. http://www.workplacebullying.org/wbiresearch/wbi-2014-us-survey/.

Nuñez, D. Carolina. "War of the Words: Aliens, Immigrants, citizens, and the Language of Exclusion." *Brigham Young University Law Review* 2013, no. 6 (2014): 1517–1562.

O'Hara, Shannon. "Monsters, Playboys, Virgins, and Whores: Rape Myths in News Media's Coverage of Sexual Violence." *Language and Literature* (July 24, 2012): 247–259.

Oliver, Kelly. *Witnessing: Beyond Recognition.* Minneapolis: University of Minnesota Press, 2001.

Ono, Kent A., and John M. Sloop. *Shifting Borders: Rhetoric, Immigration, and California's Proposition 187.* Philadelphia: Temple University Press, 2002.

Orenstein, Peggy. *Girls and Sex: Navigating the Complicated New Landscape.* New York: Harper Collins, 2016.

Palmater, Pamela. "Shining Light on the Dark Places: Addressing Police Racism and Sexualized Violence Against Indigenous Women and Girls in the National Inquiry." *Canadian Journal of Women and the Law* 28, no. 2 (2016): 253–284.

Payne, Diana L., Kimberly A. Lonsway, and Louise F. Fitzgerald. "Rape Myth Acceptance: Exploration of its Structure and Its Measurement Using the Illinois Rape Myth Acceptance Scale." *Journal of Research in Personality* 33, no. 1 (March 1999): 27–68.

Peterson, Zoe D., and Charlene L. Muehlenhard. "Was It Rape? The Function of Women's Rape Myth Acceptance and Definitions of Sex in Labeling Their Own Experiences." *Sex Roles* 51, no. 3–4 (August 2004): 129–144.

Pereira, Filipa, Brian H. Spitzberg, and Marlene Matos. "Cyber-Harassment Victimization in Portugal: Prevalence, Fear, and of Help-Seeking Among Adolescents." *Computers in Human Behavior* 62 (2016): 136–146.

Puhl, Rebecca, Jamie Lee Peterson, and Joerg Luedicke. "Weight Based Victimization: Bullying Experiences of Weight Loss Treatment-Seeking Youth." *Pediatrics* 131, no. 1 (2013): 1–9.

Powell, Adam A., Nyla R. Branscombe, and Michael T. Schmitt. "Inequality as Ingroup Privilege or Outgroup Disadvantage: The Impact of Group Focus on Collective Guilt and Interracial Attitudes." *Personality and Social Psychology Bulletin* 31, no. 4 (2005): 508–521.

Projansky, Sarah. "The Elusive/Ubiquitous Representation of Rape: A Historical Survey of Rape in U.S. Film, 1903–1972." *Cinema Journal* 41, no. 1 (Fall 2001): 63–90.

———. "Rihanna's Closed Eyes." *The Velvet Light Trap,* no. 65 (Spring 2010): 71–73.

———. *Watching Rape: Film and Television in Postfeminist Culture.* New York: New York University Press, 2001.

Pyrooz, David C. "'From your First Cigarette to Your Last Dyin' Day': The Patterning of Gang Membership in the Life-Curse." *Journal of Quantitative Criminology* 30 (2014): 349–372.

Pyrooz, David C., and Gary Sweeten. "Gang Membership Between Ages 5 and 17 in the United States." *Journal of Adolescent Health* 30 (2015): 1–6.

Rahilly, Elizabeth P. "The Gender Binary Meets the Gender-Variant Child: Parents' Negotiations with Childhood Gender Variance." *Gender and Society* 29, no. 3 (2015): 338–361.

Ratcliff, Krista. *Rhetorical Listening: Identification, Gender, Whiteness.* Carbondale: Southern Illinois University Press, 2005.

Raver, Jana L., and Lisa H. Nishii. "Once, Twice, Three Times as Harmful? Ethnic Harassment, Gender Harassment, and Generalized Workplace Harassment." *Journal of Applied Psychology* 95, no. 2 (March 2010): 236–254.

Rayburn, Corey. "To Catch a Sex Thief: The Burden of Performance in Rape and Sexual Assault Trials." *Journal of Gender and Law* 15 (2006): 437–484.

Razack, Sherene H. "Sexualized Violence and Colonialism: Reflections on the Inquiry into Missing and Murdered Indigenous Women." *Canadian Journal of Women and the Law* 28, no. 2 (2016): i–iv.

Rehman, Bushra, and Daisy Hernández. "Introduction." In *Colonize This! Young Women of Color on Today's Feminism,* edited by Daisy Hernández and Bushra Rehman, xvii–xxviii. New York: Seal Press, 2002.

Rentschler, Carrie A. "Rape Culture and the Feminist Politics of Social Media." *Girlhood Studies* 7, no. 1 (2014): 65–82.

Rios, Victor M. *Punished: Policing the Lives of Black and Latino Boys.* New York: New York University Press, 2011.

Ristock, Janice L. ed. *Intimate Partner Violence in LGBTQ Lives.* New York: Routledge, 2001.

Rodino-Colocino, Michelle. "Forum: Me Too, #MeToo: Countering Cruelty with Empathy," *Communication and Critical/Cultural Studies* 15, no. 1 (2018): 96–100.

Rose, Chad A., Lisa E. Monda-Amaya, and Dorothy L. Espelage. "Bullying Perpetration and Victimization in Special Education: A Review of the Literature." *Remedial and Special Education* 32, no. 2 (2011): 114–130.

Rute Cardoso, Ana, Paulo Guimaraes, and Pedro Portugal. "What Drives the Gender Wage Gap? A Look at the Role of Firm and Job-Title Heterogeneity." *Oxford Economic Papers* 68, no. 2 (April 2016): 506–524.

Rothenberg, Paula. *Invisible Privilege: A Memoir about Race, Class, and Gender.* Lawrence: University Press of Kansas, 2000.

Rutherford, Alison, Anthony B. Zwi, Natalie J. Grove, and Alexander Butchart. "Violence: A Glossary." *Journal of Epidemiology and Community Health* 61, no. 8 (August 2007): 678–680.

Ryan, Kathleen J., and Elizabeth J. Natalle. "Fusing Horizons: Standpoint Hermeneutics and Invitational Rhetoric." *Rhetoric Society Quarterly* 31, no. 2 (2001): 69–90.

Said, Edward. *Culture and Imperialism.* New York: Alfred A. Knopf, 1993.

Sandoval, Chela. "U.S.–Third World Feminism: The Theory and Method of Oppositional Consciousness in the Postmodern World." *Genders* 10 (1991): 1–24.

Santa Ana, Otto. *Brown Tide Rising: Metaphors of Latinos in Contemporary American Public Discourse.* Austin: University of Texas Press, 2002.

Scholz, Teresa Maria Linda. "Hablando Por (Nos) Otros, Speaking for Ourselves: Exploring the Possibilities of 'Speaking Por' Family and Pueblo in the Bolivian Testimonio 'Si Me Permiten Hablar.'" In *Latina/o Discourse in Vernacular Spaces: Somos du Una Voz?* edited by Michelle A. Holling and Bernadette M. Calafell, 201–222. Lanham, MD: Lexington Books, 2011.

———. "The Rhetorical Power of *Testimonio* and Ocupación: Creating a Conceptual Framework for Analyzing Subaltern Rhetorical Agency." PhD diss., University of Colorado, 2007.

Shepard, Alexandra. *Meanings of Manhood in Early Modern England.* Oxford: Oxford University Press, 2003.

Shepherd, Gregory J. "Communication as Influence: Definitional Exclusion." *Communication Studies* 43, no. 4 (1992): 203–219.

Sidler, Michelle. "Living in McJobdom: Third Wave Feminism and Class Inequity." In *Third Wave Agenda: Being Feminist, Doing Feminism,* edited by Leslie Heywood and Jennifer Drake, 25–39. Minneapolis: University of Minnesota Press, 1997.

Siebers, Tobin. *Disability Aesthetics.* Ann Arbor: University of Michigan Press, 2010.

Simon, Jonathan. "The Ideological Effects of Actuarial Practices." *Law and Society Review* 22 (1988): 771–800.

Slee, Roger. "Social Justice and the Changing Directions in Educational Research: The Case of Inclusive Education." *International Journal of Inclusive Education* 5, no. 2–3 (2001): 167–177.

Sobieraj, Sarah, and Jeffrey M. Berry. "From Incivility to Outrage: Political Discourse in Blogs, Talk Radio, and Cable News." *Political Communication* 28, no. 1 (2011): 19–41.

Sokolff, Natalie, and Ida Dupont. "Domestic Violence at the Intersections of Race, Class, and Gender: Challenges and Contributions to Understanding Violence Against Marginalized Women in Diverse Communities." *Violence Against Women* 11, no. 1 (February 2005): 38–64.

Spender, Dale. *Man Made Language.* London: Routledge and Kegan Paul, 1980.

———. *Women of Ideas and What Men Have Done to Them.* London: Pandora Press, 1982.

Spitzberg, Brian H., and Gregory Hoobler. "Cyberstalking and the Technologies of Interpersonal Terrorism." *New Media and Society* 4, no. 1 (2002): 71–92.

Sprankle, Eric, Katie Bloomquist, Cody Butcher, Neil Gleason, and Zoe Schaefer. "The Role of Sex Work Stigma in Victim Blaming and Empathy of Sexual Assault Survivors." *Sex Research and Social Policy* 15, no. 3 (September 2018): 242–248.

Springer, Kimberly. "Third Wave Black Feminism?" *Signs* 27, no. 4 (2002): 1059–1098.

Stotzer, Rebecca L. "Violence Against Transgender People: A Review of United States Data." *Aggression and Violent Behavior* 14, no. 3 (2009): 170–179.

Sue, Derald Wing. *Microagressions in Everyday Life: Race, Gender, and Sexual Orientation.* Hoboken, NJ: John Wiley and Sons, 2010.

Swogger, Marc T., Zach Walsh, and David S. Kosson. "Domestic Violence and Psychopathic Traits: Distinguishing the Antisocial Batterer from Other Antisocial Offenders." *Aggressive Behavior* 33, no. 3 (2007): 253–260.

Tannen, Deborah. *The Argument Culture: Stopping America's War of Words.* New York: Ballantine, 1998.

Tarule, Jill Mattuck. "Voices in Dialogue: Collaborative Ways of Knowing." In *Knowledge, Difference, and Power: Essays Inspired by Women's Ways of Knowing,* edited by Nancy Goldberger, Jill Tarule, Blythe Clinchy, and Mary Belenky, 274–304. New York: Basic Books, 1996.

Thornton, Russell. *American Indian Holocaust and Survival: A Population History Since 1942.* Norman: University of Oklahoma Press, 1987.

Tillman, Shaquita, Thema Bryant-Davis, Kimberly Smith, and Alison Marks. "Shattering Silence: Exploring Barriers to Disclosure for African American Sexual Assault Survivors." *Trauma, Violence, and Abuse* 11, no. 2 (April 2010): 59–70.

Waldron, Jeremy. *The Harm in Hate Speech.* Cambridge, MA: Harvard University Press, 2012.

Weber, Everard, Mokubung Nkomo, and Christina Amsterdam. "Diversity, Unity, and National Development: Findings from Desegregated Gauteng Schools." *Perspectives in Education* 27, no. 4 (2009): 341–350.

Welke, Barbara Young. *Law and the Borders of Belonging in the Long Nineteenth Century United States.* New York: Cambridge University Press, 2010.

———. "Law, Personhood, and Citizenship in the Long Nineteenth Century: The Borders of Belonging." In *The Cambridge History of Law in America,* vol. 2, edited by Michael Grossberg and Christopher Tomlins, 345–386. New York: Cambridge University Press, 2010.

Welsh, Sandy, Jacquie Carr, Barbara MacQuarrie, and Audrey Huntley. "'I'm Not Thinking of It as Sexual Harassment,' Understanding Harassment across Race and Citizenship." *Gender and Society* 20, no. 1 (2006): 87–107.

Wicks, David. "Institutional Bases of Identity Construction and Reproduction: The Case of Underground Coal Mining." *Gender, Work and Organization* 9, no. 3 (June 2002): 308–335.

Williams, Patricia J. *The Alchemy of Race and Rights: Diary of a Law Professor.* Cambridge, MA: Harvard University Press, 1991.

Wise, Tim J. *Under the Affluence: Shaming the Poor, Praising the Rich and Sacrificing the Future of America.* San Francisco: City Lights Books, Open Media Series, 2015.

Wolf, Michael R., J. Cherie Strachan, and Daniel M. Shea. "Forget the Good of the Game: Political Incivility and Lack of Compromise as a Second Layer of Party Polarization." *American Behavioral Scientist* 56, no. 12 (2012): 1677–1695.

Workplace Bullying Institute. "Facts About Bullying." October 14, 2014, accessed June 1, 2017. https://www.stopbullying.gov/media/facts/index.html#listing.

———. "Who Gets Targeted." October 14, 2014, accessed June 1, 2017. http://www.workplacebullying.org/individuals/problem/who-gets-targeted/.

Woods, Jewel. "The Black Male Privileges Checklist." In *Privilege: A Reader*, edited by Michael S. Kimmel and Abby L. Ferber, 27–38, 2nd ed. Boulder: Westview Press, 2010.

Index